The Transnational Capitalist Class

The Transnational
Capitalist Class

Leslie Sklair

First published 2001

2 4 6 8 10 9 7 5 3 1

Blackwell Publishers Ltd
108 Cowley Road
Oxford OX4 1JF
UK

Blackwell Publishers Inc.
350 Main Street
Malden, Massachusetts 02148
USA

British Library Cataloguing in Publication Data
A CIP catalogue record for this book is available from the British Library

Library of Congress Cataloging-in-Publication Data
Sklair, Leslie.
   The transnational capitalist class / Leslie Sklair.
      p. cm.
   Includes bibliographical references and index.
   ISBN 0-631-22461-0 (hc: acid free)—ISBN 0-631-22462-9 (pb: acid free)
      1. Capitalism. 2. Capitalism—Social aspects. 3. Environmental economics. 4. International business enterprises. I. Title.
   HB501 S619 2000
   338.8′8—dc21
                                                                00-010109

Typeset in 10/12 pt Baskerville
by SetSystems Ltd, Saffron Walden, Essex
Printed in Great Britain by TJ International Ltd, Padstow, Cornwall

This book is printed on acid-free paper.

Contents

Figures and Tables

Preface and Acknowledgments

This book has been simmering for many years. Critics of a previous book, *Sociology of the Global System* (first published in 1991, second edition 1995, third edition in preparation), correctly pointed out that its arguments were too general and that many of its claims about the globalization of capitalism had insufficient empirical support. While this might have been understandable for a book of its type, it was nevertheless true. Lacking the personal inclination to raise funds to build a research institute where the whole project could be scrutinized, tested, and improved, and preferring to work quietly on my own for the most part, I have been permanently daunted (in private, of course) by the enormity of the tasks I set myself in that previous and largely programmatic and exploratory book. *Sociology of the Global System* focused on three main institutional complexes characteristic of the capitalist global system: the transnational corporation, the transnational capitalist class, and the culture-ideology of consumerism. The salience of the choice of the first and third of these has, I think, been more than justified since then. Research on TNCs and consumerism made quantitative and qualitative leaps in the 1990s. No one now could seriously deny that an account of the contemporary world would be fundamentally incomplete without due recognition of the place of the corporations and consumerism, though not everyone would accept the connections I made between them. Nevertheless, I am quite confident that there is now sufficient empirical evidence to sustain the TNC and consumerism arguments that contributed to the theoretical framework of global system theory.

The case of the transnational capitalist class, however, is much more contentious, and that is why I have written this book. It is somewhat surprising to discover that of all the social classes, however defined and categorized, the group that has attracted least serious research is the class at the very top of the pile. Terms like elite, ruling class, and capitalist class have been out of favor in the social sciences for some time, and the idea of a "global ruling class" appears, frankly, ridiculous to many capable scholars. Some of the few remaining leftist writers in the field often sound as if they are resurrecting long-discounted conspiracy theories when they try to discuss such ideas. It is not idle to speculate why this should be so. My view is that it is intimately connected with the way in which globalization has been conceptualized as a force outside human control, in the face of which fatalism is the only rational response. Fatalism in this case is both profoundly mistaken and profoundly immoral. Globalization, like its main driving force, capitalism on a world scale, does not just happen. It is thought out, organized, managed, promoted, and defended against its opponents by identifiable groups of people working in identifiable organizations. These make up the transnational capitalist class.

I have been very fortunate to have had the intellectual and psychological benefits of many talented and enthusiastic M.Sc. and research students, some of whom have developed conceptions of globalization in their own dissertations and subsequent publications. My globalization research workshop at the London School of Economics has also been a source of inspiration and reflection for me since 1995. It is a pleasure to acknowledge my debts to the students whose research I have supervised who have successfully completed their dissertations since I started to work on globalization: Leith Dunn on gender and export-oriented industrialization in the Caribbean (1993); Ka-Ho Mok on the Democracy Movement in China (1994); Alejandra Salas-Porras on the Mexican capitalist class (1997); Yun-tae Kim on big business in Korea (1998); Carolina Ladino on women's work in Mexico (1999); Peter Robbins on the greening of the corporation (1999); and Emily Scraggs on USAID (1999). In addition, the research in progress of my current doctoral students has also contributed to my thinking and rethinking of the issues raised here.

I am grateful to STICERD, the Social Research Division, and the Department of Sociology at the LSE for supporting some of the research reported in the book; and for the assistance of Richard Shephard in Australia, Emi Tanabe in Japan, Alexius Pereira in Singapore, Alejandra Salas-Porras, Peter Robbins, Aparna Joshi and Megan Comfort in London.

Early versions of some of the text first saw the light of day as journal articles and/or conference papers. In particular I thank the editor, Diane Davies, and four anonymous reviewers for *Political Power and Social Theory* (see Sklair 1998). Many colleagues and friends made useful suggestions at various stages of the research. In particular, Bill Robinson gave detailed criticism of the whole manuscript, and Bob Conti, Jeremy Hardie, Steve Hill, Lauren Langman. Alex Pereira and Malcolm Warner commented on chapters, all very much appreciated.

I have also been very fortunate in having had numerous opportunities to discuss my ideas with and respond to criticism from groups at home and abroad, both academic and non-academic and, often, with nonsociologists, while working on the book. All of these opportunities have been valuable, but I would like to express particular thanks for sessions at Sussex University and University of California Santa Cruz (May 1997), the World Congress of Sociology (Montreal, July 1998); the Scandinavian Development Forum (Denmark, November 1998); the Center for US–Mexican Studies (February 1999), NMSU Las Cruces (February 1999); Minnesota International Relations Colloquium (May 1999); WALD in Istanbul (May 1999), and the ASA (Chicago, August 1999). I also learned a good deal from workshops on corporate citizenship organized by the World Business Council for Sustainable Development (Washington DC, February 1998) and by Chris Marsden at the University of Warwick (May 1998).

Thanks are also due to the executives of the corporations and related organizations who found the time to be interviewed on globalization and who sent me mountains of material on their versions of globalization. At Blackwell, Susan Rabinowitz, Ken Provencher, and Cameron Laux combined professionalism and enthusiasm. As always, Doro, Jessie, Aphra, and Tillie aid, abet, and subvert every line that I write.

Leslie Sklair

Chapter 1
Introduction

The purpose of this book is to explain how a transnational capitalist class (TCC) has transformed capitalism into a globalizing project. This task is approached along two intertwining paths. I endeavor to establish the TCC empirically by identifying its members and the institutions through which they exercise their powers, and also to establish it theoretically by locating the concept of the TCC within a theory of how the global capitalist system works. These are not two separate tasks but one task with two sides. We cannot have good theory without reliable empirical evidence (though this may take many forms) and we cannot generate reliable empirical evidence without good theory (and, again, this may take a variety of forms). Theory and evidence meet in the concept, and this is precisely how the concept of the transnational capitalist class is intended here: as the place where the theory (global system theory) and the evidence (the empirical demonstration that the TCC exists through its members and institutional framework) come together.

Despite an increasingly heated debate about the nature and significance of contemporary capitalism, "the free market system," there is a growing consensus that various processes of globalization are occurring. The fact that there are several different, sometimes contradictory versions of what, exactly, this globalization involves and how, exactly, it is to be explained, should not obscure the fact that it is occurring and that its effects are real for ever-larger groups of people. Many interpretations of globalization and most of its critics portray it as an impersonal force about which ordinary people and, in some versions, even national governments, can do nothing. This is both empirically false and morally fatalistic. Globalization is driven by identifiable actors working through institutions they own and/or control.

The study of globalization is beset with conceptual confusion, so it is important at the outset to define clearly what the key terms mean. The main source of confusion concerns the terms *international, transnational,* and *global.* In this book *international* refers to forces, processes, and institutions based on the pre-existing (even if changing) system of nation-states. This approach to understanding the world is often called state-centrism, and it is currently the most common approach in use in the social sciences. Most social science research takes nation-states or single societies or comparisons between them as its units of analysis. This is clearly appropriate for finding the answers to some theoretical and empirical questions. However, economic, political, and culture-ideology changes in the latter decades of the twentieth century – popularly described as *globalization* – have encouraged thinkers to look beyond the international system of states to wider and deeper levels of analysis to understand how the world is changing. Nation-states are certainly important parts of our world, but they are not the only parts and, in some theories of globalization, no longer the most important parts (see Sklair 1995; Strange 1996). The view that the role of the state (even large and rich states) is changing and its powers are declining has forced itself on to the agenda of all the social sciences. This implies that transnational forces, processes, and institutions, not based on the state, might be taking its place. The prime candidates for this role as we enter the twenty-first century are the transnational corporations. In this book, *transnational* refers to forces, processes, and institutions that cross borders but do not derive their power and authority from the state. Global system theory proposes that the most important transnational forces are the transnational corporations (TNC), the transnational capitalist class, and the culture-ideology of consumerism. The power and authority of the members of the trans-national capitalist class derive from the corporations they own and control.

For many writers the terms international, transnational, and global are used interchangeably, but this can be confusing. For example, the World Bank and the International Monetary Fund (IMF) are *inter-national* financial institutions, composed of representatives of member countries who act under the instructions of the governments of these countries. General Motors, Mitsubishi, and Unilever, however, are *transnational* corporations, owned by shareholders and controlled by Boards of Directors who can be citizens of any country. The prime responsibility of these Boards is to make the company as profitable as possible with no specific privileges extended to their states of origin. Nevertheless, many theorists argue that TNCs are in some respects bound to their national origins. This is why General Motors is often identified as an "American" corporation and Mitsubishi as a "Japanese" corporation, though Unilever, whose origins lie in both the Netherlands and Britain (and an increasing number of major "binational" corporations) would be more difficult to classify.[1]

It is now quite common to label large companies "global corporations," but it is more useful to restrict the term *global* to a very specific meaning, namely the goals to which processes of globalization are leading. The most important of these goals are the establishment of a borderless global economy, the complete denationalization of all corporate procedures and activities, and the eradication of economic nationalism. Major corporations and ideologues of globalization argue that these outcomes are essential if the TNCs are to have the opportunity to provide prosperity for all the people of the world. None of these outcomes has happened as yet and, in my view, none is very likely to happen in the foreseeable future. Nevertheless, as the research to be reported in the following chapters demonstrates, most major TNCs appear to be *globalizing* in some important respects and so the use of the term *global economy* is justified to characterize the economy inhabited and dominated by these corporations. The transnational capitalist class is the main driver of a series of globalizing practices in the global economy. It is, therefore, the leading force in the creation of a global capitalist system. The *global* is the goal, while the *transnational*, transcending nation-states in an international system in some respects but still having to cope with them in others, is the reality. The global capitalist system and the global economy exist to the extent that private rather than national interests prevail across borders.

Global System Theory

Since the 1980s there has been a flood of publications on globalization.[2] One powerful school of thought (for example, Dicken 1998; Dunning 1997) is that the transnational corporation is the dominant institutional force in the global economy and a driving force for globalization. Until the 1980s, debates around these issues in the social sciences were dominated by the conception of capitalism organized primarily through national economies and the concept of the international or world-economy, the primary thrust of Wallerstein's world-systems approach. While it is uncontroversial to argue that capitalism has always been expansionary, imperialism and colonialism were usually seen in terms of British or French or Japanese or US imperialism, and were studied in state-centrist terms. Harvey is correct to point out in his discussion of capitalist expansionism: "The outer limit to this process [the subjugation of labor to capital] lies at the point where every person in every nook and cranny of the world is caught within the orbit of capital" (Harvey 1982: 415). The "orbit of capital," while accurate, is a very abstract idea. This book will attempt to show how a new class is emerging and how it pursues people and resources all over the world in its insatiable desire for private profit and eternal accumulation. This new class is the transnational capitalist class, composed of corporate executives, globalizing bureaucrats and politicians, globalizing professionals, and consumerist elites.

Global system theory is one approach to globalization. It focuses specifically on the global capitalist system. In contrast to those visions in which globalization is seen in everything and in every phase of human history, global system theory restricts its scope to those technological, economic, political, and culture-ideology innovations that began to change the world in the second half of the twentieth century. This, of course, covers a large part of social life, but not all of it.

The global system theory propounded here is based on the concept of transnational practices, practices that cross state borders but do not originate with state agencies or actors. Analytically, they operate in three spheres, the economic, the political, and the cultural-ideological. The whole is what is meant by the global system. While the global system is not synonymous with global capitalism, what the theory sets out to demonstrate is that the dominant forces of global capitalism are the dominant forces in the global system. The building blocks of the theory are the TNCs, the characteristic institutional form of economic transnational practices, the transnational capitalist class in the political sphere and in the culture-ideology sphere, the culture-ideology of consumerism (Sklair 1995).

What drives this system? As this is a sociological study with political economy overtones it does not speculate on individual motivations. While these can be relevant, they are rarely decisive. It is entirely possible for individual capitalists to eschew excessive consumerism, indeed some of the corporate rich have been famously self-denying (mean) and others have taken obvious pleasure from giving away large parts of their fortunes. However, the global capitalist system could not survive if most capitalists behaved like this all the time. The material interests of those who dominate the system are embedded in the culture-ideology of consumerism. The viability of the system absolutely depends on being able to persuade the masses that this culture-ideology makes sense and leads to happy lives for all. Ideologies provide plausible collective motivations for groups of people who appear to be acting in similar ways, in this case actually consuming beyond their physical needs or striving to acquire the means (money, credit, barter) to do so.

The culture-ideology of consumerism is the set of beliefs and practices that persuades people that consumption far beyond the satisfaction of physical needs is, literally, at the center of meaningful existence and that the best organized societies are those that place consumer satisfaction at the center of all their major institutions. One contradictory consequence of this is that people are trained never to be satisfied in any sphere of their lives, there is always the promise of bigger (or sometimes smaller) and better and always more. The goods and services themselves become imbued with a multiplicity of meanings. If we define the good life in these terms and accept that the good life is what most of us want, then the goods and services of the corporations are the only route to its achievement, however temporary. The culture-ideology of consumerism, therefore, is the life-blood of the TNCs and those who own and control them. Global system theory sets out to explain how the system works, to show how the transnational capitalist class copes with the crises it produces, and to predict some likely outcomes.

Four Propositions on the Transnational Capitalist Class

With the outlines of global system theory in place, four propositions that structure the argument of the book can be introduced. The first is: **a transnational capitalist class based on the transnational corporations is emerging that is more or less in control of the processes of globalization**. Evidence for this proposition is presented in a variety of ways, by analyzing how the TCC works in the leading business sectors of the global economy and in several substantive problem areas.

The second proposition is: **the TCC is beginning to act as a transnational dominant class in some spheres**. This is a cautious proposition. Many scholars are skeptical about the persistence of class as a meaningful category in the social sciences and even more skeptical about its applications beyond societal or nation-state boundaries. Nevertheless, capitalism operates globally, some actors and institutions within the capitalist system have more power than others, and in many spheres of social existence those who control the forces of global capitalism do make the key decisions that affect the lives of many if not most people on the planet.[3] Even if we can demonstrate all this, it is still a very long step to the idea of a transnational dominant class, with its implications of conspiracy, comprehensiveness, and total control. There is no transnational dominant class that acts in secret to impose its will over every facet of life for everyone in the world and with complete success. However, the following chapters argue that the TCC acts like a transnational dominant class in some spheres, with a large measure of success.

The third proposition connects capitalism and consumerism: **the globalization of the capitalist system reproduces itself through the profit-driven culture-ideology of consumerism**. This implies much more than the truism that capitalists want people to buy the goods and services they produce and market. Global capitalism thrives by persuading us that the meaning and value of our lives are to be found principally in what we possess, that we can never be totally satisfied with our possessions (the imperative of ever-changing fashion and style), and that the goods and services we consume are best provided by the free market, the generator of private profit that lies at the heart of capitalism.

The inherent contradictions of a consumerist capitalism driven by the constant need to maximize private profit give the fourth proposition: **the transnational capitalist class is working consciously to resolve two central crises, namely (i) the simultaneous creation of increasing poverty and increasing wealth within and between communities and societies (the class polarization crisis) and (ii) the unsustainability of the system (the ecological crisis)**. Global capitalists (in some cases rather more than national governments) recognize the class crisis, but largely in marketing terms. In most parts of the world the absolute numbers of global consumers (and millionaires) have increased rapidly over recent decades. However, it is also true that in some places the absolute numbers of the destitute and near-destitute have also increased (see United Nations Development Program 1998) and that the gaps between rich and poor have widened since the 1980s (Korzeniewicz and Moran 1997).[4] The very poor cannot usually buy the goods and services that global capitalists sell. While there is a long way to go before consumer demand inside the rich First World is satisfied, the gap between the rich and the poor all over the world is not welcome news for global capitalists. In addition to the profits lost when poor people who want to buy goods and services do not have the money or even the credit to do so, social unrest between haves and have-nots creates many problems.

The ecological crisis is also directly connected with the culture-ideology of consumerism, encapsulated in the political and ideological struggles over the concepts of sustainable development and development itself. Chapter 7 sets out to demonstrate how the TCC has succeeded to a large extent in redefining the issue of ecological survival on planet Earth in the interests of global capitalism by creating what can be termed, after Gramsci, a sustainable development historical bloc.

Structure of the Book

This chapter has set out the logic and major concepts of the argument and introduced four propositions that connect global system theory and the concept of the transnational capitalist class. In chapter 2 a model of the transnational capitalist class will be proposed, and the relationship of the transnational capitalist class to other groups within the global capitalist system discussed. The transnational capitalist class is interrogated in terms of arguments about the current conjuncture of the world-historic struggle between capital and labor and its relationship to ideas about the national interest and the national economy in the global capitalist system.

Chapter 3 elaborates a classification of the global economy through the corporations that dominate it. This chapter lays out the methodology for demonstrating that the global economy is dominated by a number of globalizing corporations and that a globalizing elite of corporate executives is driving the process forward rapidly. Interviews carried out in a sample of more than 80 major TNCs show first, that most of them have embarked on a globalizing path and second, that different corporations have traveled different distances along this path. Globalization is defined and measured in terms of four criteria, namely: foreign direct investment (FDI), world best practice, corporate citizenship, and global vision.

These four criteria of globalization frame the arguments in chapters 4 to 8 about how the transnational capitalist class works as a whole and how each fraction has a specific part to play in building and sustaining its hegemony, always in terms of the interests of those who own and control major corporations. Chapter 4 discusses the first criterion of globalization, namely the role of those who own and control major corporations and their local affiliates in the transformation of foreign direct investment into a globalizing process. This is interpreted in terms of the decline of a state-centric global reach conception of FDI and the increasing salience of a globalizing global shift conception. Chapter 5 discusses world best practice and benchmarking. Analysis of these relatively obscure corporate practices throws light on why and how globalizing politicians have made international competitiveness such a powerful slogan for nation-states all over the world. How the professions are increasingly being restructured in terms of the norms and practices of global business is crucial for an understanding of these issues. Globalizing politicians and professionals work together to prioritize international competitiveness. As a corollary, they downgrade the value of social and community goals locally, as against the constant search for the holy grail of "national competitiveness."[5]

Corporate citizenship is the subject of chapters 6 and 7. The problematic here is the struggle between business, government, and other elements in society over the issue of regulation. The triumph of the neoliberal globalizing version of capitalism has been predicated on the argument that the state (and interstate organizations) should intervene in economic affairs only where absolutely necessary, largely to ensure social order for the pursuit of legitimate business. The slowly-emerging conception of global corporate citizenship represents the main ideological and political effort of the corporate community to persuade skeptical bureaucrats and politicians and, ultimately, the public, that they can be trusted to regulate and police themselves. They do this with the particular assistance of globalizing bureaucrats (and politicians), who act in their interests within government and the political system as a whole, to legitimate the claims of the corporate sector. These globalizing bureaucrats and politicians are often sturdily opposed by economic nationalists (shades of the mercantilists of old) who seek to defend their conception of the national interest against these globalizing forces. Evidence from recent decades suggests that the balance of power has shifted from economic nationalists to globalizing bureaucrats and politicians in most countries and in most cities. Of all the fractions of the TCC, they do look the most vulnerable to political change and public hostility. Chapter 6 focuses on corporate governance, philanthropy, employment, health, and safety aspects of corporate citizenship.

Chapter 7 conceptualizes the global shift of the TCC in terms of a substantive issue of fundamental importance, in the opinion of many the central crisis of capitalism for our times, the ecological crisis. This chapter offers an explanation of why this crisis has been taken very seriously by the corporations, how they have managed it in a variety of ways, and how they have co-opted oppositional movements. These outcomes are explained within the framework of the creation of a sustainable development historical bloc. All four criteria of globalization are relevant to the issues of how and why the transnational capitalist class, working through the major corporations, government agencies, and other social institutions, has sought to frame and solve the ecological crisis. Corporate case studies support these arguments.

Chapter 8 investigates the global vision of the corporations, deconstructed in terms of the culture-ideology of consumerism. Here the economic, political, and culture-ideology practices of consumerist elites and their allies are examined and, not surprisingly, it is here that we find some of the most visible manifestations of the globalizing process as it is disseminated from the corporations through to consumers.

Chapter 9, the concluding chapter, briefly summarizes the argument of the book in terms of the four propositions set out above. A transnational capitalist class is shown to be emerging; it does act as a transnational dominant class in some spheres; it is fuelled by a culture-ideology of consumerism driven by the insatiable desire of capitalists for private profits and by the system's need for continual expansion; and it is working consciously to resolve the key crises of global capitalism, the class polarization crisis and the ecological crisis, but failing in both these tasks. The book concludes with a brief discussion of the resistance to capitalist globalization.

Notes

1 Those who run the World Bank and the IMF can, and sometimes do, act relatively independently of the governments of their member countries or, more to the point, in the interests of some influential minorities in these countries.
2 For attempts to categorize the field see Waters (1995) and Sklair (1999). Lechner and Boli (2000) is a well-organized collection of 54 sources.
3 A leading practitioner in the field of global corporate citizenship expresses this sentiment in an interesting analysis of the "dependent populations" of states and TNCs and asks: "how long before General Motors is given a seat at the United Nations?" (Logan 1998: 67).
4 US Bureau of Census data show a dramatic increase in the gap between richest and poorest families from 1980 to 1999. In Mexico between 1993 and 1996 the proportion of the population who were "extremely poor" rose from one-third to over half (Wallach and Naiman 1998).
5 While all four fractions may be involved in all globalizing practices, globalizing bureaucrats and politicians and professionals are the most fluid.

Chapter 2
Globalizing Class Theory

Classes, however defined, are generally thought of as operating within the sphere of the nation-state. The consensus in sociology and related disciplines is that countries have classes and although the activities of some classes might spill over into other, particularly geographically or culturally contiguous countries, classes are rarely conceived outside the nation-state, a problematic but common synonym for countries and societies (Mann 1997). The main purpose of this book is to argue that a transnational capitalist class is in the making. It is domiciled in and identified with no particular country but, on the contrary, is identified with the global capitalist system.

Theorizing the Dominant Class

How do we go about rethinking the concept of class and class structure in transnational terms? The theories of national capitalist classes of Connell (1977), Useem (1984), Scott (1997), and Domhoff (1996) provide good starting places. Connell's work on class in Australia is notable for a bold if inconclusive attempt to connect the idea of a ruling class with the idea of a ruling culture, the problem of hegemony, at the conscious and unconscious levels. This is dangerous territory but it suggests how the culture-ideology of consumerism works. Global capitalism survives and capitalists prosper because people are persuaded to consume beyond their basic needs (though these needs may change and expand over time). Patterns of consumption have to be sustained that will more or less keep the mines, fields, factories, and offices of the global economy in work. As these become ever more productive due to improvements in technology and industrial organization, even more consumption is required to keep the system going. Slump and depression are not malfunctions of the economy so much as malfunctions of the social organization of consumption: to borrow and adapt a slogan from the British Conservative Party, the culture-ideology of consumerism isn't working! Therefore, the prime culture-ideology task of global capitalism is to ensure that as many people as possible consume as much as possible, by inculcating beliefs about the intrinsic value of consumption as a "good thing" and the key component of the "good life." Thus, as Ewen (1976) argued so eloquently, the captains of industry have to be reinforced by the captains of consciousness. After persuading people that the meaning of life is in their possessions, global capitalism has to prioritize the importance of constantly changing and upgrading these possessions, thus the realms of fashion, style, novelty, difference.[1]

The system is integrated through the "inner circle," the group within the capitalist class that organizes big business and promotes its interests in all spheres (Useem 1984).[2] This idea provides two direct inputs for global system theory. First, Useem's use of network analysis is one useful technique for measuring how far, if at all, the denationalization and globalization of the transnational capitalist class has gone. Second, Useem's study itself is a comparison of two cases, the USA and Britain, with obvious implications for widening the comparison, for example across industrial sectors as well as between other countries.

Scott is one of the few class theorists who, albeit briefly, even considers the possibility that the capitalist class could cross borders. He argues that until the demographic relations of national capitalist classes change so that social relations between members in different nation-states are as important as social relations between members in the same nation-state, then a transnational capitalist class cannot be said to exist (Scott 1997: 312). But this is to define class membership in terms of who marries whom, who consorts with whom, rather than in terms of ownership and control of the means of production and economic interests. Naturally, people who live in the same place, speak the same language, enjoy the same food and leisure pursuits, will tend to interact and intermarry more than people who live far apart, speak different languages, and enjoy themselves in different ways. But these differences need not be consequences of "national" characteristics. Indeed, the facts of a globalizing world are that more people are more mobile than ever before, use of a few common "global" languages (notably English) is greater than ever before, and "global tastes" in food, clothing, cultural pursuits of various types, sport, etc. are more widespread than ever before. Therefore, that members of a transnational capitalist class and their offspring who live for the most part in one country tend to marry partners and interact mostly with those who live in the same country seems less important than the fact that they also partake differentially in recognizable global patterns of capital accumulation, consuming, and thinking.

Insofar as globalization is changing the structure and dynamics of the capitalist class, it is necessary to start to explore in addition to capitalist classes in separate countries, the possibility of the emergence of a transnational capitalist class. The members of a TCC will have specific relations with national actors, agencies, and institutions in separate countries as well as actors, agencies, and institutions that cannot sensibly be described as "national." Those who own and control the means of production, distribution, exchange, and consumption have always been central to the conception of class. In the global context, the transnational capitalist class plays the central role in the struggle to commodify everything, the goal of the culture-ideology of consumerism. That some of these capitalists and their allies can find themselves, from time to time, in different and competitive class situations is a second-order problem, though it can be of decisive importance for the historical development of industries, class relations, and political systems in particular places, for example, within cities or countries or even continents. Nevertheless, for the global capitalist system as a whole, these intraclass struggles are less important than what binds the members of the class together globally, namely their common interest in the protection of private property and the rights of private individuals to accumulate it with as little interference as possible. Consequently, capitalists in the USA or Japan or Brazil or Germany or India may have more interests in common with each other than they have with their noncapitalist fellow citizens.

Domhoff's class dominance theory, a critical dialogue with the power elite thesis of Mills (1956), is the most challenging sociological account of the dominant class, and though he restricts it to the USA it provides a sound basis on which to globalize class theory. State autonomy theorists claim that the state has "interests and goals of its own, carried out by elected and appointed officials" (Domhoff 1996: 1). To this, Domhoff counters: "The idea of the American state having any significant degree of autonomy from the owners and managers of banks, corporations, and agribusinesses is a theoretical mistake based in empirical inaccuracies" (ibid., p. 3). The main empirical errors are the claims that the federal government has great independence from classes and interest groups; that independent experts are important; and that competition between parties leads them to be responsive to voters. The class dominance perspective is based on three methods of research: analysis of membership networks (the institutional connections between people and between organizations), money flows (between people and institutions), and outputs of networks (which involves content analysis of texts). Domhoff accepts Dahl's three tests for the existence of a ruling elite. Is it a well-defined group? Is there a fair sample of cases where elite preferences run counter to the preference of others? Do the preferences of the elite prevail? Class dominance theory sets out to prove that "there is (1) a small social upper class (2) rooted in the ownership and control of a corporate community that (3) is integrated with a policy-planning network and (4) has great political power in both political parties and dominates the federal government in Washington" (ibid., p. 18). The method involves a synthesis of research focused on class and research focused on organization, connected through the structured agency of boards of directors of major corporations and other central organizations.

This straightforward methodology, common in much theoretically-informed empirical social science, incorporates both agency and structure, in this case investigating individuals who are powerful by virtue of their institutional positions and the institutions from which they derive their power. Taking this into the global arena, research on the transnational capitalist class is at the same time research on corporations. The three interlocking networks of elite rule in the USA, the most thoroughly researched case, are increasingly those of the TCC globally: networks of members of the upper class, the corporate community, and the policy-planning specialists. Evidence amassed by Domhoff and others over decades (see Scott, ed., 1990), demonstrates that an upper class does exist in the USA (and elsewhere) whose members are identified through an institutional network of schools, clubs, resorts, and intermarriage, and that it is a wealth-holding class. Domhoff argues that these people bring a class perspective to the executives they meet on corporate boards, while executives bring an organization perspective to the upper class through their stewardship of the corporations. Successful corporate executives, notably those recruited onto the boards of banks and major TNCs, are not usually upper class in origins, but are incorporated to inculcate values of profit-seeking, corporate expansion and the practice of good public relations. Policy-planning networks of corporate experts, charitable foundations, and think-tanks complete the interlocking and solidarity of the elite.

Class dominance theory is highly controversial. Most sociology and politics textbooks conclude that while there might be something in elite or dominant class theory, versions of pluralist polyarchy (competing elite-like groups vying for power in a more or less open fashion) are more likely explanations of who gets what, when, and how. The differences between class dominance theory and pluralist polyarchy are small but fundamental. Both are antagonistic to the liberal democratic theory that most of the major decisions are made by politicians who simply respond to the will of the majority as expressed through democratic processes. Whereas pluralist polyarchy explains the origins and wielding of power in a nondeterminate fashion (power originates from different sources and no one source ever has a monopoly), class dominance theory argues that decisive long-term power flows from control of economic resources, more accurately from the ownership and control of the means of production. So, while military, religious, ethnic, aristocratic, political, or any other elites can and do wield power, unless they also own and control the major means of production or enjoy the support of those who do, they will be unable to hold onto their power. Their power will always be fatally vulnerable to seizure by those who do own and control the means of production, if and when they decide that their vital interests are threatened. And so, more often than not, it has proved throughout history. The capitalist class does not need to rule directly in the sense that a government or dictatorship rules, but no government or dictatorship that works actively against the interests of those who own and control the means of production can survive for long. Many governments and dictatorships have avoided this dilemma by themselves seizing ownership and control over the means of production and many more in the contemporary world thrive on turning politics into a form of business. As Robinson argues: "Promoting polyarchy and promoting neo-liberal restructuring has become a singular process in US foreign policy" (1996: 55). While radical and requiring a flexible definition of "neo-liberal restructuring," this thesis is less easy to deny now than it would have been at any time in the past for most governments.

This raises the perennial issue of the relationship between the state in capitalist society and the capitalist class. It is interesting to reflect that the Marxist thesis that the state acts like the executive committee of the bourgeoisie is actually a possible empirical consequence of pluralist polyarchy research. Some propose a stronger version of the thesis, arguing that the state is nothing but the executive committee of the bourgeoisie. In practice, the difference between these positions is not always of great importance, particularly for those who suffer when state agencies violently suppress the rights of workers and citizens as well as when they do so by nonviolent administrative means. If governments legislate in the interests of the capitalist class then it makes little difference whether they do this as if they were acting in these interests directly or not. The truly fundamental change that capitalist globalization has introduced into the state–class argument is that, for the first time in human history, there is indeed a material and ideological shift towards selling business as such as the only real business of the planet and its inhabitants. So, in the global capitalist system, agents and agencies of the state (among other institutions) fulfill the role of facilitators of the global capitalist project. James O'Connor summarizes very well a first approximation of the role of the state in capitalist society:

> the conditions of production are not produced in accordance with the laws of the market. . . . There must be some agency, therefore, whose task it is either to produce the conditions of production or to regulate capital's access to them. In capitalist societies, this agency is the state. Every state activity, including every state agency and budgetary item, is concerned with providing capital with access to labor power, nature, or urban space and infrastructure. (O'Connor 1994: 166)

Global system theory would revise this powerful statement to reflect the evidence that states are no longer monolithic bodies (even if they once were) and that the forces of globalization have pitted groups of globalizing bureaucrats and politicians and the agencies and institutions they control, against localizing bureaucrats and politicians and their bases of power and influence.[3] While there are virtually no actively anticapitalist states left, within most states and transnationally there are continuing struggles for and against capitalist globalization. These struggles take place within state and nonstate agencies, parliaments, and social movements of many types.[4] O'Connor's thesis, therefore, needs to be expanded to acknowledge these struggles.

Does class dominance theory work outside as well as inside the nation-state? For class dominance theory to be correct transnationally there is no necessity for it to be correct for any particular country. It is possible that a transnational capitalist class dominates globally while particular countries are dominated by other groups, for example elites or status groups made up of those who control the state apparatus or military or ideological or religious organizations and symbols. This may be the case in some countries with feeble capitalist classes. Further, the local capitalist class may not dominate in given parts of a country or throughout a country, but nevertheless the transnational capitalist class may dominate in strategic localities (like cities or communities with valuable natural resources). Where it sees its vital interests at stake, the transnational capitalist class can take control and exert its power even where there is no local dominating capitalist class. In such cases it often acts through alliances between local rulers and those who own and control the major corporations. An authority on the mining industry expresses this idea clearly: "The history of RTZ is thus the history of a

worldwide political infrastructure consisting of alliances between RTZ
and its potential competitors; between the company and national
governments; and between the company and power brokers within the
local communities where it operates" (Moody 1996: 47).

Extractive industries illustrate the point that whereas in the past
much of the globe was of little interest to capitalists, for contemporary
capitalism almost the whole world is of potential commercial interest,
because of intense pressure that has built up within corporations to
find new natural and labor resources and to exploit new markets. This
is a direct consequence of two world-historical forces: first, the unprecedented productive capacities of global capitalism and, second, the
hegemony of the culture-ideology of consumerism that has been constructed to solve the problem of the underconsumption of the fruits of
this production.

The capitalist system, however, is not the only global system or, more
accurately, it is not the only social system that has global aspirations. It
competes for global hegemony with the international system of states,
with global systems of religions, the global environmentalist system,
and perhaps others. Nevertheless, it is the dominant global system
precisely because the TCC owns and controls of most of the planet's
means of production.

There have been several attempts to theorize such a transnational
dominant class, and all have found a place for the transnational
corporations. Concepts of the international bourgeoisie, more or less a
staple of dependency theorists (see Frank 1972), the corporate international wing of the managerial bourgeoisie (Sklar 1987), and the
international corporate elite (Fennema 1982) have been proposed.
The Gramscian turn in International Relations has provided another
source of insight. Cox (1987: 271) writes of "an emerging global class
structure" and Gill (1990: 94ff) identifies a "developing transnational
capitalist class fraction." All of these contributions are, at best, ambivalent about state-centrism.[5] In order to move forward, I believe, it is
necessary to make a decisive break with state-centrism and this involves
a critical deconstruction of the ideas of "national interest" and
"national economy" (see below). If it is to mean anything more than
internationalization, globalization must at least mean that capitalists
(or any other globalizing forces) seek to transcend the national in
search of the global. As an attempt to build on this rich literature, the
concept of transnational practices and its political form, the TCC, is a
step towards consolidating the theoretical link between globalization
and the dominant class.

Structure and Dynamics of the Transnational Capitalist Class

The transnational capitalist class can be analytically divided into four main fractions:

1) TNC executives and their local affiliates (the corporate fraction);
2) globalizing bureaucrats and politicians (the state fraction);
3) globalizing professionals (the technical fraction);
4) merchants and media (the consumerist fraction).

The first and dominant group is composed of those who own and control the major corporations, subsumed under the generic label of TNC executives. This includes both those who are leading salaried employees of the corporations (the conventional use of corporate executives) and those who have executive power to make and influence key decisions, notably the so-called non-executive directors and other major owners and their representatives. The other three groups – globalizing bureaucrats and politicians, globalizing professionals, and consumerist elites – are supporting members of the TCC. Some Marxist scholars may object that only those who actually own the means of production can properly be called capitalists and be members of the capitalist class, local or transnational. However, the globalization of capitalism can only be adequately understood when ownership and control of money capital is augmented with ownership and control of other types of capital, notably political, organizational, cultural, and knowledge capital (Bourdieu 1996, Scott, ed., 1990).

The composition of the transnational capitalist class, therefore, reflects the different types of capital that must be mobilized to further the direct interests of the global capitalist system. While the four groups are analytically distinct in that they serve different though complementary functions for global capital in the abstract, concretely the individuals in them overlap to a considerable degree. Some TNC executives, for example, spend time as state bureaucrats (globalizing and localizing); and bureaucrats and politicians, professionals, and especially members of consumerist elites work directly for corporations. The capitalist class is defined here as those who own and control the major means of production, distribution, and exchange through their ownership and control of money and other forms of capital. In a theme that will be argued in detail in subsequent chapters, class hegemony does not simply happen as if by magic. The capitalist class expends much time, energy, and resources to make it happen and to ensure that it keeps on happening.

Together, the leading representatives of these fractions constitute a transnational dominant class in some respects. The transnational capitalist class opposes and is opposed not only by those who reject capitalism as a way of life and/or an economic system but also by those capitalists who reject globalization. Some localized, domestically oriented businesses can share the interests of globalizing corporations and prosper, but many cannot and fail to enrich their owners. Influential business strategists and management theorists commonly argue that to survive, local business must globalize (for example, Kanter 1996). Inward-oriented government bureaucrats, politicians, and professionals who reject globalization and espouse extreme nationalist ideologies are comparatively rare, despite the recent rash of civil wars in economically marginal parts of the world. While there are anticonsumerist elements in most societies, there are few cases of a serious anticonsumerist party winning political power anywhere in the world.

The following chapters aim to demonstrate that the transnational capitalist class is transnational (and globalizing) in several respects.

a) The economic interests of its members are increasingly globally linked rather than exclusively local and national in origin. The property and shares of those who own and control the major corporations are becoming more globalized as are their corporations. The intellectual products of members of the TCC increasingly serve the interests of globalizing rather than localizing capital. These outcomes follow directly from the shareholder-driven growth imperative that lies behind the globalizing of the world economy and the increasing difficulty of enhancing shareholder value in purely domestic firms.[6] The richest and most powerful corporations in the world and those who own and control them, with few exceptions, tend to be globalizing in terms of foreign economic activities, aspirations to world-class operations, the rhetoric and practices of global corporate citizenship, and global visions. While for many practical purposes the world is still organized in terms of discrete national economies, the TCC increasingly conceptualizes its interests in terms of markets, which may or may not coincide with a specific nation-state, and the global market, which clearly does not.

Purely "domestic firms" may be defined as those serving the market of one sovereign state, employing only co-nationals, whose products consist entirely of domestic services, components, and materials. That this appears to be a ridiculously narrow definition for the realities of contemporary economies suggests that the concept of economic globalization has some plausibility. Apart from small localized firms, the exceptions are mainly state-owned enterprises (SOEs) and quasi-monopolistic utility and services corporations. The facts that SOEs are being run more like TNCs and/or are being privatized and frequently sold to TNCs, and that quasi-monopolies are being rapidly deregulated, enhance rather than detract from this argument. Van der Pijl (1993: 30) traces the point when the "national identity" of the corporations "had to be abandoned" to the 1970s. While few would go this far, there is sufficient evidence to show that globalizing corporations today are not the same as the corporations of the past. There are countless explanations from economists, and from management, international business, and organization theorists (exhaustively surveyed in Dunning, 1992–4), of how and why the TNCs, under a variety of labels, differ from firms in the past. My interest here is in how the TNCs relate to the global capitalist system, which includes changing business sectors, regulatory frameworks, political regimes, and climates of opinion on social and environmental questions.

In the early 1970s, the Conference Board, a business think-tank based in New York, commissioned research on this topic. One respondent in the study stated that: "Multinational corporations are not really multinational. They are national companies with units abroad" (quoted in LaPalombara and Blank 1976: 111). In the course of my own interviews in the *Fortune* Global 500, this quotation was read out and comments invited. In the majority of cases the respondents commented, some quite forthrightly, that this was an old-fashioned and specifically American idea of how corporations operate and that no corporation aspiring to global competitiveness could afford to think in these terms any more. (This issue is discussed in more detail with respect to specific corporations in the following chapter.) Whether all those who own and control major corporations, or the corporations as they present themselves to the public, actually transcend national stereotypes is, of course, another matter.

b) The TCC seeks to exert economic control in the workplace, political control in domestic and international politics, and culture-ideology control in everyday life through specific forms of global competitive and consumerist rhetoric and practice. The focus of workplace control is the threat that jobs will be lost and, in the extreme, the economy will collapse unless workers are prepared to work longer hours and for less pay in order to meet foreign competition. This has been called "the race to the bottom" by radical critics (see Brecher and Costello 1994; Ranney 1994). While this is not new – capitalists have always fought against reductions in the length of the working day and increases in wages – its global scope is unprecedented.[7]

This race to the bottom is reflected in local electoral politics all over the world, in rich and poor countries alike, where the major parties have few substantial strategic (even if many tactical) differences, and in the sphere of culture-ideology, where consumerism is rarely challenged. Paradoxically, the rhetoric and ideology of global capitalism has become inextricably bound up with the demand for ever-rising standards of living, which makes the debate around renewable resources and irreversible environmental damage more and more difficult to engage in seriously. The central question that the issue of capitalist class control raises is: how does the TCC exert its control successfully in the interests of the global capitalist project? The answer that global system theory provides is in terms of the grip that the TNC-generated culture-ideology of consumerism has on the mass of the world's population.

c) Members of the TCC have outward-oriented global rather than inward-oriented local perspectives on most economic, political, and culture-ideology issues. The growing TNC and international institutional emphasis on free trade and the shift from import substitution to export promotion strategies in most developing countries since the 1980s have been driven by members of the TCC working through government agencies, business professionals, elite opinion organizations, and the media. Some of the credit for this apparent transformation in the way in which big business works around the world is attached to the tremendous growth in business education since the 1960s, particularly in the US and Europe, but increasingly all over the world. By 1990 there were around 200 business schools in the USA offering graduate degrees in international business. A spokesman for one of the most prestigious, the Wharton School, commented: "We wanted to be a school of management of the world that just happens to be headquartered in Philadelphia" (Carey 1990: 36). Between 26 and 40 percent of all Wharton students on graduate business programs were then from outside the USA. Research on INSEAD in Paris suggests that transnational business schools were beginning to have a significant impact on the behavior and ideology of European executives as well (Marceau 1989).[8] There is now a huge literature in the popular and academic business press on the making of the global executive and the globalization of business and management (see Warner 1997, *passim*) that confirms that this is a real phenomenon and not simply the creation of a few "globaloney" myth-makers.

d) Members of the TCC tend to share similar lifestyles, particularly patterns of higher education (increasingly in business schools) and consumption of luxury goods and services. Integral to this process are exclusive clubs and restaurants, ultra-expensive resorts in all continents, private as opposed to mass forms of travel and entertainment and, ominously, increasing residential segregation of the very rich secured by armed guards and electronic surveillance. These gated communities are being studied all over the world, in Istanbul (Bartu 1999), Bangalore (King 1999), Los Angeles (Davis 1999), and other world cities.[9]

e) Finally, members of the TCC seek to project images of themselves as citizens of the world as well as of their places of birth. Leading exemplars of this phenomenon include Jacques Maisonrouge, who in the 1960s became the chief executive of IBM World Trade (Maisonrouge 1988); Percy Barnevik, credited with the creation of ABB and often portrayed as spending most of his life in his corporate jet (Taylor 1991); Helmut Maucher, former CEO of Nestlé's far-flung global empire (Maucher 1994); David Rockefeller, the key figure in the Trilateral Commission (Gill 1990); Akio Morita, founder of Sony (Morita and Reingold 1987); and Australian-born Rupert Murdoch, who actually changed his nationality to pursue his global media interests (Shawcross 1992).

The concept of the transnational capitalist class implies that there is one central inner circle that makes system-wide decisions, and that it connects in a variety of ways with subsidiary members in communities, cities, countries, and supranational regions. Despite real geographical and sectoral conflicts, the whole of the transnational capitalist class shares a fundamental interest in the continued accumulation of private profit. What the inner circle of the TCC does is to give a unity to the diverse economic interests, political organizations, and cultural and ideological formations of those who make up the class as a whole. As in any social institution, fundamental long-term unity of interests and purpose does not preclude shorter-term and local conflicts of interests and purpose, both within each of the four fractions of the TCC and between them. The culture-ideology of consumerism is the fundamental value system that keeps the system intact, but it permits a relatively wide variety of choices, notably "emergent global nationalisms" (see below) as a way of satisfying the needs of the different actors and their constituencies within the global system. The four fractions of the TCC in any geographical and social area, whether analyzed in terms of bloc, region, country, city, society, or community, perform complementary functions to integrate the whole. The achievement of these goals is facilitated by the activities of agents and organizations that are connected in a complex network of local and global interlocks.

A crucial component of the integration of the TCC is that most of the senior members of its inner circle will occupy a variety of interlocking positions. The core of the system is the interlocking corporate directorates that have been the subject of detailed studies for some time in many countries (Mizruchi and Schwartz 1987; Scott, ed., 1990, vol. III; Stokman et al. 1985). Those in the core frequently have extensive connections outside the direct ambit of the corporate sector, the civil society as it were servicing the state-like structures of the corporations. Leading capitalists and corporate executives serve on the boards of think-tanks, charities, scientific, sports, arts, and culture bodies, universities, medical foundations, and similar institutions, just as leaders of these institutions often occupy places on corporate boards (see Scott, ed., 1990, vol. I, parts II and III; Useem 1984). While there is little evidence of widespread direct transnational (nonstate) or international (state-based) interlocking, there are indications of changes. Major corporations are beginning to see the advantages of bringing more nationalities on to main and subsidiary boards, and the idea that those who control companies headquartered in one country have to be nationals of that country is slowly eroding (see below). With the dramatic increase of cross-border strategic alliances – what Dunning (1997) calls globalizing alliance capitalism – the penetration of all social institutions by the corporations is likely to increase. It is in this sense that the claims "the business of society is business" and "the business of our society is global business" become legitimated in the global capitalist system. Business, particularly the TNC sector, then begins to monopolize symbols of modernity and postmodernity like free enterprise, international competitiveness, and the good life, and to transform most, if not all, social spheres in its own image. Table 2.1 summarizes the structure of the transnational capitalist class.

Table 2.1 Structure of the transnational capitalist class

	Economic base	*Political organization*	*Culture-ideology*
TNC executives (corporate fraction)	corporate salaries, shares	peak business organizations	cohesive culture-ideology of consumerism
Globalizing bureaucrats and politicians (state fraction)	state salaries, perks	state and interstate agencies, corporatist organizations	emergent global nationalism and economic neoliberalism
Globalizing professionals (technical fraction)	salaries and fees, perks	professional and corporatist organizations, think-tanks	economic neoliberalism
Globalizing merchants and media (consumerist fraction)	corporate salaries, perks, shares	peak business organizations, mass media, selling spaces	cohesive culture-ideology of consumerism

The particular places where the TCC operates in the unfolding era of globalization, while broadly similar in fundamentals insofar as they are parts of the global capitalist system, all have their peculiarities. So the homogenizing effects of capitalist globalization, one defining characteristic of the phenomenon, and the peculiarities and uniqueness of history and culture, are always in tension. This tension creates a globalizing dialectic. The thesis is the historical local of communities, real and imagined of all types, the relatively recent invention of the nation-state being the most prominent in the modern era. The antithesis is the emerging global, of which the global capitalist system driven by the transnational capitalist class is the dominant, though not the only, force. The synthesis is as yet unformulated. "Going global" is the tendency of contemporary capitalism, but it is neither inevitable nor irreversible.

Dominant Classes and Dominated Groups

All dominant classes in all social systems not characterized by pure democracy have to ensure their power to sustain the normal processes of interaction. So, police forces, courts of law, armies, Gods (religious and/or secular), super-ego, posterity, and other mechanisms of social control play their part to defend the integrity of the social system, to permit accommodation to change, and even (on occasion) to ensure the success of unavoidable revolutions in human affairs. While every dominant class has a siege mentality to a greater or lesser extent, which explains why they have armies and police forces and other agents of physical repression and social control, there are two specific reasons why the siege mentality of the TCC is particularly sensitive. First, the old ideological certainties of the divine rights of kings, emperors, gods, and sacred texts seriously diminished in the twentieth century. Second, the rise of democratic polities and intrusive mass media exposed dominant classes all over the world to greater degrees of public scrutiny, though not always effective democratic control, than ever before.[10]

The theoretical-historical foundations of this argument and line of research originate in Gramsci's attempt to construct a theory of hegemony and ideological state apparatuses (Gramsci 1971, see also Althusser 1971). Much of the voluminous *Prison Notebooks* can be read as a continuous critique of the assumption, not difficult to gather from the Marx–Engels classics, that ruling classes generally rule effortlessly until revolutionary upsurges drive them from power and remake everything anew. As many scholars inspired by and hostile to Marxism have pointed out, the general impression of the Marxist classics is of a rather deterministic sociology, a theory in which generic men make history but not in circumstances of their own choosing, where the emphasis is on the latter rather than the former.

It is no accident that Gramsci is associated simultaneously with a more cultural and less deterministic interpretation of Marxism, and with the concept of hegemony, for these ideas do connect. Gramsci made the connection through the role of the intellectuals in the creation and sustenance of hegemonic forms for dominant classes. He argues:

> The hegemony of a directive centre over the intellectuals asserts itself by two principal routes: 1. a general conception of life, a philosophy . . . which offers to its adherents an intellectual "dignity" providing a principle of differentiation from the old ideologies which dominated by coercion, and an element of struggle against them; 2. a scholastic programme, an educative principle and original pedagogy which interests that fraction of the intellectuals which is the most homogenous and the most numerous (the teachers, from the primary teachers to the university professors), and gives them an activity of their own in the technical field. (Gramsci 1971: 103–4, written in 1934)

While these ideas still seem to have some validity, they imply too much of a one-way process, the "directive center" asserting its hegemony over the intellectuals. Research on the transmission of ideas suggests a more dialectical process where distinct groups of intellectuals, inspired by the promises and actual achievements of global capitalism articulate what they perceive to be its essential purposes and strategies. This process is often supported and encouraged by corporate elites and their allies in government and other spheres, particularly the media. Cockett (1995), for example, shows how about 50 intellectuals of various types in the UK carried out an anti-Keynesian neoliberal counter revolution from the 1930s to the eventual triumphs of Thatcher-Reaganism and other regimes which drew inspiration from them subsequently.[11]

Cockett demonstrates in convincing detail how the revolution begun by Hayek and others in the 1930s was kept alive. Public and private meetings, conferences, academic and more popular publications, lobbying of various types, feeding the media, assiduous contacts with the politically powerful (or soon to be powerful), and, with the exception of mass demonstrations, all the techniques that research on social movements identifies were used. This is not an idealist account of social change in which the power of ideas eventually turns the tide but, on the contrary, a much more subtle argument in which the bearers of powerful ideas which have few powerful adherents work away until the material forces begin to change in their direction. The crises of capitalism and state power in the 1970s fed the widespread disillusionment with Keynesian and welfare state solutions to these crises, and the legitimation crisis in general created the openings in which activists could begin to "think the unthinkable."

Enter Gramsci, again. "A 'crisis of authority' is spoken of: this is precisely the crisis of hegemony, or general crisis of the state" (1971: 210). Gramsci, writing in the 1930s from a fascist prison, saw the latest "crisis of hegemony" resulting from the First World War and the Communist advances that followed, and would undoubtedly have seen the next crisis of hegemony for international capitalism resulting from the Second World War. Since then, theories of capitalist crisis (legitimation crisis, fiscal crisis of the state, crisis of welfare, crisis of deindustrialization, the environmental crisis, are just a few of the contenders) have been articulated from all sides. These have generally been seen as crises that need global as well as national solutions (Gottdiener and Komninos 1989; Ross and Trachte 1990). The twin processes of the collapse of communism and capitalist triumphalism, paradoxically, have increased the pressures on the capitalist system to solve all the problems of the contemporary world, quickly and globally.

The global capitalist project offers itself as the solution to all these crises and, as befits a hegemonic crisis of the first order, the solution is a new conception of global hegemony, "in other words, the possibility and necessity of creating a new culture" (Gramsci 1971: 276, written in 1930). But while Gramsci was thinking of a new socialist order, for the global age his words raise the prospect of "an emerging supranational corporate agenda" (Ranney 1994) or "transnational neoliberalism" (Overbeek 1993; Robinson 1996). The devastation of the 1970s oil shocks, the subsequent debt crises, corporate restructuring and downsizing (the race to the bottom), and the apparent inability of politicians to deal with these problems in any way other than short-term palliatives, suggest that the local effects of globalization increase the pressures on the transnational capitalist class to deliver what the culture-ideology of consumerism promises, more private possessions leading to better and happier lives for all. However, these pressures are usually refracted through the political system and the attempts of governments to get to grips with the problems of unemployment, deskilling, job insecurity, international competitiveness, law and order, immigration and emigration, multiculturalism. The culture-ideology of consumerism raises expectations that can be satisfied in at least two ways: state-driven redistribution of resources (this tends to be the social-democratic localizing solution) or market-driven increases of the size of the cake to be distributed (the neoliberal globalizing solution). An unwelcome result of the Thatcher-Reagan neoliberal experiments in the UK and US (copied widely throughout the world) has been the enrichment of many combined with the impoverishment of many more in rich and poor countries alike.[12] This has produced an arrogant overconfidence in the overprivileged and sometimes violent and sometimes fatalist reactions in the underprivileged. This is, of course, not the first time this has happened in human history.

Members of the corporate elite have commonly and with good reason felt insecure, whether from physical assault (Gladwin and Walter 1980) or expropriation (Minor 1994), particularly in the "foreign countries" where they do business. Though both phenomena declined in the 1990s, it is not very surprising that TNCs have routinely taken preemptive action to put their case before the public and local, national, and international authorities. For reasons which cannot be dealt with here, big business tends to be unpopular and its claims tend to be treated with a high degree of cynicism, so it often resorts to indirect ways of creating support for its causes and influencing public policy on behalf of its sectional interests (Beder 1997; Dreier 1982). One of the most important ideological tasks of big business is to persuade the population at large that "the business of society is business." It does this by creating a climate of opinion in which trade unions and radical oppositions (especially leftist labor, consumer, and environmental movements) are considered to be sectional interests while business groups are not. This is a large part of the creation and maintenance of global capitalist (and consumerist) hegemony.[13]

Just as Communist parties used to do in countries where they were illegal or circumscribed, big business often creates front organizations to propagate its messages. Many apparently straightforward civic organizations are largely run by and funded by the corporate elite.[14] Most of the research has been carried out on business groups in the USA and most studies focus on the ways in which both domestic corporations (Domhoff 1996; Ryan et al. 1987) and foreign TNCs (Tolchin 1993) influence the US government and its various state apparatuses to legislate in the interests of capital. Though they flirt with the now generally discredited conspiracy theory of capitalist hegemony, Eisenhower and Johnson [*sic!*] (1973) construct a useful checklist for studying the not-so-public sides of business–government relations in the US, which provides a model for similar research in other countries and transnationally:

> "Official conspiracies" are those institutionalized ways in which corporate interests shape and guide policies of the US government. . . .

The main apparatus of official conspiracies consists of organizations controlled by members of the corporate elite class that sponsor research, commission studies, publish influential journals, issue reports, engage in formal and informal dialogues with government officials, formulate policy guidelines, see that their men [and, increasingly, women (LS)] are appointed to key government posts, etc. Such organizations dealing with foreign policy include:

Corporate-controlled research-planning advising and report-issuing public affairs groups . . .
Businessmen's organizations . . .
Executively commissioned task forces, committees, and missions . . .
Citizen (read business) advisory councils and committees . . .
US Representatives to UN-sponsored panels . . .
Research Institutes . . .
Foundations.
(Eisenhower and Johnson 1973: 51–3)[15]

How does the capitalist class influence government and public opinion when it considers that its vital interests are affected? While there is a substantial literature on this general issue from a public policy perspective, there are relatively few studies that actually connect specific corporations with specific decisions. Of these, the most useful is that of Ryan et al. (1987) on the *Fortune* 500 in the USA, which proposes a three-stage model derived from research on the actual activities of some of the largest and most prominent global corporations. Stage 1 is directed towards public opinion formation, and there are various options for communication strategies that might achieve the desired end, namely to turn public opinion away from a position that harms the interests of the corporation to one that is at least neutral or, optimally, one that is consonant with the interests of the corporation. These communication strategies include one or more of the following: advocacy advertising, favorable publicity for annual reports, corporate newsletters and direct meetings with interested parties, economic education programs, image advertising, press releases, public service announcements, reports to government, special media presentations, inputs to TV and radio talk shows. Stage 2 is the arena of public policy formation, which focuses on office holders. Here, participation strategies include coalition building, lobbying, honorariums to useful allies, Political Action Committee contributions for friendly politicians, donations and support to political parties and public affairs groups, organization of public service meetings, and mobilization of trade associations. The third and final stage is public policy implementation, where the corporation has the options of compliance with new legislation, cooperation with enforcing agencies, creating a new issue to divert attention from unwelcome legislation, legal resistance to legislation or, in the last resort, noncompliance.

Ryan et al. argue that at each stage corporate actors and their allies form "iron triangles" of public interest groups, regulatory agencies, and Congressional committees, and if these are in line with corporate interests, corporations will win the battles over legislation. They report that the *Fortune* 500 are more proactive than popularly believed, a conclusion that later chapters in this book amply confirm. In the period they study, 1970–9, 11 percent of the 500 were involved in at least one major crime, and 188 charges were made against the corporations covering 163 offenses, mainly antitrust violations but also bribery, criminal fraud, illegal political contributions, and tax evasion (Ryan et al. 1987: 184–5). Larger firms were most likely to offend (but perhaps they attract most attention from law enforcers). The evidence from the USA and many other countries since then suggests that there has been no diminution in the volume of corporate wrongdoing.

Such illustrations of capitalist class strength, paradoxically, also provide evidence for the fragility at the core of capitalism. We can call this "the problem of business," and again it is best illustrated in the heartland of capitalist hegemony, the USA. From the 1960s, the age of flower power and "up against the corporate wall" (Sethi 1971), to the 1990s and the debate around the "good corporation" (Houck and Williams 1996), the issue of corporate responsibility has refused to disappear. In the 1970s corporations in the USA deliberately sought "to reverse a dramatic decline in public confidence in big business which they blame on the media" (Dreier 1982: 111). To do this, as Ryan et al. predicted they would, business mobilized through think-tanks, university business journalism courses, awards and prizes to encourage more favorable reporting, détente between business and media, advocacy advertising, and increased TV sponsorship of culture (Beder 1997; Dreier 1982). An important addition is the development of "Business Ethics" both as an area of academic research – a review by Tsalikis and Fritzsche (1989) identified over 300 sources – and as a set of responses for big business under threat, elegantly exposed, appropriately enough, in an article in the journal *Propaganda Review* by Graziano (Graziano 1989).

The reason for all this activity is that the capitalist class always faces the threat of challenge from below. No doubt at some periods, in the USA and elsewhere, big business is more popular and at other periods less popular, but the point is that capitalist hegemony needs constant support, attention, and originality to sustain it.[16] This is no less true for capitalism in the global compared with the national or urban context.

Indeed, intuitively, it appears not unlikely that "global capitalism" understood in terms of "foreign" capitalist exploitation of "our" society, will tend to be more unpopular.[17]

The parallel developments of cheap global mass media and substantial increases in various forms of transnational business relations (foreign direct investment, strategic alliances, global brands, corporate recruitment through executive and professional cross-border flows) are indicators of the unprecedented global shift of contemporary capitalism and the exposure of its promises and performance for all to see.

"National Interest" and "the National Economy"

A clear implication of global system theory is that the ideas of national interest and the national economy are both conceptually problematic and ideologically burdened. Global system theory cannot be reconciled with the view that nation-states somehow transcend the divisions of class (and related divisions of ethnicity, gender, ideology, and other differences) in the vision of a national interest. Even in the most visible manifestations of national competitiveness like war and sport, not all co-nationals or co-citizens are necessarily united against the "common enemy." Nevertheless, the rhetoric and ideology of national interest is so pervasive and so deep-rooted that it is often difficult to see through it.[18] Globalization bears a contradictory relationship to the concept of national interest.

The most common criterion for measuring economic and social well-being in the modern world is based on the nation-state. This is related to international conceptions of well-being in two senses. First, the predominance of the national economy for making global comparisons of economic performance (and the ubiquity of concepts like gross national product per capita and average wage rates) encourages international bodies, governments, and media to present some rather complex and contested economic measures in simplistic and often quite misleading forms. Second, due to what has been called space–time compression, groups with access to mass media (which now includes the large majority of the world's population) can be given some impression of standards of living in many places all over the world and can begin to compare their own circumstances with those of others irrespective of distance. These new reference groups are new only in the sense that they are a mass phenomenon today, and not the preserve of small, well-traveled minorities of past eras. This suggests that relationships between the local and the global are changing. One important marker of these changes is that globalization forces us to reconceptualize ideas like the national economy.

The idea of the national economy, like that of the national interest, appears to be intuitively obvious. Economic data are routinely collected, recorded, and constructed in the national context. One of the first signs that the idea of the national economy might be problematic was the way in which the contribution of foreign investment to the national economy came to be measured. This led to the distinction between Gross Domestic Product (GDP) and Gross National Product (GNP). GDP is defined as "the total flow of goods and services produced by the economy over a particular time period, normally a year" (Bannock et al. 1972: 187). Note that this definition does not even bother to mention that by "the economy" is meant the economy of one country; this is entirely obvious. GNP, on the other hand, is GDP "plus the income accruing to domestic residents arising from investment abroad less income earned in the domestic market accruing to foreigners abroad" (ibid., p. 188). The issues of exactly who is a resident and what income actually does accrue in the course of transactions across state boundaries, makes it difficult to decide which of these two measures refers most appropriately to the national economy.

It may be helpful to construct three ideal types of economy: purely national, international, and global. We can define the purely national economy as one serving an exclusively sovereign state-market, employing only local co-nationals, whose products or services consist entirely of domestic parts, components, and materials. An international economy would then be one made up of purely national economies, where pairs of countries export and import goods and services between themselves. What would a global economy look like? First, it would not be based on interacting national economies but on a variety of economic entities that were not national economies, like firms of various types whose aggregate business was not satisfactorily described in terms of a single national economy. Second, it would be an economy in which the key units did not in any meaningful sense express the national interest, or in which even the problematic concept of the national interest discussed above regularly did not override the interests of business corporations and those who owned and controlled them. This is a fair characterization of the contemporary global economy of transnational corporations and would be corroborated to the extent that the economic practices of these corporations were becoming increasingly transnational. The case of a rapidly growing software company in India's Silicon Valley exemplifies this well. "Infosys likes to think of itself as in India, but not run by India. . . . [The CEO says] We don't rely on local telephones, we have our own system. Our customers should not notice that the infrastructure is any different to their own – no matter where they come from" (quoted in Ramesh 2000). Infosys does almost all its business outside India, much of it with major TNCs.

The spread of capitalism as an international system of imperialism was dominated by hegemonic capitalist classes, sometimes in conjunction with state elites and sometimes in tension with them. With the advent of a genuinely globalizing capitalist system dominated by a transnational capitalist class, the ideas of national interest and national economy were revealed for the ideological tools that they were. It is no small irony that the only two great forces in modern history to have seen through political and economic nationalisms, even if imperfectly and incompletely, were the proletariat (workers of the world) organized in the feeble Internationals and the transnational capitalist class organized around globalizing corporations. Other institutional phenomena – including the great World Religions, movements for human rights and democratization, organized crime, and what Keck and Sikkink (1998) call transnational advocacy networks – may also be seen as globalizing forces in this sense. Nevertheless, none of these has the systematic and pervasive character of global capitalism. This is due to the fact that, though some of them have substantial resources and personnel, except in exceptional circumstances they cannot compete with the power and influence of the institutions that sustain the transnational capitalist class and dominate the global economy, the subjects of the next chapter.

Notes

1 See, in particular, the works of Ewen (1976), Bourdieu (1996), and Baudrillard (1988).
2 Zeitlin claims to have conceptualized and elaborated the idea of the "inner group" (in Zeitlin and Ratcliff 1988: 102 n. 49). Questions of intellectual priority aside, this is a path-breaking study on Chile, taking a systematically researched theory of the capitalist class outside the First World for the first time. Its conclusion – "What is remarkable, indeed, is that the decisive axes of the inner structure of the dominant class, successively revealed in our foregoing chapters, are here disclosed as being the axes of that class's integration with foreign capital" (ibid., p. 251) – is, of course, significant for my thesis.
3 Robinson (1996) distinguishes national from transnational fractions of dominant groups. Glassman (1999) uses the term the "internationalization of the state" for parallel processes, and gives a good account of the development of such arguments. On my definition, the state as such cannot be transnational, but globalizing bureaucrats and politicians can.

4 The literature on "old" antisystemic social movements has been regenerated by an emphasis on new social movements and identity politics (see Ray 1993; Scott 1990) and as antiglobalization movements (Castells 1998).

5 This is not difficult to explain. The military and political might of the US state (and some others), and the many occasions on which they have been used, do provide *prima facie* evidence for the continuing correctness of state-centric explanations. (And, of course, I may be wrong and state-centric explanations may be correct, but this would leave many problems raised by globalization research unanswered.)

6 Useem (1992) makes this case indirectly for corporations in the USA and I make it directly for Australia (Sklair 1996).

7 The phrase "race to the bottom" was introduced in the USA to describe downsizing and pressure on workers around 1900. Widely used in the 1990s it even found its way into the Communiqué of the G8 environmental ministers meeting in Schwerin, Germany in March 1999: "Global competition should never become a race to the bottom in environmental protection" (cited in the University of Toronto G8 website). See also Hildyard (1996).

8 International business education has spread rapidly all over the world, usually with First World partners and often with corporate support. See, for example, the report in the *Financial Times* (Oct. 12, 1998) of the partnership between two leading business schools in the USA to establish a "world class" business school in India, brokered by a group of expatriate Indian executives in the USA. Salas-Porras (1996, ch. 7) discusses the related development of the global entrepreneurial movement with reference to the globalization of big business in Mexico.

9 On globalization and world cities, see Knox and Taylor (1995), especially the chapters by Friedmann, Sassen, and King.

10 While it is generally agreed that global capitalism delivers more genuinely democratic opportunities and rule of law than any other large-scale system yet put into practice, the level of cynicism about actually-existing democracies appears to be growing all over the world. On polyarchic democracy, see Robinson (1996).

11 Cockett (1995: 306) says that "the internationalization of the work of the British 'think-tanks' was one of the most extraordinary features of economic liberalism as it developed in the 1980s," but discusses the issue only in passing. Many in the new right, of course, are suspicious of corporate capitalism.

12 Feenstra (1996) argues in the *American Economic Review* that the real wages of less-skilled workers in the US have fallen dramatically since the late 1970s. This seems likely to be true for other countries, as reflected in per capita income data (see Korzeniewicz and Moran 1997). For a thoughtful discussion of the wider ramifications of this issue, see Castells (1998).

13 Anti-big-business sentiment has existed in the US and elsewhere since at least the nineteenth century: see Piott (1985). Lipset and Schneider (1983) argue that the major institutions (business, labor, and government) all

suffer from a "confidence gap" in the USA. The relative rarity of research on how big business organizes to sustain its hegemony, compared with oppositional social movements, mirrors the relative rarity of research on the capitalist class itself.

14 Radical publications like *Multinational Monitor* and others associated with the name of Ralph Nader in the USA frequently "expose" such organizations. Rowell (1996) demonstrates this globally for the environmental field. Poole (1989) uses similar evidence to argue, paradoxically, that "Big Business Bankrolls the Left." See chapter 7 below.

15 See also on the US Council on Foreign Relations (Shoup and Minter 1977) and its French equivalent (Domhoff 1981), on the Business Roundtable (Burch 1981 and 1997), on business leaders in government (Useem 1984), on the Trilateral Commission (Gill 1990; Sklar 1980); Silva for Chile (1996); Ogliastri and Davila (1987) for Colombia; and Taira and Wada (1987) for Japan; and Scott, ed. (1990) more generally. Domhoff (1996) makes the case for a pervasive corporate dominant class whose organizations steer the state in various policy directions.

16 Evidence from other countries on the opposition to big business and capitalist hegemony can be gleaned from the general social movements literature. In an informative book on Australia, Browning (1990) claims that the left is organized in an antibusiness global network, a common and not unreasonable claim of capitalist-inspired ideologues.

17 The inverted commas signify that "foreign" capital is often owned by domestic capitalists, and often benefits elements in "our" society through profits and jobs (see Reich 1991).

18 The voluminous literature on nationalism crosscuts the issues raised here (see Holton 1998).

Chapter 3
Transnational Corporations and the Global Economy

Despite the increasing volume of theory and research on globalization (see Lechner and Boli 2000), there are still those who claim that the there is nothing new about it, that it is very much exaggerated or even that it is a myth.[1] Those who reject the idea of the globalization of the economy, in particular, argue that TNCs (variously referred to as international, multinational, multidomestic, geocentric, transnational, or global), remain overwhelmingly domestic or national companies, largely oriented to their home countries and largely constrained by home country rules and regulations.[2]

This chapter examines the extent to which these criticisms of economic globalization are valid. The point of this analysis is to show how the transnational corporations provide the material basis for the existence and power of the transnational capitalist class. To put it simply, without a coordinated global economy dominated by the major globalizing corporations, it would be impossible for a transnational capitalist class to exist. One convenient source of basic information about these companies is the list of the largest corporations by revenue published annually by *Fortune* magazine since the 1950s. In the 1990s, the editors of *Fortune* decided to combine the previously separated US and non-US corporations, and then the biggest industrial and services corporations, into one consolidated "global scorecard," the *Fortune* Global 500.[3] The rationale for the change is significant for the debate around globalization: "The world of business is rapidly transforming itself – and blurring once-valid distinctions between industrial and service companies – as a new informational economy takes hold" (*Fortune*, Aug. 7, 1995: 6).[4] In addition to Global 500 corporations, other important companies are considered, notably from the annual *Financial Times* lists based on market capitalization, the *Forbes* magazine lists of major private corporations, and smaller companies which are significant for global capitalism.

The making of the transnational capitalist class is intrinsically bound up with the globalizing of the corporations and their control over the new global economy that has been emerging over the last few decades. Analysis of Global 500 corporations is one of several possible ways to approach this emerging global economy, and it has several decisive advantages over other methods. It concentrates on (a) actual corporations rather than aggregate financial flows, (b) the actual business of these corporations (which often spreads over conventional industrial categories to take advantage of new and changing commercial synergies) rather than stock market valuation, and (c) size and its relationship to the globalizing of corporations. At all times, the distinction between the major corporations (the characteristic institutional form of economic transnational practices) and the people who own and control them, the agents of global capitalism, is treated as analytical rather than empirical. In doing this, the issue of reification is transformed from an epistemological problem into an empirical question. This clearly needs some explaining. When the CEO of DuPont made a speech about "corporate environmentalism" in 1989 (see chapter 7 below) he was speaking both for the TNC that was DuPont and for himself, an individual called Edgar Woolard. Certainly, in one sense Woolard was not DuPont, but in another sense he was then more Dupont than almost anyone else on the planet. His claim to speak for DuPont (and for the chemical industry as a whole) did reify DuPont (and the chemical industry) but in a way that exposed it to an empirical test. The test, in this case, is whether or not DuPont as a corporation and the chemical industry in general followed through on Woolard's words on "corporate environmentalism." They have done so, as chapter 7 documents. Woolard's representational claim, therefore, as an individual agent (but not just any individual agent) reflected DuPont's capacity as a powerful corporation – here, agency and structure reflect one another. This, of course, does not always necessarily happen. Woolard could have been speaking out of place, against the interests and wishes of others influential in the ownership and control of DuPont. If this had been the case, then Woolard would not have survived as CEO of DuPont, and the reification of DuPont reflected in Woolard's claim to speak for the corporate structure would have to be evaluated differently.

Another telling example of this process of corporate reification appeared in *The New York Times Magazine*. Reflecting on his interviews for an article on the moral conscience of tobacco executives, Roger Rosenblatt commented: "in dealing with these Philip Morris executives,

I felt the presence of the company within the person. In the end, I felt that I was speaking with more company than person, or perhaps to a person who could no longer distinguish between the two" (quoted in Kluger 1997: 751).[5]

The reification of a corporation differs from the reification of a class in that corporations are legal entities and specific individuals are legally entitled to speak for them. While the transnational capitalist class has no legal identity, this does not mean that it has no sociological identity. However, its sociological identity is more difficult to pin down, and that is why the charge that theories of class reify their objects of knowledge is so commonly made. Locating the institutional form of the transnational capitalist class within and around the TNCs, and the agents of this class within and around the individuals and institutions who own and control them, opens up the reification of the transnational capitalist class to empirical tests, just as the representative nature of Woolard's words on corporate environmentalism could be empirically tested. To describe the global economy and to start to explain how it works, therefore, identifying the people who count in major corporations and the transnational capitalist class, give us both conceptual handles and empirical openings. The largest corporations, as we shall see, also tend to be corporations that are globalizing. Those who own and control them and their closest allies in the state, in the political system, in the professions, and in the media and commerce, give solidity to the abstractions of global capitalist system and transnational capitalist class.

The Global Economy and the *Fortune* Global 500

Fortune lists the major corporations in the world in three main ways, by revenues, by industry, and by country of legal domicile. Many corporations today are difficult to classify neatly on all three counts. All revenues are denominated in US dollars, so when the value of the yen is high relative to the dollar, for example, Japanese companies might appear "bigger" than they really are. Many major companies are involved in a variety of industries; for example, in 1996 RJR Nabisco was a major cigarette manufacturer but was classified under food,[6] while Philip Morris was a major food manufacturer but was classified under tobacco. Some companies have origins in more than one country, usually as a result of mergers and acquisitions: for example both Shell and Unilever were domiciled in Holland and Britain.

The list published in 1996 (based on company data for 1995) presents one picture of the global economy and the corporations that dominated it at the end of the twentieth century. Corporations from 25 countries and territories were represented. Of the 500 corporations on the list, 153 were domiciled in the USA and 141 in Japan, comprising about 60 percent of the total. The rest were from Europe (171), Canada (6), Australia (4), Brazil (4), China (2), South Korea (12), and one each from Hong Kong, India, Mexico, Netherlands Antilles, Turkey, Taiwan, and Venezuela. Table 3.1 gives the geographical breakdown of the Global 500 in the 1996 list.

There is clearly going to be an element of arbitrariness in any attempt to split up the global economy into manageable parts for the purpose of analysis. One of the key consequences of globalization is the gradual weakening of the power of the state to intervene meaning-

Table 3.1 Geographical distribution of the *Fortune* Global 500 (1996)

Place of domicile	Number of companies	Number in top 100, top 250
Australia	4	0, 0
Belgium	5	0, 0
Belgium/Neth	1	0, 1
Brazil	4	0, 2
Britain	32	1, 13
Britain/Neth.	2	2, 2
Canada	6	0, 1
China	2	0, 1
Finland	2	0, 0
France	42	12, 27
Germany	40	14, 29
Hong Kong	1	0, 0
India	1	0, 0
Italy	12	3, 6
Japan	141	37, 73
Mexico	1	0, 1
Netherlands	8	2, 4
Neth. Antilles	1	0, 1
Norway	2	0, 0
South Korea	12	2, 7
Spain	6	0, 2
Sweden	3	0, 2
Switzerland	16	3, 8
Taiwan	1	0, 0
Turkey	1	0, 0
US	153	24, 69
Venezuela	1	0, 1

Source: adapted from the *Fortune* Global 500 (Aug. 5, 1996).

fully in economic affairs and the progressive diminution of national differences in the economic realm (Strange 1996). One important corollary of this is that the common split between the countries of Europe, North America, and Japan (the Triad), while still useful for some purposes, is of decreasing salience in explaining how the global economy works in each part of the world. Thus, global system theory would predict that the national origins of the major corporations are becoming less important than their relationship to the processes of globalization as predictors of their practices and rhetoric.[7] One strong nonstate influence on their practices is the sectors of the global economy in which they operate.

In 1996 (the baseline for this book), the Global 500 were divided into 44 industries plus one miscellaneous group with 6 corporations. The distribution within industries ranged from 64 commercial banks, the largest group, to 5 industries (energy, food services, hotels, insurance: property and casualty (mutual), and shipping), with only 2 corporations in each. On this basis, the global economy at the end of the twentieth century can be rearranged into five main business sectors. These are listed as follows, with the names of the industries as they appear in the Global 500 in descending order of aggregate revenues, for ease of reference.

1) The **consumer goods and services** sector (153 corporations) comprised 21 trading companies; 26 motor vehicles and parts; 25 food and drug stores; 17 general merchandisers; 11 food; 10 pharmaceuticals; 3 tobacco; 7 wholesalers; 5 forest and paper products; 6 beverages; 5 specialist retailers; 5 publishing, printing; 3 soaps, cosmetics; 2 food services; 3 entertainment; 2 hotels, casinos, resorts; 1 healthcare and 1 advertising (both in the miscellaneous category).

2) **Financial services** (132 corporations) comprised 64 commercial banks; 56 insurance companies; 4 diversified financials; 4 brokerage; 3 savings institutions; and 1 real estate (miscellaneous).

3) **Heavy industry** (84 corporations) comprised 29 petroleum refiners; 18 chemicals; 15 metals; 8 industrial and farm equipment; 3 mining, crude-oil production; 3 rubber and plastic; 3 building materials, glass; 3 metal products; 1 transportation equipment and 1 textiles (both miscellaneous).

4) **Infrastructure** (88 corporations) comprised 22 telecommunications; 16 electric and gas utilities; 13 engineering and construction; 8 mail, package, and freight delivery; 8 aerospace; 8 railroads; 8 airlines; 2 energy; 2 shipping; and 1 waste management (miscellaneous).

5) **Electronics** (43 corporations) comprised 30 electronics, electrical equipment; 8 computers, office equipment; and 5 scientific, photo, and control equipment.

The revenues of all the corporations in the Global 500 in 1996 totaled over 11 trillion (thousand billion) dollars, with assets in excess of 32 trillion dollars. The five sectors ranged from 153 consumer goods and services corporations with total revenues exceeding 4 trillion dollars to 43 in the electronics sector with revenues just over a trillion dollars. Trading was the industry with the largest aggregate revenues, and the three biggest Global 500 corporations were Mitsubishi, Mitsui, and Itochu.[8] The banks, unsurprisingly, accounted for almost half of the total Global 500 asset value. The 500 corporations employed more than 35 million people, employment rank corresponding roughly with revenues. The biggest employer was the electronic and electrical equipment industry with over 4 million, followed by motor vehicles and parts (3.5 million). Seven of the top 10 revenue sectors were also in the top 10 for employment (and 10 of the top 20).

The decision to regroup these 500 corporations from their 40-plus industries into five major global business sectors is justified in equal part by arguments on convenience and the sociologic of the global economy. The convenience argument is obvious. Five business sectors are much easier to deal with, make for greater economy of presentation, and are intuitively less confusing than more than 40 industries. The only major anomaly is the inclusion of the trading companies in consumer goods and services, for these huge corporations are something of an anomaly in themselves. It seemed more realistic to place them with consumer goods and services than in any of the other groups or by themselves. The sociological argument derives from the difficulties that the *Fortune* listers have in allotting many corporations to a single industry. For example, the three major cigarette producers, Philip Morris, RJR Nabisco, and BAT Industries were all deeply involved in other industries (see Sklair 1998). In 1995, RJR Nabisco was placed in the tobacco industry (its tobacco revenues exceeded its food revenues) but in 1996 it was placed in the food industry (that year its food revenues exceeded its tobacco revenues). The classification of the food, beverages, and tobacco industries (plus many others) in the consumer goods and services business sector preempts this difficulty (though it did not work for the tobacco and insurance conglomerate BAT until it demerged its insurance companies in 1998). As we shall see, this generally makes good sense in terms of marketing and globalization strategies. Nevertheless, there are many other examples of Global 500 companies active in more than one of these five business sectors. Several of the trading companies from Japan are interlocked with other companies (often bearing similar names) in other business sectors. Increasing numbers of major manufacturing corporations around the world are becoming major financial corporations as well, for example

GE Capital, the mighty financial arm of the mighty GE (General Electric) Corporation.

The patterning of the business sectors also makes sense. Here we find that one or two of *Fortune*'s industry groups tend to dominate in terms of revenues and numbers of corporations in each business sector. In the largest sector, consumer goods and services, two industries – trading and motor vehicles and parts – comprise about one-third of the companies and over half of the revenues of the whole sector. The importance of the car as an icon of the culture-ideology of consumerism is clear from these figures. The second-ranked global business sector is financial services. While it is not necessary to subscribe to the widely-held view that the banks have the dominant place in global capitalism (for a balanced discussion see Scott 1997, ch. 5), there is no denying that financial services of various types affect the prosperity and sometimes the viability of all Global 500 corporations, and many other companies. Of particular importance is the role of financial institutions in stock markets. So, the outcome of my classification of the global economy, that consumer goods and services and financial services together provide more than half of the Global 500 and that the aggregate revenues of all these corporations are more than 60 percent of the total, should come as no surprise. The third-placed business sector, heavy industry, is dominated by 29 petroleum refiners who account for half the sector aggregate revenues. Next comes infrastructure and its dominant industry, telecommunications, ranks seventh out of all 45 industries in revenues.

The case of infrastructure illuminates the logic of the global system analysis put forward in this book very clearly. To put it simply, if it can be demonstrated that even in infrastructure, which appears to be a naturally domestic sector, tied to and often owned by national governments, major corporations are globalizing, then this must be one good indication that the difference between the international economy based on discrete national economies and national markets on the one hand, and the global economy based on the global market and globalizing corporations on the other, is real. The global economy, however, can be and constantly is broken down into many different types of discrete markets of which national markets are certainly one type, but in some cases these are becoming less important than supranational regional markets and transnational and subnational markets of various types.

The smallest business sector by numbers of industries, corporations, and revenues is electronics, dominated by the electronics and electrical equipment industry. The distinction between this industry and the computers and office equipment industry is often difficult to maintain.

The relative smallness of electronics should, of course, be seen in the light of its novelty as a sector at all, and the view that electronics is the driving force of the contemporary global economy.

This five-business-sector classification is mainly a heuristic device to organize the analysis of how globalization operates in the global economy through the largest corporations in the world. The underlying point of this analysis is that each one of the *Fortune* Global 500 is owned and controlled by identifiable groups of people. These owners and/or controllers are sometimes individual capitalists (the very rich, entrepreneurs, non-executive directors, investment fund gurus), sometimes salaried representatives of capitalist institutions (TNCs of various types, pension funds, investment vehicles), or both. While the transnational capitalist class is comprised of several groups of actors operating through a variety of institutions and organizations, it is dominated by those who own and control the major corporations and through them, the global economy. The TNCs are the honey pot around which all those who are dependent on the capitalist global system circulate. If we are to have the tools to analyze how the transnational capitalist class works and to explain its successes and failures, then we need to identify these corporations.

Consumer goods and services (153 companies, $4.3 trillion revenues)

The consumer goods and services sector comprised the panoply of goods and services that has fueled the rise of the culture-ideology of consumerism in the second half of the twentieth century as a mass and global phenomenon. Motor vehicles and parts, one of only three industries with revenues exceeding a trillion dollars, along with trading houses, dominated the consumer goods and services business sector. The big three motor manufacturers (GM, Ford, and Toyota) all had revenues in excess of $100 billion and ranked 4, 7, and 8 respectively (1, 2, and 11 respectively in 1998). Overall, 9 motor manufacturers figured in the top 50 of the Global 500. Like the electronics industry which provides the software for virtually all major business transactions today, the motor industry provides the means of real distance movement. Most mail and freight delivery depends on motor vehicles, as does transportation to and from planes, trains, and ships; and much of the rubber and plastics industry is engaged in supplying tires and other parts for cars. The car industry is often seen as a global industry, partly as a result of the well-publicized search for a world car (notably by Ford and Fiat) to cut costs and maximize profits (Dicken 1998, ch. 10), and partly because of the centrality of the private car as the prime modernist icon of the good life. Private cars are the most expensive purchase modern consumers normally make during their lifetimes (with the exception of housing). While most people in the world are presently excluded from ownership of private cars, the aspiration to own a car appears to be almost universal. Therefore, the prospects for the motor vehicle industry and its associated goods and services look promising for the future, despite the damage that cars do to the environment. This issue will be considered in more detail in subsequent chapters.

The greatest change in the consumer goods and services sector in the last few decades has been the increasing concentration of sales outlets in general. In 1980, only 44 retailers had sales exceeding a billion dollars in the USA; in 1995 there were more than 100. These large chains are gradually driving millions of small shops out of business all over the world.[9] This has considerable implications for social life, automobile use, patterns of consumption, and for the distance that food travels from producers to consumers (food miles).

Fortune lists 25 food and drug stores and 17 general merchandisers. The largest retailer in the world in 1996 was Wal-Mart, recording an astonishing $93.7 billion in revenues and $2.7 billion in profits (it overshot the magic $100 billion revenues mark in 1997 and by 1998 was the eighth largest company in the world). In 1999 it acquired Asda, a major British-based retailer. This was portrayed in the media as a deliberate attempt by Wal-Mart to globalize its winning formula. Also on the Global 500 list of retailers and merchandisers were chain stores domiciled in several European countries, Australia, and Canada. The retail giants, though at present restricted to corporations domiciled in these countries, were active all over the world. By 1998, the France-based chain Carrefour, for example, had more than 300 stores in 18 countries, including Argentina, Mexico, Brazil, Malaysia, China and Taiwan, and Turkey.

In 1996, there were 21 trading houses (by revenues the largest single industry in the Global 500)[10] and 7 wholesalers. The preeminence of the trading industry was somewhat artificial as the top 9 corporations in the industry (and the top 3 TNCs in the *Fortune* Global 500 for 1996) were all Japan-based conglomerates involved in a large number of separate industries. For example, the number one company, Mitsubishi, had no less than 8 separate companies listed in the Global 500, and the number two, Mitsui, had 5. While the parent companies Mitsubishi and Mitsui are certainly traders, they are many other things besides. It was also notable that they generated very low returns on capital in the 1990s.[11]

The common feature of these and other corporations in this sector is that they sell directly to consumers (or provide goods and services to those who do) and, therefore, play a central and visible role in the culture-ideology of consumerism. It is here, more than in any other sector, that are to be found the global brands that have so influenced the discussion of global culture and its supposed homogenizing effects.[12]

Financial services (132 companies; $2.6 trillion revenues)

There were 64 commercial banks in the 1996 Global 500. The strength of the yen largely explains the relative dominance of Japanese banks in 1996 (6 of the top 10 and 18 overall), and the weakness of the yen largely explains their relative eclipse in 1998 (reduced to 1 of the top 10 and 7 overall). Deutsche Bank (Germany) was number one (it acquired Bankers Trust in 1998), and the top 10 also included Credit Agricole and Credit Lyonnais (both domiciled in France) and Citicorp (USA). The peculiarities of the US banking system has inhibited the growth of huge national banks, state-owned or private, that are found in many other countries. There were only 9 US-based banks in the Global 500 in 1996 (up to 11 in 1998), though significant deregulation was underway (Vietor 1994, ch. 5). The merger of Citibank and Travelers in 1998 to create Citigroup was widely interpreted as a consequence of globalization, and created the largest financial services company the world had ever seen. This merger confirmed the trend to convergence of financial services companies where the successful globalizing corporation combines securities, commercial banking, insurance, and retail brokerage functions in one global conglomerate. It remains to be seen if these megafirms can make enough profits long-term to satisfy their shareholders. The globalizing process for all the major banks was concisely summed up by the treasurer of Dow Chemical Canada, endorsing his company's choice of BankAmerica. "Dow is a truly global company and we need a truly global corporate bank – one that can coordinate the resources we need wherever we do business" (BankAmerica US Corporate Group brochure 1994).

The world financial system is not, of course, restricted to Global 500 corporations. Major international financial institutions, notably the International Monetary Fund, and the multilateral development banks, notably the World Bank, do not appear in the Global 500. Nevertheless, there is no convincing evidence that these financial institutions approach their business very differently from the Global 500 financial corporations. They tend to be led by men (rarely women) with backgrounds and interests directly compatible with those of the corporate sector in general and other bankers in particular, who often join or return to Global 500 financial corporations and/or other major institutions when they leave.[13] In the 1990s, partly as a result of pressure from political opponents in the US, the multilateral development banks began to forge more direct relationships with the private sector. Between 1993 and 1995, for example, the development banks made around $5 billion available to major corporations, including GE, GM, Motorola, IBM, AT&T, and Allied Signal, for project financing (Hildyard 1996). Just as there are conflicts of interests between and within different types of Global 500 financial institutions, there are undoubtedly conflicts of interests between them and the World Bank and IMF and others on occasion. Nevertheless, as is argued throughout this book, they all share a common and ultimately overriding interest in the continuation of the global capitalist system and the private accumulation of wealth for the members of the transnational capitalist class.

The other main financial services industries, insurance and savings, are both traditionally domestically oriented industries but, as we shall see in subsequent chapters, even they have responded in some interesting ways to the forces of globalization.

Heavy industries (84 companies, $1.7 trillion revenues)

The petroleum refining companies in the Global 500 have been historically dominated by the "Seven Sisters" (five US-based corporations plus Shell and BP)[14] who, up to 1973, controlled 70 percent of all the oil produced in the world (see Al-Moneef 1999; Tanzer 1969). The oil shocks of the 1970s and 1980s transformed the situation and a group of state-owned oil companies began to acquire or construct refineries to challenge the Seven Sisters. Thus, since the 1960s several state-owned Third World oil companies have made a moderately strong showing in the *Fortune* lists (see Sklair and Robbins forthcoming). The oil industry has always been considered to be highly "internationalized" due to its dependence on finding and extracting natural resources, both oil and natural gas, which are spread all over the planet with no regard for political boundaries. By the 1990s, the state-owned oil companies and the Seven Sisters were engaged in many joint ventures and strategic alliances in refining and marketing.

As many major private and state-owned oil companies have expanded downstream, into petrochemicals and sales and marketing of petroleum and other products, it is logical to combine the oil and chemical industries into this global heavy industry sector. The chemical industry has also been changing dramatically with an increasing split between bulk and specialty chemicals, as we will see below in connection with the restructuring of ICI. The other companies in this sector are all more or less low down on the value-added chain, their products tend to be commodities, like metals, for further processing rather than bought by the final consumer. With the exception of the fuel bought at the pumps, this is true for most of the heavy industry business sector.

Infrastructure (88 companies, $1.6 trillion revenues)

The infrastructure sector comprised TNCs engaged in telecommunications, electric and gas generation, engineering and construction, energy, and waste management.[15] A distinctively globalizing perspective on the infrastructure sector was provided by a Special Advertising Section published in *Forbes* magazine (Feb. 1997) under the title: "World-wide Infrastructure Partnerships: Productive Engines for the Global Economy." Under the inspiring slogan, "The miracle of globalization is upon us," a major conference in San Francisco (sponsored by *Forbes*, the World Bank, and various other development and finance agencies) was informed that the 1996 International Major Projects Survey had recorded 1,500 publicly sanctioned but privately promoted public works in 107 countries, valued at $870 billion. This "globalization of private investment in emerging markets . . . [is] bypassing the stage of regulatory controls." Fifty countries were said to be pursuing airport privatization, and other services such as correctional facilities, telecommunications, and water were not far behind (see also Brewer and Young 1998, table 5.3). Many of the Global 500 infrastructure corporations are in the forefront of these developments.

The top 6 of the 22 Global 500 telecommunications companies were domiciled in 6 different countries (Japan, USA, Germany, Italy, France, and Britain), the remainder comprising 10 more from the USA (mostly parts of the dismembered Bell system), and one each from Sweden, Spain, Switzerland, Netherlands, Finland, and Brazil (Telebras, privatized in the late 1990s).

There were 17 electric and gas utilities in the Global 500. In one respect, the situation of corporations in this sector is as near as one can get to a "crucial experiment" for the globalization thesis. The geographical constraints and the regulatory regimes within which these corporations have had to operate (and some still have to) appear to exclude globalization entirely and lock utilities firmly into their places of origin. However, privatization and deregulation trends all over the world and the end of actual or quasi-monopoly conditions for many energy providers has begun to change their operating conditions. The circumstances of the electricity suppliers in northern and southern

California and their overseas ventures (see below) are excellent cases in point.

The engineering and construction industry in 1996, untypically, was dominated by two companies of French origin, Générale des Eaux (known as Vivendi since 1997) and (Suez) Lyonnaise des Eaux, both of whom rapidly expanded from their base in water services to other infrastructural areas. Vivendi, for example, had a strategic alliance with BT for telecommunications services in France and is now a major multimedia investor and, like many other globalizing corporations, showing interest in the internet.

Electronics (43 companies, $1.2 trillion revenues)

For most people the electronics industry conjures up images of the almost-mythical Silicon Valley where the computer and electronic revolution of the latter part of the twentieth century is, not entirely accurately, reputed to have started.[16] The *Fortune* Global 500 distinguishes computers and office equipment from electrical and electronic equipment, but it does make more sense in a survey of the global economy such as this to aggregate these two industries (with scientific, photo, and control equipment which is now more or less entirely based on electronics) into an electronics global business sector. It may appear surprising that the electronics sector is the smallest by revenues and numbers of companies of the five business sectors in this profile of the global economy, as it is arguably, with consumer goods and services, the most visible of all the sectors in terms of the globalizing debate. (Classifying the global economy by market capitalization would probably propel electronics to the top of the list with the addition of the revenue-light e-commerce companies.)

The electronics industry was dominated by Hitachi, Matsushita, and General Electric (all with revenues in excess of $70 billion). Six of the top 10 companies in the industry were from Japan,[17] with Siemens and Philips (from Europe) and Daewoo (from South Korea) completing the ten. The industry contained many older and less glamorous corporations who have had to make the difficult transition from the pre-electronic to the electronic age, often with pre-electronic corporate cultures. Matsushita Electrical, General Electric, Siemens, Philips (renamed Royal Philips Electronics in 1998), ABB, and Rockwell, among others, did not start their corporate lives as electronics companies.

The computers sector was dominated by IBM,[18] whose revenues were almost double those of its nearest rivals, Fujitsu and Hewlett-Packard

(HP). Many of the major computer companies (HP, Apple, Intel) were located in Silicon Valley, which has spawned an interesting literature on the advantages of industrial and technological agglomeration (see Dicken 1998, ch. 11).

These brief sketches of dominant corporations in the five business sectors illustrate the contours of big business in the contemporary world. As we shall see, the separateness of these highly competitive corporations is only one side of the picture. It has to be balanced by the other side, namely a high (and apparently increasing) level of corporate cooperation in the forms of joint ventures of various types, strategic alliances, and other less visible accommodations between corporations that appear on the surface to be in bitter rivalry over markets, technology, and specialist personnel.

From "National Companies with Units Abroad" to Globalizing Corporations

The question of whether and to what extent there is a global economy based on globalizing corporations can be approached in a variety of ways. In the academic social science literature – most of which is quite hostile to the ideas of economic globalization and the global economy – the answer to the question is usually negative (Hirst and Thompson 1996; Kapstein 1994). This conclusion is normally derived on the basis of aggregate data on such indicators as the proportion of total economic activity that crosses state borders, the lack of foreign members of boards of directors, comparisons with previous periods in history, and national economic systems (variations on the theme of path dependence). These are all useful measures and, if handled properly, can teach us a great deal about how capitalism works.

Nevertheless, it is also fruitful to investigate specific corporations to discover the use and meaning of the term globalization (if any) in companies' corporate vocabularies and how these relate to corporate practices. To this end, interviews were conducted with executives and managers in over 80 Global 500 corporations, sampled from the five business sectors discussed above, around the world.[19] The interviews focused on four criteria of globalization, namely: FDI, world best practice and benchmarking, global corporate citizenship, and global vision. The first two of these can be considered criteria of economic globalization, and the other two criteria of social globalization. The logic of the argument is that while the transnational capitalist class as a whole is responsible for ensuring that all four criteria are continuously being met, the different fractions of the TCC have responsibility for ensuring that different criteria of globalization are met.

These four criteria raise issues of the differences between multinational (or international) corporations on the one hand, and globalizing (or transnational) corporations on the other. These terms are often used interchangeably in the academic and the business literature and in the press. To repeat the point made above, in this book the terms international or multinational corporations are used to mean corporations that have strong national attachments and whose foreign subsidiaries are units abroad. Globalizing corporations are those consciously denationalizing from their domestic origins in the course of developing genuinely global strategies of operation. This distinction is not always crystal clear either in the academic or the corporate literature. For example, in the influential study by Bartlett and Ghoshal (1989) the term "transnational" is used to denote corporations that appear to be more global than those denoted by the term "global." As explained above, here transnational corporations are said to be globalizing, not global, to the extent that they operate in a world made up of nation-states, though they are not necessarily dominated by them economically, politically, or in terms of culture-ideology. If nation-states were ever to disappear, global corporations might be possible, but until then only transnational, globalizing corporations are possible.

This is not simply a terminological question but a real difference of perspective central to the debate on globalization and, in particular, central to the debate over the novelty of globalization. Most writers who argue that globalization is centuries old or that it is a new name for an old phenomenon, tend to run internationalization and globalization together. We need, therefore, to find ways of distinguishing clearly between these two ideas if we are to make progress on this question. One method used to discover what the differences were for a sample of corporate executives was to present the Conference Board quotation referred to above: "Multinational Corporations are not really multinational. They are national companies with units abroad" (La-Palombara and Blank 1976: 111).[20] Respondents were asked to consider if this had ever been true of their companies, and if it was true today. The responses to this question and evidence from company publications and the public record indicate the extent to which Global 500 corporations were beginning to denationalize, one key to the globalizing process for TNCs.

The point of this discussion is not to analyze the position of each of these TNCs. That would be a very large task, even for the relatively small group of corporations (around 80) directly researched, let alone the *Fortune* Global 500 as a whole. At issue is the much more limited question of the extent to which the strategies and practices of these corporations were driven by the demands of local and/or national economic interests (the state-centrist view) or by the global interests of the corporation. A transnational capitalist class could not be built on the basis of multinational corporations that were national companies, somehow expressing and furthering the interests of "their" nation-states, with units abroad harnessed to this goal. The making of a transnational capitalist class depends on the emergence of transnational corporations that are demonstrably globalizing. Only then can they provide the material and ideological basis for transnational class action. This does not always conflict with "national" interest as expressed by state-based elites that claim to speak for it. Subsidiaries of globalizing corporations in many countries and communities often take advantage of national and local incentives for trade and investment. However, the class interest of the TCC is transnational in character, it is not necessarily connected with the specific sites where it does business and certainly not identical with the national interests of the states in which these sites are located.

One need not be a devout Popperian to be conscious of the need to specify the conditions under which these propositions could be falsified. This is simple to do in this case. The globalization thesis would be falsified if the corporations generally failed to recognize globalization (in terms of the criteria identified above) as a process affecting them. It would be falsified if corporate executives (and corporate publications) argued that corporate strategy was more influenced by the interests of the states in which they were legally domiciled than the transnational economic interests of their corporations and if their actual corporate practices bore this out. It would be falsified if they failed to see the distinction between the multinational and the globalizing corporation with reference to the quotation from the Conference Board. And the globalization thesis would be falsified if most of them reported that they were not becoming more global in any way. No doubt one could attach numerical values to all these variables and come up with a globalization score,[21] but the conviction that we are dealing with processes of transformation in still dimly-lit arenas suggests that the qualitative method pursued here is more appropriate.

The responses to the Conference Board statement that multinationals are "national companies with units abroad," brought out two vital characteristics of globalizing corporations. First, most of these corporations see themselves as both single unitary bodies and as complex collections of businesses. Thus, the decision not to categorize them for purposes of analysis in *Fortune*'s 40 plus industries but to place all the corporations into five large business sectors reflects to some extent how the corporations see themselves. Second, most respondents accepted that the statement had been true in the past (it was widely seen as an outdated "American" notion) but that no corporation with aspirations to be globally competitive could afford to operate like this any more. Jacques Maisonrouge, the first person without a North American passport to reach the highest echelons of IBM, summed this up in a much-cited anecdote. In response to criticism by the French Minister of Foreign Trade in 1966 that he should be doing more to support French industry, Maisonrouge declared: "although I am the President of a company which is a subsidiary of an American corporation, I consider myself not as a representative of American industry, but as that of a multinational industry" (Maisonrouge 1988: 151).[22] Even more tellingly, the Chairman of Dow Chemical was quoted as saying in the early 1970s:

> I have long dreamed of buying an island owned by no nation and of establishing the World Headquarters of the Dow Chemical Company on the truly neutral ground of such an island, beholden to no nation or society. If we were located on such truly neutral ground we could then really operate in the United States as US citizens, in Japan as Japanese citizens and in Brazil as Brazilians rather than being governed in prime by the laws of the United States ... We could even pay any natives handsomely to move elsewhere. (Barnet and Muller 1974: 16)

National systems of corporate regulation have converged a good deal since the 1970s, though even globalizing corporations are not yet entirely free of the state, and this is why the conventional wisdom is that most corporations are best characterized in national terms. Notions of American multinationals, Japanese multinationals, German multinationals, Indian multinationals, and so on appear to be deeply entrenched in both popular consciousness and the agenda of academic research. In recent manifestations, this old argument reappears in terms of discrete national business systems, path dependence (that is, business systems can only be properly understood in terms of the cultures from which they have emerged), and the embeddedness of firms in the specific features of their societies and cultures of birth.[23] Clearly, it would be very difficult to sustain the claim that TNCs are globalizing if most of these corporations and those who own and control them do identify themselves and their businesses primarily in nationalist terms and if systematic national differences between them really did explain concrete outcomes. As was argued in chapter 2, the ideas of "national interest" and even "national economy" are not as simple as they look, despite their regular reiteration in the media and the scholarly literature.

Japanese corporations and the Japanese economy are often characterized in nationalist terms. With the theory of Japan Inc., Johnson (1982) and others argued that the Japanese government, working through the all-powerful Ministry of International Trade and Investment (MITI), organized Japanese corporations like an imperial commercial army for the post-1945 reconstruction of the country. By the 1980s, however, MITI's influence began to wane and by the time of the crisis of the 1990s, as Callon (1995) convincingly argues, it appears to have been quite marginalized (see also Tsuru 1993). Let us, therefore, begin the analysis of the multinational/global issue with the responses of two major TNCs from Japan, Mitsubishi and Mitsui.

Global 500 consumer goods and services corporations

Mitsubishi and Mitsui were among the largest corporations in the world by revenues throughout the 1990s. A respondent from Mitsubishi, interviewed in the Australian subsidiary in 1995, remarked that the Conference Board quotation "absolutely defined" Mitsubishi in his decades-long experience with the company, but that this was exactly what the then President Makihara and his predecessor had dedicated themselves to change. The Annual Report for 1995 drew attention to the culture of change sweeping the company. The emphasis was on "Change: More than Just a Buzzword," the need "to capitalize on the dynamic forces sweeping the globe today" in a "broad "tripolar" regional framework based on Asia, the Americas, and Europe/the Middle East/Africa." The theme was reinforced in the Annual Report for 1996, where four "Principles that define Mitsubishi Corporation" were outlined. The Principles were entirely outward-oriented, all directed towards Mitsubishi's global business. This was very concretely expressed in the first Principle, the focus on relationships. Mitsubishi claimed no less than 73,000 business relationships covering about 10,000 products all over the world. The second Principle, a thorough understanding of markets, was illustrated by the examples that Mitsubishi marketed Harrods, KFC, and other premier foreign brands in Japan. The last two Principles also had an outward-directed complexion, namely a long-term perspective (illustrated by the joint venture that Mitsubishi established for producing the Proton car in Malaysia, and the fact that the company was responsible for 57 percent of Japan's LNG imports), and globalizing human resources. Of Mitsubishi's 36,000 employees, one-third were employed outside Japan. Echoing a distinction that is increasingly made in globalizing corporations, the 1996 Annual Report asserted that: "Localization involves expanding business activities at the company's nearly 180 overseas offices. Globalization means making talented human resources available anywhere in the world." International Staff and National Core Staff systems were introduced in 1996 and a new Global Leadership Program imparted skills in global thinking and managing diversity.

Many of the same globalizing imperatives appeared in the public pronouncements of Mitsui. The 1996 Annual Report stated: "Mitsui has two fundamental roles: facilitating its clients' international trading activities and drawing on its vast information, human, financial, and other resources to create new trade flows, new companies, and new industries in all parts of the world." The main goal of the company was to expand "its presence and scope as a global enterprise." Two mega-trends were particularly important for Mitsui; first, the rapidly expanding global market as free market principles were adopted all over the world, and second, the "advanced global information network society where geographical boundaries, industry distinctions, and corporate organizations have become less meaningful." As a result of the globalizing process, Mitsui was changing from a distributor of goods and services (the traditional multinational role of a trading company) to a global entrepreneur. A key aspect of this new role was that Mitsui enthusiastically searched for partnerships with companies all over the world.[24] The small operation of Mitsui & Co. (Australia) Ltd. provided conflicting evidence. About 70 percent of the business of Mitsui Australia comprised exports to Japan, responding to strong pressure from headquarters to expand the Australia-Asian business. (JETRO, long seen as a principal motivator for exports, promoted imports to Japan in the 1990s.) Mitsui's corporate strategy was to look for joint ventures with major Australian companies in third countries. Few business opportunities were excluded. The strength of the yen in the early 1990s forced Japanese companies to think of manufacturing in Australia and other places where wages and costs were lower than in Japan. Mitsui had also been approached by various Japanese companies to help set up foreign investment projects in Australia. Trading companies (like banks) become more global by servicing their globalizing clients.

Mitsubishi and Mitsui were typical of the major trading companies from Japan and elsewhere. Traders, of course, have always tended to be international by virtue of their economic conditions of existence. The history of colonialism up to the middle of the twentieth century provides many examples of quasi–imperial trading companies following the flag as more or less direct representatives of politico-economic interest groups at home, expressing the symbols and practices of imperialism and nationalism in a relatively systemic fashion. In the final decades of the twentieth century, even companies like Mitsubishi and Mitsui presented themselves much more as globalizing corporations acting in the general interests of their shareholders and global consumerist capitalism. Contributing to the welfare of Japan has not entirely vanished from the corporate agendas of companies like Mitsubishi and Mitsui, but it can no longer be said to dominate them as it once did. Callon provides solid evidence for this conclusion in his research on the changing relationships between MITI and the electronic corporations in Japan from the 1970s to 1993, notably in his analysis of the predominance of company interests over any purported national interests in the Hitachi-Fujitsu-NEC Supercomputer consortium (Callon 1995: 12 and ch. 5 *passim*). An executive from Nissho Aiwa in Hong Kong expressed this view in another but equally salient manner. The company no longer operated in terms of business between Japan and foreign countries, but "from market to market." All capitalist businesses at all times and in all places are, of course, dedicated to making profits. The major globalizing corporations of today rarely connect this with national goals. They identify with the developmental goals of the places where they and their subsidiaries are doing business rather than their states of origin. When the Toyota Annual Report for 1996 declared "Globalize Everything" it expressed a sentiment widespread among major corporations, domiciled in Japan and all over the world.

The globalizing of these corporations has consequences for those who own and control them, for their relations with their business associates and those in positions to help or harm their business prospects. Where corporate executives and large shareholders chose or are forced to operate under the directives of state agencies their relationships with these agencies and those who run them will generally preclude meaningful relationships with agencies and agents representing other states. The theory of the effective and strong developmental state dictates that corporations will act in the interests of their home states (as defined by those who control the state) even when this is against the commercial interests of these corporations. Under such conditions, a transnational capitalist class is very unlikely to emerge. Where a capitalist class starts to shake itself free from unwelcome state involvement in its affairs, or starts to shape this state involvement, new opportunities to forge transnational connections will arise. This is, however, not the only basis on which a transnational capitalist class may arise. Some corporations may be unwilling to globalize, preferring the predictability and comfort of a protected home market. In such cases, globalizing state bureaucrats and politicians may put pressure on corporations to globalize in the belief that bigger and more profitable corporations domiciled locally will serve the national interest – as they see it – better. What actually tends to happen is that outward-oriented globalizing coalitions between factions within corporations, state agencies, and political parties form to do battle with inward-oriented factions devoted to maintaining the status quo. Foreign corporations are not necessarily among the first globalizers in any economy. For example, not all the long-established subsidiaries of TNCs in protected markets in Latin America and Australia were early globalizers. Whether they were pushed into globalizing by their corporate centers or by globalizing state bureaucrats and politicians in the host countries or by some other forces, cannot be read off directly from the structures and dynamics of the global economy (see Sklair 1996). The contemporary capitalist system is global, but it does not operate in a uniform manner all over the world. The different pace and nature of opening-up and outward-orientation of economic, political, and cultural-ideological spheres in different parts of the world, means that even where corporations are ready to start or accelerate the globalizing process, they are not always able to do so. As we shall see, a central part of the work of the transnational capitalist class is to facilitate corporate globalization through economic, political, and culture-ideology work.

This has certainly been the case for McDonald's, the biggest restaurant chain in the world. While McDonald's (established in 1954) quickly became what we now would call a globalizing corporation, in many parts of the world, particularly the now defunct Communist bloc in eastern Europe and in some Asian countries, national governments refused to allow McDonald's entry. This changed dramatically in the 1990s, and McDonald's restaurants in Moscow and Beijing broke all records for turnover when they opened. This has helped make McDonald's a central icon for globalization theorists. Notwithstanding its iconic status, McDonald's is something of an enigma. Most globalization theorists see it as a powerful force for global homogenization (often reduced to Americanization) but, in fact, the company operates through local franchisees who inject significant local distinctions into the general formula of burgers and fries (compare Ritzer 1996; and Watson, ed., 1997). The hypothesis of global system theory that the search for profit, not global homegeneity, dictates the practices of globalizing corporations is robustly supported by McDonald's. Some key aspects of the business are mandatory worldwide, namely the focus on cleanliness, customer care, speed of delivery, and value for money (as taught in each restaurant and centrally through the Hamburger Universities).[25] However, franchisees are encouraged to introduce such local variations as the center considers consistent with the McDonald's global image. Control is exercised through the ultimate sanction of withdrawal of the franchise; support is offered through valuable local and global advertising and promotional campaigns. In the USA, it is claimed that around one-quarter of McDonald's franchisees have become millionaires.

Subsidiaries outside the USA generally see themselves as local companies as well as parts of what is widely referred to as the McDonald's global family. The key is the extent to which they have managed to localize the McDonald's concept. While there is little evidence that franchisees consider themselves to be units abroad of the headquarters in the USA, many strongly identify themselves with the McDonald's global family, as confirmed by direct interview in the case of the McDonald's organization in Australia (and observations elsewhere). This version of the local and the global was popularized by the parent company and implemented worldwide through many corporate globalizing practices. McDonald's corporate center has Global Boards for purchasing, marketing, information technology, construction, and design of facilities, as befits a corporation with operations in more than 20,000 communities. Franchisees from all over the world have opportunities to interact under the global McDonald's umbrella (or golden arches). Globalization comes from the top and is driven by the increasingly competitive environment in which it operates. Since the mid-1990s, McDonald's in the USA has been losing market share and has suffered some embarrassing commercial flops, though outside the USA the brand appears to be going from strength to strength. McDonald's, therefore, cannot be regarded as a multinational with units abroad.

The success of global brands in fast food and beverages appears to contradict the intuitive perception that the food and food processing industries are among the least globalizing and most locally-rooted forms of economic activity. Food is a local business and the food industry has to be aware of local culture and laws, for example religious taboos in many parts of the world, discrete culinary traditions, and food safety legislation. Food safety was widely discussed in the 1990s as a result of some well publicized and very controversial breakdowns in national and international systems of regulation.[26] The food business rests on millions of daily purchases and so global strategy is impossible to implement without considering local content. For example, some of Nestlé's brands are indisputably global, notably Nescafe, but even this product differs in composition, use, and positioning all over the world. The Nestlé respondent adamantly stated that the idea of a multinational being a national company with units abroad was a "parochial Americanism" and that the trend – both in food processing and in global business generally – was definitely moving away from this old idea of the multinational. Nestlé's own experience of rapid worldwide growth confirms the view that globalizing companies need managers with cosmopolitan outlooks, and the competition for managerial talent means that even the most successful companies must look all over the world to supplement their executive pools. This introduces a theme that will be taken up in more detail in subsequent chapters. Whereas old-style multinational firms generally ran their operations through expatriate managers from the home country, new-style globalizing corporations increasingly recruit executives from any country and increasingly train their top cadre of managers to expect to work in any part of the world. As was indicated in the previous chapter, business education (particularly through the rise of international or global business courses) is changing in response to this development.

While most types of globalizing business would find reasons to recruit local managers these days, the food business relies heavily on knowledge of local tastes. The respondent from Unilever, another major food processor, argued (like Nestlé) that the units abroad conception of the multinational was an outdated concept. Unilever had its own version of the structure of the globalizing corporation. It perceived itself as a "multilocal multinational," a more highly evolved version of the old multinational. The survival of Unilever depends on its status as a collection of local businesses that mobilizes global corporate principles, policies, and practices to serve consumers in local markets. The single global strategy for the two main companies that make up Unilever (one based in London, the other in The Hague) worked to this end. It would be difficult to argue that Unilever was a British and/or a Dutch company in any sense other than that it happened to be legally domiciled in these two countries.

Similar patterns of corporate change can be found in other consumer goods and services industries. In pharmaceuticals, Pfizer is typical of companies all over the world which have been identified as national companies. Pfizer presented itself as an American company dominated by American culture. While it had a substantial presence in many other countries, the part of the business located in the United States was still "first among equals" and the company was "informed by the American spirit." Thus far, it appears to bear out the path-dependence thesis that multinationals are national companies with units abroad. However, in the 1990s there arose a conscious recognition that the company had to globalize. The creation of Pfizer Pharmaceuticals Group (PPG), the international arm of the corporation, allowed three strategic innovations that helped to take the company into the global arena. PPG encouraged the formation of global development teams; it encouraged plan rationalization on a global basis for new drugs (the brilliant commercial success of Viagra was one result of this); and it provided the rationale for a Corporate Affairs Group, created in the mid-1990s to carry out the globalization of the company in a more systematic fashion. This replaced the Public Affairs Group, oriented more to the US political and public policy system. A new organ of corporate communication, *Pfizer World*, was one important consequence of this organizational initiative. While it would be absurd to claim that Pfizer was no longer an American company in some senses, it would be a mistake to assume that this means what it did even a decade previously. Clearly, for Pfizer and, indeed, for most of the Global 500 corporations that provide the material infrastructure for the transnational capitalist class, globalization is in no way a finished project. The inherent conflicts between the TCC and those who refuse the global capitalist project, as well as the conflicts and competition that arise between corporations and within the ranks of the TCC, will determine how far the processes of globalization will go. Nevertheless, the clear message that came from Pfizer and most major corporations was that there is no alternative to the globalizing route for businesses that wish to survive, let alone prosper.

The respondent at Colgate-Palmolive, another corporation with a strong American business tradition, strongly asserted that the Conference Board quotation reflected a position that was no longer viable for the company. Indeed, this respondent argued that, to be successful, major consumer goods companies had to focus on the whole world, which entailed marketing simultaneously across the globe. Part of the explanation offered for this view was that the technology stream is the same for all companies over a broad spectrum of industries. The world of consumers, according to Colgate-Palmolive, includes all those who have the equivalent of about US$5,000 personal income per year (enough to start buying toiletries). This is known, no doubt with entirely unintentional irony, as "trigger point marketing." This section of the world's population is growing rapidly, the prosperous part of the class polarization crisis that the TCC is working consciously to resolve. For the first time in history the number of these consumers in the Third World (though not their spending power) has surpassed that in the First World. Even in India, poor as it is, there is significant modern consumption going on.[27] These messages are delivered through the mass media, hungry for advertising revenue. In Papua New Guinea, for example, satellite TV from Australia, full of advertisements for these products, predated land-based TV. A substantial literature on consumer goods marketing all over the developing world, much of it focused on China, confirms this view (Ayala and Lai 1996, Robison and Goodman 1996, Sklair 1994).

BAT (British American Tobacco) Industries, saw the issue of the multinational in terms of the several different levels of the company's operations. BAT businesses are global, national, or regional depending on the products. Tobacco, for example, was never a BAT business in the UK and the company never focused on the UK market. However, while it employed relatively few people, the BAT factory in Southampton (England) was one of the most important exporters in the UK. On the other hand, BAT owned some of the most successful cigarette brands in the world, one or two of them arguably global brands, and some of these were directly produced by subsidiaries abroad. While the preceding discussion might appear largely academic to some readers, this issue was extremely important for BAT, as its US subsidiary Brown & Williamson was the subject of massive legal actions and public debates in several countries (see Sklair 1998). Whether Brown & Williamson is deemed to be a unit abroad of BAT or something else could eventually decide the survival or demise of the parent company.

The definition of a multinational is as much about mindset as about modes of operation in the global marketplace. Viacom (a major entertainment corporation), for example, was in the mid-1990s American to the extent that 80 percent of its revenues came from the USA. However, its publicly stated goal was to increase overseas revenues to 40 percent by the year 2000. This suggests that there was some truth to the claim that the mindset of the man who ran it (Sumner Redstone) was that Viacom must embark on the globalizing road. Redstone argued that this could not be accomplished by sitting in Viacom's HQ on Broadway, New York, dictating global strategy. Traveling all over the world meeting the local partners who help achieve the objective is an essential part of the work of globalizing executives. Viacom company lore was that this strategy was adopted only in 1996 when Redstone released the previous CEO and took over the running of the company himself. "Globalization is part of everything Viacom does" was a constant refrain.[28] Part of this was encapsulated in the claim that it sold uniquely American products with a universal appeal. (This important issue will be taken up in chapter 8, when the connection between the visionary executive, national culture, and the culture-ideology of consumerism is discussed.)

The issue of national identity and globalizing corporations is particularly acute in the company that for many epitomizes all that is wrong with media globalization, namely NewsCorp, and its inspirational founder, Rupert Murdoch. The respondent in the head office in Sydney, Australia commented: "We find ourselves a bit schizoid." This was due to the fact that the Australian government considered NewsCorp to be a foreign corporation for the purposes of regulation because Murdoch had renounced his Australian passport and taken out an American passport in order to circumvent US media ownership rules. However, the US government still considered NewsCorp to be in some senses an Australian corporation. Few proprietors go to the length of changing passports to globalize.

Few respondents expressed skepticism about the extent of globalization in their companies, but those who did tended to come from subsidiaries of Global 500 corporations rather than the corporate core. The respondent in Kimberley Clark (KC) Australia, for example, did regard it as an American company in some senses. From the perspective of the corporate core in the USA, the hub of the company was still very much to be found there. Investments abroad had been profitable, and KC considered its foreign subsidiaries units abroad to some extent, whose role was to help the company exploit commercial opportunities all around the world. However, even in this case, there were changes underway. In the 1980s, if US top management had vetoed a project, it probably would not have proceeded. By the mid-1990s, the Australian subsidiary was more likely to be proactive in initiating change. Part of this process was the growing recognition that regionalizing can accelerate commercially successful globalizing. The management of KC Australia originally reported to headquarters in the USA, but in the 1990s it began to report to the regional center (located in Bangkok at that time). The strength of the regions was a counterbalance to the dominance of the center. In particular, the view from Australia was that Asian growth was changing the relationships between the US hub and the rest of the global network of the company.[29] It seems certain that organizational power will be increasingly decided by economic contribution rather than the national origins of the company's parts. The discussion of the transformation of foreign investment in the next chapter will extend this argument in the context of the dialectical relationship between denationalization and the globalizing of the corporation.

Global 500 financial services corporations

There appears to be a growing synergy between the globalizing of the consumer goods corporate sector and what is occurring in financial services corporations. This is hardly surprising, as many scholars argue that the processes of globalization are furthest advanced in financial markets. Dicken's useful summary of the "internationalization [*sic*] of financial services" (1998: 399–421) is typical for the importance claimed for financial services in the global economy. While most states have detailed regulations covering domestic and cross-border financial transactions, a global financial system is emerging. A respondent from

HSBC put this neatly when he argued that the proposition "the bank is a national company with units abroad is true, but this is getting more false by the day and for each of the bank's businesses." One indication of this was the "Strategy Matters" report produced in London in June 1997. This was the first pan-Europe research report of its type for the bank, identifying specific companies and specific industries for their growth potential across the region. Similar reports were being written for other regions. Since 1994 there have been regular meetings of the bank's 15 heads of research from all over the world. The reason for this cross-border activity was simple: clients were driving the globalization process. This was exactly the argument of the respondent from BankAmerica, where the idea that it was a national company with units abroad had been traditionally accepted, but was no longer the case. As noted above in the remarks of the executive from Dow Canada, BankAmerica won business precisely because of its ability to follow its customers wherever they did business. An indication of the change was that the great majority of overseas managers were now local personnel or "international assignees." The bank, in common with many Global 500 corporations, no longer used the term "expatriate," which traditionally meant an American or European abroad. In a globalizing economy, major corporations can no longer afford to be seen as parochial national corporations.

Merrill Lynch, one of the most venerable of the American financial institutions, presented this dilemma in an interesting way. The units-abroad idea "is the state we are trying actively to overcome." Merrill Lynch's aim was to retain its name, valuable in an industry where reputation is everything, but also to localize its operations. It wished to be not just multinational, but multicultural. So, "while the history of the company cannot change, the way you conduct your business and the way you are perceived can change." The aim of this process was to bring to each local presence the global values of Merrill Lynch. This theme was developed in the eminent bank, J. P. Morgan, with the suggestion that what "local presence" really meant in the financial services business sector, was giving opportunities to people from outside the national circle of the founders. In the early 1970s the firm determined that a strategy of equal opportunities was the only way to attract talent, a question that will be elaborated on in chapter 6. While there were three or four different nationalities routinely represented in the top leadership of J. P. Morgan by the 1990s, the salient point was that all such nationalistic distinctions had to evaporate if a company was to be truly transnational. Clearly, people born in or holding passports from Nepal or Nigeria or Nicaragua were less likely to own and control major corporations than those born in the USA or

Germany or Japan. The point, however, was how do place of birth or civil status affect the ideas and practices of those who own and control the major corporations? The globalizing thesis is that as these corporations increasingly globalize their businesses, as more and bigger markets "emerge," such nationalistic distinctions will have to evaporate.

These changes are filtering through the whole financial system. The subsidiaries of Swiss Bank Corporation (SBC Warburg) and IBJ (Industrial Bank of Japan) in Australia were good cases in point. For the respondent from SBC the idea of a national company with units abroad appeared relevant for the 1970s but much less so today. This was partly a reflection of the expansion of the global operations of the bank (the subsidiary in Australia, for example) and changes in how banks worked in the global economy. The most important aspect of this was that functional distribution of financial products from the center was replacing products designed for national markets. The trend to globalization of management made it more difficult for corporations to maintain their national character, even if Swiss bankers running SBC from Basel or Australian bankers running SBC Warburg from Sydney saw advantages in doing so. Similarly, IBJ as a Japanese-based bank in Australia, struggled with the local and the global. There are certain expectations that have to be met as a condition of operating profitably in the global economy, wherever one operates. IBJ Australia was a self-contained company, where everyone reported to the Managing Director. The top executives were all expatriate Japanese, with Australian managers below them in the hierarchy. The President of IBJ in Tokyo in the mid-1990s did not speak good English, but the Chairman (Yoh Kurasawa, a Japanese IMF delegate) was said to speak excellent English as well as German. He was identified as someone who could push IBJ in a globalizing direction. Progress on this had clearly been slow.

Playing an increasingly important part in financial services and the global economy through their powerful position in the capital markets and management of corporate stock, are the insurance companies (see Scordis and Katrishan 1997). MetLife, a leading New York-based insurance company, typified these companies in their movement from domestic to global markets. The assertion of a MetLife executive echoed the views of many other globalizing corporations: "MetLife has the mindset of a multinational but is moving towards becoming a global corporation." This was explained in terms of a key indicator that recurred with great regularity in the corporate interviews, namely that one sure measure of globalization was the number of senior people from abroad (outside the country of domicile) who were rising to positions of responsibility in the company. MetLife was beginning to move more rapidly along this spectrum. In common with other Global

500 corporations, MetLife had introduced a Management Associates Program to recruit bright young managers with the idea of offering each one an overseas assignment to accelerate promotion. Much the same was true of New York Life, another major US insurance company, and the Prudential, domiciled in the UK but active all over the world. The respondent in the Prudential subsidiary in Australia acknowledged that in the past the Prudential might have been described as a multinational with units abroad, but not now, and that it was becoming a "globalizing" corporation.[30] Once again, movement of staff across national borders indicated change in the direction of globalization, this being most noticeable in fund management. A popular saying in the Prudential (as in many other companies) was: "go global or get left behind." The Global Investment Management Committee at that time met every two months in each center to ensure that the investment process and philosophy maintained a focus on the global. Regular video-conferencing of the Investment Review Committee, begun in 1995, helped to reinforce this globalizing structure.

Ambivalence about the ways in which financial services corporations handled multinationality and globalization was strongly expressed by the Royal Bank of Canada (RBC) respondent, interviewed in mid-1998 when the bank was in the throes of a merger discussion with Bank of Montreal, precisely in search of more global competitiveness. In the 1970s RBC had been active in Europe and other overseas markets (the multinational route), but had retrenched due to some serious business losses. Since then, the RBC strategy had been to follow its Canadian (and other) clients wherever they went around the world. For example, some important investments of these companies in Latin America had led RBC to be more active there than in Europe or Asia. However, on the other hand, significant deregulation in Canada encouraged the banks to globalize. A feature of this new situation (pointed out by the respondent from RBC) was that there had been a marked reduction of loyalty to the home base, especially for manufacturing companies as they increasingly produced for the global market. This meant that RBC was less likely to win business from Canadian corporations just because it was domiciled in Canada than had been the case in the past.

This finding was not confirmed in all cases. For example, in the Deutsche Bank subsidiary in Hong Kong a senior executive (who spoke English and Mandarin but not much German) expressed considerable skepticism about how much the rhetoric about globalization really reflected business practices. It was apparently much easier for a subsidiary to get permission from head office in Frankfurt to lend to a German company than to a non-German company wishing to make an investment in Asia. (This problem may, of course, have been influenced by the fact that the interview took place during the Asian crises of the late 1990s.[31]) Nevertheless, the acquisition by Deutsche Bank of the New York-based Bankers Trust (plus a strategic alliance with Japan's largest insurance company, Nippon Life) during this period, sent out clear messages about its response to the demands of the global economy. Deutsche Bank, despite its strong links with its base in Germany, did appear to be acting like a major corporation with globalizing aspirations.

Global 500 heavy industry corporations

The chemical and oil companies that dominated the heavy industry business sector mostly claimed to have been global from birth. The problems of their longstanding global reach raised the issue of what a multinational corporation really was. The respondent from ICI interpreted this issue in terms of what holds all the varying activities of these huge organizations together. Some ICI products required global strategies. In the case of bulk chemicals, most of the world supply of the polymers used for fibers and packaging came from one or two plants, whereas paints were manufactured in many locations. For world-traded products, increasingly those products that one company sells to other companies in the supply chain, those parts of a multinational outside the home base were more than just units abroad. They were all being increasingly seen as components in a global strategy and where they no longer fitted into it (or the strategy changed) they were discarded. Therefore, the sale in 1997 of some ICI divisions to DuPont, to finance the purchase of some Unilever divisions, was part of the global strategies of all three firms. In ICI's case, it was the decision to move out of bulk chemicals and to focus on speciality chemicals. Another consequence of this restructuring was the flotation of the ICI subsidiary in Australia. As press commentators speculated, how long would ICI retain the hidden "Imperial" (symbolic for a national company with units abroad) in its name?

The name was also problematic in the case of Shell (Royal Dutch/ Shell Group). Here, the issue of multinationality was again interpreted in terms of the excessive numbers of expatriates (from the UK, in this case) in charge of overseas subsidiaries, though the trend towards appointing more local managers in joint ventures and strategic alliances was also noted. Rather than Shell companies outside the Netherlands and Britain being units abroad, the tendency was for each Shell subsidiary to become part of the society in which it operated. This theme – that companies must earn their "license to operate," and prove their legitimacy – was common among Global 500 corporations (and in the corporate literature of most large TNCs). It was particularly common for corporations in the oil, chemical, and petrochemical industries. Companies (like Shell) that have suffered public relations reverses are very sensitive on this issue, as chapters 6 and 7 below on the issue of corporate citizenship make clear.

All the major oil companies, by the nature of their business, have crossed borders since their birth. A senior BP executive argued that most multinationals experienced a process of evolution from purely national to multinational to genuinely global companies. Indications of increasing globalization that were highlighted were when the exports of companies stop coming exclusively from the home country, and when the composition of top management became more international. The Board of BP had traditionally been mostly British, but this was changing. BP worldwide in the late 1990s had about one-third each of managers with British, American, and other passports. Company policy was that "BP long ago stopped thinking of nationality as a criterion for promotion,"[32] and BP executives and senior managers looked forward to an international career where previously they would have expected to stay in their countries of origin. This was reflected in recruitment, carried out on a transnational basis. The fact that BP presented itself as a globalizing corporation, though the culture was mainly Anglo-American, was explained by reasoning that the global business culture itself is Anglo-American. This was a very controversial claim, as was the accompanying claim that the process "has an inevitability about it." In 1998, BP merged with the Chicago-based Amoco to form one of the largest industrial corporations in the world.

Rio Tinto (formerly RTZ) acknowledged that the Conference Board statement on multinationals would have been true for them in 1976 when it was made, but that it was much less true in the 1990s. The RTZ–CRA merger (CRA was the Australian partner) in 1996 was a good illustration of the increasing irrelevance of nationality for globalizing corporations. The merger of two separate legal entities domiciled in two different countries established a new corporation. The sharehold-ers of each company were on an equal footing, apart from obvious issues like national tax policies. Two-thirds of Rio Tinto shares were owned in the UK, about 20 percent in Australia, and the rest were spread around the world. So, ownership was more dispersed than formerly, as was management, and top management was a mixture of British and Australian executives. Such outcomes may be seen as marriages of convenience, which might not work out in the long run. Those with an interest in the globalizing corporation will be studying

RTZ–CRA, Deutsche Bank–Bankers Trust, BP–Amoco, and other cross-border corporate mergers and acquisitions.

Global 500 infrastructure corporations

The deregulation and privatization of utilities all around the world as a consequence of the neoliberal revolution of the 1980s did not begin the globalizing process for infrastructure companies, but it did transform it. The global marketplace is where the utility and construction companies bid for contracts and this has always imposed some specific pressures with respect to the nationality of the companies and the currencies in which they conduct most of their business. Deregulation of the Californian energy supply industry in the 1990s, for example, led the northern California energy provider PG&E to establish what could be termed a globalizing subsidiary, PG&E Enterprises. Though this company was owned by the same shareholders, it could not simply be operated as a unit abroad of its parent company. InterGen, a global joint venture of PG&E Enterprises and Bechtel, a major privately-held construction company, operated under the evocative slogan: Local Partnerships/Global Power Solutions.

For Edison International (the new name of Southern California Edison), domestic earnings were likely to decline after the 1990s due to the competition that deregulation in California and neighboring states would bring. This decline would have to be offset by higher earnings outside the US if the company was to grow. Thus, operations in California while still dominant, did not have the overwhelming importance they once had, and new revenue generating operations overseas were not simply regarded as units abroad of the parent company. A new company, Edison Mission Energy, was established (like PG&E Enterprises) to grasp the opportunities being offered by a rapidly deregulating global marketplace. For example, in December 1995 Edison acquired First Hydro, consisting of two major pumped-storage stations in North Wales. It is difficult to see how First Hydro could in any way be considered a unit abroad of Edison International. Again, an important part of this process in Edison International was to give non-Americans their place in the top echelons of the company, a policy that was no doubt popular in Wales.

The fact that some of these Global 500 companies continued to see themselves as (mainly US) companies with units abroad while they also saw themselves as globalizing, is not surprising. The road from the multinational to the globalizing corporation is long and winding. Further, the issues of globalizing markets and globalizing corporations are easily confused. All the Global 500 in the sample were active in global markets, largely because they saw this as the best way to maximize shareholder value. Increasing deregulation and potential globalization of markets had different effects on the companies. These effects were mediated by business sector in terms of local and national regulatory environments, demand for technical expertise, corporate culture, new technologies, and changes in corporate leadership.

AT&T was typical of infrastructure companies in seeing its evolution as a globalizing process, where national companies with units abroad was a stage along a continuum and a commentary on the state of affairs in the 1970s when there were few truly global companies. By the 1990s, the AT&T respondent reflected the corporate consensus that most major corporations were attempting to globalize, but with varying degrees of success. AT&T (and many other corporations interviewed) expressed a sense of frustration that it had not yet achieved enough in this direction. Partly this was a function of the regulatory climate for global telecommunications, which began to open up effectively only in the 1990s. Schiller (1999: 42) reports that by 1995 AT&T was marketing in about 140 languages. Thus, while beverage, oil, mining, and vehicle companies, for example, have had decades to develop global networks, the learning curve for telecommunications companies has been very steep. AT&T's only truly global operations in the mid-1990s were in the US, UK, Canada, Mexico, Taiwan, India, and Russia. More were under-way, and a culture of continuous improvement was a key part of the company's globalizing efforts. As the best available standards of corporate performance become the global norm for all parts of the corporation, the distinction between home base and units abroad starts to dissolve. (The significance of the connection between continuous improvement and globalization will be discussed in chapter 5 below.[33]) This was also the case for Nynex (the New York area telecommunications company, since merged into the Bell Atlantic-GTE conglomerate). Nynex's foreign subsidiaries were still in some senses extensions of the US parent in the mid-1990s, but this was changing. In Thailand, for example, the Nynex joint venture with local partners began with 80 expatriate staff employing a few local people. However, it expanded rapidly to 25,000 employees with only 3 expatriates. The company became self-sufficient and could no longer be considered an extension of Nynex US. While this was the global trajectory that Nynex wished to pursue, it was by no means complete. Undoubtedly, its merger into a major telecommunications group was a globalizing initiative.

Many of these observations were echoed by BT. Indeed, throughout the 1990s both BT and AT&T engaged in a series of problematic attempts to forge global mergers and strategic alliances with other major telecommunications companies. One such attempt would have merged BT and AT&T (they did establish a strategic alliance for a mobile phone network). With privatization and progressive deregulation, British Telecom became BT in 1991. What was once a national monopoly, became just one, although still by far the biggest, of a number of corporations vying for telecommunications and related business in the UK and elsewhere. BT considered that the idea of units abroad expressed a decidedly American perspective, connected with the export mentality of US firms. Again, the issue of expatriate managers was raised. BT tended to employ local people wherever they were available in all their operations. All BT European companies in the late 1990s had local origin managing directors, and most of the top staff were of local origin too. As with BP, BT has retained the "British" in the company name, though the logos of these companies and most of their corporate communications refrain from drawing attention to the British connection.

Name denationalizing accelerated in the 1990s. Other companies dropping the "British" from their names were British Steel (prior to its merger with the Dutch group Hoogovens), BAe (British Aerospace), the former British Coal (the privatized rump of what was once a major company), and BAA (British Airports Authority). This issue attracted some media interest in Britain in 1999 when BA (British Airways) revealed some confusion by rebranding some of its planes with the union flag just two years after it had dropped it as an expression of its aspiration to be "the world's favourite airline." Apparently, the multicultural symbols with which it adorned its planes had antagonized its British clientele. Research by the brand consultancy, Wally Olins, of 200 of the world's leading companies, supported the thesis of global system theory that national identification was now mainly useful as a marketing tool, rather than for any serious identification with the states in which companies were domiciled. The research reported that the Italian brand added value to some foods and fashion, the German brand added value to engineering, but that Britishness failed to add value to any industry (see "Multinationals Turn Tail on Britishness," *Guardian*, June 8, 1999).

Global 500 electronics corporations

Most of the electronics companies interviewed for this study, involved as they were in some aspect of global communications, considered that the sentiment expressed in the Conference Board quotation was outdated, and usually of American origin. Philips Australia argued that some American companies still behaved as if their subsidiaries were units abroad, but if they were to globalize they would have to change. Philips itself had never been a national company with units abroad, having been created as a federation. It was not seen as a Dutch company, or an Australian or Japanese company for that matter. This was confirmed by an executive from the Netherlands, who confirmed that the company was becoming extremely decentralized. Philips used to manufacture locally for local markets, but in the 1990s it began to manufacture high-technology products in a few locations for the whole world. To do this successfully required a global organization. It was not exactly clear how the name change in 1998 to Royal Philips Electronics contributed to this end.

The view of Hewlett-Packard (HP) was that, in general, the enormity of the US market ensured that most American companies had been domestically minded. Companies from elsewhere (here the respondent referred to Philips, a competitor of HP), had no alternative to going global. HP itself was moving in this direction, becoming increasingly global in sourcing its components, and starting to relocate its manufacturing and R&D. One indication of this was that the annual Business Strategy Review had a new section on "global presence," reflecting less a push within the company than a pull from the marketplace. In the words of this senior HP executive: "It is inconceivable for a high-tech company like HP not to be globally-minded."

The same can be said for Apple, where corporate strategic positioning has largely eliminated the option of operating as a national company with units abroad. Apple Canada was cited as an example of a company that had a "branch mentality" in the past, but no longer. No Apple affiliate could now be run as a unit abroad, as Garsten (1994) demonstrated in her ethnography of Apple centers in Cupertino (California), Paris, and Kista (Stockholm). However, there is a sense in which it is very difficult for any TNC, especially one from a major economy, to avoid the type of "imperialistic condescending manner" that has historically been typical of some large corporations. Apple was striving to build executive overseas experience for all its senior management as a way to combat this.

Rockwell, whose past prosperity was largely bound up with US government contracts of various types, clearly still saw itself, in part at least, as a national company with units abroad. However, its focus was being transformed from an export to a global orientation and operating globally did create pressures to consider each market separately. Rockwell was another of those companies who claimed to be moving away from the national towards a global orientation, but accepted that it might never get there. The CEO in the mid-1990s, Don Beall, was an important driver of this globalization process. He took personal responsibility for the China market, often seen as the ultimate test of a company's global resolve. In this he was strongly backed by the Corporate Strategy Committee of the Board of Directors.

The Mexican subsidiary of Thomson, the French-based electronics company, considered that major corporations could not survive as units abroad of national corporations. Some Mexicans, for example, thought that Thomson was a Mexican company (a not uncommon claim). In fact, the issue could be reversed in that problems arise when companies are selfish and do not share information with sister companies in the corporation. In such cases, strategies of localization and globalization might conflict, but the conflicts are not over "national" interests but over the costs and benefits of centralization.

This was exemplified by the Hong Kong subsidiary of the US-based aerospace and automotive components firm, AlliedSignal. Here, problems arose because the company aspired to be global but still operated to some extent like an American company with units abroad. Despite a strong commitment to change, most of AlliedSignal's business units, according to the local respondent, continued to operate on a "silo basis," restricted by "tunnel vision," where the progress of the corporation as a whole was continually inhibited by the sectional interests of the leading parts. As all of these parts were headquartered in the USA, top management in Asia struggled to take full advantage of the opportunities in the region. For example, a new turbo-generator project for small energy needs (actually developed in the US) would have been commercially successful in China and India, but there was little corporate interest in supporting this because it was less relevant for US and European markets. The goal was to get to the point where management in Asia had the full support of the US business units for these projects. In the global economy of which AlliedSignal strives to be a part, competitive pressures would ensure this sooner or later. The problem for those corporations that were lagging in the race to globalize, was that if the necessary changes did not come soon, it might be too late. In most of the corporations interviewed, there was a tangible feeling that going global was not an option but a necessity for a successful transnational corporation.[34]

The Nonrespondents

The preceding analysis is largely based on interviews carried out in *Fortune* Global 500 corporations. (See Appendix I for details of the sample.) The interviews were conducted in the USA (California, New

York, and Washington DC), Canada (Montreal), Mexico (Tijuana and Cd. Juarez), London, Ireland, Hong Kong, and in Australia (Sydney and Melbourne). Most of the corporations that declined to be interviewed cited pressure of time or absence of the relevant executive as the reason, and some (for example, Disney and IBM) said that they never granted interviews for such purposes. It is, however, possible to work out the likely answers to at least some of the interview questions from annual reports, other company publications, and press reports. The results of this documentary research suggested that overall the nonrespondents and the remainder of the Global 500 were not radically different in any important respects from the respondents. This can be illustrated with a brief analysis of the nonrespondents in California and one other.

The four *Fortune* Global 500 corporations that declined to be interviewed in California were Safeway, Walt Disney, Pacific Telesis, and Occidental. McKesson responded to a postal survey (see below). Information about the other four corporations comes from their own publications and the business press.

Safeway Inc. is one of the world's largest food retailers, operating over a thousand stores mainly in the western halves of the USA and Canada. Its sales in the 52 weeks of 1998 exceeded $22 billion, a sum greater than the GNPs of about half the countries in the world. It owned 35 percent of the Vons chain, the largest supermarket in southern California, and a 49 percent share in the retailer Casa Ley in Mexico. The company was founded in 1926 when Merrill Lynch acquired the assets of Safeway Stores, one of the first cash-and-carry retailers in the world. Canada Safeway was established in 1929. In the 1960s the company bought up stores in Britain, Australia, and West Germany and it acquired its interest in Casa Ley in 1981. Since then Safeway has divested itself of all its interests outside North America and was taken private in 1986 via a leveraged buyout by Kohlberg Kravis Roberts & Co. (of RJR Nabisco fame). In the early 1990s, KKR, who held five of the nine seats on the board, returned Safeway to public status. None of the company's publications manifested much interest in globalization and while food retailers increasingly availed themselves of produce and products from the global marketplace, it was clear that for Safeway foreign investment and other aspects of globalization had little relevance.

McKesson was mainly engaged in the supply of pharmaceutical and healthcare products and services to pharmacies, hospitals, and healthcare networks. The written response from the company in 1997 expressed the view that McKesson was primarily focused on the North American market and, while keeping aware of global trends, had no globalizing plans for itself. This counterfactual strengthened the connection between globalization, the global marketplace, and FDI. Like Safeway, another nonglobalizing Global 500 company, McKesson restricted itself to investments in the contiguous markets of Canada and Mexico. The healthcare sector, like the food sector, was one of the few expanding markets in California and there appeared to be no compelling pressures in the mid-1990s for such companies to globalize in order to grow. The merger in 1998 of McKesson and HBOC, a healthcare informatics group, to create the world's largest healthcare services company, did present opportunities for global strategies. While 95 percent of McKesson HBOC revenues came from the US, the new company had customers in 10 other countries. It would not be surprising if the company attempted to expand its global business.

The Walt Disney Company was the major force in the global entertainment business. For some, globalization in the cultural field was largely invented by Disney through his cast of cartoon and subsequently somewhat more human characters, broadcast via an ever-increasing range of mass media. The Chair and CEO, Michael Eisner, described the global strategy (Disney synergy) in the 1995 Annual Report as follows: "how each division could promote other divisions, how each division could promote Euro Disney, how television could be used in each country as a franchise establishment . . . We did it in the US. We did it and do it in Europe and in Asia. We will start doing it in Latin America." To those who believe that Disney already exercised global reach, it was clear that the company considered it still had a long way to go. The acquisition of Capital Cities/ABC reinforced Disney's position in the US from where global operations emanated.

Disney satisfied the criteria of globalization discussed above. Euro Disney and Tokyo Disneyland represented major globalizing foreign investments and, in the case of Euro Disney, major losses borne in the short term. As *Fortune* magazine pointed out (April 13, 1997, p. 52) Walt Disney World theme parks, with 38 million visitors annually, were a bigger draw than most European countries. Disney's commitment to world best practice and benchmarking was graphically expressed by the CEO as: "Average is awful." Disney's global vision has been widely discussed, from Dorfman and Mattelart's classic (1975) deconstruction of the imperialism of Donald Duck et al. to Sorkin's assertion (1992: 205) that the aura of Disney was "all-pervasive." Within the company, Walt Disney Imagineering had the responsibility for "changing the future." This it had been doing in the theme parks for decades and developing for the new worlds of location-based entertainment and cyberspace. Whether or not Disney saw itself as an American company with units abroad is a moot point. Certainly, much of Disney was taken up with representing America to the world, but it can equally well be argued that Disney's special talent was to represent stories from all cultures and countries in a distinctive Disney fashion. The difference between the Disneyfication (or Coca-Colaization or McDonaldization) of the world and the Americanization of the world through these consumerist icons, is one important marker of the difference between global system and state-centrist interpretations of globalization.

Pacific Telesis, the California-Nevada part of the broken up AT&T/ Bell System (Vietor 1994: ch. 4) was the nineteenth largest telecommunications corporation in the world when it was acquired by SBC Communications in 1998. Its subsidiary, Pacific Bell, had about 16 million telephone access lines in California and Nevada, which accounted for most of its revenues of $9 billion plus in 1995. The push pressures of deregulation combined with the pull pressures of rapid development of telecommunications technology to turn globalization into a necessity rather than an option for Pacific Telesis, and the merging of the company into the SBC system was one indication of this. In these respects SBC was very similar to AT&T and BT, discussed above.

Occidental Petroleum (OXY), despite its name, was the fourteenth biggest chemical company in the world. Revenues from chemicals ($4.7 billion) in 1994 were almost double those for oil and gas, and more than double those for its other major activity, natural gas transmission, which explains why the company was in the chemical sector for the purposes of the Global 500. OXY produced oil and gas in 12 countries and explored for them in 23. The chemicals subsidiary, OxyChem, was a major producer of caustic soda, chlorine, PVC, and ethylene, all in high demand in the mid-1990s. In its Annual Report for 1996 its objectives were clearly stated: "Invest in profitable growth primarily in international oil and gas and speciality chemicals, with our domestic energy and commodity chemical operations providing cash to fund this growth." OxyChem was reported to be busily buying up speciality chemical companies in the US and establishing joint ventures with Sumitomo Bakelite in the US and SE Asia. In 1992 and 1994 foreign income was more than double domestic income, while in 1993 it was the other way round. It is likely that OXY has a good deal in common with Chevron and ARCO, and as the chemicals parts of their businesses appeared to be the most globalizing it is likely that OxyChem was driving OXY in the same direction.

The only *Fortune* Global 500 domiciled in Australia that declined to be interviewed was the retailer, Coles Myer. The refusal was on the grounds that the company was entirely domestic and had no interest in the issue of globalization. This may have been true in 1995 when it was approached, but a report in the *Financial Times* ("Coles Myer Sees Asia Effect by Summer," March 12, 1998) suggested that this might be changing. The company was discussing the possibility of entering regional markets with partners in Asia, even though Coles Myer had posted its best results in almost a decade. A revision of the purely domestic strategy seemed imminent. In this case, Coles Myer as a retailer without units abroad may well be globalizing with partners abroad.

This brief survey suggests that there are good reasons why Safeway and McKesson do not appear to be globalizing, while the other corporations share a good deal in common with the globalizers who did respond. There is no reason to suspect that the respondents and nonrespondents in other locations were very different. In the following chapters, evidence from the public record about many other Global 500 corporations will be presented, pointing to the same conclusion.

Conclusions

The evidence presented in this chapter suggests that the idea of globalization had a strong resonance for a sample of senior executives and middle managers in Global 500 corporations. The suggestion that multinationals were "national companies with units abroad" was roundly rejected as old-fashioned and not compatible with the demands of the contemporary global economy. Most Global 500 executives and managers in the sample considered their corporations to be in a transitional state between the multinational corporation and the global corporation, that is, they were to a greater or lesser extent globalizing.

Also clear was the finding that, in order to fulfill a "shareholder-driven growth imperative," most of the corporations considered that they had no alternative but to globalize. This was despite the problems and pain that might be caused to employees in the home country and the communities where the corporations were originally established. All of these finding demonstrate a move to globalization among the Global 500 and a certain level of success for some. Nevertheless, few of these corporations considered themselves entirely globalized. In the words of the senior executive for Asia-Pacific of General Electric: "globalization is not a natural act." The argument of this book is that the efforts of the corporations to globalize in order to survive and prosper in the globalizing world economy produce the forces that create a transnational capitalist class. These are not natural processes, but contested outcomes of struggles over economic, political, and culture-ideology resources.

Where does this leave the argument between state-centrist and globalization theorists? In California, for the utilities and BankAmerica, meeting the demands of the local economy (California, or part of it) has been until relatively recently the dominating feature of their businesses. (This also appears still to be true to some extent for Pacific Telesis, Safeway, and McKesson.) Other corporations in other business sectors, notably globally branded consumer goods, oil, and electronics, have always been more oriented to overseas markets, often as US-based companies operating and trading abroad. The globalizing moment comes when corporations stop thinking and acting primarily in terms of "developing foreign markets and meeting competition from abroad" and start to think and act more in terms of "competitive strategies for global marketing."[35] As we shall see in subsequent chapters, these new global business orientations and practices have a series of important consequences for employees at all levels, and for the communities where corporate facilities are located and where the impacts of corporate policies (employment, environmental, welfare, and others) occur.

While the important economic spaces for the corporations become increasingly dispersed all over the globe, this does not mean that specific sites of corporate activity become irrelevant. The effects of corporate practices on these sites (communities, urban conglomerations, subnational regions, whole countries, supranational regions) become more difficult to control through democratic processes, where they exist, or through bureaucratic nondemocratic processes, even where they are genuinely based on some conception of the public good. This argument connects with class, ethnic, and gender consequences of globalization, both in terms of the consequences of globalization for the workforce in globalizing corporations and also for the public at large. The impressive body of research building up on these topics (see, for example, Castells 1998; Mander and Goldsmith 1996; Smith and Guarnizo 1998) confirms that the agents and institutions of globalization are being challenged.

Globalization, in the commonsense meaning of the term (global as opposed to a restrictively local or national perspective), clearly has a central part in the corporate vocabulary of most of the Global 500 and, certainly, of almost all of the corporations interviewed for this study. Discussion of those corporations that declined to be interviewed combined with observations of global imagery in corporate publications (see table 8.1 below) strongly suggested that most major TNCs in the 1990s presented themselves publicly in global terms. The main reasons volunteered, which appeared as a coda throughout all the interviews and much of the corporate literature, were versions of the theme: if you want to grow the company you have to do it globally (or internationally). In most cases the terms "internationally" and "globally" were being used interchangeably.[36]

The argument that the biggest corporations were globalizing, in the sense that they no longer wished to be seen as national companies with units abroad, connects directly with the changing nature of the various industries within the five sectors of the global economy. In all the cases surveyed in this chapter, the biggest companies were either buying up smaller companies or making strategic alliances of various types with other major corporations and/or with smaller, more local companies and thereby locking them into their global networks. Even for state-owned corporations, similar strategies appeared to be emerging. An interesting example can be found in the 1995 Annual Report of Sinochem, one of China's great state-owned conglomerates (ranked 213 in the *Fortune* Global 500 for 1998). Citing a State Council resolution, Sinochem explains that it "has launched the trans-national conglomerate pilot project, finding its way as China's first, and has enhanced modern management by having its nucleus in finance. . . . Mainly engaged in trade, SINOCHEM will expand steadily and diversify into industry, technology, finance, information and other services, creating a truly international trans-national corporation [to] make our contribution to the prosperity of China." Sinochem carried out this policy through strategic alliances and joint ventures with many overseas companies, including Nichimen, Ciba-Geigy, and other companies in Europe, Russia, and Saudi Arabia. Time will tell whether and to what extent Sinochem and corporations like it will become globalizing corporations expressing the interests of those who own and control them, or the "national" interests of the state bureaucrats who are responsible for them.

As the next chapter argues, this no longer necessarily means (as it might have done in the heyday of imperialism) that local companies of major corporations are exploited and that the communities in which these companies are located necessarily get the worst of the relationship. Though this still can and does happen, globalization is not simply some new form of imperialism, though it does reinforce many types of exploitation by those who own and control the major means of production of those who do not. Globalization creates new forms of transnational class alliances across borders and new forms of class cleavages globally and within countries, regions, cities, and local communities in ways that do not simply reproduce the older patters of nationalistic imperialism.

Intuitively, there would appear to be at least two central determinants of globalization for companies wishing to become bigger. The first is the size of the domestic market, in the territory where the company had its origins.[37] Obviously, companies from relatively small countries (for example, Sweden and Switzerland) will have to cross national borders to win the business that will help them grow very big, whereas companies from large countries (for example, the USA and China) can grow very big merely by satisfying domestic demand. The second determinant of globalization is the business sector to which a company belongs. Oil and mining companies, for example, have always had to scour the world for the natural resources they require, while some infrastructure companies (providers of electricity and water, and telecommunications, for example) have been traditionally more tied to their home bases. While these assumptions are still true to some extent, the experience of corporate globalization in recent decades and particularly in the 1990s suggests that they are no longer entirely sound.

Changing from a multinational to a globalizing corporation is not simply a matter of putting together a collection of local capabilities, though this is a necessary part of the process. It also involves developing and implementing global strategies that would not be possible for businesses that were national companies with units abroad. These strategies involve economic-organizational, political and, culture-ideology innovations. The management and popular business literature is packed with analyses of and recipes for the successful global corporation. In the following chapters, four criteria are proposed to characterize globalizing corporations. Foreign investment, world best practice, corporate citizenship, and global vision provide the foundations for a sociological analysis of the material base of the transnational capitalist class. Transnational corporations, those who own and control them, and their allies in the transnational capitalist class are globalizing as they struggle to come to terms with the contradictions of the global capitalist system that they themselves have been instrumental in creating.

Notes

1 Notably Hirst and Thompson (1996). For critical analysis of these "myths" see Strange (1996). It needs to be noted that there is a good deal of hostility to the idea of globalization in academic circles.

2 Kapstein (1994), for example, argues this vigorously for the case of the major banks. As noted above, there is a wide variation in how these terms are used in the literature.

3 *Fortune* publishes several lists annually. The most famous is the *Fortune* 500 (which actually lists the top 1,000 companies in the US by revenue). For a

discussion of the evolution of the *Fortune* Global 500, see Sklair and Robbins (forthcoming). There have been some small discrepancies in *Fortune*'s arithmatic over the years. All revenue figures have been rounded in this chapter.

4 Citations to newspaper and magazine articles and corporate publications are given in the text, except where an author is identified. All unattributed quotations are from corporate publications or interviews.

5 This view, reported in 1994, recalls the influential "organization man" thesis of Whyte (1956) in the 1950s.

6 In fact, the food component (Nabisco) of the company was demerged from the tobacco component (RJR) in 1999, a move not unconnected with legal and reputational pressures on cigarette companies (see Sklair 1998).

7 Contributions to this debate range from those who argue that the world economy is already globalized and that nation-states are more or less irrelevant (e.g. Ohmae 1990) through those who research the conditions of economic globalization and criteria for globalizing corporations (Amin and Thrift 1994; Dicken 1998) to those who reject the idea of economic globalization entirely (Hirst and Thompson 1996).

8 One of the many effects of the Asian crises from 1997 was to cut the dollar value of most Asian currencies. This, combined with loss of business, pushed the major Japanese trading houses down the list (in 1999 Mitsui was number 5, Mitsubishi 7, and Itochu 6) and reduced overall Japanese presence in the Global 500 from 149 in 1996 to 100 in 1999. While some South Korean TNCs slipped in the rankings, all 12 retained their places in the 1998 Global 500, and 9 did in 1999.

9 A study from the State University of Iowa (cited in "The Store that Ate America," *Observer* (London) Sept. 26, 1999) found that between 1983 and 1993 more than 7,000 small businesses had closed, mostly in areas where Wal-Mart or similar cut price chains had established new stores (retail cannibalism).This is a recurrent theme in twentieth-century literature, Emile Zola's *The Ladies' Paradise* and Sinclair Lewis's *Main Street* are two in a long line of works to bemoan this phenomenon. Fast food outlets near the new stores, however, flourished.

10 By 1998, the decline in revenues of the Japanese trading houses had allowed commercial banks and motor vehicles and parts to push the industry into third place overall in the *Fortune* industries table. As noted above, these companies do not only trade consumer goods.

11 While the economic viability of global capitalism is not the central issue of this book, it can be said that the history of the Japanese trading houses in the last decades of the twentieth century does necessitate at least a partial reconsideration of global capitalism as a coherent system. If the system really is based on free enterprise, maximizing economic efficiency and competition, how long can even the largest companies survive if they do not make substantial profits?

12 Ritzer (1996) extends this argument in one extreme direction in identifying McDonaldization as the dominant motif of social organization for the contemporary world.

13 This argument is supported in an informative study of George Woods, the first President of the World Bank: "George Woods was a New York banker, not a Washington bureaucrat" (Oliver 1995: 187). None of his successors at the Bank, or those in other international financial institutions, appear to have acted against the collective interests of global capitalism, though some certainly wished to appear more "people-friendly" than others. An abundance of evidence for this assertion is available both from the Bank's supporters (see Delphos 1997) and its opponents, notably the "Fifty Years is Enough" campaign (Danahar 1994).

14 A series of mergers and/or acquisitions in the late 1990s, notably BP and Amoco, Exxon and Mobil, and Shell and Mobil in Europe, increased concentration in the global oil industry.

15 The industries usually included in the infrastructure sector are power, water, hydrocarbons, transportation,and telecommunications. For reasons explained above, hydrocarbons are located in the heavy industry sector, and transportation in the consumer goods and services sector.

16 It was.certainly the home of the semiconductor industry. On Silicon Valley and its offshoots see, for example, Saxenian (1994), Hall and Markusen (1985), and Henderson (1989). Packard (1995) is useful on Silicon Valley in general and Hewlett-Packard in particular.

17 Interestingly, the Japanese electronics corporations retained their places in the Global 500 for 1998 when other Japan-based companies suffered from the economic crisis.

18 IBM was one of the few companies that refused to grant an interview for this research, both in the USA and in Australia. "IBM receives so many similar requests to participate in surveys, questionnaires, and research projects that we have been forced to say no to all of them" (personal letter from Director, Executive and Internal Communications IBM, Feb. 3, 1997). Despite such letters from other companies, other avenues of approach did sometimes yield interviews. The literature on IBM is so extensive (see e.g. Carroll 1994; Sobel 1983) that I did not persist in this case. Korten (1995: 124) quotes an IBM executive in 1990: "IBM, to some degree, has successfully lost its American identity."

19 See Appendix I. It should be noted that interviews with TNCs headquartered in Japan were conducted in Australia, Ireland, Hong Kong, the USA, and Mexico, not in Japan.

20 The quotation is actually from one of the executives interviewed by La-Palombara and Blank whose study makes many points still relevant to corporations today. The context was the controversy raised by two influential books, Servan-Schreiber (1968), which warned that European business was being bought up by US multinationals, and Vernon (1971). For a well-informed contemporaneous discussion, see Behrman (1970),where the distinction between the (old-fashioned) conception of the international holding company approach to foreign investment is contrasted unfavourably with what he labels "the new multinational enterprise,"which has "the capacity to shift operations around the world so as to reduce costs and

improve efficiency and greater ability to expand its market penetration" (Behrman 1970: 2). This type of enterprise (now commonly called the TNC or global corporation), Behrman argues, poses a threat to national interests. For more recent restatements of these arguments, see Korten (1995) and Hirst and Thompson (1996).

21 As Hoffman and Gopinath (1994) have done, with interesting results for the distinction between "international" and "global" business orientations of CEOs of US corporations.

22 In chapter 9 ("The Global Entrepreneur") of his book on IBM, Sobel (1983: 195) quotes a former leader of IBM France to the effect: "The only thing about Maisonrouge that remained French was his accent." Sobel's argument that this proves that Maisonrouge had become "Americanized" is flimsy. Maisonrouge had become a globalizing capitalist.

23 Dicken (1998, chs. 3 and 4) directly addresses these issues and his chapters are an excellent review of the literature.

24 As a Mitsui brochure of the mid-1990s asked: "Are you looking for a business partner to help you formulate and implement your international strategies?"

25 Systematic lessons for McDonald's employees were initiated by Luigi Salvaneschi, an unemployed Ph.D. in canon law from the University of Rome and Latin University in the Vatican, who began to work for Ray Kroc when he realized that jobs for Latin teachers in the USA were strictly limited. Hamburger University grew out of these lessons: "Our first class had eighteen students. We awarded them a Bachelor of Hamburgerology degree with a minor in french fries" (Kroc and Anderson 1977: 126). It is not clear if Kroc is entirely serious here.

26 Although the BSE case in the UK was the most catastrophic in its consequences, it was only one case among many (see Adam 1998, esp. ch. 5).

27 For example, the India-based software company Infosys employed 5,000 people in 2000, of whom 200 were dollar millionaires and a further 1,800 were rupee millionaires (Ramesh 2000). For a thoughtful analysis of how this connects with rest of the labour force, see Prasad (1998).

28 Viacom's audacious acquisition of CBS in 1999 was further evidence of the company's global ambitions.

29 Regionalization is often seen as a compromise position for those scholars who cannot accept globalization, but who are no longer prepared to argue that nothing has changed (e.g. Stallings ed. 1995).

30 The fact that Prudential Australia was spun off from the parent company in the late 1990s could, however, be read as evidence for or against the globalization hypothesis.

31 See the argument of Henderson (1999) that Asian *crises* were brought on by asymmetric state capacities in the region leading to different outcomes in the face of global economic and financial pressures, a case of justified state-centrism.

32 The respondent from Chevron suggested that "the nationality of employees was becoming irrelevant" for progress in the company. This sentiment was common throughout the Global 500.

33 These characteristics were also found in Telstra, the Australian telecommunications company, that began its process of globalization and the search for world best practice in 1992 when the domestic and the international carriers merged. Partial privatization began in 1997.

34 This was vividly illustrated in the company in the late 1990s, where new structures for excellence, partly based on Six Sigma methodology, were presented as solutions to this problem (see chapter 5).

35 The sentiments are those expressed in most of my interviews with Global 500 executives and managers, the actual words are from Hoffman and Gopinath (1994: 633).

36 In common with many academic writers, most business writers appear to use the terms "international" and "global" interchangeably (see Hoffman and Gopinath, 1994: 631). I have assumed that my respondents were doing this where the context provided sufficient evidence to do so. Just the same, some respondents (as well as some academics) do distinguish between the two while continuing to indulge in the linguistic confusion.

37 This is not, necessarily, the "national" market, as some large firms in large countries can have huge markets within metropolitan areas, for example Tokyo Electric Power Company, and in subnational regions, for example Edison Electric in southern California and PG &E in northern California.

Chapter 4
Corporate Elites and the Transformation of Foreign Investment

The argument of this chapter is based on the distinction between global reach and global shift practices and interpretations of TNC foreign investment. *Global reach* is a primary stage of corporate internationalization, representing a culmination of older patterns of colonialism and imperialism. While the term comes from Barnet and Muller (1974), it is used here to denote the wide range of dependency theories that dominated the study of imperialism and (under)development from the 1960s to the 1980s. The main weakness of these theories was that their state-centrism distorted their analysis of an increasingly globalizing capitalism, although Barnet and Muller themselves were attuned to the critique of nationalism implicit in much globalizing big business. Global reach has been overtaken in practice by a more mature stage of corporate globalization that can be labeled *global shift*. While this term is from Dicken (1998), it is used here to denote investment strategies and theories to explain them that distinguish systematically between internationalization and globalization. Dicken makes this distinction, though he also argues that the state is still a key influence on the global economy (and he is skeptical on the global corporation).

Internationalization (global reach) means cross-border practices in which state agencies and actors working through national institutions, directly or indirectly state-owned, strive to achieve clearly articulated objectives of "national interest." Corporate internationalization and imperialism, on this definition, are virtually synonymous. The behavior of international or multinational corporations could thus be largely predicted in terms of the "national" interests of the governments they served. The most popular version of this argument in the twentieth century, particularly on the left, was that US multinationals and the US state went hand in hand overseas to exploit the rest of the world.

Globalization (global shift) means transnational practices in which corporate agencies and actors (principally TNC executives and their local affiliates) strive to maximize private profits globally for those who own and control the corporations. TNCs seek profits without special reference to the interests (real or imagined) of their countries of citizenship. The transnational capitalist class mobilizes the resources necessary to accomplish this objective, working through a variety of social institutions, including state and quasi-state agencies, the professions, and the mass media. The culture-ideology of consumerism is the rationale of the system.

The role of those who own and control the major corporations has been fundamental in this process as has the growth of a genuine capitalist class, sometimes transnational, sometimes multinational, rarely strictly national, all over the world. FDI (foreign direct investment) in the process of late industrialization has had a paradoxical effect. The paradox is that as states opened up their economies to foreign companies, particularly in export-processing zones, and adopted export-oriented industrialization strategies (see Gereffi and Wyman 1990) they facilitated the creation of a transnational as well as national capitalist classes. As capitalist globalization gathered pace all around the world, venerable cross-border trading companies, whose owners could be seen as members of embryonic mercantile global classes, grew into and/or were replaced by the globalizing corporations that provided the material base for a transnational capitalist class. The changes in the structures of these businesses, from somewhat informal and mobile groups of merchants into formal organizations with, literally, large amounts of fixed capital, accompanied changes in their scope of operations. One important consequence of these changes was that major TNCs, engaged in business on the fringes of the First World and in "developing countries" or "emerging markets," could no longer afford the luxury of crude imperialist exploitation, and those who ran them could no longer afford to display crass colonial attitudes. The argument is not that major corporations no longer act in these ways, but that they can no longer *afford* to do so. TNCs are generally beginning to realize that the economic benefits to be derived from such exploitative practices can be outweighed, in the long run, by their costs. For the transnational capitalist class to carry out its work effectively, all its allies have to be treated with respect and given a share of the profits.[1]

Global reach and global shift differ fundamentally in how they characterize the global economy and its constituent units. Global reach theory argued that all foreign investment, particularly from richer to poorer countries, was exploitative and that it was usually carried out to take advantage of cheap labor and/or cheap natural resources. Far from having positive developmental effects, as neoclassical and neoliberal economic theories maintain, FDI was said to underdevelop host countries and lock them into dependent relationships with the imperialist states whose interests the TNCs expressed. In an interesting but much obscured reversal of the Marxism that they sometimes purported to represent, neo-Marxist dependency theorists often appeared to argue that the TNCs were the instrument of US imperialism. The American state, in particular the military whose hardware requirements the TNCs supplied at great profit, was seen as the subject of American imperialism, and the capitalist class as its instrument. To this extent, global reach theory and the dependency framework from which it derived, were locked into a contradiction of their own making in trying to reconcile state-centrist notions of imperialism with global (or, more accurately, international) notions of economic and political practice.

Dicken's formulation of the problem in terms of a multipolar world in which states, regions, and corporations jostle for positions of power and influence, is plausible, considering the vast array of evidence available on how all these actors and institutions operate (Dicken 1998). He describes the processes involved in global shift, but does not offer any comprehensive theory of it apart from the idea that technology facilitates but does not itself cause globalization. Notwithstanding its pragmatic similarities, global shift sprouts from quite different soil than global reach and has one key advantage over it, in that it recognizes and attempts to build on the tensions between state apparatuses and globalizing corporations. All globalization theories have a problem with the state, for the simple reason that what makes globalization distinctive is that it tries to explain how and why global forces of various types displace state agencies and actors. Whereas global reach theorists see the state (particularly the hegemonic core state) as the main force driving the capitalist system forward, global shift has a much more nuanced conception of the ways that governments and corporations (or, more abstractly, states and markets) interact to drive capitalism forward. There is a considerable range of opinion on the exact nature and significance of these interactions (e.g., Dicken 1998, Dunning 1997, Krugman 1996, Strange 1996). However, what is notable about these works is their appreciation of what Susan Strange was talking about in her immortal injunction: "Wake up, Krasner [and mainstream political economy, international relations, sociology of development, comparative politics, et al.], the world has changed" (Strange 1994). Researching the *Fortune* Global 500 and an emerging transnational capitalist class is one way of starting to explain what has changed and to assess its significance.

A central weakness in both the global reach and global shift research programs is that neither deconstructs the state carefully enough. Those who study "the state" (like those who study "class") too often argue as if it is a homogeneous, if not monolithic, phenomenon. It is precisely because the state in the global capitalist system is not homogenous that it is fruitful to conceptualize the transnational capitalist class as the characteristic institutional form of political transnational practices. Within the TCC the state is represented by globalizing bureaucrats and politicians. In the age of global capitalism all states are riven to a greater or lesser extent by struggles between capitalist globalizers and capitalist (or noncapitalist, sometimes even anticapitalist) localizers, espousing various types of protectionism and other inner-oriented economic and social policies.

The Transformation of Foreign Investment

Academic researchers (Dicken 1998; Dunning 1997), international agencies (OECD 1996; World Bank 1996) and TNCs (see below) all acknowledge a general connection between foreign investment and globalization. Thus, "never before have so many firms from so many industries invested in so many countries . . . In spite of all the hyperbole about the unstoppable juggernaut of globalization, countries retain the power to prevent inward investment – albeit at an increasing cost" (OECD 1996: 47).[2] In the 1990s the preferred mode of FDI was mergers and acquisitions, accelerated by privatizations and deregulation of inward investment. Some of the biggest Global 500 corporations merged or formed strategic alliances with each other, and many smaller firms were swallowed up in the process. A widely quoted concept from McKinsey (the global management consultants) was "double the scale, half the cost" (goals not always achieved).[3] A substantial part of FDI was actually foreign earnings, unrepatriated profits (in the case of US-domiciled corporations, the OECD reported a figure of two-thirds). It was, therefore, not surprising that all the Global 500 corporations interviewed for this study acknowledged a general connection between FDI and globalization, and this finding was amply confirmed by documentary research on corporate publications. Although the reasons given for FDI differed from sector to sector, from industry to industry, sometimes from product to product, the underlying motive was uniform across all business sectors. Globalization was necessary to increase shareholder value (in some cases it always had been, in others it had become so) and foreign direct investment was the strategy through which it was most successfully accomplished for most companies.

Within this general connection that major corporations made between globalization and FDI, several themes were identified. These were (a) the importance of global brands; (b) the regulatory climate; (c) phases of foreign direct investment; (d) the home base and the foreign investment; and (e) the question of disinvestment. While all of these themes have substantial economics and business-management literatures attached, the focus here will be on the sociological context. To anticipate the findings of this chapter, all these themes around foreign direct investment pointed to the conclusion that globalizing corporations strive to become global by "being global, locally." This slogan (or some variation of it) recurred in corporate interviews, in company reports, and in business publications. It encapsulated the consequences for marketing and the promotional culture of consumerist capitalism.

Global Brands

Global brands predated globalization, but the attempt to brand a much wider range of products globally and, crucially, to globally brand the companies that produced the products is distinctive of global capitalism. In particular, global brands are at the center of the culture-ideology of consumerism that drives the capitalist system, giving the system as a whole a meaning and, in a real sense, providing a universal substitute for moral and spiritual values.[4]

While we could begin a discussion of global brands with one of many distillations of marketing wisdom that appear in textbooks or in business magazines, it is perhaps more fitting to start with the results of a 1990 survey of 9,000 consumers (5,000 from the USA, 3,000 from Europe, and 1,000 from Japan) by Landor Associates of San Francisco, a "corporate identity firm" (Horovitz 1990). This "Image Power" survey evaluated 6,000 brands on measures of recognition and esteem. While the methodology of the survey was a little hazy and we should note that the top brand, Coca-Cola, was a Landor client, the findings were nevertheless interesting. First, and not surprisingly, the top 20 brands chosen by Americans were brands produced by corporations domiciled in the USA. However, 4 of the top 10 brands for the whole sample were products of corporations domiciled outside the USA.[5]

This survey overlaps fairly closely with a more geographically balanced survey carried out by the British consultants Interbrand (1990) and is supported by my own research on consumerism in China (Sklair 1994). Table 4.1 compares the top ten brands on these surveys. The overlap requires no comment.

Table 4.1   Top ten global brands (1990)

Landor Survey	Interbrand Survey
1. Coca-Cola	1. Coca-Cola
2. Sony	2. Kellog's
3. Mercedes-Benz	3. McDonald's
4. Kodak	4. Kodak
5. Disney	5. Marlboro
6. Nestle	6. IBM
7. Toyota	7. American Express
8. McDonald's	8. Sony
9. IBM	9. Mercedes Benz
10. Pepsi-Cola	10. Nescafe

Source: Horovitz 1990.   *Source:* Interbrand 1990.

Nevertheless, the idea of a "global brand" is not universally agreed. A study in the mid-1990s of six major consumer goods companies (Colgate, Kraft, Nestlé, Procter & Gamble, Quaker, and Unilever) defined "global" as selling in 34 or more of 67 countries surveyed. On this basis, the study found that less than 4 percent of the combined total of 1,792 brands that these six companies produced could be called "global." Only six brands (Colgate toothpaste, Lipton tea, Lux soap, Maggi soup, Nescafe coffee, and Palmolive soap) sold in all 67 countries (reported in Mitchell 1996). Research findings such as these suggest that while sales are becoming more international, there are few if any genuinely global brands. But defining the globality of a brand in terms of the number of countries in which it is sold, confuses globalization with internationalization, though it does usefully remind us that the "global" is not a finished process. While there may be no global corporations and few global brands, it may be fruitful to think about globalizing corporations and globalizing brands. This refocuses attention from the number of countries in which a brand is sold to how the brand is presented to consumers, how it is positioned in the global marketplace. Very few companies will invest resources just to have their brands available in markets where there is little prospect of ever making money. However, there is a real choice between promoting different brands of similar products in different parts of the world, and creating global brands, which need not be identical, for sale in different parts of the world. Globalizing corporations selling directly to the public are more likely to strive to create global brands.

The consultants Interbrand distinguish three types of brand names: descriptive, associative, and freestanding (Interbrand 1997, ch. 2). Descriptive names, unsurprisingly, describe the benefits or attributes of the product or service (Diners Club, Newsweek, Post-it). The disadvantages of descriptive names are that they tend not to be very distinctive and that they often do not travel well outside their language and culture of origin. Associative names convey appropriate value associations that connect with what the brand offers (Visa, Habitat). However, new and powerful associative names not already in trade mark registers are difficult to find and, again, the name may not travel well. Freestanding or abstract names have no literal meaning but, when they are successfully marketed, they can become the strongest names precisely because they are distinctive to specific products or services. And they usually travel well.[6] Many names with no literal meaning whatsoever – such as Hoover, Xerox, Kodak, Sony – now have generic and virtually global status.

Freestanding names, therefore, have the most potential for global branding and Interbrand offers the following advice:

> Think global but act local – go for the "glocal" brand. The key to international branding is to maintain an international coherence but, at the same time, adapt the brand to suit local conditions. What is emphasised and communicated about the brand might be tailored to the needs of local markets in terms of promotion and packaging. The brand name is the one element of the marketing "mix" that should not be changed and is a key means of providing continuity between markets. It allows consumers to recognise the brand wherever they go (how often do we eat at McDONALD's when abroad simply because we know and trust the brand?). (Interbrand 1997: 103; upper case in the original)

It is, of course, important for globalizing corporations to be seen to be successful, to be market leaders in their major products and services. In its brochure "Introducing Unilever" of 1996 Unilever described itself as an "international" not a "global" company "because it does not attempt to enter all markets with the same product." In fact, in the mid-1990s Unilever occupied first position in its three regional markets (Europe; North America; Africa, Middle East, Latin America, Asia & Pacific) and in the Global [*sic*] market for 12 product categories. For ice-cream, tea-based beverages, margarine, and personal wash products, Unilever was number one in all these markets. For prestige fragrances and deodorants it was number one globally, but only in one of the three regional markets; and in the remaining products it had seven number one positions in regional markets. Unilever's "score" was 21 first places out of a possible 36, and 6 global firsts out of a possible 12. By the company's own definition it was, therefore, more than half way to being a global company. To improve on this performance, Unilever restructured to try to create more synergy between regional groupings for different products and product categories irrespective of geographical markets.[7] This is a good illustration of the thesis that, while truly global corporations and a truly global economy may be ideal typical, there is much solid evidence of globalizing corporations, such as Unilever, and sectors where the economy as a whole does appear to be globalizing in some respects. The recent history of the processed food and home products industries, as evidenced by Unilever (and its great rival, Nestlé, of whom more below) provides evidence for this thesis, and the promotion of globalizing brands is one important measure of it.

The creation of a global brand is one pure form of foreign investment. Success requires substantial investment in a wide range of marketing tools all over the world. According to the *Economist* "Brazil: Cost of Building Market Share for New Brands Surges" (Aug. 27, 1996) foreign companies were expected to invest US$6–9 billion in Brazil in 1996. Each 1 percent of market share for mass consumer items in Brazil was estimated to cost around $50 million. Consumer goods corporations with globalizing aspirations must be prepared to make similar investments to globalize their major brands.[8] Like those of its competitors, Unilever's products do not sell themselves; they are marketed wherever the company operates.[9] These marketing tools ranged from the obvious (advertisements on radio and television and in the print media), to the less obvious (sponsoring a multitude of popular activities to ensure maximum media exposure outside of the regular diet of advertisements). While not alone in this, Coca-Cola was certainly a global leader in most forms of marketing for its ubiquitous product. The Coca-Cola logo adorns a remarkable range of objects and activities, not least the world's most popular sports (see Pendergrast 1993),[10] and countless other events, organizations, and services that meld the company and its products into the very fabric of everyday life all over the world. The promotion of global brands is clearly an integral part of the culture-ideology of consumerism. The Coca-Cola marketing system is a telling illustration of how the cultural forms of consumerism (connecting the marketing of specific consumer goods with more or less everything that happens in people's cultural lives, however broadly or narrowly we define culture) reinforced and were reinforced by the ideology of consumerism (the values and belief system that judges our worth and meanings as human beings in terms of what we possess and consume).

The transformation of foreign direct investment for globalizing corporations, therefore, goes far beyond the longstanding activities of opening new factories and offices, acquisitions, and joint ventures of various types. FDI for the globalizing corporation today means "being global, locally" by making the brand part of the local culture and even, in some extreme cases, identifying globalizing brands with the local culture.[11]

The Regulatory Climate

All TNCs, like all businesses of any size, complain about government regulation. Indeed, one of the key thrusts of the neoliberal ideology that played such an important role in spreading the doctrine of globalization was that government should "get out of the economy" by reducing regulation of economic activities to the absolute minimum. Ironically, while the Thatcher regime in the UK and the Reagan administration in the US (and all those other governments that mimicked their actions) acknowledged their inspiration from and proclaimed their allegiance to such principles, there was no net decline in government regulation of economic activities in the 1980s and 1990s – with one noticeable exception, namely the regulation of foreign investment. Indeed, since the 1970s in almost every country in the world, it has become easier for TNCs to invest. This was the case both for the levels of investment permitted and for the range of activities open for investment. In India, for example, the rule that no foreign corporation could have a majority holding in an Indian company was abandoned in the 1990s.[12] All over Latin America in the 1990s state monopolies in several industries, notably telecommunications, were ended and privatized telephone companies were bought up by foreign corporations.[13] What has happened in mining is not exceptional.

> Under pressure from the IMF and World Bank, more than 70 countries have changed their mining laws to make themselves more attractive to foreign investment; foreign ownership restrictions have been watered down or abolished, and mining TNCs are being invited to bid for state-owned mining assets, as huge sections of the industry – from Brazil's national flagship CVRD, the world's biggest iron ore producer, to Zambia's copper industry – are being offered for sale under "free market" privatization programmes. (Moody 1996: 46)

The real issue, however, is not how much regulation there is, but what is the nature of the regulation and whose interests it serves. From the left, spearheaded by the labor movement and more recently the environmental movement, the argument has been that since the 1960s all attempts to regulate the TNCs and to legislate national and international codes of conduct to force them to act more responsibly have failed. From the center and the right, spearheaded by corporate public relations and neoliberal ideologues, the argument has been that corporations are best left to regulate themselves on a voluntary basis and that international competitiveness will benefit from this. This struggle culminated (temporarily) in 1998 in the rather unexpected defeat of the Multilateral Agreement on Investment, an OECD-sponsored attempt to give the TNCs unprecedented freedom of action to invest where and how they pleased and to inhibit local and national governments from legislating against foreign investors. The broad coalition that opposed the MAI cleverly exploited the fears of local and national politicians in many OECD countries, against the pressure of their officials and the corporate elite, that the legislation gave too much away to the TNCs and undermined local and national sovereignty. The campaign, much of it conducted via the Internet, identified the MAI with capitalist globalization and its success in stopping the MAI confirmed both the centrality of the connection between globalization and FDI and the importance of capitalist-inspired state and international regulation for understanding the processes of globalization.

It will be recalled that one of the most powerful predictions of globalization theorists of various persuasions is that as globalization intensifies, the authority of the nation-state and its capacity to act decisively in economic affairs will decline. There are two aspects of this prediction that bear strongly on the issue of regulation and foreign investment. First is the issue of whether globalization actually does undermine the authority of the state and its capacity to act decisively; second is the issue of whether the forces that produce globalization also undermine the state. The key to these puzzles lies not in whether the state regulates as such, but whose interests the state serves when it regulates or choses not to. For example, all states to a greater or lesser extent regulate public utilities (water and energy supplies, telecommunications, transportation) to control security of supply, safety, and environmental impact. However, states can decide to regulate in order to further the interests of consumers, for example to help some groups of underprivileged citizens, or to further the interests of capital, perhaps to subsidize privatized utility companies. Governments can generally be identified, albeit crudely, as pro-business or anti-business. It is of fundamental importance to acknowledge that to get elected and reelected in most parliamentary democracies (and to stay in power in other types of political systems) in recent decades it has been almost mandatory to be pro-big-business or, at the very least, not actually anti-big-business, whatever might be said in public. Instructive examples are the remaking of the Labor Party in Australia from the 1980s, New Labour in Britain in the 1990s, and the BJP in India from the mid-

1990s. Certainly, all these parties in government regulated their economies and certainly some of their legislation was opposed by specific business interests; nevertheless all three (and many more governments) can be seen as furthering the interests of global capitalism by facilitating the expansion of globalizing corporations. This was not accomplished without struggles, sometimes quite severe and divisive struggles, within these parties of government and the state structures that contained them.

It is important to distinguish between globalizers and localizers within governments, states, and international agencies. Globalizing bureaucrats and politicians share the agenda of the major globalizing corporations and have specific roles to perform within the transnational capitalist class. Localizing bureaucrats and politicians strive to promote the interests of their local constituents where these conflict with the globalizers. The major corporations naturally support the globalizers in political parties and in official positions in the state and international bureaucracies, while also trying to persuade the localizers that their interests and those of their local constituents are best served by the globalizing agenda of transnational capitalism. The slogan of the globalizing TNCs, "being global, locally," resonates powerfully in disputes about whether or not globalization serves local interests. A good example of this process at work is the "Global Sustainable Development Facility – 2B2M: 2 Billion People to the Market by 2020." This was an initiative promoted by the United Nations Development Program (UNDP) in 1998 to assist the two billion poorest people in the world. The aim was to establish an agency outside the UNDP but closely related to it through which TNCs prepared to contribute a fee of $50,000 would have access to and benefit from association with the UNDP. By 1999, 16 TNCs, including Rio Tinto, ABB, Novartis, and Dow Chemical, had signed up, and more were considering it (Karliner 1999). UNDP has always had a valuable reputation as a humanistic development agency, speaking up for those threatened by the ravages of globalization, such as subsistence farmers dispossessed by export-oriented agribusiness, indigenous peoples whose livelihoods are threatened by foreign mining corporations and unwanted dams and other major engineering works. According to their critics, these are precisely the activities that are most profitable for the TNCs that the UNDP is trying to attract (see also chapters 6 and 7 below). The fact that the newly-appointed UNDP administrator was the former public relations director of the World Bank did not allay the fears of the critics of the Global Sustainable Development Facility. The point, at this point, is not that these TNCs can never do anything that would help the two billion poorest people in the world, but that globalizing bureaucrats, in my sense of the term, appear to have gained control of the UNDP, and that their apparent identification with the interests of the globalizing corporations may be incompatible with their professed localizing goals.

This process can also be illustrated with a case of a local authority attempting to regulate the behavior of a globally powerful TNC. In 1997, the most powerful tobacco company in the world, Philip Morris (PM), owner of the world's best-selling cigarette brand, Marlboro, was fined for criticizing French antitobacco law in advertisements that the company had published in French newspapers. PM was ordered by a court in Paris to pay a symbolic 1 franc fine to each of two antismoking lobbies who had brought suit against the company. The two groups claimed that the PM campaign violated a French ban on advertisements that promote smoking. The company defended the campaign as a political discussion that was protected by guarantees on free speech. One of the advertisements showed a map of Paris with most of the city marked nonsmoking and only the tiny Ile de la Cité left for smokers, signed "Philip Morris Europe, at the service of 97 million smokers in Europe." The court ruled that the message tended to "instil the idea that smoking Philip Morris tobacco was tantamount to joining a legitimate and necessary battle against an intolerable oppression imposed by non-smokers" (Associated Press Jan. 29, 1997). What are we to make of this case? Clearly, Philip Morris could have done without the trouble and expense of defending itself in a court of law, but the derisory damages awarded and the "oxygen of publicity" for smokers' rights probably were sources of satisfaction for the company.[14] In chapters 6 and 7 more evidence is offered to support the argument that the actual effects of state regulation of big business, while they appear to be serious, are often largely symbolic, as in this case in the Parisian court.

The most important aspect of state regulation of the TNCs can be summed up in one word: protectionism. Protectionism is the theory that domestic industry needs to be protected, usually by the imposition of tariffs and/or quotas and other types of nontariff barriers (like performance or local content requirements) to reduce imports. The more protection a firm, an industry, or a country has, therefore, the less free trade there will be. There are many reasons for protectionism and against reliance on imports from foreign sources. Disruption of essential supplies during wars reminds states how vulnerable they can be without local capacities; foreign firms which dump cheap products can destroy domestic industries; and infant industries need time to grow strong before they are ready to meet more established competition from abroad. The main argument against protectionism and for free trade is that where governments protect firms or whole industries or whole economies, they tend to undermine efficiency and competitiveness. While all states have indulged in protectionist measures to a greater or lesser extent, the comparison between Latin America and East Asia has had the greatest theoretical impact in the study of development and industrialization. These issues are most fruitfully located within the debates between the proponents of various types and degrees of import substitution and export orientation as the "best" paths to industrialization and development (see Dicken 1998; Gereffi and Wyman 1990; Stallings 1995). Where do the major corporations stand on these matters?

The first fact to establish in this respect is the obvious one that business corporations exist to make profits for those who own and control them. Questions about whether TNCs prefer protectionism or free trade, or import substitution (a technique of protectionism) or export orientation (a corollary of free trade) therefore have to be rephrased in the form: does protectionism bring greater profits than free trade, or vice versa? The experience of TNCs in Australia provide a useful test case.

Australia is a paradigm example of a highly protectionist economy that was transformed through reduction of tariffs and general opening-up to free trade from the 1960s onwards into one of the most open economies in the world by the 1990s (see Pusey 1991; Rattigan 1987). However, during this period Australia had a relatively large number of major foreign TNCs operating in and, in some cases, dominating important sectors of its economy. The local subsidiaries of Chrysler, RTZ, Ford, General Motors, Leyland Motors, Lucas, Philips, Pye, Nissan, and Toyota were all well established in Australia by the 1970s, and when the call for tariff reduction and a more open economy was heard, they all campaigned vigorously against free trade (see Rattigan 1987). The position of these corporations and some major Australia-based TNCs, notably BHP, began to change in the 1980s, and by the 1990s all the major corporations doing business in Australia had embraced free trade and the globalization agenda (Sklair 1996). Thus, the experience of TNCs in Australia (and elsewhere) supports the unsurprising conclusion that corporations will espouse protectionism or free trade in terms of their own immediate economic advantage.[15] The automobile, consumer electronics, and textile manufacturers, both foreign and Australian in origin, supported protectionism as long as it was in their interests to do so, as long as successive Australian governments used high tariffs to prevent foreign competitors from threatening their domestic market. However, when pressures for free trade and subsequently globalization started to intensify, and corporations began to accept that the days of protectionism were numbered, they mostly flocked behind the banner of free trade, some more actively than others.

Why did protectionism lose its support in the political system and among the TNCs in Australia? The reasons were numerous. First, the cosy relationship with Britain started to change when the UK entered the Common Market (the precursor of the European Union) and many Australian firms and whole industries began to realize that they were uncompetitive in the world market. Second, as major corporations around the world began to embark on the processes of globalization, their subsidiaries in Australia found themselves in the anomalous position of calling for one policy in Australia while their parent companies often campaigned for the opposite policy in other markets. This was the case for Ford and General Motors in Australia, for example. And third, there was a widespread feeling in the political, academic, and business communities that reform of the highly protected labor system, particularly in transportation, was absolutely necessary and that this was intrinsically bound up with the reduction in tariffs and free trade in general.

The history of Philips in Australia is not untypical. Originally, Philips Australia investment had been self-financed. In the days before jumbo jets and fast container ships Philips had 12 factories in Australia, prospering behind tariff walls. Restructuring in the 1980s as tariffs plummeted almost destroyed the company, and corporate headquarters had to send a "couple of bucketloads of money" (in the words of a senior executive in Sydney) to help the company's South Pacific subsidiaries to survive. The result of the restructuring was that small plants in Australia and elsewhere were closed down and much bigger global plants were established in the NICs (in "newly industrialized countries" such as Singapore) and in Europe. This meant that whereas previously subsidiaries had driven the policy of their own companies locally, by the 1990s policy was mostly product driven from the center. As the Australian government gradually gave up protectionism and meaningful regulation of the activities of TNCs within its borders, TNCs increasingly began to produce for a global market. Philips Australia adopted this globalizing strategy.

ICI Australia is another telling example. The company was established in 1929 and by the 1950s it took full advantage of rapid growth in the chemical industry in Australia behind the tariff wall. When tariffs came down in the 1980s, attitudes on protection began to change. ICI Australia saw its tariffs decline from an average of 35 percent in the mid-1980s to 7.5 percent in the mid-1990s. The company, like most corporations, put pressure on the government to deliver on the other half of the reform equation, to break up the monopolies on power and other services. While tariffs were coming down energy prices were going up, and a combination of labor and employer cartels, particularly in the docks, always threatened to undermine the reforms (a factor in Labor's large electoral defeat in 1996). For ICI, the main effects of tariff reform were felt in the Botony Bay plant, the largest chemical complex in the country. This plant had been plagued with poor industrial relations for decades and when tariffs were cut ICI Australia began to downsize to cope with the competition. Enterprise bargaining was introduced and, the company claimed, the "us and them" mentality of the workplace was changed. There was no sustained union campaign against the tariff cuts, as the leadership of the union movement (ACTU) supported the Labor government, more to help it stay in office than out of any firm conviction about the benefits of free trade.

Alongside tariff reform a radical financial deregulation was implemented in the 1980s. Many foreign banks and insurance companies entered the Australian market, but few succeeded. Several major corporations – including Bank of America, Barclays Bank, Royal Bank of Canada, and Chase Manhattan – cut their losses and withdrew from the market. Citibank, the Australian subsidiary of what became Citigroup, succeeded by targeting the top half of the market, offering accounts with minimum deposits of A$5,000, later raised to $10,000, obviating the necessity for an expensive chain of branches all over the country. This strategy worked, and the average deposit in Citibank was A$30,000 (US$20,000) in the mid-1990s. Foreign banks brought in new methods and ideas that greatly benefited some bank customers in Australia, though other poorer customers may have had fewer and relatively more expensive banking options as branches closed. This, again, illustrates how changes in the regulatory framework may benefit some and work against others. Regulation *per se* is not the main issue, despite the protestations of extremist neoliberals and extremist statecentrists. The main issue is the effect of specific types of regulation on different groups in society and globally, and how they contribute to the class polarization and ecological crises in many big and small ways (O'Connor 1994).

Major corporations whose origins were in Australia were also impacted by tariff reform and the drive for free trade. The biggest company in Australia in the 1990s was BHP, the mining and metals conglomerate. BHP was always rather ambivalent about the country's high tariffs. On the one hand, it expressed doubts about high tariffs when it began to see the need to compete abroad because domestic demand, for its steel, for example, was not expected to expand very much from the 1980s onwards. Expansion meant access to overseas markets and domestic deregulation was the *quid pro quo* for this.

However, the BHP Steel Group was somewhat in favor of protection as much for its customers as for itself. The risk was that free trade might destroy its domestic market. Those running the minerals side of the business came to see the benefits of free trade quite gradually in the mid-1980s and by the early 1990s, the top leadership of the company accepted that the best prospects for growth lay abroad. By the mid-1990s, one-third of BHP's products were made in Australia and sold in Australia, one-third were made in Australia and sold abroad, and one-third were made and sold overseas. BHP has had to come to terms with tariff reform and deregulation, for which its political muscle in Australia was partly responsible. With weakening state control of its business environment, BHP began to represent itself as "a global company with headquarters in Australia" (Annual Report 1994). The result of global deregulation, or rather the gradual elimination of government regulations that impact on the opportunities of corporations like BHP to maximize profits wherever they choose to operate, starts the process of denationalization of the corporation predicted by globalization theorists. And this is largely due to the persuasiveness of corporate elites and their globalizing allies in government agencies and politics in transforming the regulatory climate in the interests of big business in the last decades of the twentieth century.[16]

Phases of Foreign Direct Investment

Many corporations have their own views of the evolution of FDI which reflect their investment experiences. A senior executive at Colgate-Palmolive responsible for Global Marketing, for example, offered a three-phase model that had started with the company's original foreign investments in the 1920s. The first phase was when the company began to export in substantial amounts; the second involved building factories and reinvestment in foreign markets; and the third was one of acquisitions. These are not necessarily chronological phases. Colgate-Palmolive was making acquisitions in Europe before it was building factories in other parts of the world.

An experienced senior manager with ICI described five stages in the development of foreign direct investment. First, an agency was established to sell the company's products; second, a branch office was set up; third, a partner was found to establish a joint venture; fourth, 100 percent local manufacture was introduced; and fifth, acquisitions were made. In the experience of ICI there is a limit to how much most companies can penetrate markets through imports so, to be successful, companies must usually manufacture locally. Exceptions to this in the chemical industry were in areas such as pharmaceuticals and chemical catalysts, where products could be easily air-freighted and where intellectual property rights required protection. This was a process that many if not most globalizing manufacturing firms would recognize. ICI in the mid-1990s had over 60,000 employees manufacturing 2,500 products in 200 sites in more than 30 countries around the world. Here, the distinction between "territorial globalization" (perhaps better termed "internationalization") and the "functional globalization" necessary to establish product dominance, was raised. This is a useful distinction. Indeed, it was the basic idea in an important book on regional development by Friedmann and Weaver (1979), and I tried to apply it in my own work on export-processing zones in the 1980s. My argument in the 1980s was that globalizing forces would transform these "development" zones from territorial into functional forms of foreign direct investment. The consequence of this change would be that, eventually, the whole of Ireland, Egypt, China, and Mexico (and most other countries) would, in effect, become export-processing zones for globalizing TNCs (see Sklair 1995 *passim* and references to earlier studies therein). These predictions have been fully vindicated by events. This is the origin of the present argument on the ways in which foreign investment has been transformed from a system characterized by the concept of global reach – TNCs representing the interests of the countries of the capitalist core – to a more nuanced system best characterized by the concept of global shift – TNCs from all parts of the world representing the interests of those who own and control them, who can be domiciled anywhere. Of course, those who own and control the TNCs are still largely concentrated in the First World.

Opponents of the idea of economic globalization argue that few TNCs have denationalized to the extent that they carry out research and development (R&D) outside their home bases. This is true, but it may be changing. The potential for change is well expressed by an ARCO Chemical executive commenting on the role of US corporations overseas: "US producers should form partnerships with customers . . . Relationships have to be expanded beyond the traditional sales–purchasing interface to involve research and development, business management and logistics information process" (quoted in *Journal of Commerce* July 12, 1996). This statement could have come from many Global 500 companies in the last few decades. There is some evidence that globalizing corporations have begun to locate R&D (and other high value-added corporate functions) nearer to their major markets, irrespective of the location of their original headquarters. It is important to escape from the burden of arguing that because IBM, for example, has not relocated its R&D to Nepal it cannot be a globalizing corporation, and to take up the argument that because Matsushita, for example, has relocated some of its R&D to Malaysia it is, in some meaningful sense of the term, globalizing. This is precisely the argument of Craig (1997), and this case repays close study for what it tells us about the role of foreign investment and the dynamics of the globalizing corporation in search of profits.

The Japan Science & Technology Agency reported in 1991 that 117 Japanese companies had established or acquired 276 R&D facilities overseas. Human resource management support services were also on the increase all over the world, a fact that traditional FDI theory misses as it focuses mainly on production.[17] Indeed, Craig's research, based on interviews with 22 Matsushita Electrical Industries (MEI) managers, is a critique of the dominant paradigm in FDI thinking, Dunning's eclectic theory, which combines ownership advantage, internalization advantage, and location advantage. Eclectic theory, Craig argues, is becoming less and less relevant because ownership advantage is weakening due to the increasing familiarity of TNCs with what is needed to make and market products successfully. The competition to corporations engaging in foreign investment comes mostly from competing nonlocal TNCs, and the point of FDI is to enhance global competitiveness in order to compete in home and overseas markets.[18] More useful is Porter's (1990) value chain, which disaggregates FDI into primary (manufacturing, sales, and after-sales service) and support activities (procurement, technology, training, and general management). The globalization of MEI combines what was referred to above as global reach (in 1996, MEI had 202 overseas companies operating in 40 countries with 45 percent of sales generated outside Japan) with global shift (by 1992, MEI had established 17 independent research facilities, although most basic research still remained in Japan). This experience gave a four-stage model of overseas expansion for MEI and, by implication, all globalizing corporations: exporting; establishing overseas manufacturing for local markets; establishing large-scale manufacturing for world markets; and, finally, linking sales, manufacturing, sourcing, and R&D overseas. The implication is that these are the phases that globalizing corporations go through.

The evolution of the corporation through these phases does not, of course, mean that MEI is no longer a Japanese company in some sense. MEI President Morishita, when directly asked about this in 1996, said: "We've grown into a global enterprise, but we still carry Japanese passports, so to speak" (cited in Craig 1997: 149). Nevertheless, more short-range R&D, technology seeking activities and product design are being carried out overseas than ever before. The aim is to build an integrated system of development–production–sales (*kai-sei-han*). Craig illustrates this strategy with two case studies. The first is air conditioner manufacturing and R&D in Malaysia, partly stimulated by the fact that Japanese R&D personnel did not want to relocate to Malaysia. The second case is the establishment of the MEI Education Center in New Jersey, USA, providing functional training programs for overseas employees. This Center also transmits the corporate culture, business practices, and philosophy of the founder of the firm, develops hybrid Japanese-American personnel and management practices, and teaches non-Japanese employees the skills needed to succeed in Matsushita.

There is widespread recognition that there are difficult problems to solve, particularly for senior non-Japanese personnel. To promote the development of North American managers, a Globalization Promotion Project was introduced to evaluate managers' potential in the company as a whole. Craig's study shows the value to globalizing corporations of linkages involving multiple units performing activities together in the same place (manufacturing, R&D, and training). Nearness-based linkages can have great benefits. This has led to "greater clustering of primary and support activities and units overseas than would occur if FDI decisions were made independently" (ibid., p. 161). In this respect, Matsushita can be seen as a globalizing corporation, a corporation evolving out of the global reach phase into a phase of global shift.

Evidence that this was not an isolated case, even for corporations from Japan, was provided by a telling statement from the 1996 Annual Report of Hitachi, then the biggest electronics corporation in the world. In its section on Global Operations, the Report explains that since the 1980s, the trend has been away from exports from Japan: "the Company has endeavored to globalize its operations by viewing the world as a single market and selecting the optimum locations for conducting its R&D, production and marketing activities." This has led to more overseas manufacturing and more imports into Japan, central features of the globalizing corporation.

The Home Base and Foreign Investment: The Case of NAFTA

It is important to distinguish the picture of foreign direct investment painted by new international division of labor (NIDL) global reach theorists, a picture often implicitly confirmed by the corporations themselves, from the picture that global shift presents. NIDL theorists argue, mostly from research on FDI from the First World into the Third World, that the main reason for such FDI is the cheapness of labor. This is a function of the poverty of countries in the Third World, the weakness of labor unions, the lack of effective worker protection legislation, and the exploitation of women. Global shift theorists, much of whose research is on FDI between countries in the First World, focus much more on FDI as a process of market penetration and resolution of internal problems of corporations that are rapidly growing bigger (Dunning 1997, Dicken 1998). Whatever the correct explanation of FDI,[19] it is always to enhance profitability, in the short or medium or long term. The sociological questions raised concern the problems and opportunities that such investment causes in the home base and in the locations of the foreign investment.

The North American Free Trade Agreement (NAFTA) signed in 1993 between the USA, Canada, and Mexico illustrates this well. Struggles over job losses in the USA caused by the NAFTA in general, and by the outward investment of US companies in the Mexican *maquiladora* (export-processing) industry in particular, illustrate well how major corporations and their allies in the transnational capitalist class deal with these questions. For the Mexican government of Salinas de Gortari, NAFTA clearly represented a chance (perhaps the last chance) for the country to establish itself as an economic power. For the more globally-oriented fractions of the Mexican capitalist class NAFTA was a wonderful opportunity to make permanent the gains they achieved under Salinas. Unlike the comprador class of the dependency theorists, the local wings of the transnational capitalist class of global system theory act like a class that believes it can fulfill its own economic destiny as part of a global capitalist system that rewards those who can play the system on a global scale. The Mexican parts of the TCC, thus, are not mere dupes of hegemonic "American" capital (the fundamental state-centrist error) but sometimes valued partners or serious competitors of TNCs (see Salas-Porras 1996), some of whom happen to be domiciled in the USA.

The expectation in the early 1990s was that high productivity combined with low wages could turn Mexico into "a Korea but with an even wider industrial base," in the words (ironic, as it turned out) of the President of Kodak Mexicana. "There is a deep personal commitment [between US and Mexican officials] driving this free-trade agreement," and the bottom line was that a successful NAFTA could reach Mexico's "untapped consumers." Ever since Mexico joined the GATT in 1986, the "Mexican middle class has been on a consumer binge for US products, sweeping in imports of Pampers and Miller's beer. Trade pact boosters now claim this demand for the small stuff will spill over into big-ticket purchases of cars, refrigerators, and washing machines" (see "Mexico, a New Economic Era," *Business Week*, Nov. 12, 1991). This exuberant journalistic phraseology expresses well the ways in which the links between TNCs, the transnational capitalist class, and the culture-ideology of consumerism are transmitted in the media.

Most of the lobbying effort for NAFTA focused on Washington, particularly in the run-up to the vote on "fast-track" approval in Congress in May 1991. Fast-track is an administrative device to prevent bills from being amended when they come before Congress; such bills must either be accepted or rejected in the form in which they are presented. Fast-track authority for the GATT was due to run out in June 1991 and the Administration was asking Congress to renew it for the GATT and NAFTA. Opponents of NAFTA argued that fast-track approval would make it unlikely that environmental and labor standards safeguards would be included (see Grossman 1998). Ralph Nader, in a letter to the *New York Times* (April 26, 1991), argued that fast-track was essentially undemocratic.[20]

It was President Bush's request to Congress for fast-track approval rather than NAFTA itself that unleashed furious lobbying efforts, both for and against the Agreement. "Trade lobbyists gear up for battle" (*Washington Post*, March 2, 1991) listed the lobbies in some detail. The pro-NAFTA lobby included the forces of big business led by their representative organizations, primarily the US Chamber of Commerce, National Association of Manufacturers, National Foreign Trade Council, US Council for International Business, National Retail Federation, Business Roundtable, and the American Farm Bureau Federation. The anti-NAFTA lobby ranged against them the AFL-CIO, various environmental groups, and some textile and farm interests (notably the protected dairy, peanut, and sugar sectors). Worries over jobs, labor standards, and the environment had made fast-track approval problematic. Carla Hills, the energetic US Trade Representative, and her staff, in collaboration with the pro-NAFTA campaign, lobbied media and business relentlessly. While the traditional rivals, labor and big business, were mostly internally united, many other groups were divided. La Raza, the Mexican-American pressure group, postponed a decision on NAFTA at this time (though later came out in favor) and some environmental groups were talking with the Administration to try to persuade it to grant environmental concessions in the Agreement.[21]

Something of the flavor of the campaign can be derived from information published in the *Washington Post* on the day of the fast-track vote. Every day in the run-up to the vote, the *Post* reported, the US Chamber of Commerce had phoned every member of Congress to ask how s/he would vote on fast track. The weight of pro-NAFTA lobbying, from clear media messages that corporate America was fully behind NAFTA to the targeting of local business groups all over the country to ensure that they made their views known to their representatives in Washington, proved overwhelming. No stone was left unturned. Even Miss Mexico spoke out for NAFTA as she was being crowned Miss Universe! AFL-CIO had conceded defeat weeks before and Alex Hittle of Friends of the Earth, a key member of the anti-NAFTA coalition, did so nearer the vote. When we consider that the main anti-NAFTA themes were US job losses to low-wage Mexicans and environmental hazards of unrestricted cross-border trade, the apparently easy victory of the pro-NAFTA campaign needs explaining.

The official Mexican government effort in Washington was headed by a Mexican globalizing bureaucrat assisted by 8 aides. "Washington power-broker" Charls Walker was hired at a salary of $20,000 per month, along with other public relations and lobby groups. One of these, Burson-Marsteller (B-M), part of the global advertising and PR conglomerate Young & Rubicam, deserves further study.[22] B-M was, in fact, already working for the Mexican government, on a US$1 million contract to improve Mexico's image on drugs. The *Washington Post* (Jan. 3, 1991) reported a B-M spokesperson's comment that this addition "to our already substantial Washington presence will provide our clients with direct access to one of the best-known and most accomplished government relations teams ever established in the Washington capital . . . [and, the paper continued] there is a 'real trend' to consolidation among politically connected lobbying and public relations firms that want to 'practice governmental relations on a global basis for clients with global needs.'" Reports that the NAFTA lobby was the biggest public relations effort of the year, and expenditure on it could exceed $100 million in all, led Democrat Marcy Kaptur, a long-time opponent of lobbies, to complain that: "The Mexican government has more access to Congress than workers in the United States" (quoted in Associated Press May 19, 1991).

The Mexican government's effort was only one part of the pro-NAFTA lobby. The US Corporate Team effort, as the *Wall Street Journal* labeled it, was even more formidable. This was led by the Coalition for Trade Expansion: "a lobbying umbrella that includes more than 500 corporations and lobbyists from five key business trade associations," the Business Roundtable, US Chamber of Commerce, Emergency Committee for American Trade, the National Association of Manufacturers and the National Foreign Trade Council (see "US–Mexico Trade Pact is Pitting Vast Armies of Capitol Hill Lobbyists Against Each Other," *Wall Street Journal*, April 25, 1991). The Business Roundtable, which comprised the CEOs of America's 200 largest corporations, was the most formidable of these organizations (see Burch 1981; Burch 1997) but they were all critical in their own constituencies. NAFTA was most wholeheartedly supported by machinery, business equipment, and consumer goods manufacturers (all well represented in the maquila industry in Mexico).

Apart from those farmers (particularly citrus and vegetable growers in California and Florida) who felt directly threatened by the prospect of "free trade" with Mexican agricultural exporters, the only other industry that was seriously split on the issue of NAFTA was textiles. Textiles, the most successful protectionist industry in the USA, had always been ambivalent over "free trade." Linda Wachner, CEO of Warnaco, a Fortune 1000 apparel firm then employing 8,000 US workers of whom 1,600 depended on 1,000 low-wage Mexican jobs, argued: "there is job creation in the United States from having sewing done in Mexico. Having a hemisphere of solid consumers and a hemisphere of flexible labor is a home run for us" (see "Splitting Protectionist Seams," *Washington Post*, May 13, 1991). The complexity of these issues was well illustrated by the contrast between the wider corporate interests of DuPont in global free trade, and its fibre division, a natural anti-NAFTA lobby. The splintering of the usually solid protectionist textile lobby played a "crucial role" in the fast-track campaign. (As it did in the tariff reform struggles in Australia discussed above.)

Each of the four fractions of the transnational capitalist class was represented in the NAFTA campaign. The Business Roundtable, a leading force in the US Corporate Team, was entirely composed of TNC executives, and their local affiliates in Mexico and along the US-Mexico border also played an important role.[23] NAFTA commanded substantial support among Mexican business elites, some of whom organized to promote their interests. A private-sector group of exporters, COECE (Coordinadora de Organizaciones Empresariales de Comercio Exterior), was formed to coordinate the NAFTA campaign for Mexican business, and hired a former US trade official as its representative in Washington (see Salas-Porras 1996; Thacker 1999).

The lobbying efforts of civil servants in the governments of Bush and Salinas provide ample evidence of the role of globalizing state bureaucrats in the campaign in both countries. Not all the bureaucrats in both governments were entirely and wholeheartedly in favor of NAFTA. Indeed, global system theory predicts struggles between those who hold a conception of capitalism circumscribed by national interests, and those actors and agencies within governments who conceptualize their interests in terms of a more open alliance with those who own and control the major corporations. Identifying the agents and agencies most active in the Mexican government's substantial lobbying efforts on behalf of NAFTA is a particularly important marker of the shift in the balance of power in Mexico from the localizers to the globalizers since the mid-1980s.

Globalizing politicians in both Mexico and the US either simply lined-up behind their governments in the voting lobbies or in some cases took more active parts in promoting NAFTA. The public relations industry and professional lobbyists, business and trade consultants of all shapes and sizes, legal personnel, and so on, as documented above, flocked to the NAFTA banner. It can be argued that such people will sing any tune they are paid to sing and this is, largely, true. But it cannot be denied that the big money was, in this case, all behind one tune. That is why this is a telling case for the argument about the transnational capitalist class. On some issues, big (transnational) business sings more than one tune, but on the issue of NAFTA and "free trade" (albeit within a relatively protectionist North American region) the fundamental interests of global capitalism were clear. To this extent, the transnational capitalist class in the US and Mexico (and Canada) was united, and the voices of the consumerist elites (merchants and media) reflected this unity in all three countries.

The campaign in Mexico and the USA on behalf of NAFTA in the early 1990s was a vivid illustration of how the transnational capitalist class, led by its principle fraction – TNC executives and their local affiliates – solved the problems of reconciling the interests of the "home base" and the target of FDI. Major corporations rarely have to defend their investment decisions individually, as in most cases where job losses are incurred in the home base due to factory closures the impact is very localized.[24] These events are occasionally discussed in systemic terms in the mass media, and here the transformation from global reach to global shift versions of foreign investment comes into play. By minimizing the importance of cheap labor as the sole rationale for FDI, though it does no harm to the capitalist cause to remind the workers in the First World that they are "overpaid," corporations try to avoid charges of super-exploitation. Instead, FDI is explained in global shift terms as maintaining the global competitiveness of "our companies" as they strive in all parts of the world to bring prosperity to the home base and provide jobs (usually portrayed as low-level, low-paid jobs) for needy folks in countries less well-endowed than "our own." Global capitalists do what is necessary to enhance profitability for those who own and control the major corporations and if "flying the national flag" does this on occasion, then they will fly the flag of national competitiveness (as I argue in greater detail in chapter 5 below). Being global, locally, means that corporations active in many countries can, where appropriate, fly different flags on different occasions. This can sometimes lead to paradoxical situations. For example, American companies sometimes do not wish to be associated with unpopular American foreign policies in various parts of the world but do wish to retain the Americanness of their products, particularly for soft drinks, fast foods, and some forms of popular entertainment.[25] Similar arguments could be made for the British-ness of products in former colonial territories. As we shall see when the issue of global corporate citizenship is discussed in chapters 6 and 7, being global, locally, is not always easy to achieve, though it is certainly necessary for the globalizing corporation.

Disinvestment

Examples of foreign disinvestment, downsizing, closure of plants, and withdrawal from some overseas markets entirely would appear, intuitively, to suggest that the corporations involved were putting any globalization they might have achieved into reverse. This is certainly one reasonable interpretation of disinvestment. There is another, however. Many major corporations present disinvestment of various types as a deliberate strategy to refocus their attempt to globalize. "To be global," in short, does not mean "to be everywhere." The explanation for this relates directly to the central goal of the capitalist system – maximum profitability for the owners and controllers of capital – and the constant necessity for major corporations to continually increase earnings for their shareholders. This means that markets and/or products and/or services that once looked promising and begin to look unpromising, or markets that do not live up to their expectations of massive profits even if they are profitable, may be sacrificed to protect share earnings. While the hegemony of the stock market is mainly a North American and European phenomenon, this peculiar business system is spreading, in a variety of forms, all over the world. The evidence is not simply that there are now many more stock markets than at any previous period in history[26] but also that with the spread of global fund management, more and more corporations depend on the confidence of investment managers for continued financial support. What can be labeled a shareholder-driven growth imperative, starting to emerge even in Japan, is a powerful force for the type of TNC-based globalization that lies at the heart of this book.

This can be illustrated by the experiences of several *Fortune* Global 500 companies interviewed in the course of the research. The products that ICI traditionally manufactured ranged all the way from consumer-oriented goods (like paints and personal care items) and speciality chemicals for consumer goods to bulk chemicals (like common salt). In the 1990s, the company began to change focus rapidly from an emphasis on the latter types of products to the former. In 1993 ICI demerged its bioscience businesses (dominated by pharmaceuticals) into a separate company, Zeneca, which soon became much more valuable in stock capitalization than ICI. This was followed by several other strategic moves, notably the acquisition of Unilever's speciality chemicals division, the sale of other heavy chemical divisions (including a swap with DuPont) and the eventual demerger of ICI Australia.

Why did ICI chose to move away from heavy chemicals and towards more consumer-oriented products? One explanation is that the cartel-like chemical industry of the decades around the mid-century began to disintegrate in the 1980s, as a host of new competitors emerged, most powerfully from the Asia-Pacific region. Under these circumstances, ICI found it increasingly difficult to be a global force in both industrial chemicals and consumer-oriented goods, and like many other corporations chose to exit one part of its traditional business rather than be dragged down. Disinvestment, therefore, suggests that some corporations tend to globalize by focusing more on their core competence as global competition intensifies. Much management literature of recent decades has been highly critical of the vast conglomerates that lumbered through the 1970s and 1980s from one crisis to another. In an extreme version of this argument, one report argued: "Japan's trading companies have been in structural decline since the first oil shock. The disintermediation of trade (in 1971 traders shipped 69 percent of exports, by 1991 this had slumped to 43 percent) and the shift from secondary to tertiary industry are just two of the factors making the trading companies obsolete" (Jardine Fleming 1993: 1).[27]

BankAmerica (BofA) is another major corporation that has disinvested. Between 1985 and 1995, the bank reduced its spread of foreign presence from 80 to 36 countries but, at the same time, it expanded its presence in key Asian and Latin American markets. Corporate income derived from outside the USA had increased to well over half the total by the mid-1990s. BofA moved to what was described as a quasi-global strategy in the late 1980s because of financial problems brought on by the debt crisis in Latin America and domestic problems in the USA. These forced BofA to abandon all nonwholesale banking activities outside the USA. Like ICI, the bank refocused on "what we did best," in this case wholesale banking, particularly corporate lending. In the 1990s BofA began to concentrate mainly on the largest corporations and biggest projects, a narrow but lucrative client base.

The theme of disinvesting to refocus also explains the recent foreign investment history of the Royal Bank of Canada (RBC). RBC was more "international" in the 1970s and 1980s, when it had branches in Latin America, Australia, and Europe, than it was in the mid-1990s. By the mid-1980s, the impact of the debt crisis forced RBC to pull back (as was the case for BofA) and concentrate on North America. Only in the late 1990s did RBC start to return to these foreign markets. In the meantime, deregulation of financial services in Canada, as elsewhere, from the late 1980s onwards gave the bank more freedom of movement and, of course, more competition. As for most banks with global aspirations, RBC adopted the strategy of following the corporations that made up its client base as they increased their overseas investments. Canadian corporations who invested in Chile and Mexico in the 1990s brought RBC along with them to service their needs. By the late 1990s, Latin America was more important than Asia or Europe for RBC. Being global, thus, meant taking advantage of market opportunities wherever they were around the world, not simply being "everywhere."

Foreign Investment as a Globalizing Practice

What does it mean to say that foreign investment, or indeed anything, is a "globalizing practice"? Transnational practices (TNP) are defined as practices that cross state borders and do not originate with state actors or agencies. Globalizing practices directly contribute to the globalizing of specific institutions, like major corporations. So, to argue that specific types of foreign investment are globalizing practices means that they contribute to the globalizing of TNCs and, by implication, to the globalizing of capitalism.

For companies domiciled in small countries (or countries with small markets, not always the same thing) the urge to globalize is a natural outcome of the urge to grow. P&O Australia, for example, explained its quest for foreign investment – "We can't get any bigger here ('here' being Australia, not Britain, of course), so we have to go offshore." However, for globalizing corporations, FDI involved much more. As we have seen, it involved being global, locally. According to a senior executive in Nestlé, one of the biggest and certainly one of the most profitable food processing corporations, the key to successful foreign investment was to be "part of the industrial tissue" wherever the company did business. This evocative phrase reverberated with all five themes of the transformation from the global reach to the global shift conception of foreign investment. Globalizing brands become successful when they become "part of the industrial tissue" in each of their markets, when they penetrate so deeply into an economy that they appear at one and the same time both global and local. And, of course, with local manufacture, design, packaging, and taste variants in so many global brands they are, in a real sense, both local and global.

Another way of expressing this, in the words of the respondent from MetLife, is that globalizing corporations are not really investors as such, but seek to do business overseas "for the long haul, not for a quick buck."

Globalizing corporations, like all businesses, have to operate under regulatory climates. As I have noted, the restrictive foreign investment regimes of the 1960s and 1970s are largely gone, and TNCs probably have more genuine freedom of movement, particularly in terms of their ability to move capital and to trade across borders, than at any time in the modern era. There are still many government regulations for FDI, but these regulations have become much less restrictive in recent decades. While there were many "foreign" corporations in the first half of the twentieth century, particularly in Europe and Latin America, who could certainly have claimed to be part of the industrial tissue of their host societies, the tremendous increase in FDI all over the world makes this much more likely today for larger numbers of TNCs.

Exporting alone is never enough to make a global product local. The phases of foreign investment identified by corporations illustrated the stages that companies have to pass through before they can be part of the industrial tissue. This varied to some extent by business sector, but the increasing commitment that some corporations show to host communities by relocating productive, administrative, and other high-value facilities as part of a globalizing strategy stands in stark contrast to the "runaway factory" conception of global reach theorists. This connects directly with the issues of the relationship between home base and foreign investment and of disinvestment. The ideologues of globalization justify foreign investment by convincing those who experience the negative impacts of corporations that FDI and/or disinvestment takes place not because of the greedy wish to exploit cheap labor and undervalued natural resources, but as part of a global strategy that will eventually bring benefits to everyone. In this way, foreign investments, like foreign disinvestments, come to have an inevitability in the never-ending quest for global competitiveness, prosperity, and the good life for all.

Foreign investment, world best practice, corporate citizenship, or global vision, do not cause corporations to globalize. This would be a circular argument, as these are criteria for and means to measure the extent to which TNCs are globalizing. The reasons why corporations consider it necessary to globalize are the increasing pressures on them to produce more and more returns to those who own and control them. These pressures are intensified by two crises with which big business constantly has to deal: the class polarization crisis and the ecological crisis. These crises, largely results of the workings and expansion of the globalizing capitalist system, are imposed on major corporations, the most important institutional manifestations of global capitalism, precisely by the need for continuous expansion and accumulation of private wealth.[28]

The corporations discussed in this chapter illustrate the central themes of the relationship between globalization and FDI. First, the globalizing corporation does not need to dominate every market of every country in the world. Many major corporations have withdrawn from some places entirely and there are still some markets in some places from which some industries, for example, media and insurance, are effectively excluded due to state regulations, though these regulations are being dismantled all over the world. What is necessary for corporations to globalize, however, is a globalizing "social" marketing strategy. This means not simply a strategy to get products into the marketplace but, much more widely, to ensure that these products and the corporations that produce them have good reputations. This entails benchmarking for world best practice, corporate citizenship for prestige, and global vision for leadership. Many major corporations will not compete where they do not have a superior position in a given local, national, or regional market. Thus, they are usually among the dominant players in all the sectors or products with which they are involved. The major corporations operate through a variety of forms of ownership and control, and these influence the forms of foreign investment in which they take part. These range from the traditional wholly-owned subsidiary pattern of companies like Unilever, enhanced by acquisitions of competitors, to forms of franchising, best exemplified by the much-copied model of McDonald's, and hybrid structures covering some quite idiosyncratic industries, like the US-based entertainment company Viacom, which owns TV channels, video rental shops, publishing houses, and film studios.

The common theme that runs through all these corporations in their efforts to globalize is their aspiration to be global, locally, to be at one and the same time a part of the local fabric yet delivering products and services of global quality and appeal. How globalizing corporations do this, through world best practice and benchmarking, and how the nation state is mobilized to this end through the ideological quest for "national competitiveness," is the topic of the next chapter.

Notes

1 This connects directly with the anxiety of many major corporations not to be seen as American or British or Japanese companies "with units abroad,"

as detailed in the previous chapter, and with the increasing impact of global corporate citizenship, discussed in chapters 6 and 7 below.

2 This is rather ironic in light of the fact that by 1995 the OECD had already embarked on negotiations for a Multilateral Agreement on Investment which would have had the effect of restricting the capacities of governments to regulate investment and the activities of the TNCs.

3 For example, the acquisition policy of Tyco aimed at cuts of at least 25 percent across the board (as reported by Raychem in Ireland). Other Global 500 acquisitions in Ireland, such as the Mitsubishi Chemical takeover of the Verbatim plant in Limerick to establish MC Infonics (for optical disc manufacture) and the Roche acquisition of Syntex, also involved downsizing, and the commercial base of both these companies was improved.

4 For an interesting development of this line of argument in the case of the Nike Corporation, see Goldman and Papson (1998).

5 Ayala and Lai (1996) describe how P&G, Coca-Cola, Unilever, and Nestlé were all striving to reach "one by two" ($1 billion annual sales in China by year 2000). In 1998, Unilever held its first board meeting ever outside the UK and the Netherlands in China as a prelude to the purchase of Lao Cai, a famous Shanghai soy sauce brand.

6 Usually, but not always. The marketing literature is full of freestanding names that failed the translation test, like the sports drink from Japan called Pocari Sweat, the toilet paper from Sweden called Krapp, and the Nova car from Ford, which translates as "no go" in Spanish.

7 In 1999 Unilever announced that it was to focus on about 400 premier brands and dispose of the other 1,600 it owned.

8 In the words of a former brand manager for Nike, its global advertising strategy was based on both "a global point of view . . . [and] a country-by-country plan to make the brand part of the cultural fabric" (quoted in Goldman and Papson 1998: 170). An interesting study of the websites of major food corporations shows that in order to promote their brands, many of these "cast the geography of their subject into a global domain" (Pritchard 1999: 15).

9 Advertising and other types of product marketing predate globalization in the sense in which it is used in this book, though I maintain that for the globalizing corporation quantitative increases in these practices have resulted in a qualitative transformation, encapsulated in the rise of the culture-ideology of consumerism. For an interesting and lavishly illustrated account of Unilever's marketing from the 1930s, see Reader (1980). On the history of promotional culture more generally, see Wernick (1991).

10 Sports sponsorship, especially the Olympics, Formula One motor racing, and football/soccer has increased rapidly (see Sugden and Tomlinson 1998, ch. 4). Prominent examples are the tobacco company, Philip Morris Asia, which has sponsored the Marlboro China Football League (supported by Samsung, the airline Asiana, Olympus, and Gillette), and Motorola, which has sponsored competitions ranging from the Champions League in Europe to youth tournaments in Hong Kong.

11 An example of this, which I borrow from an examination paper of a former student of mine from West Africa, is that until she came to London to study she had thought that the word "Bata" (the brand name of a footwear manufacturer from what was then Czechoslovakia via Canada) meant "shoe" in her mother tongue.

12 For an illustration of this process in India see Brewer and Young (1998, esp. table 5.2). In the 1970s IBM was forced to withdraw from India because of this rule. IBM refused to be a minority partner anywhere in the world, but returned to India in the 1990s in a joint venture (compare Grieco 1984 and Evans 1997). On the Maruti–Suzuki joint venture to produce an Indian car, see Venkataramani (1990).

13 The Spanish telephone company, Telefonica, was particularly active in these acquisitions.

14 While in some fields the old adage that "no publicity is bad publicity" might be true, for big business and specific corporations it is not always true, as cases such as the Nestlé infant formula affair, the McLibel trial, and Shell's problems with Brent Spar and Nigeria demonstrate (see chapters 6 and 7 below). The tobacco industry is discussed in more detail in Sklair (1998).

15 In the words of one respondent, from a mining subsidiary of Hanson in Australia: "Companies give lip-service to free trade but fight for every single per cent of their own protection." The respondent from ABB Australia argued that the reduction of tariffs and nontariff barriers in Australia had been "like a samurai sword" (resonant imagery in the Australian context) and that the government had naively gone too far too fast, albeit in the right direction.

16 While I have focused on Australia in this section, a similar case could be made for protection and regulation in many other parts of the world (see Brewer and Young 1998).

17 This omission is gradually being filled in (see, for example, Aharoni 1997).

18 Craig also offers criticisms of internalization and location advantages, but these are of less relevance here. For a useful brief account of Dunning's eclectic paradigm and theories of FDI in general, see Dicken (1998, ch. 6).

19 The underlying explanation of FDI given here is agnostic on this debate. Sometimes, even within the First World, major corporations make foreign investments that can be best explained in terms of global reach. For example, Japanese investment in the North of England in the 1990s certainly took advantage of lower wages and inferior labor protection relative to the rest of Europe, but also to gain access to the European market. Other First World corporations invest in Third World countries even though the labor content of their total product cost is minimal.

20 For a devastating critique of how crucial trade and investment legislation is handled in the US, see Nader and Wallach (1996). There is no evidence whatsoever that these processes are handled any more democratically or intelligently elsewhere. In fact, given the relative openness of the American political system, it is likely that there is less democratic accountability elsewhere.

21 See Thacker (1999) for capitalist class struggles over NAFTA.

22 Chapters 6 and 7 below discuss B-M's role in the corporate citizenship and environmental public relations industry.

23 The US-Mexican maquila wing of the TCC had campaigned vigorously for NAFTA ever since it was announced (see Sklair 1993, ch. 11). Wallach and Naiman (1998) critically assess the first four years of the Agreement.

24 One case where these local impacts were successfully brought to the attention of the national and probably bi-national audience, was the Trico factory relocation from Buffalo, New York to Brownsville, Texas and Matamoros, Mexico in the 1980s (Sklair 1993: 122–7). But this was an exceptional case and few jobs were saved. For studies of job losses, relocations, and capitalist restructuring see Ross and Trachte (1990) and Gordon (1996). These are useful sources for the debate over globalization.

25 In the course of an interesting discussion of cultural imperialism, Tomlinson (1997: 183) reminds us of Ithiel de Solla Pool's argument that the popularity of American mass culture was really "the discovery of what world cultural tastes are." While globalization is not simply Americanization, there is no doubt that the techniques of many corporations originating in the USA (often dominated by inspirational immigrant founders) bear heavily on what I conceptualize as the culture-ideology of consumerism. This does suggest that where the home base of a TNC is "American" there may be special factors involved. (See below, chapter 8.)

26 And in many unexpected places, like Shanghai and Shenzhen, in the Pearl River Delta, and, of course, all over Eastern Europe.

27 "Disintermediation" refers to the expulsion of middlemen from commercial transactions. The idea of "conglomerate" requires some unpacking, as many products and services that appear superficially to be quite disparate, have in fact considerable synergies. For example, manufacturing motor vehicles (or anything else) and lending people money to buy them, can be doubly profitable. The Japanese (and Korean) trading houses are changing, but most of them are certainly not dead yet.

28 No doubt some eagle-eyed critic will accuse me of teleological reasoning. I plead guilty, unashamedly. Yes, the global capitalist system and the capitalists and the institutions of which it is composed define their success in terms of how far they satisfy the need to expand continuously. Yes, capitalists need to accumulate private wealth. And yes, they organize (through what I am calling globalizing practices) to achieve these goals.

Chapter 5
World Best Practice, Benchmarking, and National Competitiveness

While there is nothing very new about national competitiveness, its role as a strategy for global capitalist expansion changed in the second half of the twentieth century. The changed status of national competitiveness has emerged hand-in-hand with a new world trading system built on the General Agreement on Tariffs and Trade (GATT) which gave way to the more comprehensive World Trade Organization in the 1990s. Alongside the GATT process, other related systems of economic discipline have been imposed, notably by the World Bank and the International Monetary Fund through the Structural Adjustment Programs (and also, to some extent, bilaterally between some rich and powerful governments and governments in poorer and weaker states). In 1995 the OECD began to construct a new world investment order, the Multilateral Agreement on Investment (MAI). Had it not been for an unprecedented level of mass mobilization by opposition groups from all over the world (much of it through the internet) showing national governments and local authorities in the core capitalist countries that the MAI might prove to be seriously unpopular with the electorate, this agreement would have come into force in 1998 and the "level playing field" so valued by corporate elites would already be on the statute books.

The central argument of this chapter is that it is through the quest for national competitiveness that the insertion of the nation-state into the global capitalist system is handled by the transnational capitalist class. The TCC achieves this, through facilitating alliances of globalizing politicians, globalizing professionals, and the corporate sector. Globalizing politicians create the political conditions for diverting state support of various types (financial, fiscal, resources, infrastructure, ideological) towards the major corporations operating within state borders under the slogan of "national competitiveness." Such support represents direct and indirect subsidies to the transnational capitalist class and, as was argued in the previous chapter in the context of foreign direct investment, often involves state regulation in the interests of the major corporations. Politicians deliver these aids to industry and commerce through their campaigning and votes in support of capital-enhancing labor, trade, and investment legislation. Parliamentary democracies based on geographical constituencies encourage this, resulting in "pork-barrel politics" in the USA and its equivalents elsewhere. Globalizing politicians, therefore, need global benchmarks in a generic sense to demonstrate that they are internationally competitive. Their "national" corporations and, by extension, their "nation," has to seek out world best practice in all aspects of business. Global capitalism succeeds by turning most spheres of social life into businesses, by making social institutions – such as schools, universities, prisons, hospitals, welfare systems – more business-like. Various forms of benchmarking are used in most large institutions to measure performance against actual competitors or an ultimate target (zero defects, for example). The term world best practice (WBP) is used here as a convenient label for all measures of performance, achieved through various systems of benchmarking . While globalizing politicians are responsible for creating the conditions under which WBP becomes the norm for evaluating the effectiveness of any social institution, they rarely become involved in its techniques. This is the responsibility of the globalizing professionals.

The role of globalizing professionals is both technical and ideological. Their technical role is to create and operate benchmarking systems of various types; their ideological role is to sell these systems as the best way to measure competitiveness at all levels and, by implication, to sell competitiveness as the key to business (and national) success. It is, paradoxically, the way that national economic competitiveness has been raised to the pinnacle of public life that explains the empirical link between WBP, benchmarking, and globalization.

WBP is bound to be a globalizing practice in the global capitalist system. It is quite conceivable that benchmarking could be restricted to small, localized communities of actors and institutions interested solely in providing a local service in terms of agreed criteria of efficiency. Examples of this can be found in the tourist industry, where several small competing firms offer almost identical services to unique, local attractions. They may systematically compare what they offer, and upgrade (or possibly downgrade) their services to match the practices of more successful competitors. In a global economy, however, there are relentless pressures on small local businesses to become more global, either through predatory growth or, more typically, by allying themselves with major globalizing corporations. Therefore, to become world class it is not necessary to be big but it is necessary to compare yourself with what the big players in your business sector do, and to do what you do always better (Kanter 1996). Benchmarking is the measure through which all social institutions, including the state, can discover whether they are world class.

World Best Practice, Benchmarking, and Globalization

Benchmarking is normally defined as a system of continuous improvements derived from systematic comparisons with world best practice.[1] The idea of continuous improvement was introduced by the New York University professor and soon-to-be management guru William Edwards Deming shortly after the end of the Second World War. This became the driving force behind the total quality management (TQM) movement which has had profound though uneven effects on big business all over the world (Hill and Wilkinson 1995). However, Japanese corporations working with state agencies first adopted these ideas, seeing in them the best way to rebuild their war-shattered economy. The Deming Prize for the best quality circles was established in Japan in 1951. These quality circles became a central mechanism for the spread and development of the new quality movement. By the 1990s their numbers exceeded 100,000 with about 10 million members throughout Japan. TQM, world best practice (WBP), and benchmarking were given added impetus by the increase in global competition as protectionist walls have been breached all over the world and as rapidly-growing new companies have threatened the market dominance of their older and, perhaps, less innovative rivals.[2]

These ideas did spread to the USA and Europe but through the initiatives of individual firms and occasionally trade associations rather than through state sponsorship.[3] By the 1990s, the world best practice balance may have changed. In the leading Japanese electronics manufacturer, NEC, for example, it was suggested that benchmarking had transferred know-how mainly from US corporations. NEC had chosen some competitors, customers, and supplier companies for benchmarking purposes, to exchange information on a give and take basis. These tended to be mainly from the US and Europe, rarely from Asia. NEC had given factory tours to Motorola, Texas Instruments, and others and NEC had been shown around their factories.

By 1987 the Malcolm Baldrige National Quality Award was established in the USA, along with the European Quality Award in 1991, and a veritable flood of quality initiatives covering almost all sectors of industry all over the world has followed. These gave public recognition throughout business and beyond to the TQM movement that had swept through boardrooms, office complexes, and shop floors whenever an enterprise was faced with competition, particularly from "foreign" companies, from the mid-1980s. An important aspect of these awards and quality standards and the movements they were part of was the centrality of the role of leadership, particularly the leadership of the most senior executives, in the quest for continuous improvement. Not since the robber barons in the nineteenth century had the leaders of big business been in the limelight to such an extent. And what the leaders of the major corporations were saying, almost unanimously, was that business success lay in putting the customer first and that customer satisfaction depended on quality. The implications of this will be taken up in chapter 8, when I examine the role of senior executives in promoting the culture-ideology of consumerism.

WBP and benchmarking are logical strategies for globalizing corporations because when competition can, in principle, come from anywhere in the world, it is necessary for companies who wish to hold on to their market share, let alone increase it, to measure their performances against the very best in the world.[4] An additional and crucial factor is that most major corporations are in industries in which most of their products are quite similar to (sometimes virtually identical with) those of their competitors. Thus, it was vital to ensure that any competitive advantage that a product had, however small, was matched by competitive advantages in bringing it to market. That is why WBP, benchmarking, and related performance-enhancing measures were so important. The TQM movement ensured that all aspects of company performance, from manufacturing widgets to answering telephones, from delivering and servicing the product to monitoring energy use in factories and offices, were liable to be benchmarked. The numerous criteria included for both the Deming Prize in Japan and the Baldrige National Quality Award in the USA were significant motivators in operationalizing the idea of total quality for customer-driven business. Many major corporations, as we shall see, had their own versions of these quality packages.

The pioneers in global benchmarking were technology-intensive companies whose very survival depended on continuous innovation, like Motorola and Xerox. Also influential in the theory and practice of benchmarking were the global management consultants, notably Andersen Consulting and McKinsey. Research in Australia found that benchmarking and world best practice were very much connected, both in rhetoric and in fact, by both government and companies aspiring to be globalizing (Sklair 1996). Given that much of the inspiration for benchmarking came from prominent corporations (with some government agency support) in the US, it is not surprising that this finding from Australia was thoroughly confirmed from the Global 500 in the US, Europe, and Asia.

There are literally hundreds of different quality measures, some firm specific (see below for a discussion of Six Sigma), others product or industry specific, some covering zero defects. Some cover environmental standards, others citizenship standards. Some are regional in scope (the US, UK, European Union, and Japan, for example, all have sets of quality standards) and some are virtually global (for example, the International Standards Organization ISO series). As indicated, I use WBP and benchmarking for any efforts that corporations use to compare their performance on anything with that of others.

The links between state agencies and corporations in the creation of benchmarking and best practice systems can be briefly illustrated with the cases of Australia, Brazil, and the USA. In Australia and Brazil, the globalizing fractions of the state and business were united in their belief that the protectionism of the past could no longer be maintained if they were to enter the global economy. The two governments embarked on two different paths to implement world best practice but with the same end in view, to make their companies internationally competitive. In Australia, as suggested above, best practice was seen largely as a problem of changing labor practices, and a Best Practice Demonstration Program was introduced in 1991 by the Department of Industrial Relations, working with the Australian Manufacturing Council. The rationale for the Program was clearly stated in the pamphlet "What is Best Practice?" issued in 1994: "As the Australian economy becomes increasingly integrated into the global market, Australian enterprises must become internationally competitive to succeed." This 8-page pamphlet cites DuPont, ICI, and BHP in Australia as enthusiastic supporters of the Program. The official publication of the Best Practice Program was entitled *Benchmark* and its pages in the 1990s exemplified the alliance between globalizing politicians, bureaucrats, professionals, big and small business, all striving for the quality improvements that would enhance national competitiveness.

In Brazil, the government agency responsible for quality standards was the National Institute for Standardization, Metrology, and Industrial Quality (Inmetro). The President of Inmetro declared to an international meeting in Holland in 1998 that: "The efforts made by Brazilian firms to improve the quality of their goods is linked to the beginning of competition in Brazil's economy. Up to 1990, when the economy was closed to imports, our companies did not bother about quality. After the opening of the economy in 1992, the need grew to show international standards of quality" (quoted in "Brazilian Companies Invest in Quality" [Advertisement], *Financial Times*, Aug. 26, 1998). Inmetro worked closely with the Brazilian Program for Quality and Productivity and the Brazilian Foreign Trade Association (whose President was also at the meeting in Holland), for enhanced quality in Brazil was necessary not only to compete against imports but, more importantly, to increase the potential for Brazilian exports.

In the USA, while quality standards and benchmarking have come largely from private industry initiatives, the Baldrige National Quality Award (perhaps the most prestigious mark of quality in the US) was established in 1987 as a joint venture between a government agency and industry. Although modeled on the Japanese Deming Prize, the Baldrige process was transparent and provided an audit framework which companies could use for self-assessment. By the mid-1990s more than a million protocols had been distributed, and 24 winning companies had made more than 10,000 presentations. Most states in the USA had their own awards to complement the Baldrige. Cole, from whom this account derives, has gone so far as to predict the death of the quality movement, in the "growing normalization of quality improvement as a management activity" (Cole 1998: 70), and, as we shall see below, the movement for quality, at least in the USA, may have achieved its objectives.

This is not the case outside the USA and a few major economies. While over 70 countries were reported as having agencies for accreditation and inspection of technical standards laboratories, it is commonly accepted that standards vary globally. An International Accreditation Forum (IAF) was established precisely to ensure comparability of standards and by 1998 had 18 member countries, with more applications (including Inmetro) in the pipeline. Accreditation by the IAF meant recognition for technical standards in the US, Canadian, Chinese, Japanese, and European Union markets, and a reasonable guarantee that the WTO technical rules were less likely to be used to block imports (disguised protectionism). What the three cases of Australia, Brazil, and the USA suggest is that globalizing state agents and professionals have joined forces with corporations to promote best practice in the service of national competitiveness.

While any type of WBP consciousness and benchmarking can logically be connected with globalizing corporations, there are clearly stages in these practices that indicate a lesser or greater level of globalization. In general, we can hypothesize that the wider the scope of companies that a firm benchmarks against, the higher the level of globalization achieved. As WBP/benchmarking is one of the four criteria of globalizing corporations, this looks circular. However, the argument is that corporations that are globalizing will manifest all four criteria to a greater or lesser extent and that, taken together, the four criteria provide a measure of globalization. Where corporations score high on some criteria and low on others, then this will signify tensions over globalization in the corporation.

Not all companies benchmark to the same extent. In the first place, there are those corporations who mainly benchmark internally, perhaps measuring performance in one geographical and/or functional area against that in other areas. The respondent from Alcan (Aluminum Company of Canada) posed the interesting question with respect to corporate benchmarking: "How do you act as a global company when you have operations in 30 countries; do you have 30 different surveys?" In Alcan, where increasingly Canadian employees were working outside Canada, and Brazilians, Jamaicans, Germans, and other nationalities were working for Alcan in Montreal, the answer was cross-cultural surveys, repeated every two years since 1986.

Only where corporations are aware of the existence of world best practice, can it be considered even a primitive globalizing practice. Globalizing corporations often begin by benchmarking against direct competitors, and this usually involves industry-wide standards of excellence and frequently crosses national borders. This normally leads to a higher form of benchmarking, termed here "global program benchmarking." In this case, a systematic program is introduced to transform the corporation, often an integral part of more general programs of corporate restructuring, reengineering, and the like. Global program benchmarking seeks to compare processes and outcomes irrespective of geography or business sector.[5] A brief review of benchmarking in *Fortune* Global 500 corporations will illustrate these two types.

Industry Benchmarking

There are no major corporations that appear to be satisfied with internal benchmarking alone, though some companies give a higher priority to benchmarking against outsiders than others. Apple, for example, in common with other firms that have been lauded as industry leaders, claimed to be the computer industry standard in the early1990s. This claim, while immodest, was not entirely without foundation. In the judgment of *BYTE Magazine*, quoted in Apple's Annual Report for 1995: "it would not be an exaggeration to describe the history of the computer industry for the past decade as a massive effort to keep up with Apple." However, even while this glowing testimony was being written, Apple was experiencing severe managerial crises and, in fact, sales (and stock market valuation) of the company dropped to such an extent, that it failed to make the Global 500 list at all in 1998.[6] It is uncommon for such a well-known firm to lose its Global 500 status (other companies, for example Colgate-Palmolive, illustrate that it is possible to drop out and to return). It may be the case that inattention to benchmarking and world best practice was at least partly to blame for Apple's problems. Major corporations who find themselves in trouble will turn to one or another version of benchmarking to reinvent themselves, and this is often connected with the urge to globalize, as we shall see below.

Corporations that focus mainly on their own industries for benchmarking can also be the corporations that have the highest reputations for innovation and state-of-the-art performance. Apple and other electronics and computer companies in Silicon Valley in California, as well as the leading Asian consumer electronics manufacturers, have certainly been seen in this light. Hewlett-Packard (HP) called its system of benchmarking "reengineering," and it had been in operation since the mid-1980s. In the 1990s HP regularly appeared in the prestigious top ten of *Fortune*'s "America's Most Admired Companies," a distinction shared with only one other Californian Global 500 company, Intel (see below). As an acknowledged leader in several electronic product lines, HP has often been benchmarked against (it was one of Watson's case studies).[7] Samsung benchmarked against Japanese companies, especially Sony, Sharp, and Panasonic, but in a manner described as "not closed but not open." The defect target in the Mexican subsidiary was under 3 percent and every worker was evaluated for performance. Those workers with the best records were rewarded with trips to Korea. Samsung's 16 Principles for Quality set the goal of becoming the best company globally for TV production by the year 2000. The basic quality ideas came from headquarters, but the management in Mexico translated these ideas for the local workforce to put into practice. Among globalizing corporations, there was considerable evidence to confirm the view that the benefits of benchmarking outweighed their not inconsiderable costs.

The case of Nestlé illustrated the part that benchmarking played in corporations with small home-country markets. Nestlé was established in Switzerland in 1866 and within a year had opened an office in London. By the turn of the century it had factories in Australia and the USA. A Brazilian factory was established in 1921, and so it has continued. The company celebrated its 125th anniversary in 1991 with a lavishly illustrated account of its history and its worldwide operations. Nestlé engaged in extensive benchmarking within the food industry, which was explained by the fact that most of Nestlé's products are in very competitive markets. For example, Nestlé and Unilever were fierce competitors in the global ice-cream market. As was discussed in the previous chapter, global branding is critical to the fate of many globalizing corporations. The Nestlé brand is used worldwide, and identical quality and safety standards were said to be imposed everywhere the brands were sold. Internal benchmarking was carried out regularly through an elaborate quality control system and this was a permanent part of the business strategy. Nestlé asserted that it was successful precisely because its customers could rely on stable quality wherever they saw the Nestlé name.[8] This was also evident in the acquisitions process, through bringing the firms that Nestlé acquired up to the highest standards in Nestlé or, perhaps, vice versa. This was the case particularly for cultural differences and dedication to sales in overseas markets. Having acquired the Carnation company in the USA, for example, executives from Carnation were put in charge of Nestlé in the USA and, similarly, Rowntree executives have been running the Nestlé business in Britain since Nestlé bought the firm.

At the other end of the industrial spectrum, the engineering and construction firm Fluor manifested a similar commitment to benchmarking in the 1990s. This was summed up by a former CEO as follows: "Everything is being scrutinized with the mission of performing BETTER, FASTER, CHEAPER AND SAFER than any global competitor" (Annual Report 1995, upper case in original). One example offered by the respondent at Fluor was that before it entered into diversified services for new businesses such as construction equipment and outsourcing, it first benchmarked its own likely performance against the competition. The results convinced the company that it could compete successfully.[9]

While all business sectors share common processes that can be benchmarked, different businesses raise some sector-specific problems. For most financial services corporations (commercial and merchant banks, insurance companies of various types, savings institutions) comparisons with what manufacturing companies do can be difficult. An independent organization, Greenwich Associates of Connecticut, has provided global benchmarks for banks and financial services companies around the world for decades.[10] As almost all books on globalization point out, the financial services industry is being transformed from one revolving around the accounts of individuals into an ever more concentrated system of megacorporations managing and investing enormous amounts of money in, for, and on behalf of corporate clients.

In the merchant bank J. P. Morgan (JPM), a distinction was made between benchmarking for revenues (relatively easy) and for costing (very difficult). Benchmarking risk management, the major process in big money banking today, is near the cutting edge of financial science, requiring a move from deterministic to stochastic methods of money management. JPM benchmarked employees on their compensation and on what was termed "environment" (systematic studies of how revenue-producing employees were reacting to the changing climate in the firm). The prevailing culture was that the "capital resources (i.e. the people who produce the revenues) leave the building every night." The essence of benchmarking in the banking industry, part of the corporate culture in JPM since the 1970s, was how performance was rated by specialized rating agencies on a large variety of financial measures. However, many major banks also imported their own measures into the equations.

The issue for banks like all businesses was: who does what the best? Deutsche Bank also argued that it was easier to measure processes in manufacturing industry than in financial institutions. The issue of comparability arose again in the question of who banks can benchmark against. The mergers and acquisitions process was one way that banks were able to make direct comparisons, by accessing the books of other financial institutions (as Deutsche Bank did with Bankers Trust, the New York-based bank it acquired in 1998). There are also legions of analysts who make these comparisons in the media, through the internet, and in less public forms on a regular basis. Many countries still have banking oligopolies but, as these are progressively opened up, governments help "their own" banks as the industry became more exposed to global competition. The acquisition of Bankers Trust in 1998 meant that Deutsche Bank would have to become more transparent to satisfy US regulations, and this in itself would make its performance easier to compare with other banks. As the shares of banks domiciled in different countries were increasingly listed in the same stock exchanges around the world, investors increasingly began to look for benchmarks and evidence of world best practice.

National Australia Bank (NAB) presented an interesting set of benchmarking problems. Throughout the 1990s it was the biggest bank in Australia. The deregulation of the Australian financial services sector from the 1980s onwards meant that NAB like all the other local banks in the country, were starting to be faced by competition from foreign financial corporations, for both corporate and individual business. As was outlined in the previous chapter in the course of the discussion on Citibank's FDI in Australia, not all foreign banks succeeded in Australia, indeed, several lost a good deal of money there. Capitalizing on its location-specific advantages, NAB's subsidiary, National Nominees (NN), prospered in the custodial business. This is such a peculiarly sensitive and rapidly growing global business that it is worth describing in the context of benchmarking.

Custodian banks deal with two main financial products, subcustody and master custody. Subcustody is the holding of assets like equities and fixed interest investments under one banking jurisdiction for clients from another banking jurisdiction. It is a multi-billion-dollar global business and as cross-border trade and investment grew, the custodial business grew with it. NN provided services mainly for large overseas banks investing in Australia for their own clients, acting as a subcontractor for these banks. It also performed financial services for clients, for example, collecting dividends for overseas investors in Australian companies. In the mid-1990s, NN held around A\$24 billion (about US\$16 billion) in custodial form. Most of this business consisted of investor portfolios, like pension funds. The process was that an institution, for example a pension fund in the UK, would instruct its local bank to buy shares in an Australian company and the local bank would subcontract NN to handle the transaction. Brokers in Australia also solicit business from NN.

Master Custody is the system where institutions, either government investment bodies like health insurance and superannuation funds, or private institutions like health and pension funds, employ a financial company to hold custody of their assets. In Australia, where there was a well-developed system of state superannuation insurance, pressure came from superannuation trustees to employ master custodians to hold the assets of these funds in order to separate them from the investment functions of funds managers. This was a way to limit the liability of Trustees, and meant that the client had a contractual relationship as an agent of fund managers. If fund managers made mistakes or committed errors of judgment, it was the responsibility of the master custodian to ensure that the client did not suffer financially. It is not always clear who the beneficial owners of financial assets actually are, and as this information could have important repercussions, for example for tax matters or in cases of money laundering, the custodians have to exercise considerable discretion.

In the Master Custody industry, the main competitors of NN were State Street Bank and Chase Manhattan, both domiciled in the USA and both operating globally. While a relatively small player, NAB/NN already set benchmarks in some areas of the business. As with banking in general, there was no reliable way to find out what the best standards were and custodial services, if anything, were even more competitive and secretive than other banking services. Publications such as *Global Custody Review* and, in Australia, the Australian Stock Exchange fail rates, would give some general guidance as to who was doing well and who was doing badly, but these were rather crude measures, not really comparable to the precise metrics that were characteristic of benchmarking in the manufacturing industries. The growth of the global custody industry was a good indicator of how financial globalization hit barriers erected by state legislation on financial practices and, at the same time, of how these barriers actually offered commercial opportunities to globalizing financial services corporations.

Even in financial services companies where benchmarking was in an early phase, like Fannie Mae (the Federal Mortgage company in the USA), globalization appeared to be forcing the pace. By the mid-1990s, Fannie Mae had started to benchmark against a variety of companies in the US and abroad, and a table in the Annual Report in 1996 compared Fannie Mae on several indicators with other companies outside the banking industry, in order "to avoid always being compared with banks."

Telecommunications shared some of the problems identified for financial service companies with respect to benchmarking. This was at least partly due to the increasing concentration of major corporations in these industries and the tendency for the biggest firms to expand vertically (by taking over companies at different points in the finance or telecommunications chain) as well as horizontally (taking over companies providing similar services). Congress began to deregulate the industry in earnest in 1996, opening the door for a series of huge mergers. As a result, the Bell system was split up in 1984 into the so-called Baby Bells, began to regroup (for example, the former Bell companies SBC Communications, Ameritech, and Pacific Telesis merged into a new SBC). Nynex, the New York area provider (subsequently swallowed up in the Bell Atlantic–GTE merger in the late 1990s) started to benchmark seriously in the 1980s. This was mostly against the domestic competition, notably other Bell companies in the USA. Under FTT rules there was uniformity of measurement in the industry in the US and, naturally, a series of common measures facilitated benchmarking. Nynex did benchmark globally to some extent, against BT and MCI, for example, on strategy. It is difficult to identify a world best practice in telecommunications. Efficiency was generally measured in terms of employees per 10,000 access lines, though benchmarking on the usual financial measures was also possible.

Most of the Global 500 benchmarked at least some of their activities within quality programs. Some corporations and, more to the point, some companies within corporations, took benchmarking and TQM more seriously than others. Where the quest for world best practice was seriously taken up by the top leadership of the corporation, either in advance of other indicators of the globalizing process or as a consequence of them, global program benchmarking began to dominate the life of the corporation, its constituent companies, and all its employees.

Global Program Benchmarking: Six Sigma and the Quest for Perfection

While it is not unique, the Six Sigma method for achieving excellence sums up what is meant by global program benchmarking. Six Sigma was introduced in the electronics company Motorola in the 1980s, and subsequently adopted and adapted by other corporations, notably Allied Signal and General Electric where, under the charismatic leadership of Jack Welch – one of the most successful corporate executives of the modern era – it was elevated to the status of "part of the genetic code of our future leadership" in the words of the GE Annual Report for 1997. Sony, another self-proclaimed globalizing corporation, began to apply Six Sigma to all its management processes in 1997.[11]

The origins of Six Sigma date from 1981, when the CEO of Motorola, Robert Galvin, discovered substantial differences in quality between car radios manufactured in Motorola plants in the USA and those manufactured in competitors' plants in Japan. He challenged Motorola's communications sector to improve quality tenfold within five years.[12] In 1986 Galvin set a new target of a tenfold increase in quality in all functional areas by 1989, then a hundred-fold improvement by 1991, and what came to be known as Six Sigma capability by 1992. A Six Sigma process is one that produces only 3.4 defects per million, virtually defect-free. Unlike some other quality programs, Six Sigma relied heavily on rigorous data-gathering and statistical analysis of process variations to identify sources of error and ways of eliminating them. Motorola first began to benchmark against some Japanese companies on Deming-type measures in the late 1970s, which (as noted above) gained widespread recognition in Japan long before they did so in the USA.[13] Motorola was among the winners of the first Baldrige award in the USA in 1988 (Tomas 1990), and other early winners were Westinghouse, Xerox, and IBM. Many more corporations had quality systems based on Baldrige and other criteria than used Six Sigma. One of the most advanced of these was Intel, whose commitment to benchmarking derived from the early marketing strategy of its founders to produce in huge volumes and constantly to cut costs. Intel benchmarked continually against whoever had world best practice. The Intel Quality Award is a competitive, comprehensive self-assessment, Baldrige-type internal mechanism.

Corporations quickly discovered that people who work under such a regime have to be "empowered" for the system to operate properly. The intended outcome of a successful Six Sigma program was no less than Total Customer Satisfaction (TCS), an idea that was presaged in Motorola's Partnership for Growth Program as early as 1982.[14] Motorola introduced an annual TCS competition based on team problem-solving to find the most effective solutions (in terms of money, time, etc.) for the day-to-day problems of a business under the discipline of Six Sigma. The so-called Motorola University[15] trained employees and those with whom they did business all over the world through TCS modules. By the late 1990s over 40,000 TCS teams had been created in the company. A well-publicized example of the success of these methods of benchmarking and challenging for world best practice was the Motorola factory in Tianjin, China, whose TCS team won a company gold medal for quality, to the surprise of many. Motorola claimed that its factory in Tianjin could be located anywhere in the world. As Six Sigma worked outside the company too, the company could also claim to be improving the quality of suppliers in China. If these suppliers could manufacture to Motorola standards, they could meet the standards of any purchaser globally.

Motorola worked actively with the Chinese government to upgrade its business and, by implication, Chinese business. For example, the company and the Chinese State Development and Planning Commission created a joint Center for Enterprise Excellence to implement quality improvements. The Center began with a pilot class for CEOs, managers, and technical associates from 17 state-owned enterprises that were potential supplier firms for Motorola. The class covered Motorola's key management practices, including Six Sigma Quality, Total Customer Satisfaction, Individual Dignity Entitlement (employee relations), and "uncompromising integrity" (*sic*). After a period of six months, the Chinese enterprises presented TCS projects for evaluation, and the best were admitted to a second stage of supplier development assistance. In the third stage Motorola upgraded some enterprises to become local and global suppliers. The target for Motorola in China was 65 percent local sourcing by the year 2000.

General Electric (GE) has been a leader in the application of benchmarking, especially under Jack Welch, outside and inside the company. All companies in GE worldwide benchmarked extensively. Six Sigma was part of the GE Toolkit, a package for customers and "friends" containing "the workout," a set of problem-solving techniques for decision-making by disregarding hierarchy, and other techniques like the Change Acceleration Process and Quick Market Intelligence. These were taught to customers to enable them to respond more effectively to market forces. The company willingly shared this with its business partners. Benchmarking for GE meant sharing and comparing with the best everywhere.

Six Sigma was adopted by GE in the mid-1990s. According to the Annual Report of 1997: "We didn't invent Six Sigma – we learned it. Motorola pioneered it and Allied Signal successfully embraced it." These companies shared it with GE after a decade-long "work-out" to achieve "boundaryless behavior . . . behavior that tramples or demolishes all barriers of rank, function, geography and bureaucracy in an endless pursuit of the best idea – in the cause of **engaging and involving every mind in the Company**" (bold in original). In the extravagant language of this Annual Report, GE had to "run" to keep up with the "excited charge" of employees, who had seen "the transformational magic – the rejuvenation – that this combination of rigid discipline and cheerful fanaticism can achieve in our business . . . Six Sigma has spread like wildfire across the company." GE's 350 "business laboratories" (units) broadcast Six Sigma throughout the corporation to make customers more competitive and productive. At Six Sigma meetings "zealot after zealot" shared stories, sharing quality technology, "learning is done in the boundaryless, transcultural language of Six Sigma. In this language, CTQs (critical to quality characteristics) or DPMOs (defects per million opportunities) or SPC (statistical process control) have exactly the same meaning at every GE operation from Tokyo to Delhi and from Budapest to Cleveland and Shanghai." In the words of Jack Welch, "Six Sigma is quickly becoming part of the genetic code of our future leadership. . . . ironclad prerequisite for promotion to any professional or managerial position in the company – and a requirement for any award of stock options." By 1997, in the terminology of Six Sigma accomplishment, GE had nearly 4,000 full-time, fully trained Black Belts and Master Black Belts and more than 60,000 Green Belt part-time project leaders. These and others like them were "true believers . . . drawing other committed zealots upward with them . . . We are feverish on the subject of Six Sigma."[16]

The connection between benchmarking and globalization was made explicit in a 1998 bilingual booklet "GE in Japan," where the company's new course, "guided by the compass points of Globalization" through Six Sigma, was introduced. Using an increasingly common argument (see the case of Unilever in the previous chapter), GE explained that only businesses ranked first or second in their respective markets could be given the chance to succeed. GE's three key initiatives, quality improvement through Six Sigma, Globalization, and focus on Services, were the means to achieve this success. A "Statement of nine GE values" guiding the whole process, concluded: "Have Global Brains . . . and Build Diverse and Global Teams." It is important to note that GE, like most major corporations, had been through all this before in varying forms. The success and fame of Jack Welch, like most visionary CEOs, was largely due to his ability to revitalize the company from time to time (measured primarily by increased returns to shareholders), with varying rallying calls. While he was not alone in his focus on quality, the choice of Six Sigma and the globalizing rhetoric within which it was located, was significant for the conception of the globalizing corporation. This suggests that as the pressures on corporations to globalize increase, the type of thoroughgoing benchmarking implicit in Six Sigma and similar programs will increase too.

AlliedSignal (AS), like GE, was a company with a lengthy record in benchmarking and world best practice, and its long-serving CEO, Larry Bossidy, was an early proponent of Six Sigma. AS benchmarked everything, from manufacturing processes to the functional aspects of running the corporation, both internally and externally, with a particular focus on the transmission of knowledge within the company. This was known in-house as the "quest for excellence." The Annual Report for 1997, entitled "Mindset for Growth and Productivity," described the job of "Productivity Czar" Dan Burnham: "to bring renewed impatience, energy, and resources to our Six Sigma efforts. Six Sigma means 3.4 defective parts per million – a benchmark of quality. But we've broadened Six Sigma to include all our quality and productivity efforts – and to extend them from manufacturing to all our processes, including back-office operations." According to Bossidy, Six Sigma had already saved AS an estimated $1.5 billion and had changed people's mindsets.

An AS overhead presentation on the Six Sigma Resources pyramid gives a concrete description of how this worked. At the top of the pyramid were 13 quality and Six Sigma executives assuring and supporting breakthrough improvements and employee engagement. At the second level, 100 masters trained and mentored novices, and at the third, 2,000 experts (Black Belts) drove breakthrough improvements and supporting teams. On the fourth level 18,000 managers, supervisors, and professionals (Green Belts) led process improvement, and, finally, 50,000 employees were involved continuously to increase customer value and productivity.

To the innocent outsider (and perhaps some insiders) benchmarking in general and Six Sigma with its focus on statistical near-perfection in all aspects of work must seem like a treadmill, a never-ending search for improvement.[17] According to the 1997 Annual Report: "Allied-Signal's mantra of '6 percent productivity [improvement per annum] forever' has given way to 7 percent. Why? Because [with the quest for excellence process and Six Sigma, it is] an achievable target." Like many other major corporations AS carried out regular and quite extensive surveys of employee satisfaction to measure how all these demands on employees were being seen. The 1996 survey results (reported in a special section in *Global Highways,* the in-house magazine of AlliedSignal Automotive, in 1997) showed improvements over the 1995 results. However, the overall satisfaction index of 51 percent, with 28 percent neutral and 21 percent unfavorable, revealed that, in the company's own words, "we have a long way to go." This finding confirms my own impression from interviewing executives and managers in over 80 Global 500 corporations, almost all of whose companies were deeply involved with benchmarking (though few to the degree of rigor and depth of Six Sigma). Most corporate respondents, even those clearly enthusiastic about benchmarking, either directly expressed reservations about the pressures for continuous improvement on staff health and morale or indicated in other more subtle ways that excessive benchmarking could create problems. The application of Six Sigma standards, the ultimate best practice, could also put production workers and engineers at odds with marketing personnel (usually closer to top executives). Public promises by top management about ever-better quality imposed unending pressures on those with shop floor responsibilities (see Meiksins and Smith 1996: esp. 269–72).

This was certainly the case for corporations in Australia where the Labor government of the 1980s and 1990s specifically used benchmarking and the quest for national competitiveness as a political weapon against entrenched labor and protectionist business practices. The biggest corporation in Australia, BHP, is a good case in point. A brochure, "BHP in Perspective," published in December 1994 gave an overview of BHP's position in the world's resources, commercial, and financial markets, with 17 tables of international and 32 tables of Australian comparisons. The significance of these comparisons must be considered, as argued in the previous chapter, within the historical context of protectionism that had cushioned big business in Australia for most of the twentieth century. Benchmarking was very important in Australia because many branches of the economy, notably infrastructure, utilities, and some manufacturing industries, were near monopolies. So "benchmarking against best practice overseas" was the only way (in the words of one of my more cynical respondents) to distinguish between "absolutely appalling and not quite so appalling" quality. BHP itself provided an excellent concrete example of global benchmarking. In order to improve the operation of one of its mobile equipment workshops in Western Australia, BHP discovered that the critical process was hydraulics. The world best practice site for hydraulics was found to be in Disneyland, California, and so BHP benchmarked itself against Disneyland.[18]

Procter and Gamble (P&G), the biggest soaps and cosmetics corporation in the world, saw itself in the 1990s as a data-driven company, and this was at the root of its globalizing drive. Benchmarking was an integral part of its search for data-based decision-making, and was focused on product supply, IT, and increasingly in the environmental field. P&G was seen as a leader in the advertising of consumer goods and had provided the benchmark for other companies in this area. The commercial value of benchmarking for P&G could be illustrated in a number of concrete examples, for example improvements on telephone response rates, and savings on insurance. Benchmarking on uninsured losses in the chemical industry had produced savings of more than $100 million in the 1990s through the introduction of better management systems and more efficient use of personnel. The consumer goods industry was considered especially competitive, so there was little direct benchmarking between companies selling similar products, though in matters of safety, health, and environmental impacts, sharing of information was said to be the norm. In this context, P&G benchmarked outside the soaps and cosmetics industry, having cooperated to find best practice with Coca-Cola, chemical and paper companies, and several major retailers.

In Fiat, benchmarking became "fashionable" in the 1990s. However, even in the early 1970s Fiat had sent technicians to the USA to study emission controls on vehicles. There Fiat personnel met the Big 3 US automakers (GM, Ford, and Chrysler), the Environmental Protection Agency, and other technical bodies and made what would be called today benchmarking studies. The company also established relations with other car manufacturers in Europe to tackle common problems. In the 1990s Fiat set up a formal Benchmarking Group that began to work principally in the areas of IT, costs, and marketing strategies, working alongside a corporate globalization project. The connection between benchmarking and globalization strategy was explicit in Fiat (as it was in other major vehicle manufacturers).[19]

All of the oil companies benchmarked to a greater or lesser extent. Royal Dutch Shell had been benchmarking in the area of strategic planning since the 1970s, but in other areas, notably reputation management, benchmarking was more recent. Chevron was typical in its enthusiasm for benchmarking. Prior to the 1980s, the company had been very "volumetric" but as benchmarking began to penetrate the boardroom it was realized that being the biggest was not the same as being the best. In imagery that is repeated elsewhere, in Chevron benchmarking swept through the company "cascading down to every single employee." The result was a cut in operating costs by $1 billion over the period 1990 to 1992 and the loss of 12,000 jobs. Chevron benchmarked against all major oil companies and, for specific processes like IT, outside the industry. A continuous search for world best practice was part of the corporate culture in Chevron in the 1990s.[20] Similarly, in Esso Australia (Exxon) "hardly a day goes by without some reference to benchmarking," followed by the statement, "Sometimes we feel like tearing it up"!

The Mobil subsidiary in Australia provided an interesting example of the different ways that a global benchmarking program can work out locally. The company employed a Training and Development Adviser on contract (whom we might identify as a locally-based globalizing professional). He had formerly been employed as the deputy director of a TAFE (technical and further education) college and had also worked for the State of Victoria Electricity system, so would have been familiar with both technical education practices and the workings of the public utility system. Mobil, like other major corporations, introduced a "World Class Work Culture" in the 1980s as part of a general drive to become more competitive. This was conceptualized in terms of a world best practice work regime. In the early 1990s, Mobil brought this to Australia to rejuvenate Mobil Australia. Consultants reported that while the program had improved production, both customer services and people-handling skills lagged behind. A process of highly participatory consultation at all levels of the workforce led management to reinvent the goals of the company and to promulgate a new vision for the company. No visitor to the Mobil facilities in Australia in the mid-1990s could fail to observe the blue cards proclaiming "Our Vision" all over the premises. The sentiments and aspirations expressed on the card are typical of the passion of the globalizing corporation for benchmarking, best practice, and customer satisfaction. Figure 5.1 reproduces both sides of the card.

The company produced handbooks on roles, outcomes, and appraisal – all of which were customer focused. This process was directly connected with remuneration when the pay system was transformed by the introduction of a re-earnable bonus on top of the basic annual salary. Key results were measured on CUSTOMERS, PEOPLE, PROFITS (these were usually capitalized in company publications and posters around Mobil facilities). All managers discussed these measures with their staff and "climate surveys" were carried out annually to find out about the morale and attitudes of the workforce. The re-earnable bonus of all managers depended on the scores achieved by their staff on all three factors. For Mobil, return on capital employed in the 1990s needed to be improved. Mobil's need to improve its position globally – exposed by measures published by Solomons, the major oil industry benchmarkers – showed that the company had been losing ground

Figure 5.1   Mobil Australia and Pacific Islands, Vision Statement (1995)

[side one]

Our Vision:
We will become Number 1.

Our Mission:
Our business is to satisfy our customers.

Our Values:
Our future is secured by a balanced focus on:
* Customers
* People
* Profit

[side two]

Customers:
* Customers are the reason for our existence. Every single contact is our opportunity to add value. Customers do us a favor by giving us this opportunity.
* We actively listen to our customers, respond immediately and anticipate their requirements. . . .
* We are quality driven, pursue continuous improvement and we encourage innovation in products and services and partnering with our suppliers and customers.

People:
* We value, trust and recognise our people and hold them accountable for the Company's success.
* We require a diverse team of individuals determined to satisfy their customers.
* We value innovators who continually seek out "World's Best Practices" and challenge the status quo.

Profit:
* We are committed to our shareholders to continually improve our ROCE over the long term to a level unmatched by competition.
* We operate with high ethical standards in a manner responsive to the legal requirements.

We are responsible, cost-effective and innovative in our approach to environmental, health and safety issues.

relative to its competitors. The World Class Work Culture, Mobil's global program benchmarking exercise, was designed precisely to correct this unsatisfactory situation.

Allowing for British understatement, the response of a senior executive at BP (British Petroleum) to the question about benchmarking is worth citing. "Absolutely, we are besotted by it." BP benchmarked everything within its commitment to TQM. This became deeply embedded in the company in the 1990s. As in Mobil Australia, the remuneration package of executives and managers in BP consisted in a five-year stock value scheme, based on the best-performing plants in the world of BP, all very visible through benchmarking. The company introduced a gain-sharing arrangement for all employees whereby 25 chemical companies were compared on a variety of criteria; those in the top five companies received the bonus. Benchmarking was carried out both internally and externally. There were many examples of how the system worked. One was provided by the case of toxic emissions in BP Chemicals. In 1993, BP was underperforming in this area and, as a result of benchmarking, established a target to cut emissions by half in five years. Another example concerned safety in BP facilities. The DuPont safety rate in the US was the best in the world in the 1990s, twice as good as the rate achieved by BP. BP sent a team to the USA to study the problem and returned with new practices which, when implemented, improved performance. These examples make two important points. First, benchmarks for safety and environmental hazard were freely available; and second, corporations (including competitors) were often willing to facilitate benchmarking exercises for each other.

One important issue remains – the role of WBP and benchmarking in acquisitions. The cases of two Global 500 subsidiaries in Ireland illustrate this. When Tyco acquired Raychem in the late 1990s, the factory in Ireland had already implemented systems of world-class manufacturing and TQM, and established its own Manufacturing Excellence program. Tyco, as it were, stood back and collected the profits from an already successful globalizing company. When Roche acquired the declining US-based Syntex plant in Ireland in 1994, it was an entirely different matter. Roche brought in its corporate global standards for all operations and introduced competitive tendering where all Roche subsidiaries bid against each other for the right to develop and manufacture new products. The fact that Roche Ireland has three of Roche's top ten products indicates that it is competing successfully with the best in the company. Bluntly stated, no major corporation would think of making an acquisition without a WBP program in mind.

The ubiquity of benchmarking for world best practice suggests that cooperation between major corporations is more common than the pervasive ideology of competition would suggest; indeed, benchmarking would hardly be possible if this were not so. Explicit examples of the level of cooperation received include, from the oil industry, the case of Amoco (Dedmon 1984: 94–5), and from electronics, Don Amelio at National Semiconductor. The respondent at NewsCorp Australia argued that "Newspaper businesses are like little families, hugely competitive but willing to share information, especially in manufacturing." All the big newspaper groups tour one another's plants and have always done so. And in the Royal Bank of Canada, where benchmarking was described as the "rage of the day," it was reported with pride that RBS was the only Canadian company that Microsoft invited to its benchmarking meetings!

Benchmarking was pervasive in the telecommunications industry. In BT according to the respondent, benchmarking was "completely embedded in our culture." BT's version of global program benchmarking was Project Breakout, introduced in 1994. This project explicitly set out to reengineer every aspect of BT's business through benchmarking, by moving every process forward five years to extrapolate likely results. This exercise found that costs were £1 billion too high and profits were £1 billion too low relative to world best practice. BT trawled the global consulting industry for advice on how to put this right. Three companies were shortlisted (McKinsey, Arthur Andersen, and the eventual winner, Cap Gemini). TQM had been introduced into BT after privatization in 1984 and the European Quality Association (EQA) measures drove the attempt to improve business performance. BT was, in the mid-1990s, the largest organization ever to submit an entry and win a prize in the EQA competition. The focus, as in so many other major corporations in a wide variety of industries, was on improving quality in customer interface in addition to technical standards. Most of BT's benchmarking was carried out against companies in other industries. For example, Virgin airline came out very well in measures of customer satisfaction. The finding that 98 percent of Virgin First Class passengers would fly Virgin again became a benchmark for BT, who would be very happy if 98 percent of their premium customers chose their service over the competition. BT also benchmarked against other telecommunications companies, and the regional Bells in the USA provided some industry benchmarks.

Benchmarking was also pervasive in Telstra, the result of the merger of the domestic and international telecommunications companies in Australia. Customer focus, service excellence, and investment in learning were all ongoing Telstra exercises. Telstra Learning was a specific unit that ran off-site Leadership Enhancement Programs for senior managers, to ensure that everyone was on board for the transformation of the company into a world-class globalizing corporation. In the late 1990s Telstra was linked with many major corporations, including Microsoft, IBM, NewsCorp, and AT&T, in a variety of actual and proposed strategic alliances. Much of this was attributed to the new CEO, Frank Blount, the first recruit from the USA to run a major corporation in Australia. It is significant that a state-owned company was the first to take this step in Australia, and it was quickly followed by other private companies.

Conglomerates, corporations that try to excel in a number of different businesses under one corporate structure, have specific problems with respect to globalization in general and benchmarking in particular. Rockwell, a conglomerate active in automation, avionics, communications, and semiconductors,[21] introduced a new corporate vision in 1995 defined in terms of four elements: customers, shareowners, employees, and communities. (Rockwell's "vision" will be discussed in chapter 8 below). Internally, 23 vision implementation groups were established to identify the changes needed for the company to become "the best." In control systems, for example, workers were benchmarked globally on the basis of gap analysis and analysis of how to close the gaps. This was accomplished by monitoring 12 different companies for world best practice. Like other high-tech companies (HP, Apple, and Intel for example), Rockwell was a company which others have been encouraged to emulate. In 1990 *Industry World*, a leading US magazine for manufacturers, introduced an annual award for "America's Ten Best Plants" (another indication of the growing influence of benchmarking and quality management in the 1990s). In 1996 a Rockwell plant in El Paso, Texas won this accolade for its "transition to an adaptive, agile, world-class manufacturing facility" (*Industry World*, Oct. 16, 1995). While awards are common in all industries all over the world, from the 1980s on there was a perceptible increase in their globalizing scope. "The 1995 Industry All Stars" of the magazine *Independent Energy* in September 1995, for example, announced annual awards for "companies who are meeting the challenge of global competition . . . [with] global vision." The Innovative Project Award was won by Edison Mission Energy Co. for its financing model for power projects in Asia, and the Strategic Vision Award was won by Bechtel and PG&E Enterprises for their balanced worldwide development strategy (see chapter 3 above). The message, again, was clear: to be one of America's best plants was to be world class.

These examples of how major corporations have used various forms of benchmarking in the search for world best practice demonstrate that it has become an important component of the globalizing corporations in all five of the business sectors in which the Global 500 were involved. In consumer goods, financial services, heavy industries, infrastructure, and electronics, in companies which sold directly to the public as well as those who supplied companies selling directly to the public, benchmarking for world best practice has become the norm for successful businesses and increasing profitability. The next stage of the argument is to show how globalizing politicians and professionals created the political and technical conditions for WBP and benchmarking to connect the corporate interest with the global capitalist version of the "national interest."

Politicians, Professionals, and the "Competitiveness of Nations"

The idea that different countries (or nations) have distinct management styles and economic structures is widespread and deeply rooted. The idea that major corporations are becoming more alike in the globalizing world economy is also quite widespread, though not as deeply rooted. The debate around the competitiveness of nations tries to negotiate this apparent contradiction. Big business uses the complementary skills of globalizing politicians and globalizing professionals to square the circle of economic nationalisms, booming foreign investment, and free trade in the global arena.

One need not indulge in the fantasy of conspiracy theory to understand why politicians and professionals have been so engrossed with the problematic idea of national competitiveness. In his essay "Competitiveness: A Dangerous Obsession" Krugman (1996) argues that only corporations and similar institutions can compete with one another. Nations cannot compete because they are not comparable in the ways that corporations are. The idea that nations can compete with one another is a "dangerous obsession" that interferes with the economic efficiency of the market. While Krugman's neoliberal assumptions on national industrial strategies can be challenged (see, for example, Dunning 1997, ch. 10; Dicken 1998, ch. 4 and *passim*), the logic of his case on the incoherence of the idea of "national" competitiveness seems stronger. It is a small step from the idea of national competitiveness to the kinds of quality systems practiced by the corporations, discussed above. If it is assumed that nations can compete, then it is not difficult to compute performance measures of national competitiveness much as corporate planners compute performance measures of corporate competitiveness. While the step is illogical, it is nevertheless politically central to the way in which politicians and professionals in the service of the transnational capitalist class use the state. Let us begin with the globalizing politicians.

Globalizing politicians are those politically active individuals, usually but not exclusively influential in important political parties, who accept and propagate the necessity for the permanent expansion of the global capitalist system. This worldview is often and unproblematically connected with what can be termed "emergent global nationalism." This is the view that the interests of one's nation or nation-state (the distinction can be vital, especially in ethnically divided societies) are best served if it can find a lucrative set of roles within the ever-expanding global capitalist system. If the state in question is well-endowed with resources it can compete over a wide front of industries; if it is not, it will seek a few niches that will bring in sufficient revenues to support the basic necessities of state survival. Most countries fall somewhere between these extremes. The point, however, and what distinguishes the global capitalist project from the age of imperialism, is that potential partners can come from all parts of the global system. The transnational capitalist class takes in corporate executives and their local affiliates, globalizing bureaucrats, politicians and professionals, and consumerist elites irrespective of national or ethnic origins and characteristics. The inclusiveness of global capitalism (in theory and rhetoric if not entirely in practice) is in stark contrast with previous epochs.

A telling illustration of these processes at work within the state is provided by the political trajectories of five globalizing politicians from Latin America, termed "technopols" by Dominguez (1997): Cardoso, president of Brazil, Foxley in Chile, Cavallo in Argentina (relative successes in Dominguez's terms), Aspe in Mexico (a "tragic failure"), and Evelyn Matthei (from Chile, the least influential of the five). The ideas that these five political notables take seriously "are cosmopolitan and meet normal international professional standards" (ibid., p. 3). Successful technopols have made economics "political" and they succeed by selling sound economic policy in their own countries. Technopols are technocrats but they are also active in the politics of remaking damaged social and political systems. Democratic technopols chose freer markets (read "support of globalizing business") over state intervention because their professional training (largely under the influence of neoliberal academics) provided intellectual justifications for this decision.[22] As supporters of the free market they are also more liable to favor democracy but, of course, this is the democracy of pluralist polyarchy that Robinson (1996) has described and not any wider conception of representative democracy. In a statement redolent with meaning for those who would dare to oppose global capitalism,

Dominguez argues that "only democratic political systems embody the compromises and commitments that may freely bind government and opposition to the same framework of a market economy" (ibid., p. 13). The possibility that a democratic polity might reject the "framework of a market economy" is excluded.

The careers of the five notables illustrate how technopols in Latin America (and, I would argue, globalizing politicians all around the world) are made. Five settings are of prime significance for the formation of this fraction of the TCC: elite schools, religious and secular faiths, policy-oriented teams, the world stage, and specific national contexts. The Latin American five studied by Dominguez and his colleagues all studied either directly under neoliberal mentors or were inspired by those who had (notably in the economics and political science departments at Chicago, MIT, and Harvard). They made their decisive political moves in the aftermath of the political failures of statist democrats (Alfonsin in Argentina, Sarney in Brazil, and Allende in Chile), and economic crises facilitated acceptance of some version of the neoliberal consensus. Most technopols, thus, incorporate "two international pools of ideas – one favorable to markets, the other to democracy" (ibid., p. 28). It is also important to note that these globalizers are not extreme neoliberals out to kill off the state, but politicians who want to recraft the state from "fat to fit," to encourage growth with a measure of equity. Above all, technopols understand that corporations and those who own and control them expect policy continuity to safeguard their investments. This means technopols need to develop a political agenda to establish a cosmopolitan vision that locks in their countries to free markets, international trade agreements, and globalization, and to create political openings to bring all important social groups on side for "national" development. Technopols, therefore, must "set the market rules that will meet the rational expectations of investors" (ibid., p. 35) to demonstrate that they are running their states competently.[23]

The connections between the formation of the technopols, national competitiveness, and world best practice can be elaborated as follows. The technical standards of capitalist economic relations that are intrinsic to technopol democracy are not only compatible with the types of measurements necessary to provide a convincing rationale for national competitiveness, they positively encourage them. Technopols, therefore, approach democratic politics just like their business partners approach corporate performance. Politics becomes more "business-like," processes and outcomes that can be more easily measured are privileged over those that can be less easily measured and, of fundamental importance, the system becomes increasingly predicated on the belief that there is no alternative to the free market and private enterprise. Major corporations indulge these views for obvious reasons and take advantage of the quest for national competitiveness to extract incentives to do business in every country. As has been pointed out, many Global 500 corporations interpreted globalization in terms of being global locally. The issue for national competitiveness and WBP is that each part of the globalizing corporation takes full advantage of local and national incentives to enhance its performance and profitability as a contribution to national competitiveness.

The role of the globalizing politician is to ensure that all businesses, particularly the "foreign" corporations who have traditionally felt themselves discriminated against (sometimes true, often the opposite of the truth), receive at least equal treatment. The incentives that globalizing corporations seek and obtain are often seen by economic nationalists as special privileges. These incentives, in the form of development grants, fiscal holidays, training subsidies, and other "sweeteners," are routinely justified by the argument that attracting foreign investment (as we saw in the previous chapter) will enhance national competitiveness. Success is measured directly by evidence of the addition of world-class manufacturing facilities, and indirectly by the introduction of new ideas, methods, and opportunities for local supplier industries. The ability of corporations seeking such investment opportunities to show that they are world class and thus could enhance the industrial environment they seek to enter, is a political requirement for these privileges. Without this promise of increases in national prosperity, a corollary of competitiveness, subsidies for "foreign firms" would be much more difficult to sell to local populations who might see better uses for their taxes.[24] The support of globalizing politicians, therefore, while necessary is not sufficient for WBP to be fully mobilized as a globalizing practice underpinned by the need to maximize national competitiveness. WBP must be complemented by the technical systems of benchmarking discussed above, and for this to be accomplished, globalizing professionals must be recruited to the task.

The role of globalizing professionals – lawyers, management consultants, and legions of other business service providers in private practice; statutory bodies; and knowledge institutions (research centers, universities, business colleges) – is central to the ideology and practice of WBP and national competitiveness. By the mid-1980s there were around 700 US management and consulting firms operating in over 100 countries (Stiffler 1985), and the industry has grown very rapidly since then (Aharoni 1997). Paradoxically, WBP is as central for the ideology and practice of denationalized competitiveness for the globalizing corporation wherever it does business as it is for national competitiveness. This apparent contradiction can be easily resolved, in exactly the same way that the apparent contradiction between global brands and local tastes has been resolved. Once we see that corporations generally pursue profits irrespective of extracommercial considerations, such as the national origin of their founders, the contradiction dissolves. The marketers of global brands are quite happy to alter their products to ensure maximum profitability in every market where the product is on sale.[25] Similarly, globalizing professionals work just as assiduously to make joint ventures or strategic alliances between companies identified as "national" companies in different countries the most competitive in the world, as they do to make a "national" corporation or industry the most competitive in the world. Different groups of professionals can be working for government agencies trying to make "the British" or "the Japanese" or "the American" telecommunications industry more globally competitive while at the same time advising a "British–Japanese–US" strategic alliance in telecommunications how to be the best in world.

A central sphere of operation for globalizing professionals is in the management and testing of national and global systems of quality assurance driven by an increasing focus on customer satisfaction. The professionals who administer the Baldrige and Deming awards, the International Standards Organization ISO 9000 and ISO 14000 (environmental) series and other similar tests of quality,[26] are essential supports to globalizing corporations whose interest in a global "level playing field" stems from their need to sustain the competitive advantages they already have, or regain those they are losing. These standards have both positive and negative effects for ordinary workers, consumers, and citizens. As we shall see in the following chapters, they have meant in some cases better and safer working conditions for employees, safer products, and less environmental damage. At the same time, they have also in other cases meant less congenial and more dangerous working conditions for other workers, and their misuse has resulted in more risky products, and more environmental damage. All of these affects are consequences of the pursuit of greater business efficiency, better financial performance, and in the last resort higher profits for owners of capital.

World Best Practice as a Globalizing Practice

WBP becomes a globalizing practice when politicians and professionals inside and outside of the major corporations begin to use it as a technique of social, political, and ideological control in the global capitalist system. It is no accident that the practice of benchmarking has spread out rapidly from the technical characteristics of manufacturing processes to administrative questions over a large range of industries and, eventually, to a host of non-industrial institutions such as educational establishments, medical and welfare services, and cultural bodies. In short, the ubiquity of benchmarking under various guises is a reflection of the commodification of everything.

In one form or another, WBP and benchmarking appear to be permanent conditions of existence in the global capitalist system in general and in globalizing corporations in particular. There are, however, definite contradictions between national competitiveness, based on WBP, and the ways that WBP is used to forge strategic alliances between groups of corporations of different "national origins" in competition against other, similar groups of corporations. To put this concretely, competition is routinely said to exist between the countries of Europe, Japan, and the US.[27] Hundreds of books and thousands of articles have been written about national competitiveness (see Dicken 1998, ch. 4 and *passim*; Magaziner and Reich 1983; Porter 1990). The World Economic Forum publishes an annual scorecard of measures of national competitiveness. In 1999, 59 countries were ranked on openness, government, finance, infrastructure, technology, management, labor, and institutions. The UNDP in its annual *Human Development Report* ranks more than 100 countries for social performance. However, over the last two or three decades the number of strategic alliances between corporations domiciled in European countries, USA, and Japan, has been increasing at such a pace that sober scholars like John Dunning, for example, conclude that the world economy has reached a new stage of evolution. Dunning (1997) labels this alliance capitalism (see also Gerlach 1992; Gomes-Casseres 1996). Alliance capitalism presents a theoretical dilemma for state-centric theorists, who often portray exactly those corporations most active in forging cross-border strategic alliances as the best exemplars of the national business cultures of America, Japan, Germany, Britain, et al. The much-discussed alliances between General Motors and Toyota in the NUMMI plant in California, between Ford and Mazda for the production of the Escort, and the actual merger of Daimler-Benz and Chrysler, are only three among many in the automobile industry. It is also difficult to reconcile national competitiveness within Europe with the facts of cooperative research programs among most of the major European car-makers. Strategic alliances of these types occur over a wide range of industries (Dicken 1998, Dunning 1997, Gerlach 1992, Gomes-Casseres 1996). The concepts of national economy, national corporation, and national competitiveness do require deconstruction.

The most outspoken proponent of the thesis that the global corporation has arrived and that this entails a concomitant withering away of the state has been Kenichi Ohmae, formerly the head of McKinsey in Japan (see Ohmae 1990). His somewhat exaggerated views have tended to muddy the waters of the debate, providing the raw materials for a straw man of globalization. Taking Ohmae as the standard-bearer for globalization has certainly made it easier for those who continue to cling onto state-centrist conceptions and proclaim globalization a myth (for example, Hirst and Thompson 1996). The opposition to the idea of the globalizing corporation is central for state-centrist analyses of capitalism precisely because the conception of the multinational corporation as a "national company with units abroad" is absolutely necessary for the theories of national capitalism and national competitiveness. If transnational corporations are the dominant economic institutions of the national economy in most First World countries and, increasingly, others, then unless these can be seen as national companies in some meaningful sense, the ideas of the national economy and national competitiveness start to disintegrate.

The conventional critique of the idea of the global corporation[28] is that corporations are not global because most of them still have an identifiable home country and are owned and controlled largely by co-nationals. There are both logical and empirical problems with this formulation. First, just because a company is identified in popular parlance as British (like BT) or American (like IBM) or Japanese (like Toyota) it does not follow logically that it cannot be globalizing as opposed to being national or local. Robert Reich, no friend of the globalizers, made the important point that as far as American prosperity was concerned, Toyota plants in the USA were more American than GM plants in Japan (Reich 1991). This was certainly likely to be true for the communities in which these plants were located, though the impacts on the American or Japanese economies as such are more difficult to evaluate, particularly as the inputs for and outputs from such plants would have to be tracked very carefully.

Second, the ownership and control of huge corporations with facilities in hundreds or even thousands of locations is likely to be extremely complicated. The fact that BT, IBM, and Toyota have few if any "foreigners" on their boards tells us more about logistics in the world of leading business people than it does about who owns and controls the main pillars of the global economy. Ownership of major corporations is mediated through stock markets where the custodians of massive amounts of capital, invested by fund managers, are interested primarily in return on capital invested rather than national interests, however defined. These funds are increasingly distributed around the world, though not evenly of course, and the nationality of the owners of transnational corporations may change. Even if it does not, and even if co-nationals own the stock of most major corporations, this still says nothing about the significance of ownership for the national interest or the national competitiveness of the countries where these corporations happen to be legally domiciled.[29] The assumption that the American (or any other) executives or the American (or any other) owners of the stock of a corporation legally domiciled in New York (or anywhere else) express in any meaningful sense the American (or any other) national interest, seems naive in the extreme. Yet, without this assumption, what can the idea that BT, IBM, or Toyota are national (British, American, Japanese) companies with units abroad, mean?

Problems like these have encouraged many theorists and researchers, who are still convinced of the viability of the idea of national industrial strategies, to begin to take globalization and the idea of globalizing corporations more seriously. This is due to the fact that anyone with even an elementary knowledge of the world economy must acknowledge what Dicken and others have called the global shift in finance, manufacturing, service provision, sourcing of components, and markets that occurred in the second half of the twentieth century. Undoubtedly, there are ways of diminishing the apparent impact of these developments, for example, by arguing that in some economies in the nineteenth century there were periods when foreign trade took up larger proportions of GDP than at the end of the twentieth century. Nevertheless, few people seriously doubt the argument that site-bound production systems are being replaced by regionally and increasingly globally integrated production, marketing, and distribution networks. Though these networks are often self-contained within national boundaries, they are increasingly connected to other transnational corporate networks through various forms of alliances irrespective of national boundaries. This line of reasoning provides a logical framework for interpreting empirical claims about the global economy. This is quite compatible with the view that some industries are more globalizing than others. For example, "there appear to be integrated global companies in industries such as microelectronics and consumer electronics, office machinery, household appliances, instruments, pharmaceuticals, and financial services. . . . arguably, part of a wider process of increased networking within and among enterprises . . . [including] links with customers, competitors, suppliers, and non-business infrastructure (universities, research institutions, governments, etc.)" (Brewer and Young 1998: 20, 21–2).[30] When corporations compete, therefore, they do not do so necessarily (in my view, at all) as bearers of some national interest, but as bearers of the interests of those whose capital, understood in its widest sense, is invested in the company. World best practice and benchmarking are tools to convince these investors (whether they be direct owners of shares, fund managers, executives with share options, or even those whose other forms of capital could be more profitably invested elsewhere) that they are getting the best available value for their investment. National competitiveness, following this line of argument, is a necessary fiction to carry on the pretence of capitalism as the best economic and social system for each individual country or community. Regional competition within countries and economic blocs, the creation of industrial districts, free trade, export-processing and development zones, and the struggle between local development agencies to attract inward investment, reinforce this agenda of the connection between the global capitalist system, national and subnational competitiveness, and local prosperity.

Ironically, given the fact that the quality movement began in Japan after the Second World War, neglect of international competitiveness issues was blamed for the economic crisis of the 1990s in Japan. Widespread discussions of terms such as "international standards" and "world standards" and *gurobaru sutandado* (global standards) were reported. While in the narrow sense these referred to ISO and similar measures, other economic and social indicators on which Japan was deemed to be uncompetitive were raised. "This represents a major change in Japanese attitudes. People are now conscious of a need for Japan to change its systems not in response to pressure from some other country or countries but on its own initiative" (Yamamoto 1998: 211). The subtext, therefore, is that Japan must become more business-like. In the World Economic Forum global competitiveness rankings Japan failed to find a place in the top ten in 1998 and 1999.

WBP is a globalizing practice where it is used to impose standards of performance relevant to the profitability of globalizing corporations on workers and citizens in the name of national or regional or urban competitiveness. It would be perfectly possible to benchmark in terms of other criteria – components of human happiness, or ecological welfare of whole habitats, for example – but these are rarely, if ever, considered relevant for the globalizing corporation. This is not an argument about externalities to corporate performance. Successful reputation management and corporate environmentalism, for example (as we shall see in the next two chapters), are now considered by most globalizing corporations to be intrinsic to commercial success. The corporation defines which externalities it needs to deal with, or is compelled to deal with, rather than ignoring externalities as such. This takes us into the terrain of global corporate citizenship.

Notes

1 For useful surveys of the literature on benchmarking see Barad (1997), Oliver (1997), and the case studies in Watson (1993). Cole (1995, 1998) is useful on the quality movement in the USA as a whole. See also Meiksins and Smith (1996) for an insightful approach to the role of engineers in the creation of best practice, and the possible effects of globalization on the organization of engineering in different countries.

2 Interviews with executives in the relatively newer electronic companies, and with executives in older companies that have been turned into electronic companies by virtue of technological change, suggested that this issue impacted industries as well as individual companies. For example, several respondents suggested that the automobile and oil industries were still led by managers with old-fashioned attitudes.

3 For example, during the visit of a team from Xerox to its joint venture partner Fuji Xerox in Japan in 1979, the Americans were introduced to benchmarking. This led to a Leadership Through Quality program in 1983. Xerox manufactured the first US-made product to win Japan's Grand Prize for Good Design (see Gomes-Casseres 1996: 21–2).

4 I put an early marker on the issue of what "the very best" means. It can mean "best returns on capital invested," or "best stock market price increase," or "best environmental performance," or "best employer," or any number of other things.

5 This classification resembles that suggested by the review of the benchmarking literature by Oliver (1997), but he does not connect benchmarking systematically with globalization.

6 In his book about how he transformed the US electronics corporation National Semiconductor (not itself a Global 500 company), Gil Amelio described how he "asked twenty companies for information to establish a benchmark, offering each a copy of the results and found that they all cooperated" (Amelio and Simon 1996: 241). Amelio became CEO of Apple in 1997. My copy of his book has a rainbow sticker on the front reading: "Now Transforming Apple Computer Inc." This task, however, was beyond him and Amelio left the company.

7 However, as McGovern and Hope-Hailey (1995) argue, when the company responded to adverse business conditions by some downsizing in 1992, this tarnished the image of the "HP Way," which had been much heralded in the progressive management literature.

8 Pritchard (1999) points out that in Australia Nestlé advertised Nescafe as a quality product while also promoting it as a value-for-money product. The Nestlé infant formula affair, which raised profound doubts about the integrity of the company, is discussed in chapter 6 below.

9 Bechtel, a major private construction company also interviewed, took an interesting position on benchmarking, which expressed the specific business conditions of a private company in the global construction business that had no stock price to worry about. For Bechtel, the tender process was said

to be the real benchmark, benchmarking by market forces. If the tender was not competitive the company would not win the contract. Private companies differ from public corporations, where the management team itself is benchmarked by shareholders. However, Bechtel did report benchmarking its engineering and accounting skills against world best practice, so the differences may not be as great as claimed.

10 Several industries use benchmarks from outside bodies. For example, Alcan, like many other mining companies, operated on the Best Available Technology standards of the Colorado School of Mines. There have been several best practice companies for aluminum refining over the years, Alcan and Alcoa being replaced as benchmarks in the 1990s by Pechiney.

11 Harry and Schroeder (2000) claim that Sony, Honda, Texas Instruments, Hitachi, Lockheed Martin, ABB, and others have also adopted Six Sigma. See also *Qualilty Progress*, the official magazine of the American Society for Qualilty.

12 In the 1980s Motorola had lost out to Intel in the competition to supply microprocessors to IBM, a tremendous blow to the company.

13 Deming introduced a series of quality measures focused on customer satisfaction and these became the basis for the total quality movement. In her discussion of "Foreign Manufacturing in South Carolina" Kanter (1996: 250) notes that one of her world-class entrepreneurial heroes, Roger Milliken, "who brought cosmopolitanism to Spartanburg," had started studying Deming's quality principles in 1980, "well before they caught on elsewhere." Spartanburg is famous for being the place where BMW located its first manufacturing plant outside Germany in 1992. Along with neighboring Greenville, it had actively sought foreign investment for decades.

14 A Motorola manager in Arizona quotes the Six Sigma Goal: "With a deep sense of urgency, spread dedication to quality to every facet of the corporation, and achieve a culture of continual improvement to ASSURE TOTAL CUSTOMER SATISFACTION. There is only one ultimate goal: zero defects – in everything we do" (Tomas 1990: 27, upper case in original). I am grateful to Bob Conti for a copy of this paper.

15 See the in-house magazine "Opportunities: A Motorola University quarterly publication for and about Motorola learning, training, and education" (1998). An increasing number of corporations appear to be rebranding their training facilities as "Universities." *Fortune* reported that the number of self-declared corporate universities increased from 400 in 1988 to more than 1,600 in 1998 (June 7, 1999, p. 83; see also Schiller 1999: 151 for slightly different figures). Given the demands from actual universities for corporate funding I suppose academics should be pleased, if not flattered.

16 All material on Six Sigma reproduced in quotation marks in this section is directly taken from the GE Annual Report for 1997. This is, as can be seen, rather an extraordinary document, for while many globalizing corporations do produce enthusiastic annual reports the top executive message in this one reads more like a fundamentalist religious tract. It is worth noting that Jack Welch, Chairman and CEO of GE at this time, was voted the most

respected business leader in the world in the first *Financial Times* annual survey of corporate reputation (Nov. 30, 1998). I shall analyze its implications beyond the issue of benchmarking in more detail in chapter 8 when I discuss "global visions."

17 The Motorola manager cited above gives a convincing rationale for this quest for perfection. To settle for a mere 99 percent level of accuracy would mean each year in the USA 20,000 wrong drug prescriptions, more than 15,000 newborn babies accidentally dropped by doctors and nurses, over 10 hours of unsafe drinking water, and so on (Tomas 1990: 27). He does not, however, explore the effects on the workforce of such a regime of perfection.

18 The retailer Woolworths Australia (originally modeled on Woolworths of New York in the 1920s) frankly revealed that it was borrowing ideas from Wal-Mart, and had received a good deal of friendly help from them. For details of the Australian case, see Sklair (1996).

19 The Ford 2000 Vision, which will be discussed in chapter 8, specifically says: "The focus of Ford 2000 is on process – working smarter and more effectively. It is also about adopting best practices – regardless of their origin. . . . We will practice global benchmarking – and move with agility based on the results" (Ford 2000 Fact Sheet, June 20, 1995).

20 In one of those rewarding coincidences that occur in field research, I happened to strike up a conversation with a man on the BART train into San Francisco on my way to an interview in Chevron. This man had been made redundant from his job as a middle manager with Chevron and was scathing about the consequences of benchmarking and globalization for the employees and morale in the firm in general. My interviews certainly revealed tensions within Chevron and many other corporations on these issues. The respondent from HSBC was not alone when he insisted that all benchmarking systems required a "common sense override" mechanism. Some of these tensions in how globalizing corporations deal with their own workforces will be pursued in the next chapter.

21 In an attempt to reduce its problems of conglomeration, Rockwell sold its aerospace and defense business to Boeing in 1996. Between 1994 and 1996 Rockwell made 30 other divestitures and 50 strategic acquisitions.

22 Cardoso, of course, was a prominent though critical dependency theorist in the 1970s and his conversion to mild neoliberalism came later.

23 On the Chicago boys in Chile, see Silva (1996) and for similar processes at work in Asia, MacIntyre (1994).

24 In an exposé in *Time* magazine Barlett and Steele (1998) berated corporations operating in the USA for their greedy acquisition of public funds, assisted by legions of "corporate welfare" politicians, professionals, and bureaucrats. However (and not unexpectedly) the ultimate blame is attached to politicians and bureaucrats rather than the corporations. The evidence from Intel in New Mexico suggests (as global system theory would predict) that corporations, bureaucrats, politicians, and professionals work together for these outcomes (see Southwest Organizing Project 1995, and chapter 7 below).

25 For example, the "great taste" of the major soft drinks manufacturers, a slogan that is advertised globally, is actually many different tastes put together as a result of careful and expensive market research in many localities (see Pendergrast 1993).

26 Easton (1995) is an interesting account from a Baldrige examiner. For a critique of the "bureaucratization" of Baldrige, see Hill and Wilkinson (1995: 19). Nevertheless, such standards are widely accepted and used. The (British) BSI has more than 30,000 registrations in over 80 countries.

27 A typical statement on international competitiveness is: "A less obvious, but perhaps more important factor [than the impact of energy costs on America's prosperity] has been our increasing integration into the world economy and our failure to maintain international competitiveness" (Magaziner and Reich 1983: 1). Reich served as Secretary of Labor in the Clinton administration for a time.

28 I have been careful in this book to make clear my view that there are no global corporations, only globalizing corporations. Few corporations claim to be completely global and most go only so far as to claim to be moving in the direction of globalization. My four criteria (and perhaps others that might be added or refinements of mine) suggest how this process might be measured.

29 In fact, the exact status of subsidiaries, joint ventures, strategic alliances, and other parts of globalizing corporations is often very difficult to ascertain. Corporations, of course, have an interest in obfuscating this issue, for example when they are being harassed over child labor or environmental hazards or taxes. While it is usually a simple empirical matter to establish where the headquarters of most major corporations are located, this does not necessarily have any great significance for the issue of whether they are national or globalizing corporations.

30 This is just one in a long line of arguments about which industries and, by implication, corporations, have the most globalizing potential. See, for example, Bartlett and Ghoshal (1989), Fraser and Oppenheim (1997), Dicken (1998, ch. 7).

Chapter 6
Global Corporate Citizenship

The idea that transnational corporations are responsible not just for the ways in which they conduct their business but also for the consequences of all their products and business practices, wherever they occur and whether intended or not, is of fairly recent vintage. This latter form of responsibility is what is meant by the term "global corporate citizenship." In the words of a Shell manager: "we now have to be responsible for things we could never have imagined would be our responsibility" (quoted in Greeno 1998: 6).

Most large companies nowadays acknowledge some form of social responsibility, and many, as we shall see below, make specific reference to this in their Annual Reports and other corporate publications. In a useful compendium of "eighty exemplary ethics statements" Murphy (1998) identifies no fewer than 13 separate values (ranging from commitment, through fun, to teamwork, and trust) in a broad selection of corporations. To innocent and satisfied consumers and business partners it may not be entirely and immediately obvious why TNCs (or, indeed, any businesses) take the trouble and bear the expense of corporate citizenship, global or local. There are two common explanations of this phenomenon, and they are not mutually exclusive.

First, the people who own and control big business are citizens too, and any adverse effects of their activities could be bad for them and their families and friends. This type of argument would reinforce individualist claims of the type that those who own and control corporations exhibit a high level of morality and civic responsibility. The evidence presented in chapter 2 about the unpopularity of big business, the large literature on corporate crime and misdemeanors, the suspicion that most people have about big business even when they generally support its activities, and the siege mentality of capitalism, would all suggest that those who own and control the TNCs have not become interested in corporate citizenship out of the goodness of their hearts. Further, members of the transnational capitalist class usually have the capacity to buy themselves out from the most direct consequences of corporate health, safety, and environmental hazards. They rarely suffer from living in dangerous neighborhoods,[1] and they are not victims of low wages or exploitative working conditions.

Second, it is often argued that corporations are forced to be good corporate citizens because they operate within strict regulatory regimes imposed by local, national, and international government authorities. In the next section attempts to regulate the TNCs will be considered. Suffice it to say at this point, that while the TNCs often complain that they are being regulated out of existence, their opponents complain that they are virtually free to do as they please all over the planet.

A third explanation for why TNCs are developing and disseminating mechanisms for global corporate citizenship can be derived from global system theory. This explanation builds on the ways that TNCs are globalizing, the structure and dynamics of the transnational capitalist class, the culture-ideology of consumerism, and how all three are mobilized to resolve the class polarization and ecological crises of capitalism. The first point to register is that members of corporate elites (and members of the transnational capitalist class as a whole) are probably no less or no more likely than any other groups of people to care about the effects of their actions on their workers, neighbors, consumers, or the planet. Therefore, there are likely to be some among their numbers who care deeply about issues of corporate citizenship,[2] some whose commitment to corporate citizenship is entirely cynical and others (probably a majority) who simply want to be left alone to do their jobs and accumulate capital. The argument of this chapter is that for TNCs and, more abstractly, at the level of global capitalism, there is no alternative to global corporate citizenship in a liberal democratic political system. This is because corporate crimes and misdemeanors can cost market share to those who are discovered perpetrating them and cost elections to those who are too closely identified with the offenders. Close contact with corporate elites often puts politicians in embarrassing positions. This is nicely expressed in a *Financial Times* supplement on "Mastering Global Business" (1998, week 9): "Unfortunately because the population at large may be unenthusiastic about globalisation [or, indeed, the power of huge corporations] governments risk attracting business while losing votes." Globalizing bureaucrats usually work anonymously and are usually sheltered from public exposure. The tobacco industry is a very significant example of this, and it is interesting to reflect on the differences in the ways that Prime Minister Blair and President Clinton dealt with "tobacco money." Blair, eager for a second term, took a political risk by accepting tobacco-related funding (but was later forced to return it), while the "lame-duck" Clinton publicly challenged the formidable tobacco lobby in the USA.

In most political systems there are plenty of politicians and bureaucrats who would willingly regulate the corporations. The move by the TNCs to a more proactive corporate citizenship was in some part a preemptive strike against increasing pressure on and by governments and international bodies to regulate the activities of big business more tightly. This pressure came, in the main, from the public and social movements, filtered through those within the mass media who retained sufficient independence to challenge the interests of big business in specific areas, notably employment, health and safety, corruption, community relations, and the environment.[3]

The strategy of major corporations is to avoid public contact with politicians as much as possible. Instead, they prefer to work through sympathetic officials who control the regulatory agencies, the globalizing bureaucrats who have a supporting role in the transnational capitalist class. But why would those who own or control oil companies, manufacturing industries, or merchant banks worry about what ordinary people think? The answer to this question points up the dialectical character of the culture-ideology of consumerism, the value system that drives global capitalism. All globalizing businesses, whether they serve the consumer directly or indirectly, are implicated in the culture-ideology of consumerism.[4] Therefore, issues of corporate citizenship are increasingly seen as vital to the bottom line or, as one consultant who has helped corporations develop their corporate citizenship programs put it, the triple bottom line of economic prosperity, environmental quality, and social justice (Elkington 1997). In order to understand this process properly, it is first necessary to review the history and theory of corporate regulation.

Regulating the Corporations: History and Theory

While there is no global code of conduct for transnational corporations and FDI, there are many hundreds of bilateral investment treaties governing the relations between separate countries and foreign investors. There have been several attempts to introduce binding codes of conduct for TNCs but they have all failed (see van der Pijl 1993). The codes that do exist to regulate aspects of TNC activities, notably the ILO code covering labor issues and the OECD Guidelines for Multinational Enterprises, are voluntary and, for the most part, self-administered.[5]

The evidence from the *Fortune* Global 500 suggested that industry-specific pressures, for example technical staff shortages in electronics, environmental hazards in the oil and chemical industries, threats to brand name equity and reputation in consumer goods industries, have driven changes in this sphere. Not all corporations invariably opposed regulation, particularly where they had protected positions in lucrative markets (for example, as we have seen, in Australia and parts of Latin America). What the major corporations wanted was "a level playing field" in order that those who controlled relatively open markets continued to do so and that those who controlled relatively closed markets were forced to open up to competition from outside. The Multilateral Agreement on Investment that was negotiated through the OECD from 1995 to 1998, when it was blocked by a concerted anti-big business and economic nationalist campaign,[6] was a good example of how the globalizing corporations tried to structure regulation in their own interests. They did this by mobilizing their allies in the transnational capitalist class, namely globalizing bureaucrats (friendly officials), assisted by supportive politicians representing national governments and international organizations, and the globalizing professionals. All of these groups, who share the interests of globalizing big business, meet regularly on official and semi-official committees, and many other bodies. Through such channels of communication constant pressure is exerted for friendly legislation and against threatening legislation at the local, national, and international levels. In the absence of genuinely global legal institutions (in my sense of the term) legislation can only be binational, international, and multinational (treaties between the representatives of two or more governments of sovereign territories). This implies that while the transnational capitalist class can operate globally, legal regulation of its activities can, at best, be multinational. Law, for the most part, is difficult to conceptualize outside the jurisdiction of individual sovereign states, as the difficulties with what Held (1995) has termed cosmopolitan or global law confirm. The existence of global corporate opposition to unwelcome legislation indicates that the transnational capitalist class is organized globally. The extent to which the TCC succeeds in having friendly legislation enacted and unfriendly legislation aborted is a measure of the extent to which it is in fact in control of the processes of globalization.

The issue of regulation is still very much alive for all major corporations. In the 1980s and 1990s there was one significant development that offered a potential solution to the problem of regulation for the corporations if not for those affected by their actions. This was the vastly increased activity on the part of corporations around the world in the realm of corporate governance. To put the point sharply: if governments and international institutions were to refrain from legislating the conduct of TNCs then the corporations would have to put measures in place to police themselves. Thus was born the modern corporate governance movement. In an influential study of this development Charkham (1994) argued that the time was ripe for a comprehensive system of corporate governance.[7] Charkham provides a social and historical background to corporate governance in Germany, Japan, France, the UK, and the US, details of which reveal, unsurprisingly, that business conditions vary from country to country. For example, the system of co-determination since the 1950s expanded the scope of corporate governance in Germany, while the limited role of Japanese boards of directors inhibited it. The "hard core" of major shareholders was the key to the system in France. In the UK and the US, adversarial systems and the importance of CEOs created an environment for fraught corporate governance. Charkham's conclusion is that these different conditions and systems were bad for business and bad for the public and that a major review of corporate governance was required, which governments would have to enforce. He connected this directly with the globalizing corporation (though he does not use the term): "Companies need to be truly international from top to bottom if the sterility and antagonism of economic nationalism are to be avoided" (ibid., p. 343).[8] Despite all the differences, there were fundamental similarities in all five systems: "In formal terms all five systems studied above look remarkably similar" (p. 360), except that in Germany (and other European countries) the formal separation of supervisory from management functions resulted in a two-tier board structure. Nevertheless, all are agreed that the key to corporate governance is accountability, in terms of competence and behavior of the corporations and their owners and employees. The issue of who will actually regulate the corporations, then, remained problematic. The legal system in most countries is available to prosecute those who break the law – with the important proviso that much corporate law-breaking goes unchallenged (Gantz 1998), as does some corporate implication in the globalization of organized crime, for example through the money laundering system (Castells 1998, ch. 4). But corporate citizenship and, by implication corporate governance, involves more than law-breaking: for example, perfectly legal activities that are considered by some to have seriously antisocial consequences (Houck and Williams 1996; Korten 1995; Madeley 1999).

High-level recognition of these issues came in mid-1999, when the

OECD and the World Bank established a "global corporate governance forum" in response – it was said – to the problems revealed by the Asian and Russian financial crises of the late 1990s. (This was a little disingenuous, as these were only the most recent of a series of governance crises that had struck the corporations over decades.) The OECD had previously compiled its own code, but this had not been very effective and the official charged with presenting the aims of the new forum to the public, explained the motivation behind the initiative in the following terms. "The absence of transparency, control and accountability in corporate management leads to a loss of economic efficiency overall, and undermines investor confidence in markets, and leads to the misallocation of resources to the detriment of shareholders and workers" (quoted in "OECD Spreads the Good Word," *Financial Times*, May 28, 1999). This approach to corporate governance from two of the most important international economic institutions (international in the specific sense that they are composed of representatives of national governments) suggested that some globalizing bureaucrats were becoming frustrated by the lack of progress as corporations themselves tried to deal with issues of global corporate citizenship.

Within the corporations, the central plank of the corporate governance movement's position was that corporations deserved the right to police themselves. Fundamental to this argument was the claim that outside directors on the main board of a company acted as independent arbiters of corporate behavior. A telling piece of research on this issue suggests that the argument was self-serving on the part of the corporations. Main and his colleagues (1995) tested the assumption that outside directors guaranteed better corporate governance by assessing the degree to which executive compensation (usually heavily influenced by outside directors on main boards) was linked to performance in corporations domiciled in the USA. They concluded that the assumption was invalid because it ignored extra-economic factors, notably the rather hazy legal and practical rules around the powers of Boards of Directors in all systems, and the crucial issue of CEO domination of these Boards. This domination was based on three factors: norms of reciprocity, the authority of the CEO among the other senior executives he (rarely she) had chosen to sit on the Board, and the characteristics of similarity and liking between those who occupied senior positions in corporations. Studies carried out by *Business Week* in 1985 and CALPERS[9] in 1990 (cited in Main 1995) suggested that outside directors appointed after the advent of a new CEO (compared with other directors) tended to award higher levels of compensation to the CEO and other executives. Outside directors also tended to make very little trouble for sitting CEOs, and to award more stock options to senior executives, especially restricted (risk-free) stock options (see Davis and Greve 1997 on golden parachutes and poison pills).

Evidence from the UK in 1997 suggested that this phenomenon was not restricted to the USA. These findings would appear to highlight differences between the situation in the US and the UK, and in Germany, where CEOs were never on supervisory boards and where executive salaries were much lower. However, it would be naive to assume that norms of reciprocity, the authority of charismatic CEOs, and the similarity of interests between members of Boards of Directors in Germany (and elsewhere) were never of importance when business decisions were taken. The influence of social networks on capitalist class practices is supported by the findings of almost a hundred years of systematic research in the sociology of elites (see Scott, ed., 1990).

The role of financial institutions like CALPERS in the USA and similar pension funds elsewhere in the public debate about corporate governance supplies vital evidence for the thesis crystallized by Useem (1992) on the transition from managerial to investor capitalism. Useem's argument, in some senses a contemporary revision of the debate about the "managerial revolution" that has been raging since the early part of the twentieth century, explained the impact of shareholder power on how corporations are governed. Calls to give the owners of corporations – from the proverbial old lady with a few IBM or ICI shares under the bed to the fund managers who wield enormous influence on share prices – more say in how corporations are run and what they do, will inevitably focus on how to maximize returns to these shareholders rather than how to force the corporation to accept more social responsibility, which often ends up costing the company money and management time. Despite this pragmatic truth, the move to more serious forms of corporate governance, especially in the USA, Europe, and other First World economies, has been connected with corporate citizenship.

What of Japan? In the sphere of corporate governance, as in most spheres of globalizing business, Japan (and Asian business as a whole) is often seen as an exception. While Japan is still exceptional in some respects in its system of corporate governance (and, of course, many other things), what Berggren and Nomura (1997, ch. 3) call "The End of Endless Growth" may be reducing the differences between Japanese corporations and those domiciled in other parts of the world. Two opposing forces came into play for Japanese-based corporations in the 1990s. As the so-called bubble boom collapsed, the influence of the Ministry of Finance and the Ministry of International Trade and Industry waned, giving more freedom of action to the corporations.

In the words of one scholar, "the state doesn't choose among companies; companies choose among states" (Yamamoto 1998: 211). However, the dramatic change in the business environment in Japan in the early 1990s (and the more widespread Asian crises of the later 1990s) undoubtedly weakened the corporations and made them more vulnerable to attacks on their conduct. Berggren and Nomura describe how the annual report *Contemporary Enterprises* published by the Nikkei, changed its tone from "Japan as Number 1" in 1990 to "Weakness and Crisis," the title of the 1995 report. As the entitlement (of some) to lifetime employment began to disappear, loyalty to the company eroded, and major conglomerates like Mitsui, Matsushita, and Mitsubishi were increasingly labeled as hollowed-out failures (see, for example, Jardine Fleming 1993; Smith 1995). Japanese corporations, faced with these crises, intensified their efforts to globalize. Part of this globalization was certainly related to the creation of systems of corporate governance in Japan, bringing Japanese corporations more into line with what was occurring in other major economies around the world in the 1990s (see Kakabadse and Okasaki-Ward 1996: 44ff).[10] While differences between Japanese society and societies in other parts of the world have obviously not disappeared, differences within Japan may be growing, and the transnational corporate sector, big business, is globalizing in similar ways to big business everywhere else. Without these changes globalizing corporations could not survive. The transformations in modes of foreign investment and the rise of world best practice, detailed in the previous two chapters, the globalizing of corporate citizenship that is the subject of this and the next chapter, and the creation of global visions, to be discussed in chapter 8, are all illustrations of how corporations globalize. Big business in Japan is no exception, though cities and communities within Japan as well as Japan as a sociological entity itself (like everywhere else) still obviously retain much that is specific to their place and history.[11]

It is tempting to argue that corporate governance and the whole corporate citizenship movement of which it is a central part, particularly in the world of "Anglo-Saxon" big business, was triggered by well-publicized corporate scandals in the 1980s. In the USA, the leveraged buyout of RJR-Nabisco by KKR in 1988 was exposed for all its naked greed in a *New York Times* list bestseller and made into a feature film (*Barbarians at the Gate*), and in Britain and Australia senior executives were sent to prison for insider trading and other crimes. This was certainly a contributory factor. However, the problem of corporate governance did not suddenly arise in the 1980s, it had been in the public domain for decades. As major corporations adopted more extensive globalizing agendas they needed also to be seen to be taking corporate governance and social responsibility more seriously.

More or less all *Fortune* Global 500 corporations proclaimed their attachment to good governance in company publications and in statements to the media in the 1980s and 1990s. GrandMet, one of the companies out of which the food and beverage conglomerate Diageo was forged, made specific reference to its position on corporate governance in its Annual Report for 1995. Like other major corporations with substantial interests in the UK, it gave a public commitment to comply with the Cadbury Committee Code of Best Practice and to recommendations on executive compensation from the Greenbury Committee, established to lay down a code of conduct.[12]

Competition policy is an area of regulation that presents ongoing challenges to globalizing corporations. Roche, the major pharmaceutical company, fell foul of European regulations over drug pricing and responded with a major initiative on ethical business practices. The brochure "Behavior in Competition: A Guide to Competition Law" issued by Roche in 1999 repays study in this regard. Under the heading "It is prohibited to," boxes in red with red crosses explain clearly what is prohibited, but under the heading "It is possible to," boxes in green with green ticks suggest ways in which some of these prohibitions can be circumvented under the rules. Roche, and all other TNCs, have to remain "competitive."

Financial services corporations entrusted with large amounts of other people's money clearly represent special challenges for corporate governance. In Canada, leading corporations like the Royal Bank of Canada and BCE affirmed their commitment to the principles of corporate governance, derived from the 1995 Toronto and Montreal stock exchange guidelines. For the Australian subsidiary of the Prudential insurance company the most important issue it had to face in the realm of corporate citizenship was the governance function. The Prudential, like most major insurance companies, had substantial investments in many other large companies and sought to be involved in how they were run. The chairman of the Prudential in the mid-1990s was the chair of the Corporate Governance Committee of the Australian Investment Managers Association. Such overlaps of functions are, of course, very common in most economies, but it is also a double-edged sword. The Prudential, it transpired, was subject to criticism over the salaries of its own directors. In Australia, as elsewhere, the insurance industry was rapidly demutualizing in the 1990s, which meant that some of the largest insurance companies have had to become more accountable as they took on a wider range of financial services, for example raising capital for their own expansion.[13]

In Australia, the issue of corporate governance was thrust onto the public agenda by some well-publicized business scandals in the 1980s.[14] The largest company in the country, BHP, interpreted corporate governance in terms of the pursuit of best practice in relations between the Board, management, and shareholders. Whereas in the USA and in the UK one reason why corporate governance was seen to be necessary was to limit excessive rewards to senior executives, in the rather more modest confines of business in Australia, corporate governance was mobilized for the opposite reason. "Executive remuneration is being oriented to a more international structure, given the increasing number of executives with multinational experience" (BHP Annual Report 1996).[15] BHP also illustrated an interesting trend in the globalizing of the corporations in general and of corporate governance in particular, the establishment of International Advisory Councils and similar bodies. These are usually comprised of "the great and the good," for example business associates of those who own and control the company risen to positions of public prominence and individuals from the spheres of politics and policy. Their tasks were to advise companies on how to behave and also how to win business in various parts of the world. In the mid-1990s, the International Advisory Council of BHP included senior North American business executives with "global business experience," for example the former CEO of Commonwealth Edison (himself a former Chief of Staff to the President of the USA), and senior executives from Ford Motor company, Dow, and Wells Fargo Bank. In 1998, BHP announced that it had recruited a former Chilean ambassador to Australia as its "principal adviser" for Latin America.

Dow Chemical is another company with such a body. Dow's Corporate Environmental Advisory Council was formed in 1991, and has included a former French government environment official, prominent academics in the environmental field, a former director of UNDP Asia-Pacific, a former Premier of Quebec, a former EPA administrator, and others (see chapter 7). Advising these advisers in the mid-1990s were 22 Community Advisory Panels (13 in North America, 2 in Latin America, 6 in Europe, and one in Australia).

A third example comes from one of the biggest telecommunications corporations in the world. To assist in its quest to globalize, AT&T established three International Advisory Boards, one each for the Pacific Rim, Europe, and Latin America, all comprised of local notables chosen for their abilities to oil the wheels of business.[16] A final example is from Fluor, the engineering company, whose Senior International Advisers according to the 1995 Annual Report included a foreign service luminary from Georgetown University in Washington DC, notable German, Dutch, and Venezuelan businessmen, and a former Singapore ambassador to the UN and the USA. In 1996 a merchant banker, who had formerly served as British ambassador to the USA and South Africa, was recruited.

Corporate governance for major TNCs, whether through committees of the main board, International Advisory Boards, or other bodies, must of necessity have global and national dimensions and, in some cases, subnational dimensions too.[17] The national dimension is necessary because all corporations have to be legally domiciled under a system of sovereign state law, and while few countries have specific systems of corporate governance all countries have laws that affect TNCs. The global dimension is necessary precisely because major TNCs operate under many jurisdictions and have to deal with officials at all levels. Thus, a key indicator of globalization is where a local/national concept of corporate governance is transformed into a concept of global corporate governance. In corporate rhetoric, this transformation is very often expressed in terms of applying the highest standards of business practice wherever the corporation operates (Bratcher 1999; Logan 1998).

This trend has been labeled "caring capitalism" in contrast to the idea of corporate greed that was said to have characterized the 1980s, though it would be difficult to deny that the excesses of the past provoked and co-existed with the movement to curb these excesses. In the United States the movement for caring capitalism was led by Business for Social Responsibility (BSR), an organization founded in 1992. By the mid-1990s, BSR had a national membership of 800 companies and affiliates, and operated offices in Washington DC, San Francisco, Boston, and Denver on an annual budget provided by major foundations of $2.5 million. The tone of BSR was well expressed by the theme of the 1996 Annual Conference, "Adding Values, Adding Value: Corporate Responsibility and Profitability." The argument ran like this: "With economic globalization and changing local conditions, business leaders are called upon to wrestle with complex issues that effect not only their shareholders, employees and customers but also the quality of life in local communities, our environment and people and countries throughout the world" (BSR Conference Brochure 1996). This is an excellent statement of what is meant by global corporate citizenship and, as is demonstrated below, appears generally accepted in rhetoric if not always in practice by the Global 500. The idea that maximum profits and corporate citizenship are not necessarily mutually exclusive in all cases seems gradually to be gaining ground.

There are four main components of global corporate citizenship – (i) employee relations, (ii) corporate philanthropy for community development, (iii) safety and health of all those who are impacted by corporate activities, and (iv) the environmental challenge. The first three of these will be dealt with in this chapter and the environmental challenge will be the subject of the next chapter. In what follows, the corporations discussed under each heading were not necessarily active only under that heading, though information from them provided good illustrations of how they adopted, proclaimed and put into practice these complementary aspects of corporate citizenship.

Employee Relations

The problem for globalizing corporations in the sphere of employment is twofold. First, where corporations have strong local and national origins (and most do) there is often considerable official and public pressure on them to protect employment in the home base. This pressure often fails, as the commercial advantages in closing down factories and offices and exporting the jobs to sites with cheaper labor or cheaper infrastructure or that are nearer to major markets (or all three) can be substantial. While not new, the mobility of labor and capital have intensified since the 1960s. Traditional labor forces in the First World have been displaced by immigrant labor as a result of global restructuring (see Sassen 1988), and jobs have been exported from First World industrial communities to new sites in the Third World. There has been a considerable amount of research on this phenomenon in terms of the new international division of labor (see Nash and Fernandez-Kelly 1983). The political struggles within which these changes occurred were largely over the export of manufacturing and clerical jobs, and this is still a live issue in many parts of the First World (as discussed for the case of NAFTA in chapter 4). Very few, if any, major corporations take responsibility above the legal minimum (where there is one) for communities devastated by plant closures and, in the main, the redundant workers and those who finance the state (that is, ordinary taxpaying wage-earners) have borne the brunt of the costs of restructuring.

While the export of relatively highly paid manufacturing jobs from the First World to lower wage areas in the Third World has been accelerating since the 1960s, in the 1980s and 1990s an old phenomenon with a new name, downsizing, was overlaid on this process. Downsizing is the practice of cutting employee numbers while maintaining the same level of productivity or raising it, sometimes by relocation, sometimes by introducing new technology, sometimes by increasing the speed of the production line, and sometimes by all of these (see Budros 1997; Gordon 1996; Ross and Trachte 1990). It has been imposed as part of systems of corporate restructuring through quality management in corporations as varied as Chevron and National Australia Bank. While some corporations offer counseling for workers and managers made redundant, there was no evidence of any widespread conception that protecting jobs – even in Japan in the 1990s – was an integral part of the global corporate responsibilities of major corporations. This is only surprising when we learn what other aspects of business life were considered part of these responsibilities, as we shall see.

A second issue concerning the employees of globalizing corporations, accepted by the corporations as a part of corporate citizenship, was the problem of periodic shortages of technical and managerial workers and even recruitment of executive personnel from "nontraditional" backgrounds. This was particularly intense for high-tech corporations. For example, (despite having downsized dramatically in 1992) Hewlett-Packard expressed its commitment to what it labeled *diversity* in the following statement from the CEO in the 1994 Annual Report.

> Our corporate objective on citizenship challenges the company to "honor our obligations to society by being an economic, intellectual and social asset to each nation and each community in which we operate" . . . This citizenship objective, like all our corporate objectives, is grounded in HP's core values. One of these values is a deeply rooted trust in and respect for individuals. In today's global marketplace, we bring this value to life in our efforts to promote diversity.

The subtext to this idea, shared by virtually all the high-tech Global 500 corporations encountered in this study (whether domiciled in Europe, the Americas, or Asia-Pacific), was that the educational systems of their home countries could not be relied upon to supply all the technical personnel needed to keep ahead in industries where constant innovation was a matter not simply of success, but of survival.[18] Whatever else it meant, global corporate citizenship also meant an enthusiasm for recruiting talent globally and a willingness to encourage employees from a variety of backgrounds to aspire to leadership positions. In a feature entitled "The Diversity Elite," *Fortune* magazine (Aug. 3, 1998, pp. 94–122) ranked the 50 best companies for Asians, Blacks, and Hispanics in the USA; 27 of them were in the Global 500.

Similar sentiments were found in many of the corporate statements of Unilever. In 1997 the lobby display in its London headquarters said: "Unilever's capacity to tap into the best finance, talent and technology anywhere in the world, is one of the company's greatest strengths –

making the most of international diversity is a key competitive advantage." Company publications reiterated this statement amid multicultural images of employees and consumers, all happily producing and consuming Unilever's products.

However, these processes do not always run smoothly for major corporations. Mitsubishi made public its struggle to globalize its employee relations. The official corporate position of Mitsubishi on globalizing its employee base was to open up opportunities to Japanese and non-Japanese staff equally. That this was corporate policy in the 1990s did not mean that it was accepted at all levels of the company. In the Australian subsidiary of Mitsubishi, for example, staff felt remote from this issue, and cited as evidence of their remoteness the fact that managers of Australian origin were not even included on the central register of top staff eligible to be employed internationally. This was obviously seen as a terrible snub to loyal company employees who had in some cases spent decades of their working lives in the service of the company in Australia. Even by the late 1990s, there were very few non-Japanese senior executives anywhere in Mitsubishi's global network of companies, though the creation of an International Staff cadre was claimed to be an integral part of the company's push to globalization. The policy was the initiative of the then president of Mitsubishi, widely seen as a globalizer, who tied it to the creation of an International Human Resources Development Office (IHRDO), based in Tokyo. The first General Manager of this Office was a Canadian, assisted by an Englishman. However, both of these high flyers were quickly repatriated to top jobs in their own countries of origin! IHRDO was subsequently run by a Japanese manager with only one non-Japanese staff member. Nevertheless, the company persisted with its efforts to globalize its talent base. A Global Leadership Program to identify potential top executives took place in the USA, Singapore, and Tokyo, and International Staff and National Core Staff systems were introduced in 1996. The Global Leadership Program was designed to impart skills in global thinking and managing diversity. Though personnel policies from the top echelons of the company moved decisively towards globalizing the employee base in the 1990s, evidence from Australia indicated that grassroots departments in Mitsubishi companies all over the world tended to be led by conservative managers whose traditional nationalist attitudes have not changed very much. A key symbolic event in the mid-1990s was the appointment of the first US citizen to the Board of Directors of Mitsubishi in Japan, but even he wrote in the company magazine to express disappointment over the implementation of the globalization policy overall. President Tetsuro Matsuda, who retired in 1998, went on record to admit that the future of Mitsubishi's globalization strategy was in the balance. The top leadership of the company saw globalization as a necessity for success in the world marketplace, though the rank and file of the managerial staff, particularly in Japan, were yet to be persuaded to change personnel policies throughout the company. Of the 36,000 employees in Mitsubishi in the mid-1990s, 12,000 were from outside Japan. "Localization involves expanding business activities at the company's nearly 180 overseas offices. Globalization means making talented human resources available anywhere in the world" (Annual Report 1996). Mitsubishi was not the only major Japanese corporation struggling with this issue. NEC in Hong Kong reported similar difficulties, conceding that it was "slightly behind the trend of glocalization," and had been slow to replace Japanese with local management. Major management consultants had been hired to speed up the process. However, progress had been made, and while in the 1980s it had been very rare to see a non-Japanese face at corporate headquarters, this was much more common in the 1990s.

If my general analysis is correct, then we should expect all major corporations in Japan to be in the throes of this culture change. The large trading company, Nichimen, announced its project "CREATE 98" in its Annual Report for 1996. This was a two-year effort to achieve its corporate mission of contributing to a better future for global society through the strategic objective of increasing profits. Among the measures to be implemented were reform of the Group's business structure by reinforcing ties with all of its principal customers and regions within Japan and overseas. The key support systems for the above measures were: "Continuing the localization of overseas operations and the creation of overseas affiliates capable of independent operations as local companies." This, it was acknowledged, would involve changes in personnel policies, "significantly increasing the number and responsibilities of its non-Japanese staff overseas. Concurrent with efforts to reduce dependency on business related to Japan . . ." Again, the message was clear. The globalizing corporation must expand its employee base at all levels of responsibility. For Japanese companies, traditionally closed to outsiders, this meant giving non-Japanese employees opportunities within the company and non-Japanese affiliates outside Japan more independence.[19]

Giving your business associates more independence from the parent or leading company can, however, create its own problems for corporate citizenship with regard to employees, as Levi Strauss discovered in the 1990s. (Though it is a private company and thus not eligible for inclusion in the *Fortune* Global 500, the iconic place it occupies in the global capitalist system justifies its inclusion here.) Levi's problem was how to protect its reputation as a caring employer – vital for the youthful market that the company principally appealed to – when there was clear evidence that its subcontractors were engaged in illegal and offensive practices, namely employing underage workers and treating many of their workers badly. Levi's particular problem originated with the charge that some of its subcontractors were using child labor in Asia to work in factories making clothing for the Levi label. In order to put this right, in 1992 the company developed its Global Sourcing and Operating Guidelines, which proclaimed that Levi's "commitment to corporate social responsibility will always be a global priority." This did not solve the problem and critics kept up the pressure for decisive action to put an end to child labor. One result of the pressure was a rather more explicit set of "Global Sourcing and Operating Guidelines" established in 1996. These Guidelines set out "Terms of Engagement," covering ethical standards, legal and environmental requirements, community involvement, and employment standards for all Levi sub-contractors and affiliated companies anywhere in the world. Levi Strauss, therefore, was accepting global responsibility for everything that occurred within its business network anywhere in the world – global corporate citizenship. One consequence of this policy was the company's decision to suspend business in China in protest at human rights violations. (Many companies have found China problematic – for example, AlliedSignal hired a corporate affairs executive for its relatively small operation there.)

Levi Strauss did find a creative solution to one of the labor disputes in which it was embroiled, and the company highlighted it in its corporate publications and publicized it in the mass media. When it positively identified a subcontractor in Bangladesh employing several underage girls the company did act. It paid for the girls to go to school, and persuaded the subcontractor to continue to pay their wages and hold their jobs open for them until they were old enough to work legally, 14 years of age by ILO Convention! These actions allowed Levi Strauss to claim credibility for its Mission Statement, in which the company aspired to be "the employer of choice" in its industry.[20]

Levi Strauss was by no means the only globalizing corporation to have experienced such problems. Other similar high-profile cases of First World TNCs accused of using subcontractors who maltreated workers in the Third World were Nike, Disney, Wal-Mart, Mattel and other toy factory suppliers. After a stout rearguard action, in 1998 Nike was forced to permit outside inspectors to monitor its sport shoe supplier factories in Vietnam. Mattel (a major toy manufacturer) was also subject to a coordinated campaign from minority shareholders, anti-big business campaigners, and sections of the media. This included a shareholders' resolution sponsored by the United Paperworkers

International Union (holding 126 shares) calling on the company to adopt executive compensation policies which would reward executives for enforcing minimum labor standards. Under this pressure the company adopted a set of "Global Manufacturing Principles," a code of conduct for production facilities and contract manufacturers world-wide. To enforce this code, Mattel established a worldwide independent audit and monitoring system to be developed by Dr. S. Prakash Sethi of the City University of New York. Sethi, a prominent writer on corporate responsibility since the 1970s (see Sethi 1971), is on record as a champion of global corporate responsibility: "The good corporation would be judged by the extent to which it forgoes its market power for the benefit of those stakeholders who are situated unfairly because of unequal bargaining power and leverage compared to the corporation" (Sethi 1996: 85). He accepted the brief to visit Mattel factories in various parts of the world and report on what he saw.[21] This issue has become very sensitive all over the world, but particularly in Asia. This is illustrated in the American Chamber of Commerce in Hong Kong 1998/9 *Members Directory* (1999), Section 1.14 on Universal Business Principles. Unequivocally, the publication asserts: "good ethics and good business are synonymous . . . Amcham believes that American business plays an important role as a catalyst for positive social change by promoting human welfare and the principles of free enterprise . . . We encourage members to communicate information about their existing programs and practices relative to good corporate citizenship in the markets in which they operate." These injunctions apply not only to consumer goods companies. Banks and capital goods corpora-tions have supplier codes. For example, in the 1990s the world's biggest arms contractor Lockheed Martin introduced an elaborate code, "Part-ners in Setting the Standard, Supplier Ethics and Business Conduct Guidelines," both to protect direct and indirect employees and to warn against corrupt practices.

Attempts to address these problems globally rather than on a company-by-company basis led to the establishment of voluntary social accountability standards, the most advanced of which was the SA 8000 (modeled on the ISO standards discussed in the previous chapter) by the Council on Economic Priorities. This was monitored by the Swiss-based international testing and quality assurance company SGS. The first facility to be certified SA 8000 was an Avon Cosmetics factory in the UK. Sainsbury, the Global 500 grocery chain, has also been active in the SA 8000 movement. With the Department for International Development (an agency of the British Government), Sainsbury helped establish an Ethical Trading Initiative to encourage corporations doing business in the Third World to adopt higher sourcing standards. These are promising moves for the cause of genuine global corporate responsibility.

Many companies have explicit rules about the behavior of their employees when in positions of responsibility abroad. Colgate-Palmolive (C-P), for example, insisted that its subsidiaries operated under a written company code of conduct as well as under the laws of the places where they were located. The company had strict rules about political practices, so employees were never permitted to give bribes or contributions to political causes. (Few companies, naturally, admit to giving bribes, but it is notable that some major corporations in the 1990s explicitly refer to bribery in codes of conduct or similar publications.) In addition, C-P specifically insisted on equal treatment for all its employees, irrespective of gender, race, or any other characteristic. Company publications strongly expressed the need to employ all types of people and openly claimed that some of its commercial success was due to these open-minded employment policies. Though conceding that the company was "never far enough along" in implementing the policy, the incidence of locals running subsidiaries – a key measure of its open employment policy – was increasing. C-P called itself a "truly multinational global business." Being global, locally, worked as an employment policy as well as a policy for foreign investment. Colgate-Palmolive's global human resource system aimed to provide common ground for 500 human resources professionals working in nearly 200 countries. The motivation behind these initiatives was the same as for the electronics corporations, namely that in the search for all available technical and managerial talent, a policy of "diversity" was inevitable. For those interested in equality of opportunity, therefore, this was a positive consequence of globalization, at least for those who got better jobs.

Though most of the attention of those concerned about how major corporations treat their employees has been focused on consumer goods corporations, the actions of those in other business sectors have also been monitored. In the financial services sector a rarified version of what I have called the class polarization crisis of capitalism has been evolving over the last decades. The rapid spread of electronic money-handling and data transfers in the sector has caused both the elimination of hundreds of thousands of routine clerical banking and insurance jobs and the creation of tens of thousands of new financial transaction jobs all over the world. When the merchant bank J. P. Morgan stated that "the assets of the company walk out the doors every night," the idea of human capital took on a distinctive meaning. In general, as the average level of worker skill rises, and as the laws pertaining to employee compensation for injury and sickness at work and to dismissal become more equitable, corporations are more likely to consider it in their commercial interests (humanitarian questions aside) to look after their more highly skilled workers. The class polarization effect of globalization, however, means that for every worker who benefits from these advances there are many more, globally, for whom these jobs with protections are not available.

The necessity for and the difficulties involved in globalizing human resources management have been recognized at least since the 1970s. Many TNCs found that while globalization of human resources management was conceptually attractive, it could also be operationally unmanageable. The establishment of a regional personnel office was one step towards a global perspective without sacrificing management control and effectiveness. But regionalism had its own problems because most of the "regions" of the world are far less homogeneous than what the term "regionalism" assumed them to be. If this is true here, then the suggestion that some International Relations theorists have made that regionalism is a sort of halfway house between globalization and state-centrism, would require unpacking (see Stallings 1995). Nevertheless, effective management of human resources is critical to the success of TNCs, and the RPO can be an important step in expanding the global perspective and worldwide effectiveness of the firm. In the 1990s, these issues were being debated with increased focus on the global dimension (Schuler 1997).

Corporate Philanthropy and Community Development

One old-established way in which businesses have traditionally expressed corporate citizenship has been in the form of philanthropic contributions, usually to the communities in which they originated and/or where their major facilities were located.[22] This was such a common practice that it is likely that every single member of the *Fortune Global 500* did this to a greater or lesser extent. It becomes a globalizing practice when it expands in geographical and social scope. Geographically, globalizing corporations take responsibility not only for the home base, but also for places overseas where the company has business interests and, eventually, everywhere that the company's products and influence reach. In addition, globalizing corporations begin to take responsibility for a wider range of social needs. The Founders values of Alcan, reproduced in the Code of Conduct booklet, were described as time-tested values and ethics which have been in place since the founding of the company. They derived from the problems of operating in remote areas where the company was responsible for employees, their families, and their communities. As Alcan put it, "we are only as healthy as the communities in which we operate." This principle extended all the way from a mine site in Jamaica (a major source of bauxite) to corporate headquarters in Montreal. A written code of conduct covering community affairs has been available since 1978, and an environmental code was added in the late 1980s.

In the case of Coca-Cola, the geographical scope was virtually all permanently inhabited parts of the planet and the social scope was also global. One extended illustration of the range of its community development activities will suffice to make the point. A single issue of the company newsletter for Asia-Pacific, "Coca-Cola Asia Pacific Update" (third quarter 1998), then in its twelfth year of publication, contained the following examples of Coca-Cola's corporate philanthropy and community development.

i) "First Lady says thanks for Project Hope assistance." (Project Hope helped underprivileged children to get an education in China. The Coca-Cola system was a strong supporter of this project, and Hillary Clinton on a visit to China thanked the company for its good work.)

ii) "The Real Thing refreshes the Filipino spirit." (The Coca-Cola parade "stole the show" in the 100th anniversary celebrations of Philippine independence in Manila. It was the first company in the soft drinks industry to get involved in the Centennial Movement, a grassroots [sic] organization to raise awareness of the anniversary among the people of the Philippines.)

iii) "Indian summer cools with Coca-Cola." (Music and movie presentations were sponsored by Coca-Cola across India; along with Coke, Thums Up, a leading local soft drink, was also promoted.)

iv) "Drinking a toast to Pahela Baishakh." (Coke helped to celebrate Bengali New Year in Bangladesh.)

v) "Let the games begin." (Coca-Cola has sponsored the youth sports games in Fiji for the last 20 years. This was the biggest event of its kind in Fiji.)

vi) The company sponsored the Korean Football Association, and the Coca-Cola Soccer village in Singapore. (The company also supported many other sporting events and associations all over the world.)

Such activities were not uncommon, though the range and geographical spread for a single company were unusual. Coca-Cola was one of the most relentless corporate philanthropists and community developers in the world of big business, and was widely recognized for its efforts (it won a Council on Economic Priorities Corporate Conscience Award in 1995 for social responsibility). Such activities raise the issue of the dividing lines between advertising, promotion, and philanthropy. Purists will argue that any support in which the company name or product is identified is promotion, not philanthropy. This sounds logical, but is not realistic under the conditions of global business. Corporate sponsorship of the arts, which is widespread all over the world, is a good case in point. Sponsorship by major banks or oil companies or vehicle manufacturers of operas, art exhibitions, or musical productions, all actual cases, certainly does promote the products of the companies in general terms. However, these sponsorships are also seen as acts of corporate philanthropy. When corporations donate money and equipment to educational or medical institutions or fund infrastructure, products can be and often are promoted, but these acts are also seen as contributions to community development. An example of this is the growing corporate sponsorship of schools, some quite discreet, some less discreet. The following excerpt from a letter sent to a school principal in Colorado Springs in the USA by the district executive director of "school leadership" for (again) Coca-Cola is an extreme example of a tendency that has alarmed educationists.

> Here we are in year two of the great Coke contract. I hope your first weeks were successful and that pretty much everything is in place (except staffing, technology, planning time and telephones).
>
> First, the good news: this year's installment [*sic*] from Coke is "in the house" and checks will be cut for you to pick up in my office this week.
>
> Now the not-so-good news: we must sell 70,000 cases of products (including juices, sodas, waters etc.) during the first three years of the contract.
>
> The math on how to achieve this is really quite simple. Last year we had 32,439 students, 3,000 employees and 176 days in the school year. If 35,439 staff and students buy one Coke product every other day for a school year we will double the required quota.
>
> Here is how we can do it:
>
> 1 Allow students to purchase and consume vended products throughout the day. If sodas are not allowed in classes, consider allowing juices, teas and waters.
> 2 Locate machines where they are accessible to the students all day. Location, location, location is the key.
> 3 A list of Coke products is enclosed to allow you to select from the entire menu.
> 4 A calendar of promotional events is enclosed to help you advertise Coke products.

I know this is "just one more thing from downtown," but the long-term benefits are worth it. (Quoted in Brazier 1999: 11)[23]

Not all sponsorships or contributions to community development raise such serious issues, however. Coles Myer, the largest supermarket chain in Australia, reported in 1995 on contributions to the Australian War Memorial, the National Heart Foundation, the Cancer Institute, the Royal Victorian Institute for the Blind (in its home state), Shine Australia (teaching job skills to unemployed youth in cooperation with government departments), and the K-mart Wishing tree (providing gifts to the needy at Christmas). It also sponsored the Suntops program for children with cancer, among other philanthropic acts. These were all based in Australia, but as Coles Myer began to look overseas to accelerate its growth (see above) its philanthropic activities can be expected to follow its foreign investment.

Many Japanese-based corporations had impressive records of corporate philanthropy. The major Japanese insurance company, Sumitomo Life, "is committed to providing top-quality services and fulfilling its responsibilities as a good corporate citizen in each of its host communities overseas." Vision 21, its five-year plan for the mid-1990s, was based on originality, profitability, and the aspiration to be a comprehensive service provider. Sumitomo Life's overseas presence involved support for a broad range of charities, including community welfare organizations, cultural activities, exchanges with local universities, scholarships, waste collection, and children's art. In words that echo those of dozens if not hundreds of major corporations: "Our goal is to be a full-fledged member of each community in which we operate." Corporate citizenship in Sumitomo was encapsulated in a new philosophical concept – "humony" (a combination of humanity and harmony) – expressed, for example, in its support for the universal power of music. Sumitomo opened the Izumi concert hall in Japan in 1990, and hosted an annual Vienna Music Festival in Osaka. In similar vein, in its Annual Report for 1996 the Japanese trading house Itochu proclaimed its Credo: "ITOCHU – Committed to the global good, by connecting economic benefits, societal benefits and individual benefits." The Itochu Foundation (most major corporations have Foundations to distribute their largesse) focused on youth with a Children's Libraries Aid Project, an Overseas Students Aid Project, a variety of research projects and a Youth Recreational Center.

Diageo gave corporate citizenship a very high profile in its literature. As the merger that created the company was being discussed, the Annual Report of 1995 proclaimed: "GrandMet continues to take a leadership role in community involvement, protection of the environment and social responsibility," and spent over 1.5 percent of its profits on community action, with a focus on empowerment. In addition, GrandMet International Foundation supported charitable foundations in emerging markets. A conversation between the retiring and the incoming chairmen reproduced in the Annual Report reinforced this point. GrandMet in the mid-1980s was a successful, largely British conglomerate. The decision to go global with branded food and drink products seems obvious now, but it was not obvious then. As part of its globalizing drive, the retiring chairman remarked: "I rank setting up GrandMet's community programme as one of our most remarkable achievements." An independent Corporate Community Involvement Study ranked GrandMet's Community and Environment programs number one in peer review in the UK.

Diageo followed up on this work by releasing a set of corporate citizenship guidelines under the interesting title "Global Brands, Local Citizens" in June 1999 in which it expounded one of the most complete justifications for global corporate citizenship of any major company.

> What is corporate citizenship?
> Companies are part of society. They enjoy certain rights to trade freely but, like individuals, they also have certain responsibilities for the wider public good. What is understood by corporate citizenship has evolved significantly in recent years. It is no longer seen as just charitable giving; it is now viewed as encompassing all the ways in which a business and its products and services interact with society. In the broadest sense, it is an attitude of mind which informs behavior and decision-making throughout a company.
> Increasingly, companies need to make public their policies and actions in corporate citizenship. Consumers, special interest groups, governments and others feel they have the right and need to judge how companies operate. What they think matters, and companies need to be responsive to this.

Diageo put these policies into practice with a wide variety of projects, including the Cities in Schools and Burger King Dragon Award in London, the Foyer Federation for Youth, and the GrandMet Trust. Outside its home base, notable programs in the USA included KAPOW (Kids and the Power of Work), REACH (Recognizing Employee Actions in Community Help), the Pillsbury Customer partnerships, and the Burger King Academies. The Smirnoff Foundation supported job skills programs in Russia and Eastern Europe, Gilbey's "Building a Nation" program funded education and housing in South Africa, and in India the company was a founding member of the Indian Business Community Partnership. An ethical approach to business based on evaluating the company's impacts through the use of social audits was established, and the company was the inaugural winner of the Social Commitment Award of the Institute of Grocery Distribution in Britain for community relations work in the UK and India.

In common with other corporations involved in controversial products (in this case alcoholic beverages) Diageo paid particular attention to safeguarding its reputation. Establishing itself as an advocate of moderation in alcohol use was very important to the company. It was a founder member of several "social aspects organizations" (as they are known in the alcoholic drinks industry) to counter reckless and underage drinking (the Portman Group in the UK, the Century Council in the US, and the Amsterdam Group in Europe). In common with the oil and chemical industries and the tobacco industry, Diageo and other purveyors of alcohol have not been entirely successful in distancing themselves from the consequences of their legal commercial activities.[24]

The efforts of Mitsubishi to globalize its employee base and the ways in which its employees related to the company (and vice versa) were discussed above. The company had also been grappling with other aspects of corporate citizenship in the 1990s. The Annual Report of 1994 set out the policy of the company on the issue of "Contributing to Society." The policy was created by the company's Committee of Philanthropy, and was defined as: "seeking to contribute to local communities both in Japan and overseas in ways that preserve harmony with local customs and cultures." This included support for institutions as wide-ranging as Martin Luther University in Germany and Cambridge University in England, and Friendship Camps for Mothers and Children in Japan (for single-parent families and parentless children). Mitsubishi was the first Japanese company to support Médecins sans Frontières, and it also supported many cultural and educational programs in Japan and abroad, the Blind Society of Australia and learning packages for Australian schools, for example. Funding decisions were taken in Japan on the basis of applications from local groups, and local employees were generally involved. The philanthropy program in Mitsubishi Australia grew in the 1990s along with the business of the company there. The ethic of Working for the Betterment of Society was central to the company's global self-image. Employee Volunteer Clubs in Tokyo mobilized 700 staff weekly. "Reflecting the global orientation of our business operations, we are involved in numerous philanthropic activities around the world" (for example in Dalien, Jakarta, Johannesburg, Dubai, Sydney, Chile). The focus on forging better relations between Japanese businesses and the local communities in which they operated illustrated the essential problem that globalizing corporations that wish to move in the direction of denationalization in order to grow, face every day.

The annual report for 1996, entitled "The Principles that Define Mitsubishi Corporation," took these commitments further. The principles were organized under four headings: a focus on relationships, thorough understanding of markets, long-term perspective, and globalizing human resources. The policy on global corporate citizenship, which connects with each of these guidelines, mirrored its faltering steps from being a Japanese company, full stop, to becoming a globalizing company with its origins in Japan. The policy was based on three central ideas. The first was responsibility to society, realized through its public-interest activities focused on the company's Committee for Philanthropy (as described above). Mitsubishi asserted a central precept in the globalizing of its corporate citizenship. It accepted a general responsibility to society – the Mitsubishi Committee for Philanthropy required no connection with the business of the company as a condition for its giving. Its conception of global corporate citizenship was summed up in a conversation reported in the 1996 Annual Report with the then President Minoru Makihara: "We realize that we must live in the same world in which we work: it's only natural that we care."

The second idea was its acceptance of environmental responsibility, and the third (the most important for business strategy) was relationships, specifically the 73,000 trust-based relationships the company had with its partners for the 10,000 products that it traded. These three ideas were forced into a blaze of unwelcome publicity throughout the 1990s when an environmental pressure group, Rainforest Action Network (RAN), targeted Mitsubishi for its logging activities in the rainforest. An analysis of how this dispute was settled to the evident satisfaction of both parties – a landmark compromise in the sometimes violent history of big business versus the environmentalists – will be presented in chapter 7. Suffice it to say at this point that the language and organizational structure of the RAN–Mitsubishi settlement confirmed that globalizing corporations appeared to accept a substantial measure of global corporate responsibility. Whether language and structure translate into permanent changes in behavior is, of course, another matter, and that will be discussed too.

Many other major corporations also provided evidence for the thesis that under the conditions of globalizing capitalism, big business had no option but to be seen as responsible globally. Indeed, an executive of ICI argued that: "If you look back . . . social responsibility was one of the key elements of the founders of many global companies – it was about providing employment for people, looking after them, and also looking after the communities in which they lived" (in Greeno 1998:

6). Significantly, a commentary on this statement drew attention to the changes brought about by globalization in the ways that companies have developed their capacities in this realm (ibid.). In the financial sector, BankAmerica claimed to see global corporate citizenship "not so much as an issue, more as a necessity." To put this judgment into practice, the bank gave weight to the level of investment and length of domicile it had in each location. The Bank of America Foundation offered grants and loans for a wide variety of local community development and inner-city projects, and was rated highly in California for its efforts to serve lower-income credit needs (reported annually and in its quarterly newsletter "Community & the Bank"). Most of this activity was US-based but the Foundation reviewed requests for grants worldwide (see Gladwin 1993: 31, 35). Global banks in Britain, for example HSBC (Midland) and Natwest, also had active community development programs.

TIAA-CREF, a nationwide retirement system for around 6,000 education and health-related institutions in North America that was also a Global 500 corporation, connected its commitment to corporate governance and good citizenship through its Social Choice Account. This was the largest investment fund in the USA to use social criteria (Annual Report 1995). A senior consultant for corporate governance monitored all 2,500 companies in the portfolio, not only in the US but also overseas. CREF Global Equities Account had about 60 percent of its assets outside the USA. The CREF Growth Account made its first foreign investment in the mid-1990s, buying shares in ABB (Asea Brown Boveri). TIAA's largest single holding was in Mall of America (Minneapolis) and it also had property investments in Europe. The Social Choice Account avoided investment in environmentally harmful activities, weapons, nuclear energy, alcohol or tobacco, and (in Northern Ireland) non-fair-employment companies.

Fluor realized the value of corporate citizenship in the 1950s but in this case the motivation had come from the employees as well as the executives. A former CEO described this in his brief company history as follows: "The corporate personality took on an additional stature when our employees established an in-plant federation to support charitable organizations in their communities. We also started a formal program for corporate contributions to charitable causes, education and civic betterment in 1952" (Fluor 1978: 19–20). However, untypically for a *Fortune* Global 500 corporation, nowhere in company publications in the mid-1990s was there any mention of corporate philanthropy or community development.[25]

Such reticence was certainly not the case for BP, which acquired the US-based Amoco in 1998 to form one of the largest oil and chemicals conglomerates in the world. As BP presented itself as a leader in the field of global corporate citizenship, further study of its policies and practices is appropriate.[26] The booklet "BP in the Community" (1996) made the position crystal clear. "Companies are an important, integral part of society, and we accept the challenges and responsibilities which our position places upon us ... Our guiding principle is mutual advantage ... We seek profitability – but not at any price" (John Browne, Group Chief Executive). BP's first International Community Report (1995) won the Worldaware Business Award for Effective Communication, one of many such awards created around the world to encourage corporate citizenship.

Examples of international programs supported by BP and its employees included many global conservation projects (mainly through the organizations BirdLife International and Flora and Fauna International). In the "Working together for a better world" scheme 70 pence (about one US dollar) from each BP calendar sold in 1997 went to UNICEF (70,000 copies of the calendar were distributed in 20 countries). BP has also supported Save the Children Fund, WWF, and role models for the young in a Student Mentoring Project in association with the British Council, which was taken up by BP companies in Singapore, Malaysia, Australia, New Zealand, South Africa, Tanzania, Russia, Belgium, and the Czech Republic. BP made valuable contributions to the Prince of Wales Business Leaders Forum,[27] and its Science across the World programs in Europe, Asia Pacific, America, and Africa covered hundreds of schools and over 1,000 teachers in 40 countries in the mid-1990s. Seventy percent of BP's total expenditure on community projects took place outside the UK. BP was also a pioneer in benchmarking corporate philanthropy and community development programs. The Value Assessment process, used widely in industry and business schools, improved on these programs and helped adapt them to local conditions. The company was a member of the London Benchmarking Group and its performance was externally monitored.

In 1997, BP produced a landmark "Social Report" taking off from "BP in the Community." In it, the Group Chief Executive John Browne, driving the process from the top, stated: "Our intention is to move from a simple description of our work with local communities to a full account of BP's impact in the world covering all aspects of our operations. This is an ambitious undertaking – and this document should be seen as work in progress. We have much more to do." The distinctive feature of the report was its focus on measurement, how to evaluate more than 1,300 community programs with more than 900 national and local partner organizations. 125 of the company's employees were involved in these programs and they were estimated to affect

10 million people. BP spent £19.5 million (about US$30 million) on these projects in 1997, which represented 0.5 percent of pretax profit.[28]

While most of us will be understandably impressed by this record of corporate philanthropy and community development, former BP employees and their dependants in Lima, Ohio and oil workers in Colombia might be more cynical about BP's actual commitment to community development.[29] In 1997, despite claims that there were four potential buyers, BP closed down its refinery in Lima, Ohio, amidst angry protests that it had betrayed the local community. The BP executive in Lima who had built the plant up and defended it against closure was reported to have lost his job. While BP still operated a chemical plant in the city, the economic prospects were bleak. The journalist who researched the story concluded: "Making a profit is no longer enough for the global giants. With shareholders – our pension funds – breathing down their necks, they have to constantly ask themselves if they could use their cash more profitably." Factory closures are happening all the time, of course. Corporations cannot be expected to support indefinitely plants that fail to produce satisfactory profits, and the damage to or even destruction of the communities that rely on the economic activity these plants bring is a price that has to be paid to defend this form of capitalist rationality. However, globalizing corporations also spend tens or in some cases hundreds of millions of dollars to support good works around the globe, which includes funding arts and university institutions some might consider overendowed already (including my own).

BP has also been subject to allegations concerning violent links between the army and BP operations in Colombia. In common with many TNCs in Colombia, BP is said to have paid left-wing guerrillas not to attack company installations and paid the military to protect their interests in the country.[30] BP's behavior in Colombia has been compared to Shell's behavior in Nigeria by a member of the European parliament. It was alleged that the company paid the military $1.25 for every barrel of oil produced and over $5 million in a "3-year voluntary agreement of cooperation" for the army to protect company property from guerrillas. BP has also been accused of ambivalence in its denial of charges of condoning gross human rights violations and causing environmental damage (cited in Madeley 1999: 126).

Again, BP and all other companies placed in similar situations cannot win. Either they get out of Colombia and risk the type of community damage for which they were so bitterly criticized in Lima, Ohio, or they stay and do business, provide jobs, perhaps upgrade the local level of skills, perhaps help to support local and national democracy and human rights groups. Without presuming to judge others, it is still possible to pose the question: are these contingent features of a basically good and socially worthwhile economic and social system or are they intrinsic features of a flawed system that is not sustainable?

This question is given a somewhat different but equally sharp focus by the case of Unilever. Like BP, it was proud of its record on corporate citizenship and publicized its activities through company publications. Unilever saw its role in two ways: satisfying consumer demand everywhere and acting in a socially relevant way, so that it was "a force for good in the world." This meant aspiring to values of quality, diversity, and technology, beyond the products that the company manufactured. This was made concrete in its report, "A Sense of Community" (Feb. 1997), which asserted that corporate philanthropy had always played an important part in Unilever's history and that there was a continuing corporate commitment focused on youth, education, and the environment. Corporate philanthropy in Unilever was based on spending at least 1 percent of the company's pretax profit in cash, kind, or time in the UK. In 1997 a decision was taken to concentrate on fewer projects, which was painful, but (reminiscent of BP's interest in benchmarking its social performance) Unilever expected that this would add greater value to its philanthropy program. Funding was concentrated in education (an example was support for the organization Investors in People in Schools); environment (Young People's Trust for the Environment, for example); arts sponsorship (projects in Merseyside, where the company had substantial investment, the Shakespeare Globe Theatre, and the Open Air Theatre in Regents Park, London, for example); enterprise (the Prince's Trust, and the London Enterprise Agency, for example); brand sponsorship (the Flora London marathon, Persil Funfit, and Timotei Plantlife, for example); and employee involvement (Save the Children Fund, the school governors project, and various activities around the company's facilities in Port Sunlight).

The Annual Review (Report) of 1995 stated Unilever's case firmly. "The brands we make serve people's everyday needs, when it comes to what they eat and drink, the way they look and how they keep their clothes and their homes clean. That's what has turned those brands into household names and made us one of the largest consumer goods companies in the world." Unilever products sold in over 150 countries. For example, Organics shampoo was first launched in Thailand in 1993 after joint development work by Unilever's Hair Innovation Centers in Bangkok and Paris. By 1995, the brand was selling to the value of £200 million in more than 40 countries. "Success [the 1995 Annual Review asserted] depends on providing the right mix of international and local brands for the local consumer," like Good Humor Breyers ice-cream, Elizabeth Arden, Calvin Klein, Omo, and Lux, plus the relaunched local Viso detergents range in Vietnam. There is nothing original about my commentary on this. Unilever and all other consumer goods corporations have their own conceptions of what "people's everyday needs" are and how to satisfy them. They also have their own conceptions of what development is. As the corporate conception of sustainable development is the focus of chapter 7 below, I shall not offer any detailed discussion of this tired but fundamental issue here. Suffice it to say that there has to be an argument about the place of Organics shampoo in the development priorities of Thailand, about the place of Viso detergents in the development priorities of Vietnam, and about the mix of global and local brands for development as a whole. The controversy over the invention of the toothpaste pump and the brilliant sales strategy of its promoters (prominent among whom was Unilever) is one among many symbols of this difficulty of reconciling the culture-ideology of consumerism with the genuine needs and prospects for sustainable development of communities all over the world.

Unilever's fine record on corporate philanthropy and community development coexisted with what most globalizing corporations have had to do to remain competitive in the global economy. Unilever has had to replace permanent workers by contract workers in its plants all over the world, to speed up production lines, and to purchase plantations to secure supplies of raw materials. The positive and negative effects of all these practices on different groups within local communities sit uneasily beside the claims of corporate citizenship. Two superficially similar but ironically different images sum up these paradoxes. First the corporate view of how Unilever served its consumers: the front cover of the Annual Review of 1995 showed a group of black schoolchildren neatly presented in green school uniforms brandishing with glee a Unilever brand of ice-cream. Next, the critical view: the cover of *New Internationalist* magazine's withering assessment of the company's activities showed two rather blank-faced children amongst a forest of Unilever products, holding confectionary in their "sticky fingers."[31]

Most of the computer and electronics corporations focus their corporate citizenship efforts, not surprisingly, on education and global communications in some form or another. Notable among these was the computer company Apple, which had mixed fortunes in the 1990s. Apple had a rather distinctive individualistic conception of corporate citizenship, marketing its products as people-friendly under the logo "Changing the World, One Person at a Time," a cutting-edge global image. Its corporate HQ was located at 1 Infinite Loop, Cupertino, California, a campus-like complex which included the Apple University, Museum, company store, and fitness center. In corporate HQ in Silicon Valley a Worldwide Community Affairs department provided Apple technology to nonprofit groups and schools and enlisted employee volunteers for service in their local communities. The company reported similar activities in South Africa, Singapore, and Denmark, and with the Hispanic community in the USA through LatinoNet. Apple's impressive contribution to the NGO Forum on Women in China in 1995 was a major public relations coup and a vindication of corporate citizenship through technology. During the 10-day conference more than 2,200 people a day used Apple products, Apple's WorldScript gave access in 27 different languages, and more than 2,000 journalists filed their stories directly via Apple technology through the internet (Annual Report 1995: 47). Gladwin (1993: 29, 35) confirmed that Apple (and Hewlett-Packard) deserved their reputations as good corporate citizens.

Nevertheless, most electronics companies suffered from two related problems that conflicted sharply with their exciting, clean, almost clinical images. First, their record on the health and safety of their production workers has attracted a good deal of scholarly research, mostly with conclusions unfavorable to the companies; and second, the environmental impact of their production processes, particularly the issue of how they deal with the toxic wastes they produce, has been criticized.[32] Again, there does seem to be a disjunction, to put it no more strongly, between the images and practices of global corporate citizenship broadcast by these corporations, and their actual performances in and around the places where they make their products.

Pfizer (previously noted for its position on corporate governance), also prominently displayed its commitment to corporate philanthropy in a report entitled "Pfizer Philanthropy" (1996–7), where it announced a new strategy of Venture Philanthropy, "charitable endeavor based on risk-taking, innovation, and entrepreneurial spirit." This was mostly US-based, but a "Global Disaster Relief" program (bringing assistance to victims of the Yunnan earthquake in China and the Kobe earthquake in Japan, and to refugees in Rwanda) signaled a globalizing tendency and attention to its emerging markets in China and Japan. The organizational restructuring from which these new initiatives emerged is of significance to this argument (see above). This was driven as much by the need to maximize market penetration as by the need to globalize the corporate citizenship effort. My point is, precisely, that globalizing corporations do not separate these two needs. Those who do so risk missing a fundamental truth about the globalization of the corporations.

It is easy to be skeptical, even cynical, about corporate citizenship pronouncements. Some corporate philanthropy is used for tax purposes, and with the help of creative accounting, corporations can actually make money through tax write-offs by giving it away. Most corporate philanthropy is, to a greater or lesser extent, promotional either directly, to advertise products, or indirectly, to create good feelings towards corporate activities. For example, in the Walt Disney Corporation Annual Report for 1995, the CEO proclaimed: "During fiscal 1995, a total of 27,435 Disney cast members [Disney-speak for employees] worldwide, working through the Disney VoluntEARS Program [*sic*], donated 227,102 hours of community service in 361 separate projects." It is likely that most people affected by these projects were aware of the Disney connection. However, it is still valid to ask why popular global icons like Disney (and most other Global 500 and smaller corporations) bother to engage in such activities which, after all, deflect financial and personnel resources from the main business of capturing markets and making profits. The answer to the question is that the boundary between business (especially globalizing business) and everyday life has been progressively blurred as capitalism has globalized. TNCs, as the prime carriers of the practices of the global capitalist agenda, consider it necessary to engage in these extracommercial activities for commercial and reputational reasons.

Another way of putting this is that sponsoring popular culture, the arts, and education is an effective way to reach consumers. This was true all the way from oil companies to computer companies to cigarette companies, even if their logos were hidden or not prominently displayed. Mining companies, like cigarette companies, have suffered a bad press for most of their active lives so it is not surprising that they make special efforts to create goodwill for themselves wherever they operate. RTZ explicitly considered global corporate citizenship to be a particularly important influence in the move to globalize management structures. How companies related to governments, the public, and NGOs, for example, were matters of increasing significance for RTZ . These issues were defined as matters for core management competence and not left to specialists, as had previously been the case in the company. What had been seen in the past as soft issues, such as health, safety, environment, and community development, were all bracketed together and had much higher priority. Rio Tinto (the new name of RTZ-CRA) placed particular attention on its community relations – in the words of the Annual Report in 1997: "Wherever the Group operates, good relations with its neighbors are fundamental to long-term success." These relations were said to be based on the principles of mutual respect, active partnership, and long-term commitment. This policy was pursued in parallel with the company's Health, Safety, and Environment (HSE) policy. During 1996, for example, RTZ-CRA invested $22.7 million in community projects around the world. In

Australia these projects included the CRA Aboriginal Foundation, the Flying Doctor Service, the Australia Science Olympiad, and a partnership with Earthwatch (a local environmental group) for regional fellowships. In Southern Africa (where RTZ has had a long and stormy history), the company funded a Worldaware award for sustainable development, and an irrigation scheme in Zimbabwe. In Canada, the Conference Board (a leading business organization) selected a high school funded by RTZ for "The Global Best Award." And in the UK, RTZ was the leading corporate supporter of the New Earth Galleries at the Natural History Museum in London, as well as of the Lord Mayor's Dragon Award for a Green Information Technology project. The company proclaimed its commitment to high standards of corporate governance.

However, for decades critics of the practices of mining companies in general and critics of RTZ in particular, have been collecting evidence and making physical protests on issues that bring the high standards that RTZ sets itself into serious doubt. If even a fraction of the allegations about Rio Tinto were true, the company's claim to leadership in the sphere of global corporate citizenship would ring hollow.[33]

Safety and Health of Consumers and Citizens

All corporations, probably all businesses, began to become more aware of their responsibilities with respect to the safety and health of those who consumed their products and those who were affected by the ways in which these products were produced in the second half of the twentieth century. Some of the responsibility for this can be attributed to the pressure of consumer movements around the world. The term "consumerism" is commonly used in two almost diametrically opposed ways both in academic research and common parlance (Sklair 1995: 84). Here it refers to an uncritical obsession with consumption and, of course, it lies at the heart of the culture-ideology of consumerism. It is, however, also used in an almost opposite sense to denote suspicion of and a wish to monitor the safety, value, and comparability of consumer goods and services. This is how the consumer movement uses the term and it can – though does not always – lead to a radical critique of consumption patterns.[34] "Consumerism" is used here always in the first sense, the term "consumer movement" refers to the second sense. Concerns about how corporations impact the safety and health of consumers and citizens is a central focus of the consumer movement.

The case that has attracted most ongoing media and scholarly attention is certainly the Nestlé infant formula affair that began in the

1970s over allegations about unethical marketing of infant formula in poor countries. A powerful breast-feeding lobby joined forces with anti-big-business campaigners to harry Nestlé around the globe, while Nestlé responded through the legal system and public relations. Infant formula producers were subjected to boycotts all round the world. The ongoing story of this conflict has a permanent place in the annals of corporate irresponsibility and corporate citizenship.[35] Nestlé, of course, is not the only transnational corporation to have become embroiled in controversy far from its major shareholders and executives. The marketing and dumping of inappropriate and/or out-of-date drugs in Third World countries has also attracted criticism to some major pharmaceutical companies (Medawar and Freese 1982). However, more recently, several companies have gone some way to rebuilding the reputation of the industry by making valuable and generous donations of medications to developing countries, notably Johnson & Johnson, Merck, and Pfizer (who freely distributed $60 million worth of antitrachoma drugs in 1998).

Two names that are inextricably linked in the annals of corporate catastrophe are Union Carbide and Bhopal. This is one of the most written-about tragedies in corporate history.[36] In the 1980s Union Carbide was one of the largest chemical corporations in the world, headquartered in the USA and operating globally. Bhopal is a city in the state of Madhya Pradesh, central India. On the night of December 2/3, 1984 toxic fumes containing methyl isocyanate, hydrogen cyanide, and cyanide leaked from the Union Carbide pesticide plant located in a densely populated district of Bhopal, about three kilometers from the central railway station. The fumes affected about 250,000 people, and the death toll has been estimated at between 15,000 and 20,000 people.[37] Many of those who have written about Bhopal accuse the company of double standards. The main charges are that Union Carbide produced toxic chemicals, banned in some (usually richer) countries, in India where the environmental regulations were not so strict or could more easily be ignored, and that safety provisions in the Bhopal plant were substandard.[38] The Union Carbide Company had been operating in India since the 1940s, and owned 50.9 percent of Union Carbide India Ltd. (foreign companies at that time were not permitted to own more than 51 percent of any company in India). The Bhopal plant was opened in 1979 to supply fertilizers, pesticides, and other inputs for the Green Revolution that was to transform agriculture in some regions of India. Despite many warnings that the plant should not have been built in such a densely populated area, the lure of investment and jobs proved too strong for the authorities responsible for investment decisions.

Bhargava (1988) analyzes the catastrophe in three parts. First, the main causes of the accident were generally agreed, even by some Union Carbide managers. The Bhopal plant had safety standards and emergency systems that were significantly inferior to those operating in comparable Union Carbide plants, notably the major facility in Institute, West Virginia. Second, the reasons for the extremely high death and injury toll were also generally agreed. There was no system for ensuring public safety in the event of a major incident; there was no satisfactory evacuation plan; and there was little immediate response on the spot from Union Carbide itself, or the local or national government, or the army. Third, the loss of life and health, and the financial losses suffered by the victims and the local community as a whole, have never been properly addressed. The aftermath of the Bhopal catastrophe is a sorry and tragic tale of international legal tangles, corporate prevarication, and negligence by agencies of the Indian government responsible for representing the victims and their families. The only shred of good to come out of Bhopal, in Bhargava's view, was that: "The whole world's attitude about uses, production, and storage of hazardous materials is being altered as a result of this incident, and chemical companies have been put on notice that the world is watching" (Bhargava 1988: 2).[39]

Transnational corporations did not suddenly become aware of their impacts on the safety and health of consumers and citizens in the late 1980s. Events in the 1960s and 1970s in many parts of the world had clearly signaled these problems. The publication of Rachael Carson's book *Silent Spring* in 1962, even though it focused narrowly on pesticides (perhaps precisely because it focused narrowly on pesticides) and corporate attempts to suppress the book's publication and discredit it, were clear indications that there were serious questions to be answered (McCormick 1992: 55ff). Sensational publicity and sober scientific research combined to heighten public consciousness about the perils of industrial production and to put the corporations on notice that they would be held accountable for their actions on the world stage as well as in the communities where disasters had occurred. The media began to publicize thousands of environmental incidents that had profound local impacts and some that had wider repercussions, notably catastrophic oil pollution off the coasts of England and California, explosions at chemical plants in Seveso, Italy and at Flixborough in England, the Three Mile Island nuclear scare in the USA, mercury poisoning around Minamata Bay and toxic poisoning elsewhere in Japan (for which Mitsui was eventually ordered to pay compensation in 1972). In Japan, 1970 was "the year initiating the era of environmental challenge" (Tsuru 1993: 129–38).[40]

Nevertheless, Bhopal appeared to have had a more profound global impact on the corporate sector, and especially the chemical industry, than any other catastrophe. This was probably due to a coincidence of factors. The timing was clearly of great significance. By the end of 1984 the World Commission on Environment and Development was well into its work on creating a new and universally acceptable conception of sustainable development which big business could not easily ignore. Location was also important. First World corporations producing dangerous products in the Third World had long been suspect just for being there.[41] A third factor was that Bhopal had been a public relations disaster for Union Carbide, the chemical industry, and the pattern of industrialization that it represented. Union Carbide representatives were unhelpful and at times callous, initially trying to blame the accident on Sikh terrorists or disgruntled employees. The adverse public reaction to the long-term reluctance of the company to accept full financial and moral responsibility for the destruction of the community near the plant rang alarm bells in corporate boardrooms around the world. And, finally, although nothing on the scale of Bhopal had ever happened in the First World, many people (no doubt, including shareholders, executives, corporate professionals, globalizing bureaucrats, and politicians at all levels) were beginning to wonder: could it happen here? A chilling commentary is Perrow's seven ingredients model of Bhopal: toxic substance, residential area, gas cloud, particular weather pattern, most people home in bed, no alarm sounded, and unawareness of toxicity of the gas. Perrow argues that four or five of these conditions are present in accidents that happen regularly in the US (and, no doubt, everywhere else). "But one day all seven elements will combine, and America will know at first hand what happened in Bhopal" (cited in Bhargava 1988: n. 15). A health catastrophe that has already happened "here" (for those living in the First World) and is being exacerbated by TNC marketing in the Third World, is the scourge of tobacco-related deaths and illnesses (Sklair 1998).

Global Corporate Citizenship as a Globalizing Practice: Deconstructing Shell

The thesis of this chapter is that like FDI and world best practice (and global vision), global corporate citizenship is an intrinsic feature of the globalizing corporation. As we have seen, many major corporations have focused their citizenship efforts on corporate governance, relations with their employees, corporate philanthropy, and community development, or on health and safety issues for consumers and citizens. Some major corporations, however, have developed comprehensive programs for global corporate citizenship and they exemplify the process of transforming corporate citizenship into a globalizing practice.

Early in 1998, Shell produced a 56-page glossy report under the title "Profits and Principles – Does There Have to be a Choice?" Everything about this report, from its provenance to its structure, from its choice of typefaces to its graphics, from the way it was publicized to its reflexivity, expresses the dilemmas and contradictions that face globalizing corporations in their efforts to resolve the growing crises of class polarization and ecology in contemporary global capitalism. It can, therefore, be taken as a leading exemplar of the quest for global corporate citizenship, as state of the art in this realm at the end of twentieth century. The following analysis of the Shell Report 1998 is predicated on the assumption that all globalizing corporations aspire to the views expressed in the Report and that, in its way, it serves as a benchmark for the policies and practices of global corporate citizenship.

The Shell Report 1998 was a direct and deliberate response to a series of dramatic events that involved the company in the mid-1990s. The Report begins: "We were all shaken by the tragic execution of Ken Saro-Wiwa [a prominent writer and human rights activist] and eight Ogonis by the Nigerian authorities. We were ill-prepared for the public reaction to plans to dispose of the Brent Spar off-shore storage buoy in deep water in the Atlantic" (p. 2). In both cases the company claims that it acted "honorably" but that "the conviction you are doing things right is not the same as getting them right" (p. 2). Under the title, "Shareholders Shame Shell" the *Guardian* newspaper (May 6, 1997) reported that Amnesty and WorldWide Fund for Nature had attacked Shell at a seminar organized by Pensions Investments Research Consultants (Pirc), ahead of the Annual General Meeting. This was said to be the first time a company in the UK had faced a shareholder resolution on environment and human rights. Amnesty was represented by Sir Geoffrey Chandler, a former Shell director, and the President of the WWF was the Duke of Edinburgh. Serious opposition indeed! The AGM in London was disrupted by human rights and environmental protesters amid considerable publicity. The anti-Shell campaign gathered momentum.[42]

The Shell Report 1998 claims that a planned process of change, "Transformation," had begun in 1994, predating these crises. Information and ideas for Transformation included a global consultative exercise aimed at two issues: first, society's expectations of multinational [*sic*] companies, and second, the reputation, image, and overall standing of Royal Dutch/Shell Group. This involved 7,500 members of the public in 10 countries, 1,300 opinion leaders in 25 countries, and 600 Shell employees in 55 countries – a considerable investment in money and management time and energy. The tone of the Report is that Shell had made mistakes while acting in good faith, that it took seriously the need to learn from these mistakes, and that this would be a continuing process involving all its stakeholders. Stakeholders are employees, those who own shares in the company, and everyone else who might be affected by anything the company ever does, in short, the majority of the population of the planet. In 1998, Shell companies had an interest in operations in more than 130 countries, the other 60 or so countries are mainly very small and poor.[43] Much is made of the fact that Shell first published a Statement of General Business Principles in 1976, subsequently revised and translated into 34 languages, and that the core values on which the Principles were based have been maintained from the beginning. So, the impression given is that the Report is part of an ongoing process of corporate citizenship, not a hasty response to the Nigerian executions and the Brent Spar fiasco, both of which resulted in large amounts of adverse publicity and some loss of revenue for the company.

Most environmental and human rights activists will find it difficult to believe that Shell would have reacted in the ways that it did had not these problems reached critical importance, which means to say that they were prominently publicized in the mass media and were affecting profits and the share price. This is probably a mistake. More than 100 major corporations had published dedicated corporate citizenship reports of one type or another in the 1990s (the majority focused on the environment and corporate giving). The fact that Shell issued the Report is not unusual, though it is in some respects a model of its kind. Nevertheless, two pieces of evidence demonstrate that Shell wished to draw maximum publicity to the Report when it was released in April 1998. First, the Report did contain at least one newsworthy item which was picked up by most of the financial and business press, radio, and TV. Twenty-three staff had been sacked in 1997 for soliciting bribes, mostly in Nigeria, Latin America, and Asia, plus at least one in the North Sea oilfields. Second, and certainly even more newsworthy to environmental activists, on the day the Report was released Shell announced that it was withdrawing its US subsidiary, Shell Oil (then the largest foreign company by revenues in the US), from the Global Climate Coalition.[44] Thus, generally speaking, Shell achieved a "good press" for its Report and won an important respite from its critics.

The structure of the Report and its reflexive nature are of considerable interest for any analysis of how the globalizing corporation deals with corporate citizenship. The Report is divided into an Introduction proclaiming that "This report is about values" and eight sections. The first and by far the largest section, "Living up to our Principles" (pp. 5–30), outlines the Statement of General Business Principles (see above) and the extent to which the company lives up to them. "Principle 1, Objectives" tells us what the business is about, namely Return on Average Capital Employed (ROACE), the key performance measure of most commercial enterprises. This is absolutely standard in all corporate citizenship publications and is the critical clue for solving the puzzle of what, exactly, is the most important target audience for such reports. The answer is: the financial community, those who influence the share price. This impression is confirmed by "Principle 2, Responsibilities," in which Shell recognizes five areas of responsibility: to shareholders, to customers, to employees, to those with whom they do business, and to society.[45] "Principle 3, Economic Principles" transmits the messages: "Without profits, no private company can sustain principles. Without principles, no company deserves profits." "Principle 4, Business Integrity" contains the information about bribery that was noted above. Principles 5–9 (Political Activities; Health, Safety, and the Environment; the Community; Competition; and Communications) complete the list.

The second section comprises "Tell Shell" reply cards, where readers are invited to comment on these Principles and how Shell approaches them. This is discussed below, when the reflexivity dimension of the Report is considered. The third section, "Issues & Dilemmas," covers six "critical social and environmental issues facing the Group," namely human rights, climate change, globalization and the role of multinational companies, operating in politically sensitive regions, dealing with industrial legacies, and renewable resources. This section is introduced with a quotation: "to fail to do good when it is in one's legitimate power to do so is rightly condemned by the world." This is attributed to Sir Geoffrey Chandler, chair of Amnesty UK, one of the critics of the company at the time of the trouble surrounding the 1997 AGM. Each issue/dilemma is briefly outlined and Shell's approach is presented. There is no attempt to argue that any of these problems can be solved to everyone's satisfaction. Shell's approach is to open up all the problems to discussion, involve as many stakeholders as wish to be involved through reply-paid responses and the company's website, and introduce administrative procedures and action plans where appropriate.

The fourth section (pp. 46–7), "Contributing to society," is a statement by John Elkington, chairman of the environmental and management consultancy SustainAbility, that introduces his idea of the triple bottom line. Here Elkington describes how he was wooed by Shell, turned them down on several occasions and finally, obviously impressed by Shell's commitment to change and acceptance of the logic of the triple bottom line, agreed to work with the company.[46]

The fifth section is a "Message from the Chairman," Cor Herkstroter, with a Road Map of the Group's plans to manage and measure Shell's contribution to sustainable development and social accountability (pp. 48–51). The Report concludes with an Auditors' Report by KPMG in The Hague and Price Waterhouse in London, an Annex listing Group publications and structure, and the reply-paid envelope for comments. The back page reinforces the message with the words: Join the global debate.

The structure of the Shell Report-1998 is, therefore, what modernist sociology would term reflexive modernization. "The reflexivity of modern social life consists in the fact that social practices are constantly examined and reformed in the light of incoming information about those very practices, thus constitutively altering their character" (Giddens 1990: 38). Business, especially foreign investment and exporting, has always been reflexive in this sense, as reports from salespeople and managers in the field, and the practices of market research, demonstrate. What is different about the globalizing corporation is that, for the first time, information from a wide variety of stakeholders is being systematically collected globally and is constitutively altering the character of business practices. All the way through, the Shell Report 1998 exhibits built-in reflexivity. The first page consists entirely of the following message in reader-friendly green handwritten script:

> We care about what you think of us.
> We want you to know more about how we work and how we strive to live up to our principles.
> This report is part of a dialogue, and we will continue to seek your views.

The second page explains how "Debating expectations" in the move from a "trust me" to a "show me" world have changed the ways that multinationals must respond to their critics. Evidence that this was being taken seriously by Shell comes from the details of the consultation process (described above) involving thousands of stakeholders all over the world. Within the company, reflexivity operated through various "Letters" that top managers are required to sign to commit them in writing to the Statement of General Business Principles. This process began in 1978 with the introduction of the Letter of Representation which every Chief Executive and Chief Financial Officer of every Shell company was required to sign. In 1997, all Boards of Shell companies were invited to adopt the Group Business Principles as their own company policy. In addition, all country chairmen [*sic*] were required to sign a new Business Principles Letter, committing them to company principles, with specific requirements for different countries. This process was still underway by the time the 1998 Report was published, when 127 of the total of 129 Business Principles letters had been received. These letters were discussed with management teams, though it is uncertain how comprehensive these processes were. Discussion of the Principles (see above) is punctuated with messages in the green handwritten script. For example: "We strive to be good corporate citizens but we sometimes make mistakes" and "Our commitments are to the communities and the nations in which we operate, not just to the government of the day."

Discussion of the Principles is concluded with three tear-off pages itemizing nine questions and issues on the one side and space for "Your view" on the other. Respondents are asked to tick a box for each of the possible nine views if they would like their views posted on the Shell website. These opportunities to express views are structured somewhat like seminar or exam questions. Readers are asked to debate: Shareholder value versus social investment? Go in or stay out? When is a fee a bribe? And, of course, What do you think of this Report? On each of these pages (between pages 30 and 31) the same message is presented down the left-hand margin framing, literally and discursively, the context in which views are sought.

> In considering many of the following questions you may find it helpful to put yourself in the position of the manager of a local operating company of a multinational corporation. Imagine that your company has been present in the country in question for 75 years. It has assets of some US$500 million and 1,000 employees of whom 98 percent are local staff. The revenue generated for the local government by your operations represents some 20 percent of the national GDP. Over the last 50 years there have been several different regimes in power. These situations are typical of those faced by some managers in the everyday conduct of their business and the factors they have to take into account when making decisions.

Shell strives to give the impression that it is worthwhile for readers of the Report to take the trouble to respond. The reply-paid envelope for views on the nine issues was valid in all countries except Canada, Congo, and Laos (they do not subscribe to the international reply-paid system). "We really do want to receive your views [the envelope flap assures us]. Your comments will be taken into account and published on our website, if you so wish." No one should be in any doubt that Shell Report 1998 was part of an ongoing process of corporate global citizenship, in which the views of all stakeholders can get a fair hearing.[47]

The typeface and graphics of the report have been commented on above. Given the amount of time, effort, and money devoted to the look and style of corporate publications, it is obvious that corporations take these matters seriously, and so should we. The cover picture shows a herd of caribou crossing a tundra pond. I am sure that I am not alone in finding this a beautiful image. Shell provides its own deconstruction. "This picture captures the vulnerability of life; of communities moving and changing as they go. It serves to emphasize the respect, care and sensitivity which companies, governments and all other influential bodies must exercise. And for us, it also illustrates our fundamental belief that we do not have to choose between profits and principles." In one sense, this is baffling. Does a picture of caribou crossing a tundra pond resolve the issue of profits versus principles? It does not. But asking this question misreads the point of the picture on the cover of the Shell Report. The point of the pleasing image is to mediate between the question and the answer that the company immediately gives. Shell proclaims its "fundamental belief that we do not have to choose between profits and principles." So, while this highly reflexive Report is full of invitations (join the global debate) and concrete opportunities (send your views in the reply-paid envelope, put them on the internet) for all the stakeholders to let the company know what they think, it answers the question and provides soft closure of the issue on the inside front cover. Despite its protestations that all questions are open, everything can change, Shell has already decided on the answer. Fundamental beliefs are not normally open to genuine debate.

This is an excellent illustration of the representation of reflexivity in the global capitalist system, and may be familiar to those who have experienced consultation exercises in institutions striving to find progressive, non-authoritarian solutions to their problems. "We hope, through this Report and by our future actions, to show that the basic interests of business and society are entirely compatible" (p. 3) is an exemplary statement of what we can call "reflexive closure." That is the presentation of a position that in itself is not open to question (that you do not have to choose between profits and principles) and the recognition that people, even friends, still have to be persuaded. The issue is closed, but the process of persuasion, testing, measuring, matching actions to promises, matching policies to principles, is open and ongoing for all stakeholders wherever they may be. The international reply-paid envelope ensures that (with the possible exception of those in Canada, Congo, and Laos who cannot afford a stamp) everyone who can read and write can join in.

The Report is lavishly illustrated. Snapshot photographs are captioned with handwritten script messages (20 million customers a day; Shell community support in the Philippines; Street protest, London; Encouraging road safety in Thailand; Sponsored teachers in Nigeria, etc.). Tables and figures, for the most part, clearly show how business and social targets of various types have been achieved. The only picture of a senior Shell executive is that of Cor Herkstroter, Chairman of the Committee of Managing Directors. This picture accompanies his message, his credo, "There does *not* have to be a choice between profits and principles" (p. 48, underline in original in handwritten script), and a Road Map [*sic*] of the details and timings of Shell's plans to satisfy its Principles. While rather confusing at first sight, this Road Map repays study.

Part of the confusion is in the title. It is not so much a Road Map as a flow chart of company history from the 1950s to the year 2002 illustrating how far financial, environmental, and social systems in the company have evolved from immature (represented by a white band) through developing and mature (getting darker) to integrated (green, of course). Most of the maturity (with the exception of financial accounting and standards) and integration appears to be concentrated in the late 1990s and the future. The bottom of the chart is labeled "Engagement" (defined as "encouraging a dialogue with critics and interested parties"), and shows how external and internal engagement have evolved since the 1950s. The point of the Road Map appears to be to provide a checklist against which the corporate citizenship aspirations and achievements of the company could be measured. As such, it is useful, but again as part of a global consultation exercise it does give the impression of closure, that the direction and structure of change are established at least up to the year 2002. The Road Map is, then, another graphic representation of "reflexive closure."

The Shell Report, therefore, was certainly one of the highest expressions of global corporate citizenship produced in the twentieth century. This analysis of its substance, style, and form of argument shows how Shell has turned global corporate citizenship into a powerful globalizing practice. Other major corporations are not far behind. How the corporations have measured up to the environmental challenge is the subject of the next chapter.

Notes

1 "As the Citizens Fund reported in September 1992, '230 times more toxic waste was emitted in the neighborhoods near the plants of the fifty largest industrial toxic producers in New Mexico] than in the communities of the

chief officers of the companies [responsible for the waste].' Seventy percent of these executives lived in communities where toxic emissions from industrial facilities were zero. . . . as study after study has recently shown, the burden of living in unhealthy communities falls disproportionately on people of color and on working and low income people" (Southwest Organizing Project 1995: vii). See also Westra and Wenz (1995).

2 In the next chapter I develop the idea that there are "embattled green minorities" in many globalizing corporations who appreciate the contradictions in the corporate version of sustainable development, but who are unable to cope with them. My interviews inside the corporations suggest that there are also social-democratic minorities in most major corporations whose pressure over the years for corporate citizenship is only now bearing fruit.

3 Thus: "American activist groups, which have largely focused on the domestic social performance of major corporations, are now turning their attention more intensively on international trade and investment operations. This interest is symbolized by the recent launching of *Multinational Monitor*, a new monthly magazine published by Ralph Nader's Corporate Accountability Research Group. This magazine represents the globalization of US activist demands for corporate responsibility and accountability and offers a continuing vehicle for comparable groups around the world to exchange information and publicize firms that are the targets of their campaigns" (Barovick 1980: 53).

4 Not all businesses welcome the culture-ideology of consumerism. It is not necessarily in the interests of small merchants and those who supply them to sell ever more of their products, which may necessitate longer hours of work, more staff, more administration, more stock, more debt, more waste, and so on. An example of this is the sometimes unwelcome pressure on organic and craft producers to supply supermarkets on a scale that undermines the reasons for going organic or crafty in the first place.

5 A survey carried out by the Council on Economic Priorities in 1998 on the codes of conduct of 71 US companies, revealed that 40 made no attempt to monitor their labor codes, and very few used external auditors to check that codes were being followed. I expand this discussion in the section on "Employee Relations" below.

6 This was the first important victory for the antiglobalization coalition that developed rapidly from the mid-1990s. For details see Mander and Goldsmith (1996: 533–6). The campaigns for and against the MAI can be followed on the internet.

7 Charkham was a former director of PRO NED (a group to promote non-executive directors in the UK). He was seconded from the Bank of England to serve on the Cadbury Committee which attempted to establish best practice for corporate governance in Britain in 1992 with, it may be said, a good deal of support from big business. The organization Transparency International campaigns on the topic through its publications and website.

8 This is a very clear example of where "internationalization" really means "globalization" in a non-state-centrist sense.

9 CALPERS (California Public Employee Retirement Scheme) is a major investor in a host of US and, more recently, overseas companies and a scourge of underperforming corporations and their boards. Its first foray into the Japanese equity market was in 1994.

10 Gomes-Casseres (1996) in his book *The Alliance Revolution: The New Shape of Business Rivalry* discusses how Japanese TNCs are working with as well as against their "competitors." He makes the useful point that some, though not all, strategic alliances need and develop their own systems of collective governance and that this may bring some reluctant Japanese and other corporations into the fold. The point is that where some globalizing corporations do implement good citizenship measures globally it is in their commercial interests to ensure that all their competitors do so as well. See also Kester (1991) for the differences between the US and Japanese systems of corporate governance and "change without convergence," and Mallin and Rong Xie (1998) for evidence that corporate governance in China is being influenced by the Anglo-Saxon model. The journal *Corporate Governance: An International Review* is useful on these issues.

11 See also "globalization of Japan" in Castells (1998, ch. 4).

12 The Greenbury Report of 1995 recommended a code to tie executive compensation to specific performance criteria. After an initial flurry by corporations in the UK to improve their practices, research by the remuneration specialists New Bridge Street Consultants in 1999 suggested that discredited share option schemes appeared to be on the increase again and that failing executives were continuing to award themselves massive pay increases.

13 In fact, Prudential Australia was spun off from the parent company in the UK in 1998, presumably in the belief that it would do better as a separate, but perhaps not entirely separate, company.

14 The entertaining book by Sykes (1994) provides strong evidence for the claim that of all the contenders for the country in most need of a system of corporate governance (at least in the First World) Australia took first place.

15 It was subsequently stated in the *Financial Times* ("Broken Hill Chairman Apologises for Poor Performance," Sept. 23, 1998) that shareholder groups demanded and got the resignation of both the CEO and the chairman. They were held responsible for a loss of 40 percent in the company's share price between the start of 1997 and September 1998. Corporate governance with a vengeance!

16 Not wishing to be misunderstood on this sensitive issue, I am not implying that members of such boards engage in corrupt practices (although this cannot be entirely excluded). My meaning is that they are increasingly necessary precisely because of the increasing reputational costs of corrupt practices. For a useful review of the US Foreign Corrupt Practices Act twenty years on, see the whole issue of *Northwestern Journal of International Law and Business* 18 (Winter 1998). Of particular relevance is the paper by Gantz (1998), a sober assessment of the problems and prospects for solving them.

17 For example, in the USA each state has its own business legislation, Delaware being traditionally the most permissive; in some regions of Europe there are special concessions for incoming corporate investors; and in China, cities, provinces, and national rules for TNCs differ to some extent. In what follows I shall focus on the national and global, but the point about subnational differences is another timely reminder of the inadequacies of state-centrism.

18 "Pressure on Congress and the White House to increase the immigration quota for information technology workers rose yesterday as the Senate judiciary committee heard warnings from Silicon Valley that jobs could move overseas and the US could lose out in the global IT market unless the cap is lifted" ("Senate Told of Shortage of IT Staff," *Financial Times*, Feb. 26, 1998). In Ireland, electronics companies have lobbied the government to change tax laws to permit more attractive stock option plans for top technicians. At the other end of the spectrum, the proportion of US companies offering remedial maths and reading skills rose from 4 percent in the late 1980s to 18 percent in 1998 (Schiller 1999: 153).

19 An interesting example of this is the Sumitomo subsidiary, Sumicem, manufacturing fibre-optic couplers in Ireland. Sumicem considers Sumitomo, to whom it sells some of its production, more as a customer than as a parent company, and gives it no special privileges.

20 In his angry denunciation of corporate power, Korten (1995: 233) has a rare good word to say about the then CEO for this laudable resolution of the problem in Bangladesh. Nevertheless, Korten goes on to point out that Levi Strauss lost its place in a listing of the 100 best companies to work for in the USA when the compilers visited the Levi's plant in El Paso to discover that the benefits reported by headquarters staff were not, in fact, enjoyed by Levi's workers in El Paso. The twin cities of El Paso and Cuidad Juarez have long been sites for low-wage women garment workers (see Sklair 1993, ch. 5).

21 I am grateful to Professor Sethi for details of this case. For a list of 224 shareholder resolutions to 151 companies in the USA with their sponsors compiled by Interfaith Center on Corporate Responsibility, see Bratcher (1999). Most of these are on human rights abuses and environmental issues.

22 I remember as a schoolboy in Thornliebank, a small industrial village outside Glasgow, Scotland, reading on occasion in the Crum Memorial Library. Crum was a local engineering family with substantial interests in nearby industrial estates. Andrew Carnegie, another notable Scottish philanthropist, built many libraries all over the World.

23 Coca-Cola faces steep competition. In 1992, Penn State University gave exclusive marketing rights on campus to Pepsi in exchange for about $8 million for scholarships and buildings.

24 Diageo has also been active in the field of diversity (for example, through its Burger King Diversity Action Council to encourage business relations with ethnic minorities) and sustainable community development (through

its decision to build up its supply of Irish cream when sales of its major brand, Bailey's, expanded rapidly, rather than sourcing the cream from elsewhere).

25 My respondent, interviewed in California in 1996, was not forthcoming about this either. It is possible that Fluor preferred to give quietly. My informant at the private company Bechtel, along with Fluor among the biggest in this industry, made the point that his company did not publicize its corporate philanthropy. Perhaps they were both well known for good deeds among their significant others. Bechtel, certainly, was well known in some quarters for corporate crimes and misdemeanors.

26 One important indication of the company's genuine interest was the establishment of the BP Corporate Citizenship Unit at Warwick University Business School. Chris Marsden, formerly Head of BP Community Affairs, was the first Director of this unit, and I am very grateful to him for discussions on corporate citizenship. BP's environmental policy and practices are discussed in chapter 7.

27 This organization works extensively all over the world to encourage and facilitate corporate support for community development, with a good deal of success (see Nelson 1996).

28 To put this in perspective, this is exactly the sum that BP committed to invest in the new "BP Institute" of petroleum sciences at the University of Cambridge. For details, see "Super-deals Put Cambridge on the Corporate Funding Map," *Financial Times*, April 23, 1998). The headline is somewhat misleading – as the article notes, in the 1940s Shell gave Cambridge the equivalent of £20 million in today's money to establish a department of chemical engineering.

29 These cases were not widely reported, but see "Heartbreak in Sundown City," (*Guardian*, April 12, 1997); and "Oilmen Dread Colombian 'Kiss,'" (*Observer*, Nov. 3, 1996). I consider a third case of principles and profits for BP, the aftermath of the Exxon Valdez oil spill in Alaska, in chapter 7.

30 For case studies of the social and environmental consequences of oil industry activity in Latin America, see Gjording (1991) and Sabin (1998).

31 See "Unilever's Sticky Fingers: Inside a Multinational," *New Internationalist* (June 1987). An official history of Unilever is Reader (1980). Konings (1998) is a rare critical analysis of a Unilever subsidiary in Cameroon that illustrates richly the complexities of foreign direct investment and the follies of rushing to judgment on specific cases. It is most ironic that two manufacturers of luxury products, The Body Shop (cosmetics) and Ben and Jerry's (speciality ice-creams), are widely considered to be leaders in the fields of corporate citizenship and sustainable development.

32 On the US–Mexico border, see Fox (1991) and Sklair (2000). The discussion of "worker-blame discourses" in matters of occupational safety in Hall (1996) is of considerable relevance here. These issues are revisited in chapter 7, where the case of Intel is discussed.

33 For a more detailed analysis of Rio Tinto's policies and problems in the environmental sphere see chapter 7 below.

34 The two extremes of the consumer movement in Britain are exemplified by the Consumers' Association, whose influential campaigning is part of an ever-expanding commercial empire that never challenges consumption in general, and the radical *Ethical Consumer* magazine, a valuable resource on consumer boycotts and the real costs of consumption. Similarly, in the USA the work of the Consumer Association can be contrasted with the organizations and publications associated with Ralph Nader.

35 These boycotts continued into the 2000s (see the newsletter of Baby Milk Action in the UK and the <babymilk> website). In October 1999, Nestlé's new CEO, Peter Brabeck-Letmathe, began a PR offensive with a series of information packs on the infant formula issue, including a Report to the Director-General of the WHO reproducing supportive letters from government agencies in over 50 countries allegedly confirming Nestlé's compliance with the WHO code.

36 My account here is based mainly on Pearson (1987, esp. chs. 10 and 11), Bhargava (1988), Hartley (1993), and the continuing Bhopal update, accessible via the Corporate Watch website. McCormick (1992: 230n58) correctly notes that the attention drawn by Bhopal overshadowed another catastrophe, with some features in common, that took place in a suburb of Mexico City shortly before. We may also note that in its 1998 Environment Report, BHP actually builds into its incident severity rating system, "public/media" reaction, where "Public concern restricted to local complaints" is one of 8 criteria of level 1 (low severity) and "Probable public or media outcry (with national or international coverage)" is one of the eight criteria of level 5, the highest severity level (Appendix G). For interesting discussion of how health and environmental issues are treated in the media, see Adam (1998, ch. 5).

37 As of this writing, people are still dying from the effects of the catastrophe. According to the Bhopal website, Indian Council of Medical Research reports from 1998 estimated that almost one-quarter of the exposed population still surviving was chronically ill. Union Carbide (subsequently renamed Eveready Industries India Ltd.) dismantled and sold off most of the original factory in 1998 amid claims that vital evidence was being destroyed. The legal proceedings drag on.

38 Rowell (1996: 96n141) cites a source from 1992 naming several corporations who were guilty of similar double standards while claiming noble environmental credentials. These included BASF, Ciba-Geigy, Dow, DuPont, ICI, Monsanto, and Shell. It is likely that some of these were corrected during the 1990s.

39 The same sentiment is expressed more dramatically in a study of social movements in India. "Bhopal was the major disaster that revealed for the whole world the murderous nature of the multinational companies and of the capitalist 'development' that was the major ideological base of postindependence third world regimes" (Omvedt 1993: 149).

40 Tsuru (1993: 249n5) explains that the widely-used Japanese term *kogai* (environmental disruption) literally means "disamenities and damages inflicted on the public."

41 "While the Bhopal methyl isocyanate poisonings have raised a red flag for producers and regulators of hazardous chemicals, smaller yet similar flags have been raised by reports of commonplace poisonings and sloppy application of hazardous chemicals in Mexican export agriculture" [and in many other countries, LS] (Goodman 1987: 94). Here Goodman refers to Bayer of Mexico products. This, of course, raises the central question, asked to powerful effect by the manufacturers of guns, cigarettes, infant formula, powerful cars, and many other potentially dangerous goods: how can we control how people use our products?

42 Protesting outside or, where possible, inside the AGMs of large corporations is a familiar form of opposition. In the 1990s RTZ (now Rio Tinto), Barclays Bank, HSBC, British Aerospace, and Hanson among others have been attacked in the UK in this way; in the USA, buying shares and putting challenging resolutions to shareholder meetings is a popular method (Bratcher 1999); and there is some evidence that even in Japan shareholders are beginning to protest (Kakabadse and Okasaki-Ward 1996: 44–55).

43 As with so many ideas in everyday use, the term "stakeholders" has a profoundly ideological aspect.

44 This organization was widely seen as an obstructionist corporate lobby dedicated to blocking regulation related to climate change. Shell's decision was enthusiastically welcomed by Greenpeace and other environmental organizations. I shall return to this issue in the next chapter.

45 Although I consider typography later, it is worth mentioning here that the first two areas of responsibility are in bold black type, with commentaries in green while the last three are in fading grey type, with no commentaries at all. These typefaces and formats are reversed on subsequent pages where the other areas are discussed, but the initial impression of the typography confirms that of the order of listing: two important responsibilities (to shareholders and customers) and three less important.

46 SustainAbility has been working with major corporations for some time. For example, the 1992 issue of its in-house magazine *SustainAbility News* features a cartoon on the cover highlighting the consultancy's role in the environmental reports of BT, Dow, BP, ICI, IBM, British Airways, Union Carbide, Monsanto, and Norsk Hydro. The firm promotes what I would term a green culture-ideology of consumerism through the bestselling *Green Consumer Guide* and its various spin-offs. It is, therefore, difficult to understand why there was so much agonizing about the Shell business.

47 By January 2000 about 100,000 English-language copies of the Report had been distributed, plus translations into several other languages. These numbers include internal distribution to *circa* 80,000 employees of the company. Frynas (2000) raises disturbing issues for Shell in Nigeria.

Chapter 7
The Transnational Capitalist Class and the Struggle for the Environment

Business corporations have had legal obligations to safeguard the health and safety of their employees for more than a century. Indeed, it was the reports of the Factory Inspectors in nineteenth-century England that Marx used to such devastating effect in his moral indictment of the barbarities of the capitalist system. The British Factory Acts of 1847 and 1874 were among the first halting steps towards a still incomplete system of protection for the health and safety of workers. Chapter 6 (above) argued that an intrinsic part of the globalizing of the corporations is their acceptance of some measure of global corporate citizenship. Globalizing corporations routinely tell us about what they have done to safeguard the rights and improve the conditions of their employees and those affected by their activities. The idea that corporations should also share responsibility for the health and safety of the planet – a further dimension of global corporate citizenship – is of much more recent vintage. This chapter investigates the ways in which the globalizing corporations have dealt with environmental challenges that have been building up over the past decades.[1]

The chapter is organized in four sections. First, the history and theory of corporate environmentalism, the most significant TNC response to environmental problems, are considered. The second section discusses the corporate capture of some parts of the environmental movement through the creation of a "sustainable development historical bloc." In the third section, the policies of some major corporations are compared with their practices on specific environmental issues. The final section deals with the corporate ideology of sustainable development as a globalizing ideology through an analysis of the ecological crisis of consumerist capitalism.

Sometimes it is convenient and appropriate to use the terms *environ-*

mental and *ecological* interchangeably. However, there are instances where it is important to distinguish them (see, notably, Dobson 1990). The transnational capitalist class has successfully resisted the pressures from ecological radicals to move from piecemeal responses to separate environmental problems that global consumerist capitalism can handle, to a coordinated response to a singular ecological crisis, which is far more threatening to the global capitalist system.

History and Theory of Corporate Environmentalism

The evocative phrase "corporate environmentalism" was coined by Edgar Woolard, then CEO of DuPont, in 1989. The shock of Bhopal globally (see chapter 6 above) and the Superfund legislation in the USA, were important triggers for the concept and the ideology of corporate environmentalism.

The Superfund legislation of 1980 was intended to make corporate polluters pay for the Environmental Protection Agency (EPA) to clean up their mess. This was, as Dowie observes, "a major defeat for corporate America, and – but for the immediate and very strategic creation of the Superfund Coalition – it would have been a major triumph for the environment movement" (Dowie 1995: 89). The Coalition was created in 1987 by Dow, DuPont, Monsanto, GE, Union Carbide, and major insurance companies, and was influential in the reform of the Act that created partnerships between corporations and regulatory authorities to clean up toxic sites, reducing industry's burden. Superfund was certainly very important, and it failed because of the conflict over who would pay the toxic debt, estimated by one scholar at over $100 billion. The "failure of legislators and regulators to take effective and timely action is related to the economic and political power of major corporate polluters: the power to use government as an instrument of self-interest and the power that derives from a central role in capitalist development" (Barnett 1994: 2). Barnett identified among the major polluters the oil companies Exxon, Mobil, Texaco, Chevron, OXY, Amoco, and ARCO and the chemical companies DuPont, Dow, Union Carbide, and Monsanto. Of the 12 companies associated with the largest number of sites, 8 were petrochemical majors (including DuPont, Monsanto, Union Carbide, Mobil, and Exxon) plus GE, Westinghouse, Ford, GM, and Shell Oil. Superfund highlighted the global problem of the environmental impacts of the major corporations in pursuit of their business goals.

For decades, theorists of singular ecological crisis and multiple, but manageable, environmental problems have argued over the future prospects for life on the planet. Major corporations always tried to keep these ideas apart, but the argument climaxed in the late 1980s and early 1990s under the pressures of globalization. Corporate environmentalism, in all but name, had already become the key concept for those corporations trying to cope with the environmental problems that had been identified over the preceding decades in their various industries. As noted in chapter 6, many commentators date the key event that began to create significant public awareness of the emerging ecological crisis as the publication of Carson's bestselling critique of the chemical industry, *Silent Spring*. The fact that Monsanto and other corporations tried unsuccessfully to suppress the book gives some indication of the high stakes involved.[2] In his authoritative history of the global environmental movement, McCormick (1992) names one of his chapters "The Environmental Revolution (1962–1970)," giving *Silent Spring* pride of place. Subsequent disasters, like the *Torrey Canyon* (1967) and Santa Barbara (1969) oil spills, toxic contamination that provoked hundreds of antipollution suits in Japan in the 1970s, Bhopal in 1984, and *Exxon Valdez* in 1989, reinforced these problems. At the same time, sustainable development was emerging as the key concept for those who were thinking about almost any issue with an environmental aspect (for a comprehensive review see McManus 1996).

This view received dramatic confirmation in one of the key texts of the movement animated by the ecological crisis interpretation of the future of the planet, *For the Common Good*, by Daly and Cobb (1994). In the conclusion of their award-winning book they appealed to several groups of people for support:

> There is still another group whose support we covet. This is that rather small group of persons who have a deep and knowledgeable concern for the Third World. . . . We have in mind specifically the kind of people who co-operated in writing the Brundtland Report (*Our Common Future*), which calls attention to the idea of sustainable development . . . As the concept of sustainable development is further defined, we believe it will begin to resemble our outline of an economics for community. (ibid., p. 371)

Although this might sound a little disingenuous – sustainable development became a major industry while their economics for community sank almost without trace – it clearly expressed a fundamental truth: sustainable development was seen as a prize that everyone involved in these arguments wanted to win. The winner, of course, gets to redefine the concept.

We can trace the first indication that some members of the corporate elite were beginning to take the ecological crisis seriously to the publication of *Limits to Growth*, sponsored by the Club of Rome (Meadows et al. 1972). This gave a modicum of business respectability to the profoundly anticapitalist thesis that growth had limits; but, in general, those who spoke for global capitalism were able to shrug off the deeper lessons of the "limits to growth" school as alarmist and naive. However, the problem would not go away and the more forward-thinking members of the global business community knew that they were going to have to deal with it, eventually. By the late 1980s it became clear that sustainable development was the answer and, as will be demonstrated below, it was eagerly taken up by globalizing corporations as they tried to cope with the emerging force of the arguments around the singular ecological crisis.[3]

The corporate response in the US and Europe to Bhopal and the problems it had so catastrophically highlighted evolved gradually throughout the 1980s. The chemical industry was clearly under pressure to be seen to be taking decisive action. An initiative of the Chemical Manufacturers Association (CMA) in 1988 in the USA resulted in the Responsible Care Program.[4] (The idea was first articulated in 1984 by chemical companies in Canada.) This was adopted by more than 170 members of the CMA (including Union Carbide) and announced to the investing public and concerned citizens in full-page advertisements in the *New York Times* and the *Wall Street Journal* on April 11, 1990. The British Chemical Industries Association had adopted its Responsible Care Program in 1989.

The analysis of ecological modernization theory – a modernist sociological rationale for corporate environmentalism – in Mol (1995) focuses on the chemical industry. The project of ecological modernization was to modernize modernity "by repairing a structural design fault of modernity: the institutionalized destruction of nature" (ibid., p. 37). In opposition to environmentalist counterproductivity or demodernization theories, hyperindustrialization[5] where ecological criteria drive industry was recommended. As the state had largely failed to take control of these processes, Mol argues, it is up to the corporations to do so. The role of state agencies changes from bureaucratic, top-down dirigism to "negotiated rulemaking and the creation of favorable condition for such transformation processes" (Mol 1995: 58). Environmental NGOs must change their ideology and become more cooperative, and as ecological modernization becomes increasingly interdependent with globalization, deindustrialization initiatives are marginalized. The chemical industry's Responsible Care Program certainly promoted this agenda, one entirely compatible with the maximization of profits.

Not only industries but international organizations of various types took it upon themselves to "do something" about the environment. The European Community introduced a Community-wide environmental auditing scheme in 1993. The World Bank (for whom Daly had been a senior economist) had been discussing the environmental aspects of their lending since the 1970s, with controversial results (see Rich 1994). The record of the OECD on environmental rules for transnational corporations is also instructive. The Environmental Committee of the OECD began to discuss the issue in the early 1980s. In January 1985, shortly after Bhopal, the Committee proposed that an environmental management chapter be added to the OECD (voluntary) Guidelines for Multinational Enterprises, first introduced in 1976. The proposal was strongly supported by all the governments of the OECD, with the exception of the UK (the US offered only lukewarm support). The strongest opposition to the proposal came from the Business and Industry Advisory Committee (BIAC)[6] which managed to block it (Gladwin 1987: 26). As the new millennium dawned the Environmental Committee of the OECD was still trying to legislate for a comprehensive system of environmental protection.

Why has it proved so difficult to enact effective legislation to protect the environment? One factor was clearly the phenomenon of poacher turned gamekeeper in the leadership of some bodies charged with environmental protection. Schrecker (1990) gives the example of the appointment of an Imperial Oil (Exxon) executive as adviser to Canada's Minister of the Environment, and Dowie (1995) gives many examples from the USA. However, it is clear from the evidence of the 1980s that even antiregulatory right-wing governments like those of Reagan and Thatcher could no longer entirely ignore environmental violations. For example, while the Reagan Administration was pulling the teeth of the EPA, at the same time it permitted the establishment of a powerful Environmental Crimes Unit in the Department of Justice (see Burch 1997, Part A, pp. 205–15). Schrecker speculates on a potential "environmental corporatism of the future" and describes the Canadian National Task Force on Environment and Economy (a response to Brundtland) in terms that are worth quoting. The Task Force:

comprised the federal Environment Minister and a number of his provincial counterparts, one academic, two representatives of non-governmental environmental organizations, the head of the Ontario Waste Management Corporation, and business representation including senior executives with some of the worst polluters (and most aggressive opponents of environmental regulation) in Canada. The Task Force completely excluded representatives of organized labor, thereby indicating the government's perception of their irrelevance. (Schrecker 1990: 184)

This is a good approximation of the local wing (in Canada) of what can be termed the "global environmental elite," though it is not always necessary to exclude labor-movement representatives. Job blackmail is a common tactic when business is threatened with serious enforcement of unwelcome environmental laws. In such cases, an alliance of: "Workers, corporate managers and local businessmen tend, with some exceptions, to line up on the same side of such issues. The other side . . . are often from outside the immediate area, and their immediate livelihoods are conspicuously not at stake" (Schrecker 1990: 186). Environmental politics is a distinctive form of class politics where the global and the local frequently intersect.[7]

Driving a wedge between the labor movement and the environmental movement has been a fairly successful strategy of the transnational capitalist class. Dewey (1998) argues cogently that the history of relations between environmentalism and labor in the USA (and elsewhere, to be sure) is rife with misperceptions. Unlike the traditional greens, from the 1940s to the 1960s labor-environmentalists connected conservation and the struggle against pollution under the rubric of the health and safety of workers and citizens. The history of early labor campaigning against air and water pollution – part of the attempt by unions in the USA (and Australia, for example) to take their work into the wider community – has many valuable lessons for explaining the outcomes of contemporary struggles. The AFL-CIO represented labor at the first two National (US) Conferences on Air Pollution in 1958 and 1962, and the union movement continued to take environmental issues seriously, under the leadership of Walter Reuther. Just before his death in 1970, Reuther warned of an impending environmental crisis and the need for these issues to be raised in union negotiations. The United Automobile Workers Union sponsored the first national environmental teach-in at the University of Michigan, two months before the first Earth Day in 1970. Amazingly, the UAW joined the Sierra Club, Wilderness Society, National Audubon Society, Environmental Action, Friends of the Earth, and Zero Population Growth in a letter to Congress calling for "air pollution control standards so tough they would banish the internal combustion engine from autos within the next five years" (quoted in Dewey 1998: 56). However, the oil embargo of 1973, chronic stagflation, and the pressure of foreign competition drove a wedge between labor and the emerging green movement. "Worried workers moved closer to management's anti-environmental views [in the 1970s], and both unions and environmentalists largely abandoned the earlier vision of a common front for social, economic, and environmental reform" (ibid., pp. 46–7). The alliance between organized labor and the environmental movement collapsed in the mid-1970s under the "industry-promoted argument that the nation could not afford the luxury of environmentalism" (ibid., p. 58). Environmental job blackmail became an important business tactic that is still in use, though by the 1990s corporations more commonly argued that environmental concern protected existing jobs and created new jobs. Ironically, Thatcher and Reagan's war against the unions in the 1980s drove some parts of the labor movement back towards the environmentalists. The campaigns against NAFTA, the MAI, and the WTO since then continued the process of reconnecting some parts of organized labor and greens in the USA and elsewhere.[8]

The major corporations were not, of course, standing idly by while the struggle over the environment was accelerating. Globally, big business response was orchestrated by the International Chamber of Commerce (ICC) based in Norway, which had been promoting an environmental agenda since the first UN environment conference in Stockholm in 1972. The ICC had members in more than 100 countries, though it was most active in Europe. It founded its own Commission on Environment in the 1970s, and its first World Conference of Environmental Management in 1984 attracted 500 leaders of industry, government, and environmental groups from 72 countries. The ICC was chosen to give the official business community input to the Bergen Ministerial Conference that led to the report of the UN World Commission on Environment and Development where the concept of sustainable development was firmly established. In the frank words of an ICC analyst of this process: "the Brundtland Report called on the cooperation of industry . . . the business community is willing to play a leading role, and to take charge" (Willums 1990: 3). And take charge of sustainable development it did.

An immediate consequence of the work of the ICC was the Global Environmental Management Initiative (GEMI) of 1990 formed to implement the Business Charter for Sustainable Development. Nineteen leading US transnational corporations announced their support for GEMI (including Union Carbide, desperate to rebuild its reputation after Bhopal). GEMI soon took on an institutional form in Washington DC.[9] While the organization that eventually resulted from these ICC environmental efforts, the World Business Council for Sustainable Development (WBCSD), was probably the most influential of the so-called "green business networks," it was one among many. Rowell (1996: 105) counted about 40 green business networks by the mid-

1990s.[10] For all their differences – local, national, or global, general or industry-specific, well or less well resourced – they all had one thing in common, their emphasis on self-assessment and voluntary codes where possible, but a decisive input into regulation where necessary. The consensus that came out of a colloquium of major corporations brought together by the consultants Arthur D. Little (Greeno 1998: 8) expressed this sentiment: "In fact, you don"t have to explore sustainable development very long before realizing that today's existing government structures cannot cope with many of its elements." In this respect, the globalizing neoliberal revolution associated with the Thatcher–Reagan attempt to mould state legislation to promote rather than to restrict the corporate interest (or "free enterprise" as it was ideologically constructed) was very successful.

The roots of the distinctive global capitalist theory of sustainable development can be traced to the discussions around the Brundtland Report, *Our Common Future*, presented to the General Assembly of the United Nations in 1987. The uneasy compromise between conceptualizing the problem as a set of environmental challenges and as a much more serious singular – indeed, planetary life-threatening – ecological crisis suited big business very well. An insight into corporate thinking on the issue was given by Stephan Schmidheiny, a Swiss billionaire who was to play a crucial role for big business at the Rio Earth Summit in 1992. His contribution to a pre-Rio ICC book – "The Entrepreneurial Mission in the Quest for Sustainable Development" (Schmidheiny 1990) – bears close scrutiny.

Until recently, Schmidheiny argued, environmental protection had been a defensive, negative, antiprogress concept. But now environmentalists and industrialists were beginning see each other's points of view and to compromise. Thus, the idea of "sustainable growth" had replaced the idea of "conservation" and industry could get on with its job. Limits to growth were not, as originally thought, limits on supplies, but "mostly on the side of disposing of resources which have been used and transformed in the productive process" (ibid., p. 36). How, Schmidheiny asked, can the industrial entrepreneur assist in sustainable development? Accepting that industry had to operate within existing frameworks, it can, nevertheless, act to use these frameworks for its own advantage. In the case of laws, rules, and regulations, business must "adopt an offensive attitude and creatively contribute towards ecological legislation" (ibid., p. 39), and where public opinion was concerned, industry must meet the "emotion of the ecologists" with "concrete solutions" and "facts." With a sentiment that roundly confirms the argument in previous chapters about the crucial change in direction that characterized global business, he concludes: "the most important outside input guiding the development of a business originates from the consumers" (ibid., p. 40).[11]

Thus, the negative environmentalism that Schmidheiny identified, that forced industries to respond to radical challenges on pollution and toxic hazards, gave way to more general conceptions of "sustainable growth" and "sustainable development" (entirely compatible concepts, in his analysis). Corporate environmentalism, therefore, both as a social movement and as an ideology, coexisted easily with this moderate conception of sustainability. From this powerful conceptual base big business successfully recruited much of the global environmental movement in the 1990s to the cause of "sustainable" global consumerist capitalism. This achievement is an object lesson in how dominant classes incorporate potential enemies into what Gramsci called new historical blocs. Historical blocs are fluid amalgamations of forces that coagulate into social movements to deal with specific historical conjunctures, reflecting concrete problems that have to be confronted by different social groups (Gramsci 1971). In the struggle for hegemony, historical blocs form and dissolve and reform. Big business mobilized a sustainable development historical bloc against what it saw as a threatening counterculture organized around the powerful idea of the singular ecological crisis, the "deep green" or ecological movement.

Corporate Capture of the Environmental Movement or Constructive Dialogue: The Creation of a Sustainable Development Historical Bloc

The global capitalist system exists in order to ensure the conditions for the continued accumulation of capital and its legally guaranteed conversion into private wealth. This it does globally through the economic institution of the TNC, politically through the transnational capitalist class, and through the culture-ideology of consumerism. How does the global environmentalist system work? Its characteristic institutional forms are what can be termed transnational environmentalist organizations, transnational environmentalist elites, and green consumerism.

The relationships between the global capitalist and the global environmentalist systems can be conceptualized in terms of coalitions that cluster around points along a continuum, rather than two mutually contradictory and irreconcilably opposed sets of social forces or historical blocs. A central struggle between these forces is over the ownership, redefinition, and effective monopoly of the public appropriation of sustainable development. Corporate environmentalism is the main weapon of those working for the global capitalist system to establish ownership of sustainable development and with it, bring the agents and agencies of global environmentalism over to its ways of thinking and doing. The transnational capitalist class, therefore, organized the sustainable development historical bloc. The main ideological and practical tasks of the members of this bloc are to deflect attention from the idea of a singular ecological crisis and to build up the credibility of the idea that what we face is a series of manageable environmental problems. Sustainable development, then, can be achieved piecemeal by meeting all these separate problems as they arise. On the other side of the argument are those within global environmentalism who cling to the idea of an impending singular ecological crisis and argue that it can only be averted by taking action to change the "system" as a whole (not always conceived as the global capitalist system). The argument that sustainable consumption is the key to sustainable development is most forcefully expressed at this point.

It would be incorrect to suggest that what I am calling the sustainable development historical bloc entirely ignores the problem of consumption. For example, Unilever and a few other companies have begun to elaborate "cradle-to-grave" (lifecycle) profiles for each of their main products. Without such analysis it is impossible to assess the environmental footprints of any business. One of the leading forces in the bloc, the World Business Council for Sustainable Development, of which Unilever is a member, has had this as an area of special study for some time. There is some indication that the secretariat and some of the corporate representatives (the embattled green minority), though not those who own and control the TNCs who make up the membership, see this as a major problem. As a Procter & Gamble executive put it: "The challenge we are all struggling with is how to bring sustainable development into the core of our businesses, so that it truly starts to create a force to push for competitive advantage and business success" (in Greeno 1998: 10). As we shall see below, this process has some way to go in P&G.

The connections between the characteristic institutions of global capitalism and global environmentalism grew dramatically in the 1980s and 1990s. These connections straddled the spectrum from direct and indirect TNC sponsorship of transnational environmental organizations (TEOs) to downright hostility and occasional violence between the parties and their allies. A first approximation of TEOs would include those in and around the UN system, notably the United Nations Environment Program, the Commission (subsequently Division) on Sustainable Development, and the Global Environmental Facility; and NGOs, notably the World Conservation Union, WorldWide Fund for Nature, Friends of the Earth, Greenpeace, and the International

Organization of Consumers Unions.[12] To this list must be added the myriad of smaller and usually specific issue-oriented organizations that mushroomed around the Brundtland Report and the UN Conference on Environment and Development in Rio in 1992, and its aftermath. While these are not necessarily all global, many of them are part of the global environmentalist network.

The sustainable development historical bloc began in earnest in the period leading up to the Earth Summit in Rio in 1992. The close relationship between Maurice Strong, the virtual CEO of the Earth Summit, and Stephan Schmidheiny is a matter of public record. The environmental arm of the ICC, the Business Council for Sustainable Development, represented big business in Rio (see above, and Willums 1990) and was successful in keeping any potential criticism of the TNCs off the official agenda.[13] There was, as a consequence, formidable corporate input into the formation of the UN Commission on Sustainable Development (CSD), the major institutional result of UNCED. The CSD has become a major transnational environmental organization in its own right. It evolved into a Division for Sustainable Development at the UN, and its major task was to monitor how member governments tested, developed, and used over 100 indicators of sustainable development. The extent to which it redirects attention away from the singular ecological crisis that threatens the very existence of global capitalism onto the multiple environmental problems that corporations can cope with and global capitalism can live with, will be a critical test for the success of the sustainable development historical bloc. The signs are not promising for deep ecologists. The basis on which the CSD approached its task of measuring consumption and production was as follows:

> Sustainable consumption and production are essentially two sides of the same coin. Sustainable consumption addresses the demand side, examining how the goods and services required to meet peoples' needs and improve the quality of life, can be delivered in a way that reduces the burden on the Earth's carrying capacity. The emphasis of sustainable production is on the supply side, focussing on improving environmental performance in key economic sectors such as agriculture, energy, industry, tourism and transport. (United Nations 1998)

From the ecological point of view this approach is based on a series of fallacies. The first is the anthropocentric approach itself (sustainability for people and societies taking precedence over sustainability for the planet). The second fallacy is the idea that "sustainable consumption" and "sustainable production" are essentially two sides of the same coin (for ecologists, the real issue is not "sustaining" production and consumption, but reducing them absolutely). In addition, ecologists argue that it is fallacious to assume that "meeting needs," "improving quality of life," and "improving environmental performance" are parts of the solution to the ecological crisis. They are not. They are parts of the problem, particularly in terms of distinguishing real from artificial needs and establishing universal norms for an ecologically sound quality of life. It need hardly be said that those who hold these views – radical ecologists – are a small minority, even in the environmental movement.[14]

Many important decisions relating to the regulation of the activities of TNCs take place in the rather secretive meetings of international trade organizations, notably the WTO, the successor of the GATT, and these are particular targets of the sustainable development historical bloc. Useful research has been done on how these powerful bodies are advised. Of the 111 members of the three main trade advisory committees to the US government on the 1979 Tokyo round of the GATT negotiations, 92 represented corporations, 16 were from trade industry associations (10 from the chemical industry), and 2 were from trade unions. The environmental advocacy seat was not filled. Of the 92 corporations represented, 27 had been assessed fines by the EPA for environmental offences and five (DuPont, Monsanto, 3M, GM, and Eastman Kodak) were then on the EPA top ten list of hazardous waste dischargers. All of these companies had lobbied against environmental legislation (Hilliard, cited in Korten 1995: 177–9). Studies of advisory committees for the Codex Alimentarius Commission and other regulatory bodies have noted similar patterns of representation (Avery, Drake, and Lang 1993). Repeated examples of industry errors (to give the companies the benefit of the doubt) that endangered health and damaged the environment in recent decades have forced significant changes in how corporations are regulated, but the system is still far from adequate.

At the national and local levels the process of global capitalist capture of the environmentalist movement accelerated on all fronts. In 1991, the premier US advertising magazine listed the connections between the hundred leading national advertisers and environmental groups, detailing cash donations and promotional programs. This demonstrated how deep the commercial dependence of local environmental groups on the corporate sector was (*Advertising Age* 1991). Further research by Dowie (1995) and Beder (1997) confirmed that the trend grew in the 1990s and that it was not confined to the USA. The extent to which local, grassroots environmental groups can resist the trend to corporate environmentalism and stay out of the sustainable development historical bloc is clearly a very fruitful topic for research (see Yearley 1996). The sustainable development historical bloc was based on the alliances that were forged between members of the transnational capitalist class and their representative organization, and the four groups that make up the transnational environmentalist elite – transnational environmental organization executives and their local affiliates, globo-localizing green bureaucrats, green politicians and professionals, and green media and merchants. The relations between these groups and the four fractions of the transnational capitalist class can be analyzed within the context of global capitalism's class polarization and ecological crises. While some leading figures in the transnational environmental elite had strong records of criticism and political organization against global capitalism on class and ecological issues, the connections between TEO executives, international organizations (particularly agencies of the UN), and TNCs (and other capitalist global organizations) certainly increased in the 1990s. Although the revolving door between transnational corporations and the green movement may not be as marked as that between TNCs and state agencies, channels of communication have grown rapidly. Dowie (1995) notes that by the 1990s most environmental lawyers worked for corporations, not for the NGOs that the original environmental lawyers created to sue the corporations for environmental crimes. This undoubtedly led to tensions within the environmental movement. Manes, in his evocatively titled book *Green Rage*, described how the radical Earth First! movement grew out of "disillusionment and exasperation with the reform environmental movement and its *idée fixe*, credibility" (Manes 1990: 66), and he documents the rise of "ecotage" (environmentally motivated sabotage). Rowell (1996, ch. 6) also documents the chilling corporate and corporate-implicated response to Earth First! and other environmental radicals.

Globo-localizing green bureaucrats play a crucial role in the struggle that ensues when the interests of global capitalism threaten the global environment. This group consists largely of those who have an official duty and moral commitment to protect and enhance the environment against the onslaughts of those who would damage it. Research on the major international and national environmental treaties and legislation provides ample evidence that few of these treaties and pieces of legislation threaten the ability of global consumerist capitalism to continue more or less as it has been doing over the past few decades. (See below for evidence from the struggle over global atmospheric change.)

The third fraction of the transnational environmental elite is composed of green politicians (leaders of Green parties), and the large numbers of non-Green party politicians who, for one reason or another, have jumped on to the green bandwagon in their local and/ or national and/or supranational constituencies. These were comp- lemented by the growing legions of green professionals (lawyers, academics, journalists, ethical investment analysts, consultants, etc.) dedicated to spreading the environmentalist message. Muckrakers delight in exposing politicians who appear to propound green mess- ages but are, in fact, working behind the scenes to further the interests of environmentally-suspect corporations (see, for example, Cockburn and Silverstein 1996, on "Greens and the Color of Money"). The establishment of the President's Council on Sustainable Development can be seen as a key moment in the creation of the historical bloc, at least in the USA. Dowie interprets this as a strategic maneuver by which Clinton distanced himself from the (marginally) more radical Gore by linking sustainable development and economic vitality. The Council was packed with corporate executives (for example, from Dow, DuPont, Ciba-Geigy, and Chevron), and "balanced" by green movement nota- bles, including "some of America's most accommodating pro-corporate environmentalists" (Dowie 1995: 184), all but one of whom had sup- ported NAFTA.

This phenomenon is not restricted to the USA (see Beder 1997). John Elkington, the founder of SustainAbility, a core member of the sustainable development historical bloc in Britain, has argued that big business is beginning to take its environmental and ethical responsibil- ities more seriously. SustainAbility produces an Annual Benchmarking Survey on corporate environmental reporting, and claimed that by 1998 more than 500 TNCs had published environmental reports. Elkington illustrates his argument with evidence of collaboration between corporations and environmental organizations. For example, BP worked with Greenpeace to develop solar power; Shell invited Greenpeace and others to seminars with senior managers to discuss Brent Spar; and Forum for the Future, a consultancy set up by Jonathan Porritt and Sara Parkin, former leaders of the Green Party, offered its British corporate members reduced consultancy rates. According to Porritt: "The old approach of trying to buy off environmentalists by pretending to be green is just not credible any more" (quoted in "Big Business Works for its Green Card," *Observer*, Feb. 22, 1998). Such statements from well-known green luminaries are music to the ears of the corporate creators of the sustainable development historical bloc and their allies in public relations.[15]

The fourth fraction of the transnational environmentalist elite con- sists of the green media and merchants, those who use environmental- ism to sell and promote products and services (Vandervoort 1991). Since the 1980s the green consumer has become a significant target for big business. Alliances between the merchants and media of global capitalism and the green merchants and media of the global environmentalist elite are common. For example, major supermarket chains (like Sainsbury's and B&Q in the UK) present themselves as environment-friendly with the support of environmental campaigners, while encouraging consumption without limits. Such activities tend to blur the contours of the critique of capitalism through rejection of the culture-ideology of consumerism, rarely a popular line of argument under the best of conditions.

The four fractions of the transnational environmental elite, including elements within traditional "back to nature" and "conservation" movements that previously spoke for and nurtured the environment, were transformed as a consequence of the relentless insertion of the whole world into the global capitalist system. It remains an open question whether and to what extent the global environmental elite can mount an effective challenge to protect and enhance environmental, let alone ecological, interests in the face of the unrestrained expansionism and resource profligacy that is inherent to the global capitalist project.

The widest context possible of this problem is global climate – the atmosphere in which planet earth and all living things exist. In 1973, the WHO established a global program of air-quality monitoring, with a group of 14 countries supplying data on sulphur dioxide and suspended particulate matter. This became part of a more general Global Environmental Monitoring System (GEMS) in 1976, supported by the United Nations Environment Program, and in 1985 the Global Resource Information Database was launched to distribute all the information collected. GEMS organizes the results of over thirty monitoring networks covering more than 140 countries. Tens of thousands of scientists from all over the world have participated in the program. The consensus of scientific opinion is that there is cause for concern in all five areas that GEMS monitors – climate change, transboundary pollution, natural resources, oceans, and health consequences of pollution.

Few environmental issues have engendered as much controversy as acid rain, the greenhouse effect, and global warming. They all connect with the undeniable fact that industrialization and present patterns of production and consumption have increased emissions of carbon dioxide, methane, nitrous oxide, and CFCs, collectively known as the greenhouse gases. Ninety-seven percent of greenhouse gases are water vapor, but it is the other 3 percent that scientists and many people who know very little about the science involved (including myself) are worried about, and these make the most headlines. Computer-based projections of temperature rises from 1 to 6 degrees fahrenheit over the next century alarmed politicians so much that a global climate treaty was signed in Rio in 1992. The 38 developed countries (more or less the First World plus the former Soviet bloc) who signed the Rio Treaty agreed to try to stabilize their greenhouse gas emissions at 1990 levels by the year 2000. Developing countries, notably China, India, South Korea, Brazil, and Mexico, were exempt. By mid-decade it was perfectly obvious that these targets were not going to be reached, and a new global climate conference at Kyoto, Japan (1997) set new targets, but this time they were to be legally binding on the 38 signatories. Once again, developing countries were exempt. Global climate treaties pitted environmentalists and the corporations against each other (if the worst-case scenario was correct, then many basic industries would have to change dramatically, perhaps go out of business). There was also disagreement about whether First World producers and consumerist lifestyles or Third World dirty industries and population pressure were most responsible.[16]

While the activities of the major corporations are by no means the only cause of climate change, their effects are generally agreed to be significant. Pressure on the corporations to be ever more environmentally responsible, therefore, grew steadily from the 1970s and as it grew individual companies, trade and industry associations, and their allies also started to organize to defend themselves in what Newell and Paterson (1998) label the fossil fuel lobby. One of the most effective members of the lobby and, thus, of the sustainable development historical bloc, was the Global Climate Coalition (GCC). GCC was formed in 1989 and by the mid-1990s claimed a membership of 60-plus major corporations and organizations representing more than 230,000 separate firms.[17] GCC had official status at major national and international meetings, including the Rio Earth Summit. It has also testified at US Congressional hearings and other high-level US governments meetings. Its claim to be "the lead business voice on climate change issues" was thus well founded. While the GCC was based in Washington DC and comprised mostly of US-based organizations, it represented global capitalism against attempts to restrict First World growth (essential, it argued, for growth in the Third World) through climate control regulation. It campaigned successfully against proposals to limit carbon dioxide emissions in the developed countries but not in the developing countries. GCC was widely blamed (or credited) for the inability of the Kyoto conference to reach a satisfactory agreement on limiting greenhouse gases.[18] This was achieved primarily by arguing that the Kyoto Treaty proposals would raise energy prices and cost millions of jobs in the First World.

Greenpeace and other environmental organizations campaigned against it and various boycotts of GCC members, in particular Exxon/Esso, Chevron, Ford, GM, Goodyear, Mobil, and Texaco, were declared. It is difficult to ascertain how effective these boycotts were, but they may have played some part in the decisions of Shell Europe and BP (followed by GM, Ford, and Amoco) to leave. A Business Environment Leadership Council was set up to challenge the GCC in the USA. BP and then Shell publicly repudiated the GCC stand at Kyoto against mandatory controls on greenhouse gas emissions and, in doing so, highlighted the real contradictions inherent in the ideas of "the entirely environmental corporation," sustainable development, and the future of global capitalism. In 1999, before a House of Commons environment select committee, a BP Amoco spokesman distanced the company from an Esso UK (Exxon) spokesman on the issues of the urgency of the problem of climate change, and the utility of a trading system for emission permits, which BP Amoco had begun to introduce (see "BP Clashes With Esso Over Action On Global Warming," *Guardian*, April 15, 1999). Newell and Paterson (1998) make a convincing argument that the main reasons for splits in (and the likely defeat of) the fossil fuel lobby were the gradual delinking of ever-increasing energy use from economic growth and insurance industry fears of weather-induced disasters. How long before someone sues the oil or auto companies over an avalanche in Europe, or floods in China or Mozambique?

Just as there are many differing and even antagonistic parts of the global capitalist system, the global Green system is not all of a piece. The distinction introduced at the beginning of the chapter between separate environmental problems and a singular ecological crisis is fundamental at this point. O'Riordan (1991: 6) argues that environmentalism has evolved through dry, shallow, and deep green phases, oriented to the problem of sustainable development.[19] Dry greens believe in the manipulation of the marketplace through benign self-regulation, while shallow greens criticize this "reinforcing of the pernicious status quo" and focus on community-based reform, eco-auditing, and environmentally benign consumerism. Among environmentalists, O'Riordan argues, only deep greens reject, by implication, the culture-ideology of consumerism and the whole global capitalist project.[20]

Does deep green ideology offer a real alternative to global capitalism and the culture-ideology of consumerism? Dobson's (1990) version of the distinction between environmentalism and ecologism builds on the seminal analysis of deep ecology by Arne Naess (1973), where the distinction between shallow instrumental concern with pollution and resource depletion and deep intrinsic concern with ecological principles was first drawn systematically. Dobson argues that the debate took two turns between 1973 and 1990. First, a theory of the intrinsic value of the environment was developed and, subsequently, a critique of this in terms of the need for a change of consciousness with respect to our relationship to the natural world. Deep ecologists are radically non-anthropocentric in the sense that they do not accept that human beings are the center of the universe. Generic mankind is replaced by some other concept of the whole biosphere. The growing strength of the corporate-led sustainable development historical bloc has increasingly marginalized all forms of radical ecological thinking and organization. Deep green environmentalism or ecologism does represent a radical rejection of global capitalism and the culture-ideology of consumerism, but its viability as a practical alternative to these is at present inhibited by its political weakness. Ecologism lacks a program that would appeal to those in the Third World who are presently without ready access to the consumer goods enjoyed by the majority of people in the First World, and to those in the First World who feel relatively deprived in terms of their spending power.

In the absence of a credible ecological alternative, globalizing corporations with the sometimes enthusiastic, sometimes reluctant assistance of major environmental organizations have created a sustainable development historical bloc. For many corporations, this has meant presenting a rather new environmental face to the public and green movement gaze but, as we shall see in the next section, the policies and principles of the corporations with respect to the environment and their actual practices are not always in perfect harmony.

Environmental Policies and Practices of Major Corporations

Historically, TNC environmental policies have largely been responses to official attempts to regulate the environmental impacts of business. In addition to national governmental initiatives in many countries, some international and transnational bodies have also moved into this arena. This has occurred, in particular, through the United Nations system since the 1950s (McCormick 1992; Weiss and Jacobson 1998). Two important developments in the 1990s were the Benchmark Corporate Environment Survey (not completed) and the Montreal Agreement on CFCs (quite successful). The Benchmark Survey was a project of the UN Center on Transnational Corporations to discover what environmental policies TNCs had in place and what TNCs were doing to improve their environmental performance. Data from 163 TNCs with sales of over one billion dollars were collected and analyzed before the project was aborted (Robbins 1996).[21] The Benchmark Survey was never completed because it was seen as a threat to major corporations, who had always been somewhat suspicious of the Center's attitude towards them, particularly in relation to TNC activities in the Third World. This suspicion was not entirely unjustified, particularly in the early days of the Center's work.

The Montreal Protocol of 1987 on the protection of the ozone layer was a very specific intervention into an activity that was restricted to a part of one, albeit major, industry. While the chief US negotiator was quoted as saying, "the signatory countries sounded the death knell for an important part of the international chemical industry, with implications for billions of dollars of investment and hundreds of thousands of jobs in related sectors" (cited in Benedick 1991: 1), the actual Protocol and subsequent agreements did not, in fact, damage the international chemical industry very much. Phase-out periods were generous and well supported, alternatives were found, and few if any companies suffered very much. The key to this success was that the US government and the major corporate producers were in agreement about the commercial viability of the plan to phase out CFCs. This did not threaten the evolving sustainable development historical bloc, indeed it strengthened it by showing the major corporate supporters of ozone layer protection in a bright green light.

The task for the historical bloc was to turn corporate environmentalism into an acceptable form of sustainable development, leaving space for the culture-ideology of consumerism. Therefore, it is important to reflect on the theoretical possibilities open to globalizing corporations that considered it necessary to respond to the ecological challenge. One attempt to construct a typology of corporate environmental policies (in Canada) focuses on the issue of anthropocentrism, the worldview that puts people (generic man) at the center of the universe. Dion (1998) identifies four types of corporate environmental policies, two characterized by strong and two by weak anthropocentrism. The first is what Dion labels neotechnocratic. He argues that the technocratic enterprise which "dominates nature and exploits it for its own sake without any environmental concern" (ibid., p. 153) no longer exists because of environmental regulation,[22] though the neotechnocratic enterprise (he gives the example of Canadian Pacific Railways) is thriving. Its key characteristics are conformity to laws and regulations, corporate transparency, collaboration with community groups, associations, and governments, and emphasis on individual responsibility.

The second type of environmentalist policy is techno-environmentalist. Such corporations try to develop means and mechanisms for self-regulation that facilitate both protection of the environment and short-run profitability (for example, Alcan). These have all the characteristics of neotechnocratic corporations, plus environmental programs and emergency plans, quasi-legal mechanisms, environmental training for their personnel. They also support scientific and technological innovations involving environmental protection. The third type is what he calls, unflatteringly, the pseudo-environmentalist. These corporations develop prevention mechanisms and management methods for products and raw materials to use natural resources in a socially responsible way (General Mills and Tetra Pak are examples). They are characterized by all the previous factors plus recycling, recuperation and reuse, reduction in the volume of products and materials, safe elimination of waste, and means and methods of prevention. The fourth type is the quasi-environmentalist. They are "generally committed to ecological ideals and the strategies needed to achieve them . . . Such companies (Shell Canada, Colgate-Palmolive, IBM Canada) are the most extreme examples of business corporations characterized by the pursuit of profit together with the development of ecological consciousness within their corporate culture. . . . Ecological consciousness is raised to the level of a practical concern for nonhuman beings in their own right" (ibid., p. 156). In addition to all the characteristics of the first three types, they manifest ecological ideals and the strategies needed to achieve them, they support green research and development, and they pursue educational objectives.[23]

Dion's research is significant because it is one of the few efforts to theorize corporate environmental policies. His fourfold classification works as well for the *Fortune* Global 500 in the mid to late 1990s as it did a few years earlier for corporations operating in Canada. In the late 1980s and the early 1990s, corporate responses to the environmental challenge gradually evolved from simply ignoring the fear of a looming ecological crisis post-Brundtland reinforced by Rio, to a more mature corporate environmentalism. Dion's research catches these changes in their early phase. For example, a Booz-Allen & Hamilton survey of 220 executives of major corporations in 1991 reported that three-quarters of them had published formal environmental policies, but half of these only in the previous two years. Dion's analysis of the corporate focus on anthropocentrism is very important for the clue that it provides to the relationship between corporate environmentalism and sustainable development, between coping with multiple environmental problems and confronting a singular ecological crisis. The difference is the dawning realization that the culture-ideology of consumerism has to be dealt with. The problem for global capitalism is that it cannot be dealt with in an ever-expanding global economy, despite the seductive powers of sustainable development.

Dion's main conclusion is that corporations began to take the environment more seriously in the 1990s (in my terms, expanding the scope of the sustainable development historical bloc), and that finding is certainly borne out by my own research and the research of most of those who write on the subject. The 1990s witnessed an outpouring of books, articles, new journals, Ph.D. theses, conferences, and new institutions devoted to the relations between business and the environment. While there was no diminution in the volume and harshness of the attacks on corporations and their damaging (often catastrophic) impacts on the environment, there was a definite increase in research and discussion based on the dual and reinforcing premises that big business was implementing genuine environmentally friendly policies and that, in general, the corporate conception of sustainable development was politically viable. In light of the argument above, this is all evidence of the success of the sustainable development historical bloc.

There are, undoubtedly, several positive consequences of environmental learning for major corporations. It can, for example, enhance competitive advantage (Banerjee 1998) and the popularity of the Total Quality Environmental Management approach attests to this (Shrivastava 1996; Smart 1992). A green corporate image (as Ben & Jerry's and the BodyShop found) sells well all over the world, and cooperative alliances (for example, that between Dow Chemical and the Nature Conservancy) opened up doors for both parties. Nevertheless, the key issue persists: "Is it possible for an enterprise to be an 'absolutely environmentalist' enterprise?" (Dion 1998: 159). Dion's research was restricted to the level of policy articulation: what the corporations said with respect to the environment and their impacts on it. But what do the corporations actually do with respect to the environment? How do their actions relate to their policies? Answers to these questions will be relevant for the most important question: Is global consumerist capitalism, as represented by the practices as well as the policies of the major corporations, sustainable?

While fully recognizing that the global capitalist system is not the only source of environmental crises (and in some cases not even the main source, for example where state agencies, encroaching pastoralists, and others damage the environment), it is nevertheless true that global business (like all human activities) has environmental impacts. Some sectors – notably mining, chemicals, oil, motor vehicles, and agribusiness – have been identified as having more serious effects than others (see Brower and Leon 1999; Leonard 1988; Madeley 1999; Pearson 1987). As I have argued above, there is an ongoing tension within the environmental movement between those who see these issues as the seamless web of a singular ecological crisis and those who see them as related but essentially separate problems, each of which is capable of technical solution or, at least, improvement. By focusing on major corporations rather than specific environmental issues, it is possible to gain useful insights into how the global capitalist and the global environmentalist systems work and why they work as they do. The creation and operation of the sustainable development historical bloc and the role of the transnational capitalist class in it are central factors in this analysis. With this in mind, we can now move on to some brief case studies of how corporate policies and principles match up to actual practices in the environmental sphere. The method of analysis is straightforward. First, the environmental policies and principles of the corporations are presented – often in their own words – and then these are compared with some examples of their practices.[24]

Procter & Gamble

Environmental policy has been a priority for Procter & Gamble (P&G) since the 1970s. This was a consequence of longstanding chemical industry problems with media images of "mountains of foam on rivers" and a large part of water environmental science came from the efforts of the detergent industry to solve these problems. Since the 1970s there has been a significant culture change in the chemical industry. Chemical companies proactively discuss environmental issues and P&G has gone so far as to claim that it has changed from being perhaps the most secretive to the most open company in the industry.

P&G played an important role in the creation of the sustainable development historical bloc. It was courted by both organizations that subsequently united to establish the WBCSD and became deeply involved in its work. This commitment came from the very top of the corporation. The Environment and Social Responsibility section of the 1995 Annual Report asserts: "P&G believes that environmental quality and economic progress are interdependent, and that industry must lead by example." Two examples were offered of its attachment to these values. First, the company had reduced waste by 52 percent over the previous five years and, second, it had been instrumental in the formation of the Federation of Environmental Management Initiatives, through which trade associations from Mexico, Venezuela, and the US provided education and training for local industries in Latin America.

P&G's commitment to environmental improvement is clearly stated in the 1995 Environmental Progress Report, a document that was subject to independent outside review. It was introduced by the then CEO: "P&G's success in the global marketplace is driven by our ability to provide the world's consumers with products that offer superior performance and value. Not only do we strive to excel at meeting consumer needs, but we firmly believe that our long-term success is closely linked to environmentally responsible growth." This 27-page report spoke of problems as well as successes. In common with similar reports of other companies, reading between the lines leaves the impression that the substantial improvements in environmental performance of the early 1990s were beginning to level out. Annual Environmental Progress Updates, under the title "Continuing Environmental Leadership," detailed both present and future goals and performance. In 1997, for example, present goals were savings on plastic and carton board, eliminating amounts of shipping containers, increasing recycling, developing advanced wastewater treatment, and submitting at least 100 new "Design Manufacturing Wastes Out" projects.

P&G was one of the few companies to grasp the nettle, albeit tentatively, of the relationship between consumption and sustainable development. "We believe progress lies not necessarily in 'consuming less,' but in consuming differently" – that is, products with less damaging environmental effects, a theme that the company pursued with WBCSD. In this respect P&G illustrated perfectly the contradictions inherent in being a globalizing corporation. As noted above, its publications were full of fine sentiments and its policies have attracted much praise in the annals of corporate greening. P&G won almost 50 awards for environmental performance between 1990 and 1995, from national organizations (for example in Turkey, France, Canada, Italy, and the USA), as well as from other corporations (such as the DuPont Award for Innovation). While all these awards were being judged, won, and presented, however, the P&G Buckeye pulp mill in Perry, a small town in northwestern Florida, was at the center of an environmental and community crisis.

The crisis revolved around the Fenholloway river into which, ever since the mill had started operating in the 1950s, untreated effluent had flowed. Knowledge about this case, one of thousands all over the world, would probably have remained local but for a series of articles in the *Tallahassee Democrat* (March 17, 24, 31, 1991) which attracted national media attention. Around this time a staff reporter for the *Wall Street Journal* covering P&G, decided to write a book about the company (Swasy 1994), and this gave Fenholloway and other skeletons in the company's cupboard a good deal of publicity. These sources, and subsequent violent events, alerted greens in the USA that a major campaign issue might be developing. This did not occur, however. P&G continued to win prestigious awards and the company's green image, while dented, survived to be polished anew.

Fenholloway, like so many other campaigns of the weak against the strong, is a story of a few local characters with no previous history of social-movement activity militating for justice, and being met with overwhelming force, some directly from the corporation they accused as the creator of their misery, some from other persons.[25] It is also a story of the local power of globalizing corporations (providing a good living for some local people) in communities they and their allies all but control economically, politically, and ideologically. Along the Fenholloway, P&G as the major employer dominated local business. Politically, the pulp mill could mobilize the Perry-Taylor Chamber of Commerce and the county commission (2 of whose 5 members in 1992 worked for P&G) whenever the need arose. Ideologically, any attack on P&G was seen as an attack on the free enterprise system. The local radio station and the *Tallahassee Democrat*, both of which had given publicity to the company's responsibility for pollution on the Fenholloway, were put under pressure to retract. The most serious incident that occurred was the harassment, rape, and attempted murder in 1992 of one of the local campaigners, Stephanie McGuire. The company denied any connection with the attack and later offered a $5,000 reward for information on it. The police dropped the case soon after. In the mid-1990s, as part of a move out of raw material production, P&G sold off the Buckeye mill. At the end of the 1990s, the Fenholloway campaigners and victims were still waiting for legal redress. It is possible that P&G has not heard the last of this remote corner of Florida and its ordinary people.[26]

P&G has been widely written-up as a success story for corporate environmentalism (see Vandervoort 1991), but Fenholloways are rarely discussed in the business literature. Despite drawing attention to P&G's enormous advertising budget, leading to "overconsumption," Shrivastava (1996) does not mention Fenholloway. While he does note that there were "clashes between environmentalists and workers at P&G plants," he avoids substantive issues of environmental destruction and corporate responsibility. Commenting that the company "seeks to maintain harmonious community relations . . . [yet] these relations have not been uniformly harmonious" (Shrivastava 1996: 106), does not suffice. The emphasis on P&G's Total Quality Environmental Management system globally is clearly incomplete without a serious analysis of how the company actually deals with environmental crises in its own backyard. The same criticism can also be leveled at Smart (1992). The defense that Fenholloway is a detail, inappropriate for such overviews, will not succeed. Shrivastava quotes approvingly the detail that P&G supported wildlife projects along other rivers in northern Florida.

One of the highest-spending advertisers in the world, P&G has used green marketing, environmental education in schools, and advocacy advertising to powerful effect. It formed its own film production company in 1949, and teamed up with the Paramount TV Group in the 1990s to promote its image. This may help to explain why P&G has won so many environmental awards yet at the same time was accused of polluting the Fenholloway River, was being boycotted by animals rights groups, and was being sued over toxic shock syndrome. P&G exerted strict control over the placement of its advertisements. Gloria Steinem of *Ms* magazine claimed that it stipulated "its products were not to be placed in any issue that included any material on gun control, abortion, the occult, cults, or the disparagement of religion" (cited in Beder 1997: 192). *Ms* declined the advertisements, but few media outlets were in a position to resist one of the world's biggest advertisers (see Schiller 1999, ch. 3).

Mitsubishi

Mitsubishi, in the top ten of the Global 500 throughout the 1990s, has had global aspirations at least since the 1970s when its chairman sat on the executive committee of the Trilateral Commission. A section entitled "Meeting the Global Challenge of Sustainable Development" in the 1994 Annual Report highlighted partnerships in the environmental field with Daimler-Benz in a pulp mill joint venture in Canada, and experimental reforestation in Malaysia, Chile, and Brazil. Throughout the 1990s, Mitsubishi promoted an image of environmental responsibility, through being an active member of WBCSD, through its chairmanship of the Environmental Committee of the Japanese Association of Corporate Executives, and through its financial support for WWF-Japan and other environmental organizations.

The 1995 Annual Report reaffirmed the "Primacy of the Natural Environment," noting that its Environmental Affairs Department had been established in 1990, and that it was deeply involved in rainforest regeneration projects in Malaysia and Brazil. The company also supported sustainable development projects in the USA, and organized the Marunouchi Environmental Forums for Citizens. There was further evidence of the importance of the environment for Mitsubishi in "Your Road to Success," a conversation with the President, Minoru Makihara, reprinted in the company's magazine *MC Globe* in 1995. His answer to the question, "How is Mitsubishi Corporation responding to global environmental concerns?" was: "As a concerned corporate citizen, we are all well aware of the importance of the environment . . . We realize that we must live in the same world in which we work: it's only natural that we care."

Why, then, has Mitsubishi been a prime target of environmentalists? Karliner (1997, ch. 4) gives several answers to this question. Most controversially, Mitsubishi has been logging the rainforest all over Asia and shipping timber to Japan and other markets. The struggle between the Rainforest Action Network (RAN), a transnational environmental organization, and Mitsubishi was one of the most keenly fought and closely followed in the 1990s. While the main issue for the environmentalists was the destruction of the rainforest, for the corporations and for the transnational capitalist class there were wider issues at stake. As Madeley points out in his brief but effective discussion (1999: 72–4), there are often minerals and other resources under trees, and in the mid-1990s Malaysian timber concessions were already being turned into mining concessions. While Mitsubishi Corporation directly logged the rainforest through its own companies and others in which it had an interest, it is important to note that several other companies within the Mitsubishi Group, which totaled more than 150 separate legal entities, were also implicated in rainforest destruction. Mitsubishi's Bank of Tokyo financed rainforest exploitation, Mitsubishi Paper Mills pulped the timber, and other subsidiaries built roads and provided services that made logging possible (see Holzer forthcoming). The RAN-organized boycott in the USA affected the sales of many Mitsubishi products, including motor vehicles, Kirin beer, and Nikon cameras, and Mitsubishi lost a lucrative contract at San Francisco International Airport. The boycott was called off after an historic agreement between the parties signed in 1998. However, the agreement was actually between RAN and two US subsidiaries of Mitsubishi, not the Mitsubishi Corporation itself, against whom RAN continued to campaign. Company publicity, including a full-page statement in the *New York Times*, used the corporate logo to advertise the settlement. If, as is entirely possible, the boycott has to be reactivated (as happened in the case of Nestlé) it will be much more difficult to mobilize all those people who have the image of the RAN–Mitsubishi settlement firmly implanted in their psyches.

It is not exclusively for logging the rainforest that Mitsubishi was known in Malaysia. Operation Lallang, originally created to combat communist terrorists, started to be used against environmental activists in Malaysia in 1987. Among those arrested and allegedly tortured were campaigners against the radiation from a factory operated by Asian Rare Earth, jointly owned by Mitsubishi. The factory processed raw monazite, a banned substance in Japan, and Malaysian and overseas experts had declared the storage sites unsafe. Environmentalists, backed by thousands of local residents, fought a protracted battle in the Malaysian courts to force the company to make the factory safe, winning some decisions in lower courts but losing in the more political Supreme Court. Eventually, the company gave up the struggle and closed Asian Rare Earth down after almost two decades of hazardous operation. Neither Mitsubishi nor the Malaysian authorities came out of this affair with much credit (Rowell 1996: 260–4). In its 1999 Annual Report, Mitsubishi continued to claim that "Environmental responsibility is an integral part of Mitsubishi Corporation's corporate philosophy," and proudly announced that the corporate Head Office had been certified ISO 14001 (the international standard for environmental management systems). This was an impressive achievement, but it highlighted rather than resolved Mitsubishi's relationship to the global ecological crisis.

Monsanto

Monsanto, the leader in genetically modified organisms (GMO), has been called the Microsoft of biotechnology. Like Microsoft, it has been hailed by the stock market as one of the truly heroic innovators of the twentieth century (see Kloppenberg 1988, chs. 8–10), while it has been reviled by environmentalists as a prime exponent of corporate manipulation and planetary degradation. In 1990 the Monsanto Pledge, "our environmental vision," was announced as the company strove to gain the moral high ground (see Smart 1992, ch. 5).

The company certainly has been innovative, not only in its science, but also in its reaction to its opponents. In 1997 the CEO, Bob Shapiro, invited three of its leading critics to discuss GMO issues with the company in London. Shapiro was described as a man with "the reputation of a brilliant, caring liberal who enthuses about ecology as much as about business. . . . he talks of reinventing business around the idea of 'ecological sustainability' and of 'cold, rational' business logic delivering new industries to save the world."[27] He was a member of at least two influential bodies in the US, the President's Advisory Committee for Trade and Policy Negotiations and the Trade and Environment Policy Advisory Committee. Shapiro argued by videolink to the Greenpeace Business Conference in October 1999 (available on the Monsanto website) that biotechnology was problematic, but he celebrated its potential for solving the problems of the world.

Like most other major corporate targets of environmental and social movements, Monsanto has claimed leadership in the environmental and humanitarian fields. The company has presented itself as a careful steward of the environment and as an important actor in the struggle to feed the world. The President of the company, in an address in 1997 to the National Academy of Sciences "Forum on Nature and Human Society" (also available on the website), put the position in terms that are paradigmatic for the leading members of the sustainable development historical bloc.

> Corporations – like plants, animals and ecosystems – must be concerned with their own survival and improvement. They cannot afford to live only for the moment. They must continuously evolve, to ensure they have a viable future.
>
> That's why Monsanto, and a growing number of corporations like ours, have begun to take more than a passing interest in biodiversity. Biodiversity is the key to sustainable development, and our focus in it is rooted in self-interest. It's a way of looking at the future, and understanding emerging trends, *so that we can minimize threats to our survival . . . and set the stage for continued growth.* . . . Why is Monsanto interested in sustainability? The simple answer is that we believe current models of economic growth are a dead-end street. We know the human race can't go on consuming resources the way we have for generations, due to absolute constraints on the earth's biological and physical systems. . . . We are staking our future on the concept of sustainable development . . . by pursuing a business model which allows us to address *the two imperatives of growth and sustainability.* (Hendrik Verfaillie, Monsanto website, speeches/ 97oct30, italics mine)

The problem, of course, is whether growth driven by the culture-ideology of consumerism and sustainability can be achieved within the global capitalist system.

One place where these claims are being tested out is India, where Monsanto has been engaged in business since the 1960s, mainly supplying herbicides. However, "since it moved into genetic engineering and seeds under the slogan 'Food, Health, Hope,' it has expanded rapidly and is now set to become the most powerful force in Indian agriculture, moving into water supply and growth hormones for cattle. In place of the publicly controlled Green Revolution, Monsanto heralds the onset of a privately led genetic revolution" (Vidal 1999: 12). Monsanto's stated aim in India, as for the whole world, was to feed the people through GM food. However, two sets of events conspired to impede, at least temporarily, Monsanto's global vision in India in the late 1990s. First, Indian environmentalists managed to stop field trials of GM cotton in several states due to the company's inattention to the minutiae of Indian laws on permissions and safety procedures for such trials. Second, the patenting of so-called terminator seeds (seeds that do not germinate after their first growth, thus ensuring that farmers always have to buy new seeds every year, from Monsanto for example), spread dismay among farmers. This resulted in the mobilization of a movement against the company and GMO science in India (although the extent of this may be exaggerated). Monsanto has also met public opposition in Bangladesh, where the Grameen (microcredit) Bank was forced to withdraw from a planned Grameen–Monsanto Center for Environment-Friendly Technologies to safeguard its image, though indirect links continued. This will undoubtedly be one of the most fiercely fought battles between ecologists and globalizing capitalists in the new century.[28] Kloppenburg puts the central issue very well in his discussion of Ciba-Geigy biotechnology research:

> Does the Sudan really want access to a Funk Seed Company sorghum line that, through recombinant DNA transfer, has had a bacterial gene added that provides resistance to a proprietary herbicide produced by Funk's corporate parent, the transnational agrichemical giant Ciba-Geigy Corporation? Access to the elite lines developed in the advanced capitalist nations might simply reinforce processes of social differentiation among peasant producers, facilitate the global elaboration of factor markets, accelerate environmental degradation, and deepen relations of technological dependence between North and South. (Kloppenberg 1988: 287)[29]

The issues over GMOs that have caused so much public unrest and political confusion in Europe at the turn of the millennium were exactly the same issues that caused public unrest and political confusion a decade earlier in the USA, as Kloppenberg makes clear. The fact that in the USA the GMO corporations overcame opposition cannot be unrelated to the effectiveness of the coalition for GMO created in the USA for Monsanto, Ciba-Geigy, and the rest by prominent environmental public relations firms (Beder 1997, ch. 2) as part of the sustainable development historical bloc. It remains to be seen whether or not the political systems in Europe and/or the EU prove resistant to this powerful strain of corporate persuasion.

While Monsanto attracted a great deal of publicity in the late 1990s in the context of genetically modified organisms, it would be a mistake to assume that this was the first major controversy with which the company has had to deal. As noted above, Monsanto was one of the main actors in the campaign to discredit Rachael Carson in the 1960s. E. Bruce Harrison, the public relations specialist who coordinated the attack on Carson, worked on behalf of Monsanto and the chemical industry in the "war against the environmentalists" (Proctor 1995: 48–52; see also Rowell 1996: 107–8 and ch. 4 *passim*). In 1977, Monsanto launched a $4.5 million media campaign to reassure consumers into believing that chemicals were natural and safe. Proctor (1995: 102–3) reports that the positive image rating of the chemical industry rose by 6 percent in the two years following the campaign. Similar campaigns of advocacy advertising have been used by TNCs and industry associations for decades (Beder 1997; Sethi 1977). Monsanto was also active in the campaign for public acceptance of the bovine growth hormone, orchestrated by Burson-Marsteller (B-M) and aided in this task by other public relations companies. One of these special-ized in tracking the activities of environmental activists for major corporations (including Shell, Monsanto, and Philip Morris) and co-opting some of them to further corporate ends. PR Watch alleged spying on consumer groups and dairy farmers to counter the bovine growth hormone scare (Greer and Bruno 1996; Rowell 1996: 111).

In this campaign, B-M used classic public relations strategy. First the illusion of public and expert support is created for what appears to be a food-cheapening technology, but one whose risks have not actually been properly assessed. B-M built a grassroots network ("astroturf"). "Business executives and lobbyists; biotech company executives; farm-ers; veterinarians; university professors; high school teachers; Chambers of Commerce and elected and appointed officials" are mobilized (internal B-M document cited by Rowell 1996: 113).[30] Cockburn and Silverstein (1996) provide a wide range of evidence on the ubiquity and duplicity of environmental public relations in the USA. For example, Carol Tucker Foreman, the founder of the Safe Food Coalition and formerly an assistant secretary of agriculture in the Carter Administration, was also a discreet lobbyist for Monsanto, assisting its attempts to reduce regulatory controls on the production of food (ibid., pp. 129–30). The attention of the environmental public rela-tions industry to the detail of potential and actual opposition to the corporations and the capitalist way of life is certainly impressive. Beder (1997, ch. 10) cites one typical example of a vigilant Monsanto manager who persuaded the education authority in his locality to withdraw a high school text, *Environmental Science: Ecology and Human Impact* on the grounds that it was "anti–industry."[31] Monsanto's claim to environmen-tal leadership is not convincing and the company has failed to persuade most environmentalists (let alone ecologists) that its version of science for the public good is benign.

Intel

The 1996 document "Environmental Health and Safety at Intel" is a comprehensive approach to Environment, Health, and Safety. Four long-range goals were proclaimed: to be an EH&S leader in communities and the industry; to prevent all injuries to employees; to measurably reduce the environmental burden with emphasis on source reduction; and to deliver products to the marketplace with a vision of product stewardship. Concrete short-term goals included reducing volatile organic compound emissions by 50 percent per unit of production, reducing work injuries and illnesses by 20 percent worldwide, and recycling 50 percent of solid waste by 2000. Good progress was made on all of these. The company worked closely with US agencies, it helped to craft the Closed Cycle Substance and Waste Act in Germany, and it has assisted small companies to recycle in Israel.

Intel is a relatively young company. It formalized its first combined EH&S policy in 1991, and revised it in 1995. In the mid-1990s, 225 professionals worked on safety engineering, ergonomics, and environmental engineering. The company supported the development of ISO 14000, the British Standard 7750 (in its facilities in Ireland, subsequently closed down), and the European EMS standard. Intel's Strategic Chemical Council monitored standards over all company sites. In various company documents Intel has committed itself to prioritize source reduction over end-of-pipe solutions both in its own operations and through the key role it played in the Semiconductor Industry Association and EPA committees. Interest was also expressed in lifecycle policy, and a take-back scheme introduced in Germany to encourage the return of used electronic products. Intel has won numerous environmental awards, for example from the Malaysian Ministry of Human Resources, from Ireland's National Industrial Safety Organization, and the states of Oregon and Arizona.

An environmental award from Arizona might have come as a surprise to residents of the neighboring state of New Mexico, where a citizens' group, South West Organizing Project (SWOP), has been criticizing the company since the 1980s, when Intel became the largest private employer in the state. The growth of Intel stimulated suppliers like Sumitomo to move wafer production to New Mexico. All this industrial development required expensive infrastructure, which was paid for out of taxes, though most of the corporations that benefited paid little or no tax. SWOP estimated that Intel alone had been exempted from hundreds of millions (perhaps as much as two billion) of dollars in tax payments. Community advisory panels were handpicked by Intel to neutralize the challenge from groups like SWOP. While Intel produces a clean product, electronics is by no means a clean industry, the processes of production are dangerous for workers and produce toxic wastes. Local groups find it difficult to counter the highly sophisticated public relations strategies of major corporations. The reason for this is simple. The many commercial opportunities that major facilities of large corporations bring are very attractive to many groups. The local allies of the transnational capitalist class stand to profit from such development and, of course, new industry brings jobs. The Intel Chairman, commenting on negotiations around the building of a new facility, made the connections between the local and Federal allies of the company. The local newspaper reported that that he had "received assurances from the 'Environmental' Vice-President, Albert Gore, that the permit process for the plant would be streamlined: Intel uses 'some pretty noxious chemicals . . . it's important . . . we move rapidly and . . . make sure unnecessary red tape didn't stand in the way . . . We just wanted to make sure the administration understood the problem.' Had the meeting gone the other way? 'We would have gone outside the US.' " (quoted from *Albuquerque Tribune* in SWOP 1995: v).

New Mexico is one of the poorest states in the US, and has long been dominated by military supply installations, many highly polluting. The EPA had previously named three Intel facilities in Silicon Valley plus one in Arizona as Superfund sites. Added to this, the facts that the San Jose community of Albuquerque (the location of a GE military supply plant) had also been designated a Superfund site and that over 200 GTE workers had been poisoned in another New Mexico electronics plant (Fox 1991), should have been a warning on the dangers of electronic production. The potential for environmental racism, the siting of polluting facilities in underprivileged ethnic minority communities (Westra and Wenz 1995), was also clear. While officially promoting the benefits of pollution prevention in its corporate publications and public pronouncements, Intel's marketing strategy for a fast-changing industry depended on persuading local authorities to make rapid decisions on planning and environmental issues. Despite Intel's poor environmental record, the New Mexico Environment Department granted the Albuquerque facilities a permit for 356 tons of toxic emissions per year. While Intel had replaced CFCs with nontoxic alternatives and was phasing out glycol ethers, the use of many other toxic chemicals was still common in its plants.[32]

Intel's New Mexico facilities were located at Rio Rancho, originally developed as a residential community by a company one-third controlled by the family of the then Governor of New Mexico. Intel adjoined Rio Rancho and was subsidized by a battery of tax incentives, notably Industrial Revenue Bonds sold by the county to an Intel affiliate. Because the county was the "nominal owner" of the land, Intel paid no property or state sales tax. Intel also established a Foreign Trade Zone, receiving more tax incentives. When the new factory was planned in the early 1990s, Intel circulated several US states in a bidding war to obtain the most generous incentives (a common example of the race to the bottom). New Mexico provided an Intel Ideal Incentive Matrix to attract the plant at a stated cost to public funds of $114,000 per job (other estimates suggested a much higher figure). By this time, public pressure on the county had resulted in two minor concessions wrung from Intel, namely the right of officials to inspect Intel property and supplemental rent of $5.5 million over 17 years. Despite the short life of most electronic products, the Intel lease was for 30 years and if the company went bankrupt, the county (the nominal owner) would be responsible for cleaning the polluted site.

New Mexico won the race for the new plant, with 17 Intel employees on the state's team. The head of the New Mexico Economic Development Department was subsequently recruited to manage the lobbying team at Intel. A letter from him (reproduced in SWOP 1995: 114) demonstrated his complete attachment to the interests of Intel. The new Governor of New Mexico in 1994 was also closely connected with Intel, controlling a company that had been dependent on Intel for the bulk of its construction work since the 1980s. In 1993, even before the new plant was in production, Intel was found in violation of emission standards at its existing semiconductor fabrication plants, on its own figures.

Under these circumstances it is not surprising that there was a serious lack of political will to monitor environmental hazards. Superfund Right to Know laws were incomplete, and states had to fund implementation themselves. In New Mexico, environmental regulations were supervised by the State Emergency Response Commission (SERC) and Local Emergency Planning Committees. In the 1990s, SERC was chaired by the President of Rinchem, a hazardous waste storage company, under contract to Intel! New Mexico had passed a law to fund the computerization of Right to Know information through a hazardous chemical trucking fee. As of the mid-1990s, none of the money collected had been used for this purpose. Intel was granted permits to increase emissions into the relatively clean New Mexico air. The logic behind this decision, not unique to the USA, was that expressed by Lawrence Summers: "underpopulated countries in Africa are vastly underpolluted, their air quality is probably vastly inefficiently low compared to Los Angeles or Mexico City" (quoted in SWOP 1995: 53, from a World Bank memorandum in 1991). As public pressure grew in affected communities, the New Mexico Air Pollution Control Bureau began to levy fines of $15,000 a day for periods in 1992–3. After appealing to the Federal government, Intel was permitted to settle for $40,000. SWOP (1995) concludes that the EPA does not exert sufficient pressure on Intel (or many other polluters). The Occupational Health and Safety Bureau of New Mexico, for example, had 10 full-time inspectors to monitor 34,000 businesses. The interests of native peoples and people of color are not a priority. Intel's public response to its critics has been minimal.

Dow

It is somewhat ironic in light of subsequent events that Dunn (1979) described Dow Corning's success in the realms of public affairs as "total communications." Dow Corning was a joint venture of Dow Chemical and Corning Glass established in 1943 for the development of silicones. In the 1970s it was a very well-educated company, with 25 percent of all personnel having one degree, and 10 percent holding advanced degrees. Dunn describes how the Company Code was circulated to managers all over the world for comment, then regional guidelines were developed on the basis of these comments. The company had a low public profile, though this was to change in the 1990s when the silicone breast implant crisis forced Dow Corning to file for protection under the US Chapter 11 bankruptcy laws (see below).

Dow showed an early interest in pollution control. Indeed the chairman of the company went on record in the early 1970s to say that pollution control could save enough money to break even on its costs (see Barnet and Muller 1974: 344). Dow (like 3M, Chevron, and others) was later to claim that it had saved hundreds of millions of dollars through greening measures.[33] An EH&S Committee of the main Board was formed in 1983, followed in 1991 by a Corporate Environmental Advisory Council. Members of this body included a former environment official of the French government, academic environmentalists, a former UNDP Asia-Pacific director, a former Premier of Quebec, and a former EPA administrator. Dow has played a leading role in the President's Council on Sustainable Development.

The 1996 Progress Report on EH&S asserted definitively: "Sustainable development is a global business goal." This committed Dow to implement its Codes of Management Practices globally by 1997, to promote the Responsible Care ethic among major business associations, customers, suppliers, and policy-makers and to advocate global regulatory harmonization. An example of this policy in practice was the establishment of Dow's Value (industrial) Park near Leipzig, where a start was made on using the waste from one industrial plant as the raw material for another. Dow's goal, thus, was to "incorporate principles of sustainable development and eco-efficiency into business strategies." The 1997 Progress Report on EH&S set goals for 2005 in which Dow announced the establishment of an EH&S Management Board with six top executives working on three commitments: responsibility and accountability, preventing EH&S incidents, and increasing resource productivity.

To what extent have Dow's excellent policies on environmental stewardship been borne out in practice? Dow Chemical is perhaps best known among environmentalists as the company that manufactured the broad-spectrum herbicide Agent Orange for the US military to defoliate Vietnam, and for its lengthy struggle to avoid responsibility for the deadly effects of the dioxin Agent Orange released. (Dow and the other companies involved eventually paid $180 million to military veterans while denying liability.) It is not surprising, therefore, to learn that Dow has also been an active member of the dioxin lobby. It is surprising, however, to learn that at the height of the struggle over liability for those who suffered from Agent Orange, Dow was awarded the World Environment Center's 1989 Gold Medal for Corporate Achievement.

What are we to make of the claim that while corporate greens from Dow and other major corporations sat on prestigious bodies like the President's Council on Sustainable Development and on the boards of some of the most important environmental organizations, their companies were also funding the anti-environmental backlash through the Wise Use movement and the public relations firms specializing in undermining radical environmentalists? According to Deal (1993), Dowie (1995), Karliner (1997), and Beder (1997) this was the case. Predictably, Dow has been a target of green and corporate responsibility movements all over the world. The company is in a sensitive area of production and many of its products are intrinsically hazardous. *Multinational Monitor* included Dow in its list of ten worst corporations in 1995 for its role in the silicone breast implant crisis that had affected thousands of women. The responsible company, Dow Corning, was 50 percent owned by Dow Chemical. Unluckily for Dow, the husband of one of the women affected was a Dow Corning corporate ethics officer. He had challenged company attempts to suppress evidence of much higher implant complication rates than anticipated, and was so disturbed by the company's response that he exposed it publicly (Byrne 1995, Angell 1996). As more evidence accumulated and the numbers of legal suits against the company grew, Dow Corning filed under Chapter 11 in May 1995. Dow Chemical claimed that it had never been directly involved in the implant business, and considered itself safe from litigation. This belief was rudely shattered later that year, when a court in Nevada awarded over $14 million in damages against Dow Chemical in an implant case. As with tobacco litigation, the legal and scientific aspects of the case are highly complex and contentious.[34] Part of Dow's evidence that silicone breast implants were not the cause of the medical problems reported by the litigants derived from an epidemiological study which was later discovered to have been carried out by researchers who had agreed to act as consultants to Dow (and may even have been in Dow's employ at the time). This would not, of course, necessarily invalidate the results of the research. Further, Dow had donated at least $7 million to Brigham and Women's Hospital where the research had been conducted (Mokhiber and Wheat 1995: 13–14). In another instance of potential conflict of interest, Dow loaned one of its research scientists as a staff member to the House Commerce Committee. This was the committee that oversaw the work of the EPA and the Food and Drugs Administration, government agencies deeply involved in attempts to regulate the types of products that Dow manufactured. The EPA had levied the largest fine in its history on a Dow subsidiary (DowElanco) in 1995, for failing to report information on the hazards of the insecticide Dursban (INFACT 1997: 38–42).

Corporations such as Dow defend themselves with reasonable arguments. Of course they want the best-qualified researchers to advise them; of course they donate funds to institutions carrying out scientific research relevant to the safety of their products; of course they wish to share their expertise with official bodies. Conflicts of interest only arise where people cannot be entirely trusted to subordinate their own personal interests and/or the interests of those who directly or indirectly employ them, to the public interest (never easy to define exactly). The point of corporate responsibility, according to the corporations, is that such conflicts of interests should never be permitted to arise.

Suspicion is inevitably raised by the ubiquitous use of lobbyists and front groups, created for corporations by public relations consultants. Dow Chemical has been singled out by many commentators on these grounds. The 1997 Annual Report of INFACT, the corporate accountability research and campaigning group based in Boston, numbered 51 lobbyists at the Federal level, plus 36 registered lobbyists in 13 US states for Dow. This was in addition to the substantial lobbying efforts of the Chemical Manufacturers Association. INFACT listed seven trade associations and lobbying fronts that Dow and other major corporations funded and worked through. For example, the American Tort Reform Association, the Global Climate Coalition, and the Coalition for Improved Environmental Audit were extremely active in campaigns to undermine public health and environmental legislation in the USA and globally (INFACT 1997: 36–43). The Foundation for Public

Affairs, funded by Dow (with Philip Morris, Exxon, Mobil, and Shell), monitored hundreds of public interest groups for advance warning of possible opposition (Beder 1997). In fairness, it might be said that Dow (and many other major corporations) do desperately need the services of public relations experts in the litigious cultures of the global capitalist economy. Madeley (1999: 46) reports that Dow, Shell, and Occidental Chemical were being sued by 16,000 workers in 11 countries on the health hazards of a single pesticide (DBCP), banned in the USA in 1979, but marketed in the Third World in the 1980s. In the USA, many of the country's leading medical authorities argued that the balance of scientific evidence does not support the link between silicone breast implants and the medical problems on the basis of which courts have awarded billions of dollars in damages (Angell 1996).

As indicated above, Dow has been deeply involved in the controversy over dioxins. There are at least 75 dioxin compounds, all of them potentially dangerous, as byproducts of waste incineration, chemical manufacturing, chlorine bleaching of pulp and paper, and smelting. Thus, it can be easily seen that many interests are at stake. From the 1950s when dioxins were discovered to 1995 when the EPA acted to control them, the corporations have attempted to reassure the public about their dangers and to influence legislation. Proctor, in his book on the politics of cancer, provides evidence that in the 1980s officials from Dow successfully interfered with an EPA scientific report on dioxin levels in the Saginaw Bay area, where Dow's major Midland complex is located (Proctor 1995: 80). Dow executives have been instrumental in mobilizing the Chemical Manufacturers Association, the National Association of Manufacturers, and the US Chamber of Commerce to oppose dioxin control legislation through its Visible Scientists Program and various front groups (notably the Alliance to Keep Americans Working and Citizens for a Sound Economy). Along with other members of the dioxin and related lobbies it has undermined attempts to achieve environmental justice by the use of strategic lawsuits against public participation (SLAPP) litigation. In the 1980s the chemical industry and the EPA under a new Reagan-appointed leadership collaborated to lower the toxicity risk levels in general (see Proctor 1995, ch. 4). However, as scientific evidence against dioxin mounted the global chlorine industry and its allies (such as the so-called Chlorophiles – chlorine workers in Belgium and Holland) began to mobilize. Their strategy was similar in respects to the strategy of the tobacco lobby (see Sklair 1998). The five main arguments of the chlorine lobby are that dioxin occurs naturally, we cannot ban chlorine from the planet, chlorine-based products are very beneficial, the case against dioxin is emotional not scientific, and that nature produces many substances like dioxin. The Citizen's Clearinghouse for Hazardous Wastes reported that in 1993–4, 24 out of 28 members of the House Subcommittee for Dioxin hearings had received money from dioxin producing industries through Political Action Committees. There is little doubt that there has been a serious lack of global corporate citizenship over dioxin in which Dow, as well as DuPont, Monsanto, and BASF, are implicated (see Beder 1997, ch. 9; Gibbs 1995).

This volume of unfinished business calls into question Dow's aspirations to be a leader in matters of environmental and corporate responsibility. However, Dow's place as a senior partner of the sustainable development historical bloc is assured.

RTZ (Rio Tinto)

When RTZ and CRA merged in 1995, the company asserted that it was

> a world leader in the mining industry. . . . In order to deliver superior returns to shareholders over many years, RTZ-CRA takes a long term and responsible approach to exploring the earth . . . In this way, we help to meet the growing global need for minerals and metals which contribute to essential improvements in well being. Accordingly, we set ourselves high environmental and community standards. Our commitment to health, safety and the enhancement of the skills and capabilities of our employees is second to none in mining. We seek to make lasting contributions to local communities and to be sensitive to their culture and way of life. (1996 Annual Report)

The 1996 Health, Safety, and Environment policy of the merged company was specifically intended to apply to all subsidiaries, and in each company the implementation of the policy was the responsibility of a senior executive. The policy was communicated to all employees and made available to the public. Joint ventures and other companies where the Group was involved but did not have operating responsibility were encouraged to fall into line. The Environment and Community Relations Committee of the RTZ-CRA Board would ensure that the policy was put into effect throughout the company. The 1997 HSE report (of what was by then Rio Tinto) discussed the 280 responses generated by the 1996 Report, noting many helpful comments on land management, water protection, and policy implementation, a good illustration of the corporate reflexivity that was noted for the Shell Report 1998. Progress was claimed on all 1996 priorities and detailed tables listing environmental impacts of all mines were supplied. The consultants Arthur D. Little confirmed that the committee of the board on social and environmental accountability was composed entirely of non-executive (outside) directors, that a revised formal process for reporting serious HSE incidents had been established, and that a new groupwide system for HSE assessments and audits had been put in place. These were all responses to previous difficulties. The main problem was said to be to ensure that all these new mechanisms worked properly at all the Group sites. "This remains an improvement opportunity for the Group."

One "improvement opportunity" might have been the experience of RTZ in the Cerro Colorado copper mine on the lands of the Guayami people in Panama, which began in 1980, when it took a 49 percent stake in the mine (the Panama government owned the rest). It ended in 1991, when the mine was abandoned. In his careful study of the project, the ethnographer Gjording analyzed the actual effects on the local population, some of which had occurred before RTZ's involvement. There was substantial loss of land and relocation of some communities, water damage, road building, and traffic damage. On balance, therefore, the project as far as it went did not directly threaten the physical existence of the Guayami people. However, the real issue was that the mine "was completely foreign, it operated on completely foreign mindsets, it served completely foreign goals" (Gjording 1991: 154). By "foreign" Gjording did not mean outsiders as opposed to "Panamanians" (the dependency model), but all those who were "foreign to the Guayami people" including elements in dominant Panamanian ruling groups (much nearer a local-global type of analysis). The balance sheet of losses incurred by a single local family as a result of a penetration road to the mine illustrates the huge complexities of measuring economic and ecological impacts in this and thousands of similar projects. In the sphere of environmental rights, the native people were not well treated. CODEMIN, the Panama government agency responsible for the mine, did not negotiate with the Guayami, but presented them with a series of *faits accomplis.* While the project did co-opt some local leaders, this gave the community very little in concrete terms. Despite benefits for a few local people, the Guayami as a whole were left feeling powerless.[35]

When RTZ arrived it promised to carry out local impact studies to its high global standards, but in light of its poor existing record most activists and local leaders not directly identified with the mine did not take the company's promises seriously and communicated this skepticism to the local population. This skepticism received partial confirmation when RTZ proposed high-grading, taking out the best ore first, and leaving the lower grades for when the Panama government eventually took over the project. The Guayami people realized they needed help if they were to prevent the mine destroying their traditional way of life, and the Panamanian Bishops' Conference gave it. Survival International in London, the Russell Tribunal in Amsterdam, and many other groups also took up the cause. Shareholders' resolutions to RTZ and Fluor (who had been hired to do the construction work on the project) increased the pressure,[36] and in 1981 the Guayami people's Forum brought their case to Panama City, amid considerable publicity. Gjording correctly points out that the Guayami needed protection from dominant groups in the nationalist Panamanian majority population as well as from rapacious TNCs. "The populations of less-developed countries commonly face national governments and wealthy elites who are allied with foreign interests" (Gjording 1991: 259). When the pro-union labor law in Panama threatened to interfere with company plans to exploit the mine, one of RTZ's lawyers was reported as saying, "We"ll get rid of the law" (cited in Moody 1996: 50). This was not necessary. RTZ abandoned the project in 1991 and left the Guayami people with a despoiled environment. The company, apparently, took no continuing responsibility for this failed Panamanian project. Sabin's comment on the history of Amazonian oil development is apposite here. Neither case is "a simple tale of capitalist penetration and pristine native resistance. . . . Here, as in other instances of extractive development, native groups complain that there has been too little of the right kind of development and too much of the wrong kind" (see Sabin 1998: 144; also Bunker 1988).

The case of the Cerro Colorado mine provides evidence for both the class polarization crisis and the ecological crisis. Undoubtedly, a minority of Guayami people did benefit economically from the mine, while the welfare of the majority did decline, but not catastrophically. Ecologically, the environment around the mine suffered with few benefits, so the usual anthropocentric trade-off argument that some environmental damage is compensated by improvements in human welfare, cannot be made. Even if the project had been completed, it is doubtful that the welfare of the Guayami people as a whole would have benefited sufficiently to balance out their ecological losses. RTZ and the Panamanian government agency responsible for the mine would, no doubt, reject both these gloomy conclusions. Cerro Colorado, it can be argued, showed the prospect of modernity to the Guayami. It left them with roads, experience with machinery, and a taste of the industrial culture necessary for their development. It is reasonable to pose the questions: What is the alternative for such people? Does the globalizing of the capitalist system simply accelerate the inevitable process of getting to the modern world? The next example of Rio Tinto's practices takes this argument a step further.

The open-cast copper and gold mining complex at Grasberg in Indonesian Irian Jaya is owned jointly by Freeport McMoran corporation (based in New Orleans), the Indonesian government,[37] and RTZ. This is one of the biggest and most valuable mines in the world. While RTZ had a minority stake in the project, its importance for the company was evident from Annual Reports. In 1996 RTZ-CRA and Freeport obtained permits for expansion of the mine. RTZ-CRA had a 46 percent interest in this expansion (and 12 percent of Freeport). The Freeport mine has been a target for environmentalists and human rights campaigners for decades (see Moody 1996, Madeley 1999, Rowell 1996). It had all the ingredients of the classic corporate exploitation of the rainforest, neglect of the needs of the existing Amungme population (certainly those who did not get jobs in the mine), and environmental despoliation. In the words of the 1996 RTZ Annual Report: "Mining operations at the Grasberg mine involve significant environmental challenges," though there is no mention of the equally significant human rights challenges (or of Grasberg) here or in the glossy "Health, safety and environment report" published by the company in 1997. The Ajkwa river was so badly polluted from the mine that the company itself warned local people not to drink the water or eat food crops growing by the river. Local leaders filed suit in Louisiana (the home state of Freeport) and the company offered a minimal trust fund payment to quiet the protest. The local population rejected the offer of a 1 percent share in the mine as "an insult to us as human beings with rights and as Indonesian citizens."[38]

In 1996, the frustration of the local people spilled over into violence against the security office at the mine after years of abuse of Amungme leaders and mine workers. The area around the mine was the most highly militarized district in Indonesia and allegations of serious human rights violations, including torture and murder on corporate property, have been made by the Australian Council for Overseas Aid, the Catholic Church, and the National Human Rights Commission of Indonesia. Freeport and RTZ denied these allegations and condemned the actions of the military. The mine has also been condemned by groups in many parts of the world. In the University of Texas at Austin and Loyola University New Orleans, to both of which Freeport made generous donations, student protests embarrassed the company and raised public awareness of the issues. Similarly, the World Development Movement in the UK has campaigned to protect the local people around the mine. While it is difficult to boycott gold and copper as such, many well-known financial services companies, including Prudential, Norwich Union, and Commercial Union (all Rio Tinto shareholders) have been targeted. RTZ appears to attract opponents. In a revealing address to the centennial conference of two prestigious mining institutions in 1998, the chairman of Rio Tinto indicated that he was well aware of these problems. Admitting that the mining industry had become complacent in recent decades about the environmental and social effects of its activities, he said:

> increasing globalisation of development opportunities has brought with it a new challenge that we have been slow to recognise – namely how best to generate development benefits from our investments, including the specific interests of indigenous people and the promotion of human rights. This has come at a time when the creation of global information space has thrust mining into a much higher profile. . . . far too often we have found ourselves on the back foot trying to defend past actions against current standards – never an easy task. *We have become less adept at capturing the reputational benefits of better social and environmental performance than we have been at improving that performance itself.* (Wilson 1998: 3, underline in the original)

RTZ is in a similar position to many other corporations engaged in environmentally hazardous projects in vulnerable Third World communities. Citing the RTZ chief executive in 1995, Moody (1996: 49) documents "problems everywhere" for the company. These include Grasberg, the Bingham Canyon copper smelter in the USA under a Superfund clean-up order, the Rossing uranium mine in Namibia where the company is fighting off charges of lung disease and cancers in former workers, pollution in a gold mine in the Czech Republic, the ongoing struggles in Bougainville PNG, and the impending ecological damage in Lihir PNG, where RTZ wants to develop the world's largest unexploited gold reserves.[39] Rio Tinto and other mining TNCs cannot win – if they close down, economic hardship follows, if they persist, they have to do business in fraught conditions, as best they can. Behind all these cases lies the race to exploit natural resources to feed both genuine needs and excessive wants. These contradictions cannot be resolved within the system. A search for "Grasberg" on the internet illustrates this poignantly. McIntosh Redpath Engineering, on contract to Freeport, under the slogan "Advancing Underground Excellence," relates how it can provide a hoisting system capable of lifting up to 40,000 tons per day from 500 meters deep in the earth. Under another slogan, "A Picture speaks a thousand words," www.moles.org illustrates what the original mine looked like and its present appearance as a water store for the much larger Grasberg mine. An aerial photograph shows "how the mine's 'overburden' – the ground the Amungme once called home – is just dumped over the side of the mountain to pollute and silt up downstream watersheds and the land that was once the rich home of the Komoro people." Neither the class polarization crisis nor the ecological crisis can be resolved within the global capitalist system, however much RTZ and corporations like it try to clean up their operations.

Broken Hill Proprietary (BHP)

In its 1996 Annual Report BHP expressed an aspiration to be "the world's best resources company. . . . [to] link resources and technologies for the benefit of customers and communities worldwide. . . . contributing to the communities in which we live and work, and a high standard of care for the environment. . . . value safety, honesty and excellence in all we do." In order to meet what it termed "the Global Business Challenge," it proclaimed: "We aim to achieve leadership in our performance in every aspect of our business. Safety and environment are our highest priority and our most serious commitment. With this approach, we will meet changing community expectations." BHP made its first public statement of environmental principles in 1991, and its Community Relations policy appeared in 1997. In BHP's Environment Report for 1998, in some respects an exemplary model of its genre, the CEO states the company's shared commitment:

> Our business is non-renewable resources. Our commodities and products are generally in abundant supply and, in some cases extensively recycled. In the end, however, they are finite.
>
> Our products are also essential. They are the raw materials of industry, transport and construction, of our way of life.
>
> Our job is to provide the resources the world demands in a sustainable manner – in an economically, environmentally and socially responsible way.
>
> To be sustainable we must provide returns for our shareholders today, as well as investment for the future.

While this statement appears to be saying that when the resources run out, as they are bound to do, then "our way of life" (arguably global capitalist consumerism) will end too, the implications of this are followed through in the 1998 Environment Report. The Report confines itself to some general statements about the possibility of reconciling profits, environmental care and remediation, and community interests. Like other major corporations in hazardous industries, BHP has responded to its critics by introducing best practice for safety all over the world, and by putting in place an advanced system of environmental management and pollution reduction. In the Annual Report for 1996 it claimed that the environmental problems it had been experiencing in Tasmania as a result of a coastal oil spill and in the Ok Tedi copper mine in Papua New Guinea (PNG) were both under control. It is this latter claim that is of interest here.

In its Annual Reports and other corporate publications in the mid-1990s BHP projected an image of the positive developmental effects of the mine. Pictures of the serious young Papuan Chief Surveyor at Ok Tedi, and of the Papuan nursing sister supervising outpatient care for local mothers and infants in the hospital complex constructed and managed by Ok Tedi Mining Limited, conveyed these effects strongly. BHP had also learned the value of reflexivity insofar as it noted that there had been problems at Ok Tedi. In the "Copper" section of the 1996 Annual Report the compensation scheme negotiated with the PNG government for those villagers "whose lifestyles have been affected by the mine's operations" was mentioned. And, in a brief section on "Environment," it was acknowledged that there was a problem with "tailings and overburden disposal" at Ok Tedi. So, BHP did not ignore its problems entirely. The question is, did it deal with them in accordance with its own high principles.

BHP was a major actor in the mining industry in PNG. The Ok Tedi copper mine, in which BHP had a controlling stake, had been both a source of large profits and a running sore for the company since its opening in the 1980s. Shortly after the Australian government granted independence to PNG in 1975, Ok Tedi Mining Limited was established. The promise of revenues and jobs persuaded the PNG government to exempt the company from most of the country's environmental laws. Unsurprisingly, the mine has become an environmental hazard. According to the Australian Conservation Foundation in 1991, the head of the Ok Tedi River system was almost "biologically dead" after years of exposure to crushed rock, cyanide, and heavy metal wastes from the mine. The livelihood of about 30,000 landowners downstream from the mine had been seriously impaired and in 1994 they filed suit in Australia against BHP. The company, which accounted for about 30 percent of PNG federal revenues, was later found in contempt by the Victoria Supreme Court (BHP was headquartered in Melbourne) for its involvement in legislation that was drafted for the PNG parliament making it a criminal offence to sue BHP! For this behavior BHP was included in *Multinational Monitor*'s list of the ten worst corporations of 1995 (Mokhiber and Wheat 1995). The company and the PNG government eventually set up a multimillion-dollar compensation fund for those plaintiffs prepared to opt out of the law suit.

In December 1995, the Compensation (Prohibition of Foreign Legal Proceedings) Act was passed in PNG, making it illegal for landowners affected by any resource project in PNG to pursue future legal action in a foreign country.[40] In 1996 the litigation was settled and special compensation programs were put in place. Nevertheless, the controversy dragged on and was sufficiently serious for BHP to issue a Discussion Paper, "BHP and Ok Tedi," in August 1999, reviewing the dispute and admitting the difficulties of bringing it to a conclusion that would satisfy all the parties.

Once again, there is no simple resolution of the issues of globalizing corporations wishing to exploit resources in fragile environments with the support of local authorities and some local people, and opposed by other local people and environmentalists and human rights activists from all over the world. But once again, it is difficult to reconcile the facts of Ok Tedi with the principles that BHP has proclaimed for itself, though the 1998 Environment Report did go some way to acknowledging these problems.

BP (BP Amoco)

As discussed in the previous chapter, BP is a company that claimed to be a leader in social and community affairs. My analysis of its policies and practices concluded that, while these claims were not entirely without foundation, there is an element of double standards at work, particularly in its operations outside the UK (in the US and Colombia). What of its environmental record?

BP's goals, reiterated in many corporate publication, were extremely ambitious: "no accidents, no harm to people, no damage to the environment ... good HSE performance is crucial to our business." The 1996 HSE Report paid specific attention to sustainable development, charting its evolution through the 1980s and 1990s and highlighting the fact that BP was a leading member of the WBCSD. "Sustainable development [the Report proclaimed] has been described in terms of the triple bottom line – economic prosperity, environmental protection and social equity, and the need for a balance between these objectives." BP has committed itself to performance measures in its Annual Reports and other company publications on these three bottom lines. The HSE Report for 1997 set the goal for BP to play a leading role in supplying the world's growing need for energy "without damaging the environment." Conscious of the importance of communicating these policies and best practices throughout the company, in 1997 BP distributed to employees a 12-point Operations Integrity Assurance

System, "Getting HSE Right." Also in 1997, BP Chemicals issued an impressive set of Site Reports, with measures of safety performance and on-site and off-site emissions for about 70 chemicals.

The merger of BP and Amoco at the end of December 1998 gave the new company an opportunity to present itself to the investment community and the public at large. The 1998 Annual Report set out goals for the new group: "The world's need for energy is growing steadily day by day. Energy and materials, used safely and efficiently, are essential to the prosperity and growth of every country and every region in the world. Sustaining and enhancing our quality of life depends on them. BP Amoco's goal is to play a leading role in meeting these needs from oil, gas, solar power and petrochemicals without damaging the environment." Special mention was also made of dialogue between BP Amoco and other organizations, including Amnesty International, Christian Aid, Friends of the Earth, Greenpeace, Human Rights Watch, Oxfam, Save the Children Fund, and WWF. Further evidence that BP took the environmental effects of its activities seriously came from its Environmental and Social (E&S) report for 1998. This was assisted by the consultants ERM Social Strategies (responsible for the collection of independent commentary on previous reports)[41] and auditors Ernst and Young (who provided attestation statements and the data annexe). These outside verifiers were recruited to provide independent confirmation for the company's claims, in response to market research showing that people did not entirely trust companies to monitor themselves. (This lesson has not filtered through to the wider issue of regulation, apparently.)

Another lesson from market research is that corporate pronouncements on the environment had most credibility when they emanated from the top of the company. The statement of Sir John Browne (Group Chief Executive) in the 1998 E&S report was, therefore, of significance:

> The key area where action is necessary is the environment. Although the science is still provisional, the legitimate concerns about the risks of a fundamental change in the earth's climate are too serious to be ignored. Precautionary action is justified and necessary. . . . I believe it is possible to demonstrate that oil and natural gas can be found, produced, refined and used without causing harm to the environment.

In addition to a variety of environmental performance targets achieved, the Report announced that 30 company sites had been certified to the ISO 14001 environmental management standard.[42] The target was to reduce greenhouse gas emissions by 10 percent from 1990 to 2010.

The company was part of the group that contributed to a World Resources Institute report on "Safe Climate, Sound Business," another small contribution to the construction of the sustainable development historical bloc.

The case studies in the 1998 E&S report were of particular interest for the fact that BP (unlike some other companies) did not avoid dealing with problematic issues. In the section entitled "How we measure up," the performance of the company in Alaska was examined. This site had provided up to 20 percent of BP Amoco worldwide production in the past, but was declining. In direct response to unfavorable media stories, the Report robustly declared: "Alaskans have high expectations in corporate citizenship, environmental stewardship, jobs and business opportunities. Public opinion surveys have consistently shown that most Alaskans believe we are performing responsibly." BP Amoco was the state's biggest taxpayer, and every Alaskan received an annual dividend from the earnings of the Alaska Permanent Fund ($25 billion from oil revenues as of 1998). Attention was drawn to "antidevelopment groups" expressing concerns about more energy projects in the area. The company's response was that numerous independent surveys had indicated little adverse impact from the last 20 years of development on Alaskan wildlife and that Alaskans were more worried about jobs and business opportunities than damage to the environment. In any case, the plan was to exploit less than 0.5 percent of the 8 percent of the Arctic National Wildlife Refuge that was open for development. BP Amoco rated well on ethical conduct, employee development, relationships with contractors, and HSE, and the few incidents that had occurred had all been dealt with properly. The State of Alaska had even recommended the company-operated Prudhoe Central Power Station for its first State Voluntary Protection Program Award.

ERM Social Strategies conducted inquiries to test out BP claims in Alaska. It reported that the most comments were positive, but there were some "vague statements" [*sic*] from critics on ethics and relationships, native communities, HSE, and employees. The only specific point from critics that was cited related to two "environmental advocacy groups" who argued that the company should "get serious about developing renewable resources." Though it is clearly a central issue for BP's commitment not to damage the environment, this point was ignored. This is not surprising, as it is difficult to see how BP Amoco (or any other oil company) could stay in business if it really decided to stop all activities which were demonstrably "damaging the environment." Leaving the Global Climate Coalition, as BP did in 1998, was an important gesture. Working seriously to develop energy sources that do not damage the environment and phasing out those that do (particularly petrol) would be positive action.

It is difficult to ascertain the whole truth about BP Amoco's role in the Alaskan oil industry. Nevertheless, the way the company has handled the issue suggests that it does have a case to answer. This case once again highlights the deep contradictions of globalizing corporations in global consumerist capitalism, and the ways in which the sustainable development historical bloc has evolved in this remote fringe of the world. While the 1998 HSE Report focused on Prudhoe Bay, on the North Shore of the Alaskan pipeline, there was no reference to Chugach native village on Chenega Island in Prince William Sound near Valdez, at the southern end of the pipeline.[43] This tiny village was devastated in 1964 when a tidal wave washed every home out to sea. Disaster struck again in 1989 when the oil tanker *Exxon Valdez* broke up, destroying the subsistence fishing of the 27 returned families. Research in Alaska implicated BP and its local subsidiary, Alyeska, for failing to prevent the oil spill in 1989 and for failing to clean it up properly. Native files are alleged to prove a catalog of criminal acts, of which executives in BP headquarters in London were aware (Palast 1999a). The exploitation of Alaskan energy can be seen as a tale of two corporations, BP Amoco, one of the largest in the world, and the Chenega Native Corporation, one of the smallest. By the late 1990s, BP Amoco owned 49 percent of the Alaska Pipeline. Gas is the key to Alaskan energy superprofits, but as it is under the tundra and cannot be transported, its book value is zero. But gas can be liquefied, piped, and shipped out. Under a 1970s court order, pipelines were declared illegal in Alaska, but by one vote the US Congress overturned the order. This reversal was attributed to the success of BP, ARCO, and Exxon in persuading Congress to accept their commitments to protect the environment, namely the promise that they would not build a gas pipeline once they had built the oil pipeline. This dilemma split the local population. Some Chugach villagers were opposed to a new pipeline because of fears of another major spill, while the President of the Chenega Native Corporation, which owned village land and the surrounding wilderness, was a keen supporter.

The Chenega Corporation was, in fact, a creation of BP and its oil industry partners, established after the 1969 Prudhoe Bay oil find to give the local people a stake in the development. "By turning their tribes into corporations, the oil companies explained, natives could become shareholders and dividends from contracts with the oil companies could sustain the villages" (Palast 1999b). Impoverished Chugach villagers could not refuse the offer, and the land was sold to the oil companies. By 1999, of Chenega Corporation's 69 shareholders only 7 still lived on the island and many local people believed that the plan had been designed to fail, in effect to bribe the local population to move out of the area. The Chenega Corporation sold off 90 percent of the village's territory to a trust fund established by Exxon and Alyeska, the BP-controlled consortium, to "preserve" the land, and Chenega became an oil services center. The fishing was almost dead, and islanders who used to catch their food for free became dependent on air-freighted supplies. To survive, they had to be on the BP-Aleyska payroll. However, oil jobs were seasonal, and 70 percent of the local population were on public assistance. The President of the Chenega Corporation operated from his corporate headquarters, Chenega Towers in Anchorage, where he directed logging and tourist concession businesses.[44]

Former Governor Walter Hickell has said that Alaska is "the owner state," paying an annual dividend to each resident. Alaskans were "stockholders in a resource-rich enterprise." He was US Secretary of the Interior when the ARCO chairman, R. O. Anderson, promised not to build a gas pipeline in Alaska. After Governor Hickell left office he teamed up with Mr. Anderson to form the Yukon-Pacific Corporation whose corporate purpose was to build the gas pipeline! Palast asks the question: Is BP trying to turn Alaska into a colony? His answer is no. "BP would never turn the state into a restless colony so long as it can operate Alaska as a well-run subsidiary in which it owns the majority of shares" (Palast 1999b). In early 2000, three Greenpeace activists from a group monitoring the BP Amoco Northstar oilfield were arrested by Alaska state troopers and charged with criminal trespass, alleging collusion between the company and police.

BP has engaged in what Greer and Bruno (1996) label "greenwashing," for example with other major oil companies in funding the National Wetlands Coalition. While this may sound like an organization devoted to the protection of the wetlands as, of course, it was intended to, Rowell (1996: 88) claims that it "exists to weaken legislation that protects wetlands and promotes drilling for oil and gas on wetlands." Once again, what is an oil company to do? In order to thrive – make good returns for its shareholders, keep its employees in work, provide energy for our apparently insatiable needs – it must find new resources to exploit. If these happen to be in wetlands or in Alaska, places to which greens are emotionally attached, then it must find a way round the opposition to exploiting these resources. The National Wetlands Coalition and thousands of similar organizations all round the world simply make the work of the TCC in promoting global consumer capitalism a little easier. Amoco, now part of the BP corporate group, has funded what Rowell (1996: 93) labels "two of the most active anti-green right wing think tanks," the Competitive Enterprise Institute and the cleverly-named Political Economy Research Center.

BP's record on the environment is, at best, mixed. On the one hand, it was ranked as the fifth largest polluter in the USA on the EPA's 1989 Toxic Releases Inventory. A BP facility in Texas was one of the worst offenders. On the other hand, progress was certainly achieved in some respects on pollution emissions in plants all over the world in the 1990s. The Texas chemical facility at Green Lake illustrates this well. Total emissions fell from over 15,605 tonnes in 1990 to 9,459 tonnes in 1997 according to a BP Chemicals Site report for 1997. However – typical of corporate environmental reporting – while the fact that emissions per tonne declined from 1.9 percent in 1996 to 1.7 percent in 1997 is highlighted in a side panel, the fact that actual emissions in this period rose by 1,625 tonnes is buried in a table. In this case, most of the increase was due to off-site disposal. Also buried in the table is the fact that emissions to air in this facility were virtually unchanged from 1996 to 1997, and the 1997 figure was higher than the figures for 1990 to 1994 inclusive.

Let the last word here on BP (and these brief examples) rest with Rodney Chase, Managing Director of BP, spoken when he was chairman of a group of 90 major corporations meeting in Paris under auspices of the international Chamber of Commerce seeking to influence the post-Rio debate on the environment. His personal concerns focused on "late 20th century consumerism [and] the problems of short-lived commodities which generate waste which stays around for a long time" (quoted in "Big Guns to Fire Green Shells," *Financial Times*, Oct. 6, 1993). While neither BP nor any other major corporation has come to grips with Chase's question, the sustainable development historical bloc has so far managed to ensure that the question is rarely raised in the mainstream of social and political life in the global capitalist system.

Sustainable Development as a Globalizing Ideology

In his analysis of the multiple meanings and uses of sustainable development, McManus writes that it "has become a dominant discourse for anything remotely environmental in the 1990s. While the term originated in a specific historical context, its apparent universality is an important reason for its mobilising power" (McManus 1996: 48). In the early 1980s, Michael Redclift put forward the then rather unfashionable argument that "it is the poor [of the South] who are the losers in the process of environmental depredation" (Redclift 1984: 2).

By 1992, even the CEO of Dow Chemical was theorizing: "Sustainable development recognizes that poverty is the ultimate polluter and that hunger has no environmental conscience" (cited in Grossman 1998: 9). Today there is a growing body of opinion that sees the singular ecological crisis exposing contradictions in the inner logic of industrial societies. However, it is exactly at this point that the key contradiction between the capitalist version of sustainable development and ecological survival emerges. To put the issue bluntly, many researchers now seem convinced that any attempt to raise consumption standards in the rest of the world to the levels of the First World, or even to maintain present First World levels, is insupportable on environmental and resource grounds. A growing band of radical thinkers is calling for the very concept of development to be abandoned and the concept of postdevelopment is gaining increasing currency (Sachs 1992).

The claim that there is a contradiction between global capitalist development and global survival appears to have *prima facie* plausibility. If this is indeed the case, then the corporate version of sustainable development cannot be maintained. The transformation of the green vanguard of global capitalism from dry to shallow environmentalism signaled the fact that some ecological crisis messages were getting through to the transnational capitalist class and that serious attention was beginning to be paid to programs to take the crisis out of the environment. Clearly, the dominant agents in the global capitalist system had no option but to believe and act as if the contradiction between global capitalism and sustainable development could be resolved by a combination of economic-technological, political, and culture-ideology means. A central aspect of this solution involved the way that the global capitalist system could use the whole planet (particularly the Third World) to resolve the contradiction, and it is in this sense that sustainable development became a globalizing ideology for the TCC.

There are many examples of how this has worked out globally. Traditionally, TNCs have used the Third World as a place to relocate their most hazardous and polluting production processes, to establish pollution havens. However, it is likely that many, perhaps most, major TNC subsidiaries in developing countries achieve higher environmental standards than local firms. Despite this, pollution havens and their corollary, industrial flight, clearly persist.[45] This is certainly one way that the TNCs could continue to resolve the contradiction of ever-increasing development and ever-worsening ecological crisis for the countries of the First World. However, a combination of international political pressures, the global nature of many environmental hazards, and the unwillingness of Third World governments and their peoples to tolerate such behavior, makes it unlikely that this could be a long-term solution for the core capitalist countries.[46] Nevertheless, what the UNCTC once labeled "unregulated waste tourism" persists. The 1989 Basel Convention on the Control of Transboundary Movements of Hazardous Wastes and Their Disposal was an attempt to regulate abuse in this field, but central to the question was the myth that everything is cheaper in the Third World. Labor is, but other inputs for hazardous waste management can be much more expensive, so the foreign currency shortage that drove Third World governments to such desperate measures may increase rather than decrease as a result of these activities. Already, we can see such problems emerging in the international attempts to implement the well-intentioned Agenda 21 aspirations of the Rio Earth Summit. The hypothesis that it is the culture-ideology of consumerism that drives the system and, thus, provokes the contradiction between capitalist development and global survival, helps us to explain why TNCs produce and treat their wastes in such a cavalier fashion and why governments and elites in the Third World are so desperate for foreign currency, partly to finance imports of consumer goods or the means to produce them.[47] This is certainly one side of sustainable development as a globalizing ideology.

The other side is the genuine developmental efforts that major corporations make to create new markets and stimulate existing ones all over the world. Here, it is important to maintain the distinction between state-centric explanations of elites from First World countries despoiling Third World countries and the globalizing thesis on the structure and significance of the TCC. The globalizing of the transnational capitalist class means that corporate, political, professional, and consumerist elites in Third World countries want to keep their own private communities clean and safe and to protect those parts of their own countries that are special to them. Lucrative exploitable resources may be more likely to be developed in Third World countries than elsewhere because the people who occupy the land are not the elites in these places. As we have seen, such development tends to intensify more than resolve the ecological crisis for most populations and for most habitats (the effects on the class polarization crisis are not so clear-cut). A question raised about the record of Rio Tinto can justifiably be asked of all transnational corporations wherever their profit-seeking and employment-creating activities impact natural and social environments. "If today's mining industry cannot even finance the clean-up of mining wastes from the recent past (which US experience of the Superfund has shown to be true), what chance is there of its safeguarding future generations against the even bigger wastes it is now planning to create?" (Moody 1996: 52). The evidence reviewed in this chapter on the historical records of major and respected corporations manufacturing personal and household products, the food we eat, the electronics that enrich our lives, and the minerals without which few of these products would be possible to make, shows that all these major corporations have a case to answer. The rapid growth of global corporate citizenship and its specific application in the creation of the sustainable development historical bloc suggests that the ways in which some major corporations have chosen to answer their critics has more to do with protecting the reputations of the corporations than solving the problems. This raises a fundamental issue for the global capitalist system, namely is the global vision of the major corporations, and those who own and control them, irredeemably flawed?

Notes

1 This chapter has been influenced and informed by Peter Robbins' doctoral research on the greening of the corporations, and the forthcoming dissertations of Michelle Bellers on Greenpeace and Friends of the Earth, Claudia Granados on sustainable development along the US–Mexico border, Boris Holzer on corporate environmental discourse, and Aparna Joshi on Monsanto and GMO in India and the West.

2 Beder (1997) suggests that this was when "greenwashing" (environmental public relations) began, and Monsanto has been active in this cause ever since. See also Greer and Bruno (1996).

3 An update of the original report in 1992 had very little impact, being swamped by the umbrella idea of sustainable development.

4 For example, "According to a senior vice-president of a United States chemical TNC, Bhopal has changed TNCs' consciousness about what they need to do to make their operations safer" (United Nations 1988: 16). This was confirmed to me in several interviews, for example, Roche set up an International Task Force to cope with the aftermath.

5 Sociologists of development might see this as a Warren thesis of the environment!

6 This little-known organization, representing major corporations, was an influential lobbyist on behalf of the Multilateral Agreement on Investment. Its existence supports a central thesis of this book, that the transnational capitalist class is not opposed to regulation of local, national, or global business, it simply wants the right to ensure that any regulation imposed is in its own commercial interests. There is urgent need for more systematic research on BIAC and similar organs of global capitalism.

7 These issues are being taken up by the global environmental justice movement (Dobson 1998; Gibbs 1995; Westra and Wenz 1995).

8 See Brecher and Costello (1994). The campaign against capitalist globalization has also succeeded in bringing labor and ecological activists together (Mander and Goldsmith 1996).

9 The original 19 included Allied-Signal, Amoco, AT&T, Dow, Dupont, ICI Americas, Procter & Gamble, and Union Carbide. Others, such as IBM and Johnson and Johnson, also signed up.

10 These are of very different types. Compare, for example, Deal (1993) and Nelson (1996).

11 See also Schmidheiny (1992), which has become a standard reference for the global corporate response to the environmental challenge.

12 National Wildlife Federation, National Audubon Society, and Sierra Club, all based in the USA, are among the largest environmental organizations in the world. Although they are not global as such, they all have global agendas.

13 For a critical assessment of Rio see Panjabi (1997) and Dalby (1996) on how the reporting of the Rio Earth Summit in the most influential newspaper in the USA reinforced the environmental status quo.

14 I would not wish to appear entirely negative about the Division on Sustainable Development. The annual "Success Stories" (1997 onwards) are quite inspiring. They might be read in the spirit of "pessimism of the intelligence, optimism of the will" that inspired Romain Rolland and Antonio Gramsci (and me too).

15 Another telling example is the policy of Friends of the Earth in England, in its magazine *Earth Matters*, to work with companies that appear to be responding to environmental pressure, notably BP Amoco and B&Q, the UK-based "do-it-yourself" store (Juniper 1999). However, in a previous issue of *Earth Matters* (Alley and Taylor 1999), the type of policy and practices for which B&Q is commended in its sustainable wood products are shown to be a sham for similar products elsewhere. See also Lenskyj (1998) on the Sydney 2000 "Green Olympics" and the involvement of Greenpeace in the "environmentally sound Olympic Village." These organizations are in a very difficult position.

16 For a subtle analysis of the disagreement between the Washington-based World Resources Institute and the New Delhi-based Centre for Science and the Environment over allocation of First World versus Third World "blame" for global warming in the early 1990s, see Yearley (1996: 102–7). On the actual environmental consequences of many common activities, concluding that motoring is by far the single most destructive activity, see Brower and Leon (1999).

17 Including the *Fortune* Global 500 companies Amoco, ARCO, BHP, BP, Chevron, Chrysler, Exxon, Ford, General Motors, Goodyear, Hoechst Cela-nese, McDonnell Douglas, Mobil, Shell, Texaco, Union Pacific, and USX. Union Carbide was also a member.

18 In a vote of delegates and green groups at Kyoto, the GCC was named as the organization that had done most to wreck the agreement. Exxon was placed second, followed by Tokyo Electric (TEPCO), and the major vehicle manufacturers. A spokesman for the GCC was quoted as saying: "We regard this as an honour ... It shows we are an effective lobby group" (see "Temperature Rises at Global Warming Talks," *Guardian*, Dec. 5, 1997).

19 O'Riordan is in an excellent position to comment on these issues as he connects the academic and corporate wings of the sustainable development historical bloc through his membership of Dow Chemical's Corporate Environmental Advisory Council since its formation in 1991

20 Understandably but perhaps a little prematurely, O'Riordan excludes socialist environmentalism from his account of "evolution of environmentalism." There are several versions of the socialist environmental alternative (in O'Connor, ed., 1994, for example), but it is not at all clear how they can cope with the critique of industrialism (Dobson 1990, ch. 5). Contributors in Peet and Watts, eds. (1996) connect these issues with social movements through the motif of liberation ecologies.

21 The UNCTC was disbanded and moved to Geneva in the early 1990s where it became a Division of UNCTAD. It no longer has any monitoring role with respect to the TNCs though it does continue to produce useful publications on TNCs and the global economy, for example the annual *World Investment Report* and the journal *Transnational Corporations*.

22 This is debatable. There are many examples of major corporations that have relocated to avoid environmental regulations (see Leonard 1988, Clapp 1998b). Leonard is correct to argue that pollution havens are not a viable industrialization strategy for developing countries, though they still exist in considerable numbers.

23 A notable contribution is the ten-point Environmental Project Management Tool of S. C. Johnson. While not a Global 500 company, Johnson Wax is a recognized leader in the spheres of environmental stewardship and community development in many parts of the world. (It has the added distinction of nurturing its problem-ridden headquarters in Racine, Wisconsin designed by Frank Lloyd Wright, and opening them up for free public tours.)

24 Where no direct references are given the information in these cases is based on interviews (all but Monsanto), corporate publications, press reports and websites of companies, locations and campaign groups.

25 This account comes mainly from Swasy's book which, it should be noted, was based on more than 300 interviews of current and former employees, scores of interviews with people professionally and commercially knowledgeable about the company, and a very thorough review of legal and public records (see "Reporter's Note," Swasy 1994: vii–x). P&G apparently purchased 200 copies for internal distribution. Fenholloway takes up only one chapter; others are concerned with allegations about the excessive control the company exerts over its employees and the communities where it is based, and its global aspirations, "Pampering the World."

26 Rowell (1996: 175) provides further harrowing testimony on this case, one of many incidents of physical attacks on environmental campaigners he connects with the Wise Use movement.

27 "Vision of a Hi-tech Fix for Society" (*Guardian*, Dec. 16, 1997). I cannot resist quoting the concluding paragraph of this article. "The meeting broke up after two hours. The head of Monsanto Europe took Lang [a prominent

British food policy academic and activist] aside. 'Hey Tim, do you read Jürgen Habermas. . . . You sound just like him.' "

28 At the end of 1999, in the face of mounting public pressure and the potential threat of future lawsuits, Monsanto announced that it was discontinuing its efforts to commercialize sterile seed technology and changing its name. However, as environmentalists pointed out at the time, new forms of genetic modification with similar effects were not ruled out.

29 Despite my admiration for Kloppenberg's work, it would be inconsistent for me to ignore the state-centrism inherent in this formulation. While the corporations domiciled in the USA and Europe are clearly dominant, there is a good deal of important research on GMOs being conducted by scientists and local companies in the South, some working with Monsanto and some against (see Vidal 1999).

30 B-M appears to be prone to leaks. The text of a Burson-Marsteller report, "Communications Program for Europabio" (a coalition of major agrifood bioindustry corporations, including Monsanto), dated January 1997, can be found on the <corporate watch> website, detailing exactly what Beder and others mean by "global spin."

31 A related example of the dioxin lobby concerns two resolutions against dioxin from a Texas PTA convention in 1995. Six "concerned parents" circulated material to undermine calls for action against dioxin. In fact, three of these parents were members of the Chemical Council, one was an employee of DuPont, and the others were also connected with industrial interests. Consequently, one resolution was diluted and the other postponed (Beder 1997: 157–8).

32 In 1992, Intel announced a new plant in Silicon Valley, and "streamlined regulatory permit processes" (permissions granted in 3 rather than the normal 18 months) were credited with this development. Subsequent research revealed that Intel and the Governor of California had pressured the Bay Area Air Quality Management District to override technical objections to proposed emission levels (SWOP 1995: 17–19). These levels were much lower than those granted for the New Mexico facilities, where similar allegations were made.

33 Summed up in a typical article in the Samsung *Magazine* for December 1999, "It Isn't Easy being Green? But It Can Be Profitable," and, more cynically, by an environment executive of Loblaw, Canada's largest food distributor: "If we made a lot of money destroying this planet, we sure can make money cleaning it up" (quoted in Vandervoort 1991: 14).

34 See Angell (1996). The company newsletter, *Around Dow*, shows that Dow was winning more implant cases than it was losing in the 1990s.

35 Gjording (1991, ch. 10) on "Outside Agitators" is a thoughtful account of the problems of representation in such struggles.

36 RTZ has been subject to several hostile minority shareholder actions since the 1970s. Rowell (1996: 74–5) reports that in the mid-1990s RTZ began to consider how to consolidate shares into blocks of 100, thus excluding small investors entirely and preventing shareholder opposition.

37 Hiscock (1997: 268–9) reports the involvement of one of Indonesia's leading businessmen, Mohamad Bob Hasan, in the Freeport mine. This is a good example of how a member of the local corporate elite interacts with globalizing executives and politicians.

38 See the Corporate Watch website, where details of Freeport are continually updated. On the other hand, the *Balanco Social/Social Report* of Rio Tinto Brasil (1997) presents an entirely different and benign picture of the company's overseas operations.

39 Popular agitation that led to the closure of the Bougainville mine in PNG so discouraged bankers that Rio Tinto and partners were forced to rely on financing from the World Bank's Multilateral Investment Guarantee Agency to exploit the new gold mine in Lihir Island, PNG. On the expected environmental destruction of this remote place see Hildyard (1996: 178).

40 The March 1996 issue of *Multinational Monitor* contains several articles on PNG, concerning BHP, Chevron, Freeport, and the Porgera gold mine.

41 ERM conducted independent reports on BP's operations in Alaska, China, Egypt, and South Africa. The Report notes that ERM annual turnover was in excess of $250 million, and at no time in the last five years had BP business been more than 1 percent of this turnover. Independence is clearly a sensitive issue.

42 For a deconstruction of the ISO 14000 series and, by implication, other standards, see Clapp (1998a).

43 My sources for what follows are two newspaper articles by Gregory Palast (1999a; 1999b) based on four unpublished volumes of his research materials, and articles in the *Guardian* newspaper on July 12, 1999.

44 There is no mention of Alyeska or Chugach in BP's 1998 Environment and Social Report, which discusses the Alaskan operations. The only reference to Alyeska in the BP Amoco information pack for 1998 appears to be in the Site Summaries section of the HSE Data 1998 Report, namely "Crude oil loading (Alyeska)-Alaska, vapor emissions: Valdez terminal."

45 For a balanced comparative analysis, see Leonard (1988) usefully updated by Clapp (1998b). It is worth noting that opposition to NAFTA was spear-headed by environmental groups on precisely these grounds (see Dowie 1995, ch. 7). For analysis of the related question of the environmental impacts of export-oriented industrialization, see Sklair (2000).

46 "Just between you and me, shouldn't the World Bank be encouraging more migration of the dirty industries to the LDCs?" These leaked words of Lawrence Summers, then chief economist at the World Bank and latterly Clinton's Secretary of the Treasury, were headline news in 1992 (see Yearley 1996: 75–6). See also Westra and Wenz (1995: xvi and *passim*). As Leonard (1988) shows, economists had been arguing this for some time.

47 I am, of course, aware that much of the available foreign currency is spent on weapons and other instruments of repression, but it is not difficult to connect this to the need to sustain and protect the consumption of elites.

Chapter 8
Global Vision and the Culture-Ideology of Consumerism

Many major corporations have a vision (or mission) statement, and the expression of a global vision is the fourth criterion for the globalizing corporation. Global visions come in a variety of shapes and sizes and from a variety of sources, but most of them have one thing in common. They all serve, directly or indirectly, the culture-ideology of consumerism, and its role in sustaining global capitalism based on mass (if not quite universal) consumerism forever. This line of argument helps to explain the vogue of theories about the end of ideology or the end of history from the 1950s to the present. Whatever else might change or however social systems might diverge, the argument went, people would all agree on one principle, namely the desirability of consuming more and more goods and services. Globalization, therefore, could be seen as a new convergence thesis. Rulers could guarantee social peace (even in the absence of civil liberties in some parts of the world) by ensuring the conditions for people's material desires are met. The creation of these desires (the demand side of the equation) could safely be left to consumerist elites (the fourth fraction of the transnational capitalist class),[1] and the production of goods and services (the supply side) could be safely left to the ever-more-productive organs of global capitalism. In the words of a senior corporate executive, responsible for some of the world's most successful brands: "Once television is there, people of whatever shade, culture, or origin want roughly the same things" (CEO of H. J. Heinz, quoted in Beder 1997: 184).

As the previous two chapters have shown, most globalizing corporations claim to accept the obligations that global corporate citizenship brings. The analysis of the global vision of globalizing corporations (often publicly articulated by CEOs) provides an important guide to the values that underlie these conceptions of global corporate citizenship. Domestic or multinational corporations have little need of global visions. The key problem of a domestic corporation is to ensure its local market. Multinational companies need to ensure the foreign markets they serve, whether by direct exports or through local manufacturing and/or services. A globalizing corporation needs a global vision precisely because it is in the process of denationalizing, redefining its ties to its place of birth, and forging new ties with its global markets and partners. Most Global 500 corporations strive to achieve a global vision, but many concede that in practice they are falling short of the goal.

It is a widely-held misconception that globalization and localization are mutually exclusive and contradictory processes. Those who draw attention to the vitality of local entrepreneurs and cultures as evidence against globalization are correct to the extent that some globalists predict the demise of the local as global forces inexorably create a homogenous global culture (see Lechner and Boli 2000, Parts VII and VIII). This argument has no place in the theoretical framework that underlies this study. The global capitalist system is predicated on the accumulation of private profits on a global scale and the leading actors in the system have no particular interest in destroying or sustaining local cultures apart from the drive for increased profitability. Where local or national agents threaten profitability capitalists certainly destroy them, as colonial powers have done in the past wherever local enterprise interfered with their expansionist plans. Economic globalization has changed this to some extent by making it easier for globalizing corporations to integrate local partners into their cross-border networks and to take advantage of local talents and resources, an advantage that can be shared with local elites. Always to see opposition between the local and the global is the result of a rather naive static view of traditional practices and cultures. Global forces certainly change local cultures but this does not necessarily mean that they destroy them, though sometimes they do.

While the underlying rationale for corporate global visions is to be found in the culture-ideology of consumerism,[2] these visions can be expressed in at least three different ways. First, some corporations actually do make direct connections between their global vision and the greater good of humanity through the medium of their global brands. No doubt most corporations would like to do this, given the value of the most successful global brands, but the world market is still sufficiently diverse to make this difficult for all but a few products. Nevertheless, consumer-oriented global visions for humanity have been articulated by several major corporations and global system theory would predict that we can expect many more to follow in the years to come. A second expression of global vision can be labelled industry-oriented, where corporations structure their visions around the industries of their main products. This connects with the culture-ideology of consumerism through the goal of being world number one or the best or the most respected in the industry, measured in terms of the sales of these products and the ways in which they enhance the quality of people's lives. This is not so different from the first, but the manner in which these corporations express their global visions tends to be rather more modest. A third expression of global vision is best labelled organization-oriented. In this case, the corporation has a vision of being better-organized to fulfil its destiny of global success. Service to customers (as well as other stakeholders) is an important part of this vision, in some cases the stated point of the vision, providing the link with the culture-ideology of consumerism. These distinctions are not rigid. Consumerist visions often contain industry-oriented and/or organizational features.

One further issue requires attention and this is the role of the visionary executive, usually the CEO or the President. In some corporations, particularly those which have experienced traumatic reverses in their fortunes (even profitable stagnation can be a trauma for global capitalists), specific individuals with proven track records in corporate success have been recruited to turn the company round. The most important reason for this is to improve the stock price of the corporation and this has often been accompanied by the articulation of a global vision. The visionary executive succeeds by convincing three key groups that he (rarely she)[3] has the solutions to the corporation's problems. These groups are the Board of Directors (with power to hire and fire, and to decide remuneration), the financial press and the investing community. This varies to some extent from country to country but major corporations are increasingly dominated by financial institutions rather than individual investors. The evidence from the Global 500 is that the rhetoric of visionary CEOs connects directly with the culture-ideology of consumerism.

Consumer-oriented Global Visions for Humanity

According to Luthans and Hodgetts (1997, p. 414): "Perhaps the most important pillar of the world-class organization is its customer-focus. The organization puts the customer at the center of its strategy, and all systems and personnel are organized to serve the customer." The best-selling management guru Rosabeth Moss Kanter puts the same idea in a more dramatic form: "THINK LIKE THE CUSTOMER: THE

GLOBAL BUSINESS LOGIC" (Kanter 1996, p. 48, upper case in original).[4] As we shall see, these are exactly the rhetorical devices of the major corporations.

Philips (renamed Royal Philips Electronics in 1998), provides a good starting point for discussion of consumer-oriented global visions. Under the slogan: "From vision to reality. Let's make things better",[5] the company attempted to reposition itself in the global marketplace to serve consumers all over the world. Philips was explicit about this global vision. "Let's make things better" was intended to be a holistic view of betterment in the community, for employees, and others. This went beyond the product as portrayed in the previous corporate theme of "let's make things better at work, home and away."

Founded in 1891 in the Netherlands, Philips was actively involved in 60 different businesses and sold its products in 150 countries. Its commitment to the culture-ideology of consumerism was clear. "As one of the world's leading electronics companies, Philips believes it bears a special responsibility to help ensure that the world ahead will be better and that people can look forward to an improved quality of life." In the mid-1990s Philips launched its first global promotional campaign, as a support for the corporate decision to transform its efforts in the North American market. The campaign brought together symbols and emotions familiar in the consumerist canon. The focus was on the personal, the individual, the unpredictable consumer, connected to others in a series of virtual consuming communities. Targeting people who want to project "a new-look me," the technology unleashed by Philips gives the consumer the confidence to say: "I can do it [more or less anything I want] myself." This signified the rise of the "re-abled" (empowered) consumer. But this vision was also a caring vision, giving each one of us the means "for conserving energy . . . my energy." The vision was grounded in a new generation of personal digital assistants, including pens that download written and spoken notes into personal computers, and what the company called, poetically, "personal emotion containers".

Philips projected its vision not only inside the company, but also outside in strategic locations. Agreements with the UN Development Program were undertaken to provide training services in China, Argentina, Mexico, and India. This involved preparation for ISO certification and other quality processes. The company was quite open about the benefits of this work – such projects made good public relations sense and provided valuable networking opportunities with the authorities. In short, these projects created opportunities to work with globalizing bureaucrats and politicians and to globalize local bureaucrats and politicians all over the world.

This global vision played out in subtle ways in Philips Australia, where it was turned into Vision 2001, Philips' aspiration to be "Australia's Leading Electronics Company by 2001." To achieve this, five core values were to be implemented: namely, delight customers, value people as our greatest resource, deliver quality, achieve premium return on equity, and encourage entrepreneurial behavior at all levels. The global vision was, therefore, at one and the same time both a general Philips global vision and a specific Australian Philips vision. But for both, the customer and the satisfaction of consumer desires came first.

Disney's global vision has been discussed in many contexts (Dorfman and Mattelart 1975, Sorkin 1992). Disney, along with McDonald's and Coca-Cola, is, of course, widely regarded as an icon of globalization. Within the company, Walt Disney Imagineering had the responsibility for "changing the future." This it had been doing in the theme parks for decades and in the mid-1990s began to develop "new worlds of location-based entertainment and cyberspace," a prime component of what Langman (2000) calls "cyberfeudalism." The modern theme park is a distinctively global phenomenon, combining the capacities of globally-dispersed industry for the production of the merchandise with the symbolic potential of the culture-ideology of consumerism. The production and marketing of sports goods has boomed in a similar way. Here, the acknowledged leader, Nike, has turned its slogan "just do it" and its "swoosh" into core cultural symbols in their own right. Nike's creative use of sporting icons (particularly African-Americans) has projected a global vision that goes far beyond the materiality of its products, as Goldman and Papson (1998) argue and illustrate in fine detail.

The global vision of Colgate-Palmolive (C-P) is expressed almost entirely through the lens of consumerism and what this entails for production and profits. A senior executive with substantial "international experience" argued this case in the form of a nine-component narrative that bears repeating in its entirety, less for its distinctiveness than its representativeness and completeness as a corporate expression of the consumerist global vision. The first component refers to the five core categories of the consumer products markets in which the company competed globally (oral, personal, household and fabric care, and pet nutrition products). The second component was the need to understand global consumers by looking for common features – for example, teeth-cleaning is almost universal but different people clean their teeth in different ways. The third component was the relentless quest to develop technically relevant products, and the continuous search for value-added, especially in the developing world. C-P's interest in Brazil, for example, stems from the fact that it has 100 million relatively prosperous consumers (and about 70 million poor people). The fourth component lay in the company's global brands, brands that could be promoted in all markets. This led logically on to the drive to standardize manufacturing processes and products – like many other producers, C-P noted that decreasing tariffs facilitated global patterns of production, not necessarily fewer factories but certainly more efficient production. Next came the need to squeeze costs out of the supply chain. It is important to note that for C-P labor costs were not always the key to cost control, for many products energy and transportation costs were more important.[6] The seventh component was the globalization of trade partners. For C-P, a corporation with revenues in excess of $9 billion, a mere 50 business partners (huge retail chains such as K-Mart, for example) accounted for one-third of total sales. The eighth component was highly trained, flexible, multi-cultural management, "people prepared to move around the world," with language skills and cultural sensitivity. The connections between this and the issue of diversity may be noted (see chapter 7 above). The final component of C-P's global vision, for public consumption at any rate, was the return to shareholders, the factor that drives all growth companies.

Just as everyday personal consumer goods companies like C-P express their global visions in terms of consumerism, computer and electronics companies do so too, but with a rather different focus. Intel, "Architect of the Microcomputer Revolution," saw itself doing for the current revolution what the inventors of the steam engine did for the industrial revolution. Despite its near-universality, the digital world penetrated differently in different places, though it was undeniable that many people were buying PCs who had not previously been in the market. Intel's top management made regular tours of the Far East and other so-called emerging markets to monitor commercial opportunities and to spread the vision of the microelectronic age. At the beginning of 1996, for example, six senior officers toured the Far East, India and Japan and met about 1,000 people at all levels, from top government officials and business leaders to ordinary computer users. This was a fairly common occurrence. As was noted in chapter 4 in the discussion of global brands, Intel was most unusual in enjoying high consumer recognition for a hidden component. The "intel inside" sticker that adorns so many computers keeps the name and the accompanying vision in the public eye.[7] Responding to the challenge of the internet, by 1998 Intel's vision had been refined in terms of "getting to a billion connected computers worldwide," all with Intel inside.

There was some corporate recognition that the electronic revolution has created an elite class of information-rich consumers who had left the masses behind all over the world.[8] This was an idea specifically discussed in an interview with a middle-level manager at Apple's gleaming campus-like headquarters in Silicon Valley, who contrasted the reality of computer use and access to the internet with the Apple vision of personal computers for all. This global vision, for Apple, was directly related to the idea of education as "a lifelong and globe-spanning activity" enhanced, perhaps even made possible on a mass scale, by what Apple has to offer. The educational and communitarian possibilities of the internet are obvious, but the commercial potential – making the culture-ideology of consumerism electronic – is more likely to dominate this new medium (see Schiller 1999). The global visions of electronic corporations are, therefore, of significance for the trajectory of global capitalism.

One interesting local manifestation, replete with the positive and negative consequences of globalization, is the Information Age Town (IAT) created in Ennis (Ireland) in 1997 when the town won a I£15 million (about $20 million) award to help put its people on-line. The scheme was financed by Telecom Eireann, the national telecommunications company, and by 2000 over 80 percent of homes in Ennis had internet access. Prime amongst the main factors that won the competition for the town against over 30 competing entries was the existing links of Ennis to the global economy, notably through the nearby Shannon airport, the dynamic presence of Shannon Development Corporation, and the fact that over half of the local manufacturing workforce were employed in TNCs. In the words of the local chamber of commerce, Ennis had already begun to "migrate into the global" and the IAT was a spur to maketing on a global basis. Local schools and colleges provided computer skills training and the chamber of commerce ran courses on e-commerce, all with attractive subsidies. However, not all local businesses were enthused by the stark choice between going on-line or going out of business. The major TNCs in the region (and there are many) are involved in a variety of ways in the IAT, for example the chairman of the organization is a senior executive of Roche Ireland.

The role of the corporation in making the world a better place through continuous technological advances in consumer goods and services was a common theme for electronics corporations. This was vividly conveyed in the booklet "NEC Global Vision. C&C [Computers & Communications] for Human Potential." Through its technology and imagination, Nippon Electronic Corporation's global vision integrated three objectives. The first was to "empower lives to make contributions to society." The illustrations of how this was being accomplished in the mid-1990s were telling. For example, in Texas Tech University Health Sciences Center in the USA, the NEC Global Network Class "Gakkos" integrated internet-based global classrooms all over the world (school pupils were enjoined to "Be a Global Citizen" on screen). NEC's second objective was to connect people through global networks; the third was to create innovative tools and new potential for people and societies, all similarly illustrated with global images from around the world. "Our vision at NEC is that of a world unified, where the possibilities for human enrichment are virtually endless. Transforming this vision into reality is the true role of NEC multimedia." NEC introduced its C&C vision in 1977, one of the first systematic corporate statements of how the power of computers could be integrated with the scope of global communications. This was the logical consequence of the three core technologies in which NEC was a world leader (computers, communications and semiconductors), all vital to the creation of the Global Information Society.

In contrast to some other Japanese companies, NEC claimed that its employees tended to follow the ideas of top management on the need to globalize. There was less evidence (in public, at least) of the resistance to globalization that has occurred, for example, in some of Mitsubishi's constituent companies. In NEC, the global message was reported to have been generally effective all through the company. If accurate, this may well have been due to the systematic efforts of senior management to communicate the vision regularly throughout the company's far-flung empire with monthly corporate strategy meetings where results were fed back to each division, through video, e-mail, personal presentations and other means. However, another and possibly decisive difference between NEC and general trading companies, was that the business sector in which NEC participated – electronic communications – was much more global and "visionary" to start with, which gave an advantage over conglomerates like Mitsubishi. "Just imagine" was the NEC Multimedia slogan, the future was encapsulated in terms of imagination. "Imagine a global communications network that can instantly bring individuals and institutions closer together, regardless of language and culture. Imagine a world where even the most routine work can bring genuine pleasure and enhance productivity" [*sic*].

Dell Computer articulated its global mission in the statement of its visionary founder Michael Dell: "to be the most successful company in the world at delivering the best Customer Experience [capitals in original] in the markets we serve." This was driven throughout the corporation under the slogan "the Direct Model," highlighting the goal of dealing directly with customers and employees all over the world. In practice, this could be observed in the Focalpoint center in Dell Ireland, a multimedia customer experience. The strategy clearly works. A hundred dollars invested in Dell in 1988 was worth $56,470 in January 1999!

Given the high visibility of telecommunications in public and academic conceptions of globalization, it is not surprising that many of the major corporations in the industry promote themselves with global visions. For example, MCI claimed to have articulated the first internet-based global vision.[9] AT&T, on its own admission, had struggled to articulate a global vision and shake itself loose of its traditional roots as an American telephone company. Its strategy and mission statements were "unrelentingly communicated around the world," its vision was "bringing people together, anytime, anywhere." This, it was claimed, was more than just an advertising slogan (though it was certainly an advertising slogan whatever else it might have been). To make sense of this as a global vision, once again, we must connect it with the culture-ideology of consumerism. Communication itself has been turned into a form of mass consumption and, as a result, has been dragged into the culture-ideology of consumerism via the ease of superfluous communication (easy but not inexpensive). The mobile phone, for all its socially valuable attributes, is the highest material embodiment of this process to date. AT&T's vision of "bringing people together" expressed the commercial interest in this process exactly. Like NEC, it promised a world where: "even the most routine work can bring genuine pleasure and enhance productivity."

The global vision in Motorola, another corporation that invested heavily in global telecommunications and mobile phone networks, was "bringing modern communications to the world." Motorola conceded in the late 1990s that this vision was not sufficiently well articulated. The explanation offered for this shortcoming was very instructive. As Motorola had traditionally been driven by engineers the company had fallen behind in marketing (see the discussion of Six Sigma in chapter 5). Despite the fact that the company introduced the first handheld portable cellular phone (in 1984), it lost the commercial initiative in the 1990s. Realizing the magnitude of its mistakes in this regard, Motorola became a major invester in cellular phones and initiated a campaign to teach engineers and marketers to be interdependent to promote and achieve the global vision. In Motorola's subsidiary in Hong Kong, the entry point for the China market, the issue was put in graphic terms. Globalization was a "train that has left the station"; no one could afford not to be on board. No company could afford to be "just an American [or Japanese, or Chinese] company." The global challenge had to be met, and Motorola responded in many ways, for example by introducing Iridium, the world's first handheld global satellite phone and paging network.[10] Even in Motorola, however, there was some resistance to the globalization script, no doubt spearheaded by "American engineers." While corporate managers "talk the talk of globalization very compellingly," their actions did not always match their words. Nevertheless, these globalizing visions allowed pro-globalizers in companies such as Motorola to use the language coming from the top to spur their laggard colleagues into action. As the global vision was driven from the top, rewards and recognition based on the global vision were becoming more common. Motorola, like an increasing number of major corporations, encapsulated its vision in a credit-card-sized reminder, for employees and customers, reproduced as Figure 8.1.

Financial services companies, banks in particular, tended to articulate their visions in terms of their business sectors, but there were some interesting exceptions. Merrill Lynch (M-L), for example, articulated a broad global vision under the title "The Promise of the Global Marketplace."

> once segmented markets are joining into regional blocs, which in turn are coalescing into a single vast global market. . . . Indeed, as this global marketplace grows, fed by the revolution in information technology and the erosion of international trade barriers, it will actively foster winners. . . . For Merrill Lynch, the globalization of the capital markets has the paradoxical effect of leading us to pursue a strategy of becoming more *local* at the same time we are becoming more global. While this dual strategy may sound contradictory, it is not. To help both investors and issuing clients reap the full benefits of globalization, we must be global in the products, services and intelligence we bring to bear, but we must also be local in our relationships and our ability to participate in key local market activities, which are growing rapidly. (1996 Annual Report)

The Annual Report of 1997, entitled "Partners in Human Achievement," expanded the vision through the belief that the company had a larger purpose than making money. This had a distinctly ideological (though not exactly surprising) bent, however, as it was embedded in the argument that: "There is no viable alternative to capitalism as an economic structure." M-L's vision drove it to promote economic growth and development. Fortunately for financial services companies, the imperatives of economic growth and development create an enormous demand for capital. M-L prospered while doing good in terms of its

Figure 8.1 Motorola "Total Customer Satisfaction" card

(front)

> # OUR FUNDAMENTAL OBJECTIVE
> ### *(Everyone's Overriding Responsibility)*
>
> ## Total Customer Satisfaction
>
> **[logo] MOTOROLA**

(back)

> **KEY BELIEFS** – *how we will always act*
> * Constant Respect for People
> * Uncompromising Integrity
>
> **KEY GOALS** – *what we must accomplish*
> * Best in class
>   - *People*
>   - *Marketing*
>   - *Technology*
>   - *Product: Software, Hardware and Systems*
>   - *Manufacturing*
>   - *Service*
> * Increased Global Market Share
> * Superior Financial Results
>
> **KEY INITIATIVES** – *how we will do it*
> * Six Sigma Quality
> * Total Cycle Time Reduction
> * Product, Manufacturing and Environment Leadership
> * Profit Improvement
>
> Empowerment for all, in a Participative, Cooperative and Creative Workplace

global vision, as exemplified by its lucrative involvement in the privati-zations of the telephone systems in Peru, Hungary, and Portugal, other privatization business in Brazil (the largest in Latin America in the 1990s), INDOSAT in Indonesia, and the entry of Deutsche Telecom in the US market. The visionary CEO, David Kominsky, was profiled in *Forbes* magazine as a "common man with global ambitions" ("Merrill-izing the World", Feb. 10, 1997).

The most widely-publicized global financial event of the 1990s was the merger of Travelers Group (the insurance and stockbroking con-glomerate) with Citicorp (one of the world's biggest banks) to form Citigroup. In the words of one analyst: "This is the first move in the global end game. It is a classic case of thinking the unthinkable" (quoted in "Big and Bigger" *Financial Times*, April 7, 1998). Citigroup marketed itself as the premier financial services group for consumers, customers, institutions and government agencies worldwide. The new company's organization chart (reproduced in *Fortune*, Nov. 23, 1998) illustrated its global vision by placing Global Corporate Business, Global Consumer Business, and Asset Management as the next layer down from the joint CEOs and the board. The accompanying picture showed the two CEOs, hands on a large globe.

BankAmerica (BofA) explicitly employed a version of the "think globally, act locally" slogan which swept through the corporate sector in the 1990s. BofA's version was articulated as "global vision, local hand." The rationale was that it is important, even for a global bank, not to lose sight of local differences, and that it is vital to be able to change the reference point from the local to the global and back again when necessary. To accomplish this, the bank introduced a system of intensive briefings for executives attending top-level meetings with Finance Ministers and other high officials in the places where it was doing business. As with all globalizing corporations, the Board of Directors was a source of extensive global experience. For example, Board member Tom Clausen's period at the World Bank was clearly of significance in this regard.

In Shell, the idea of corporate vision was widely discussed in the 1990s. The Shell Global Scenario team and its various visions of the future connect with the analysis in chapter 6 of the Shell Report 1998, where information was given on Global Forums involving thousands of Shell stakeholders. One suggestion as to why the company had expended so much time, effort and resources on these issues emerged from interviews with members of the scenario and reputation management teams. The idea of vision did not traditionally resonate in Shell because the company was full of engineers and accountants (the implication was that they were far too busy to sit around worrying about such arcane matters). However, the increasing problems of operating globally forced the question "what does Shell stand for?" onto the agenda in the 1990s. At least three images of Shell were evident. These were the exciting image of a bold company drilling oil wells at sea; an image of security (summed up in the advertising slogan "you can be sure with Shell"); and the image of a global corporation with joint ventures and strategic alliances all over the world. All these had to be accommodated in a single global Shell vision. The restructuring of the company in the 1990s was driven by the recognition that its financial performance (return to shareholders) was inadequate and that this was because of the forces of globalization. The 1995–2020 scenarios were based on three absolute certainties, continuing globalization (defined mainly in terms of FDI and privatization); liberalization of trade (the prediction was that this was not going to be reversed); and rapid technological progress (especially in communications). Any vision generated by the company, therefore, had to incorporate these certainties (see Davis-Floyd 1998, and compare Frynas 2000).

Honda's global vision was clearly consumer-oriented. The company principle from Honda's corporate philosophy summed this up in a rather understated fashion: "Maintaining an international viewpoint, we are dedicated to supplying products of the highest efficiency yet at a reasonable price for worldwide customer satisfaction" (quoted in Mair 1994: 45). Honda was widely regarded as the originator of the global-local corporation, and particularly noted for its success in transplanting factories and ideas from its home base in Japan to its subsidiaries in the USA and Europe. Honda gives us an excellent example of the three key elements of the consumer-oriented global vision. First, the "international" (here we may read "global") viewpoint deliberately denationalizes the vision, more significant for a corporation of Japanese origins than for those from some other countries. Second, the promise of products of the "highest efficiency and reasonable price" recalls the continuous search for world best practice without which the globalizing corporation is doomed to failure. And third, the point of the whole activity, "worldwide customer satisfaction," locks the vision securely into the culture-ideology of consumerism.

This section concludes with the visions of Ford and BT, companies that successfully combined reference to two (very different) industries with globalizing consumer-oriented visions.

In 1994 Ford gathered its top 1,800 global managers for an unprecedented meeting in Florida to discuss Ford 2000, the company's vision of its future. While the vision – to ensure that Ford would become the world's leading automotive company by the year 2000 – was couched in terms of the motor industry, it was as much a globalizing consumerist vision as an industrial one. Indeed, the 1998 Annual Report had the words "Consumer Focus" emblazoned on its cover, reinforced by the message: "As we drive to deliver superior shareholder value in the 21st century, Ford is developing an intense *Consumer Focus*" (underline in original). The message of the chairman neatly combined the key themes of global vision that were characteristic of the most globalizing corporations:

> The company is expanding its definition of customer satisfaction – beyond products, and even beyond the sales and service experience. . . . A good company delivers excellent products and services, a great one delivers excellent products and services and strives to make the world a better place. Great companies understand that to fully meet the expectations of consumers, they must address the concerns of society. That is the only way to ensure sustainable development and growth. It also is the best way to richly reward shareholders. (Annual Report 1998)[11]

The reference to sustainable development is important for the value that it places on the company's attempts to address the undisputed environmental impact of motoring and need to support the sustainable development historical bloc. Two initiatives illustrated this theme. First, Ford added a new logo to the ubiquitous elegantly-scripted *Ford* that adorns millions of vehicles all over the world – a leaf and road symbol (bright green leaf growing out of a blacktop road motif) which "represents harmony between the environment and transportation. This Ford trademark is used on a variety of Ford products and literature to show Ford's commitment to protecting the environment." Second, Ford acquired a majority interest in PIVCO Industries (based in Norway), the manufacturer of the two-seater TH!INK [*sic*] electronic car, a zero-emissions vehicle "designed for those who want an environmentally friendly small car." Ford committed itself to helping PIVCO introduce this car in Scandinavia.

The Ford 2000 Vision also specifically connected diversity, for Ford's employees and for its customer base, with globalization, acknowledging that this might create difficulties. "Although we presently have a diverse workforce, creating an environment that fosters and encourages diversity will require a long-term cultural change" (Ford 2000 Fact Sheet, June 20, 1995). The Ford 2000 Timeline, entitled "The Road to Globalization," stretched from 1903 when the company sold its first imported model in Britain to 1995 when the North American and European operations were merged and "launched as a fully functional global operation." The global vision permeated to all parts of the Ford family of companies, for example to Visteon, the Ford captive parts supplier which, like GM's Delphi, is looking to capitalize on the parent's vision and techniques while trying to capture auto parts business from other major car manufacturers.

The global vision produced by BT as part of a comprehensive review of all its operations embarked upon in 1998, similarly combined industry issues and customer focus with the potential impact of the company on society as a whole. This was accomplished through the categories of Vision, Mission, Values and Style. The BT Vision was to be "the most successful worldwide communications group." The BT Mission through which the Vision was to be achieved consisted in the effort "to generate shareholder value by seizing opportunities in the communications market world-wide." The first BT Value was: "We put our customers first." The BT Style began with the assertion: "We are: One big global team [with a] global perspective." These statements were set down in the pamphlet, "Realising Our Vision" (May 1999), one of a series through which BP started to reconsider its vision, mission, conception of sustainable development, and business practices.[12] The motif that ran through all these publications was that, in the words of the CEO: "The pursuit of sustainable development is not an option – it is nothing more or less than a necessity for our economic and social survival."

The case of BT was not raised in the general discussion on sustainable development in chapter 7. The reason for this was that as a telecommunications company with a faint ecological footprint, BT could afford to adopt a rather more ecological conception of sustainable development than corporations with much deeper footprints. A telling illustration of BT's openness was that the company discussed both the widening gap between the rich and the poor (the class polarization crisis) and the environmental rebound effect, where reductions in environmental impacts are lost due to increased consumption (an important part of the ecological crisis). One excellent example of environmental rebound cited by BT is when improvements in traffic flows due to the application of new electronic road monitoring equipment result not in the reduction of traffic but in the generation of new traffic flows (from "Changing values," September 1998). However, the analysis of rebound effects gives BT the opportunity to speculate that increased use of the types of services that it offers, notably video-conferencing and electronically facilitated home working, might reduce business travel and thus the environmental impact of vehicle use. This would increase the profits of BT but might reduce the profits of petroleum companies, vehicle manufacturers and airlines. While this would certainly be an environmentally beneficial development it is not one with which the oil, auto, or airline industries have yet come to terms. As the analysis of the Shell Report 1998 demonstrated, an oil company like Shell (and a motor company like Ford) has a much harder time justifying its principles and its vision than a telecommunications company like BT. Here, again, we have an example of the potential for one industry (telecommunications in this case) to take advantage of the environmental challenges to business to undermine the prospects for another industry (transportation). BT's capacity to integrate these issues into its vision of the new wave corporation, therefore, can be understood in terms of its location in the telecommunications industry as well as its aspiration to be a globalizing corporation.[13]

Industry-oriented Global Visions

Some corporations project their global visions more modestly in terms of what their industries and products have to offer on a global scale. ICI, for example, proclaimed its vision to become: "the industry leader in creating value for customers and shareholders" (Factbook 1997). ICI aimed to achieve this through a checklist of aspirations, namely market-driven innovation, winning in quality growth markets worldwide, inspiration and rewarding of talented people, exemplary performance in safety and health, responsible care for the environment, and relentless pursuit of operational excellence. Most major corporations aspired to these objectives. The significance of ICI in the late 1990s, from the point of view of the present discussion, was that this global vision emerged as the company started to restructure away from its traditional heavy bulk chemicals businesses to the more consumer-oriented end of the market. As a result, the global territorial vision, to cover the globe with its factories, became secondary to a more functional global vision related to consumer products based on its speciality chemicals. There was clearly an element of short-termism and anxiety about cash flow at work here. In its rationale for this change of focus, ICI explained that a polymer plant, for example, cost hundreds of millions of dollars to build and took many years to be fully operational, while a fragrances plant cost about 10 million dollars to build and was up and running in a year or so. The rhetoric was of the rebirth the company, driven by the search for new markets. This restructuring was fundamental for the credibility of the new global vision and was based on enormous changes in the material resources of the company. In what was described as a "reverse take-over by Unilever," ICI bought Unilever businesses valued at $8 billion and sold off $5 billion worth of its own. The new visionary CEO of ICI, Charles Miller Smith, came directly from a senior position at Unilever.[14]

In a similar fashion, companies as different as Lufthansa, BHP, Metlife and TEPCo (Tokyo Electric Power Company) articulated their visions in terms of what their business sectors had to offer the world. Lufthansa projected itself in terms of "More Mobility for the World," both as the well-respected airline centrally, and in terms of its airline-related subsidiaries, for example, Lufthansa Shannon Turbine Technologies (Ireland) where the valid point was made that local success is necessary for the global success of the company to be assured. In "Our Vision and Values," BHP sought to be "the world's best resources company. . . . [to] link resources and technologies for the benefit of customers and communities worldwide. . . . committed to employees, customers, contributing to the communities in which we live and work, and a high standard of care for the environment. . . . value safety, honesty and excellence in all we do." Metlife's Global Vision was "to be the leader in solving people's financial security problems." This was a value-added process and the company's contribution was to spread risks and to manage money. The idea that money management is at the leading edge of globalization has sharpened the global visions of many companies in financial services. TEPCo, one of the world's major nuclear energy providers, projected a vision focused on the development of nuclear power, "indispensable for the future of the world".

The Rockwell vision was to be "the best diversified technology company in the world." The vision starts from four elements observed in the visions and missions of many other corporations: customers occupy first place, then stockholders, employees, and communities. As described in chapter 5, Rockwell monitored 12 different companies all over the world for best practice on such indicators as financial performance and reputation, and benchmarked on what it labelled the "supplier of choice" index, a measure of what made Rockwell the supplier of choice of a variety of products and services to its customers. When the Rockwell vision was introduced in 1995 there was a good deal of "cynicism" reported. The company specifically emphasized that it was not just another "program of the month" but a serious attempt at restructuring, precisely because it was a global vision. The pressure for a global vision came from the recognition that businesses like Rockwell could no longer operate simply as American corporations. "Foreign" firms were moving into US markets to compete with Rockwell and there were problems of different international standards when Rockwell (or any other US-based company) went overseas to compete in "foreign" markets. The "number one driver" was "market dynamics," with its attendant opportunities and competitive threats. Throughout the 1980s, Rockwell had been mainly oriented to the US aerospace market, largely dependent on government contracts. By the mid-1990s, government contracts made up only about one-sixth of the company's business and, as a result, new markets were essential to sustain growth (for example, Rockwell became one of the largest manufacturers of modems in the world). While the roots of Rockwell are still firmly planted in the USA, its new global vision reflected a measure of denationalization forced on it by changing conditions of business. The globalizing corporation globalizes because it has no other way of growing and increasing its returns to shareholders – even in the USA, the largest market in the world.

Tyco, the infrastructure conglomerate, exemplifies this globalizing shift exactly. A recent entrant to the Global 500, Tyco made over 100 "smart, disciplined acquisitions" in the 1990s, including Raychem (Ireland), itself a globalizing corporation with businesses in 50 countries. The first page of Tyco's Annual Report (1998) has planet earth in the background and superimposed, the text: "Tyco focuses expansion efforts on specific market segments where we are, or can be, a global leader."

Many consumer goods and services corporations expressed industry-oriented global visions. Johnson & Johnson (J&J) articulated a global vision to be the biggest health care provider in the world, satisfying needs for health-related consumer goods, pharmaceuticals, professional devices and services. J&J constructed an interesting rationale for this vision, one that can be fruitfully connected with the discussion of corporate responses to environmental challenges in the previous chapter. In all areas of health, J&J argued, the health of the individual depends on the health of the environment. Therefore, the health of the planet is the basis for individual health. This belief was put into practice through the company's extensive program of corporate contributions in many spheres all over the world.

Finally, some industry visions are rather more existential in character, while still firmly focused on the market. For example, the mission of Salomon Brothers at the corporate level was "to know who we are." Acknowledging increasing consolidation in the financial industry, Salomon was content with its "niche player" image. Under the corporate umbrella of its mission statement, some divisions had generated their own market-generated "visions." In general, the driving vision of the company was that technology would eventually eliminate many jobs in financial services and companies like Salomon Brothers would have to learn to adapt. In a world where, in all likelihood, "kids will be doing their own investment on the Internet in twenty years," prospects were at best uncertain.[15] Thus, questions about identity needed to be raised. Salomon was later merged into Travelers Group (and subsequently Citigroup).

Existential questions were at the root of indecision about the articulation of visions in many Global 500 corporations. Some freely admitted to such problems, while accepting that it was necessary for a company with globalizing aspirations to have a global vision. For example, according to a senior executive in the Hong Kong subsidiary of Nissho Aiwa, the company had found the articulation of its global vision "very difficult." The main issue here was that every division in the conglomerate aspired to a worldwide trade network; some succeeded in achieving this but some did not. While most managers and workers thought primarily of their own divisions, only top management saw the whole picture and was thus capable of developing global vision. This is clearly an ongoing problem, but its roots appear to be functional (why are we in this business?) more than geographical (why are we doing business here?).

These industry-oriented global visions all had elements of the wider aspirations of globalizing corporations to serve the global consumer. In the case of Salomon Brothers, the potential loss of the market for its services (when even kids might be investing directly and leaving finance houses with little to do) meant that constructing a corporate vision or mission led logically in a more introspective direction. For ICI, the decision to withdraw from bulk chemicals and to focus on speciality chemicals led to the articulation of a new global vision for new (consumerist) business opportunities.

Organization-oriented Global Visions

The differences between consumer-oriented and organization-oriented global visions were rarely clear-cut; they were often a matter of emphasis. The five business sectors, it will be recalled, contained over forty separate industries denominated by the compilers of the *Fortune* Global 500 in 1996 and it was not always clear, even to TNCs themselves, to which industry they primarily belonged. Some corporations focused their visions more on organizational issues than the contributions their products or services made in satisfying consumer needs globally but, nevertheless, most of these visions had elements of global consumerism.

Marubeni's New Medium-term Plan, VISION97 (introduced as a three year program in 1995) was an example of an organization-oriented global vision. The first objective of VISION97 was to optimize management resources through a Group Network Management strategy. A globalizing corporation operating in a "global, borderless economy" (a clear reference to Ohmae's concept), must organize its business units into one comprehensive network. In order to do this the second objective of Marubeni's vision – organizational decentralization – came into play. What made this a global vision was the acknowledgement that, "As we go about these tasks – as an organization and as individuals – we are mindful of our obligations as corporate citizens of the world."

Programs, plans and visions for the new millennium were not uncommon in Japan-based corporations. Toyota, in its Annual Report for 1996, described two programs unveiled during that year. The first, the Global Business Plan, called for overseas plants to manufacture two-thirds of the vehicles sold outside Japan by 1998 (less than one-half were in 1994). The second was the vision for the year 2005, a "conceptual blueprint for invigorating corporate culture, raising global efficiency, diversifying business portfolio, and establishing an identity as a contributing member of the community in every nation." This was an organizational vision directed towards making Toyota a better company rather than making the world a better place in general or through the motor industry. A significant aspect of what was deemed to be necessary to achieve this vision was the company's exhortation: "Globalize Everything" (Annual Report 1996). This was explained in terms entirely focused on the organization of the company. In the history of Toyota, marketing came first, local production came next, design and development became international in 1970s, and in the 1990s Toyota was globalizing management. "Globalize Everything" was illustrated with a series of images from all over the world. Rapid growth in the USA was illustrated by Indiana's governor at the launch of a pickup truck production line in his state. Developments in Europe were illustrated with pictures of the former British Prime Minister, John Major, holding one "R" spade in the C-O-R-R-O-L-A Plant Groundbreaking Ceremony in Derbyshire, England, and of a new service station in Moscow. Asian growth was symbolized by the joint venture for the production of auto engines in Tianjin, China (a first step towards a fully-integrated Toyota automobile plant). The organizational vision here connects directly with the production and use of Toyota vehicles all over the world. Motor vehicles, it need hardly be said, are prime components of the culture-ideology of consumerism everywhere.

A third Japan-based corporation that exhibited an organization-oriented global vision was Tomen, whose global vision was, precisely, to become a global company. Tomen had been trading with companies all over the world for 75 years but increasingly had become involved in a much wider range of activities. In 1990, it announced a ten-year long-term business agenda, the ACT-21st Plan (Aggressive Challenge to the 21st Century). "Our vision for the 21st century is to elevate the traditional concept of a soga shosha to a higher level and become a diversified yet highly integrated global enterprise . . . keywords of our successful global strategy are change and create . . . where we combine multinational business functions as we conduct business enterprises on a global scale."

Kimberley Clark, the US-based personal products company, operated with a top-down vision of the relationship between present practice and future goals. However, this was not imposed on individual companies in the group, and was not inconsistent with customized local visions, such as that developed in Australia. The mission statement of KC Australia emerged from consultations with a large sample of employees. The Corporate Communications office in the Australian company produced regular videos, with messages from the CEO, who was reputed to have made over 100 presentations on the mission statement around the country. Each unit in the company also had its own mission statement with mechanisms to involve every employee. The key to success for KC was the "ownership of aims".[16] The organizational character of the global vision was summed up in the axiom: "The only way to get world class performance is to have world class people." This vision was tied in with career development all through the company, not simply in terms of vertical movement (promotion) but also horizontal movement (across companies and across territories) in the group. It should be noted that in the view of the Australian subsidiary KC was still very much an American company with units abroad (see chapter 2). However, a form of globalization through regionalization was said to be occurring in which the US headquarters was gradually ceding authority to the regions, particularly in Singapore, the center of Asian operations. Thus, a global vision with regional elements was gradually emerging and this created tensions with the far-flung subsidiary in Australia caught between two power centers of the corporation. Many other Australian TNCs (few big enough to appear in the *Fortune* Global 500) were also struggling with regionalization and globalization, for obvious geo-economic reasons. This was certainly the case for three Global 500 corporations from Australia, the retailer Woolworths, and National Australia and ANZ banks.

The conclusions drawn from these cases can be reinforced through the study of corporate Annual Reports, one of the few vehicles that corporations have to present themselves to their shareholders, to the investment community as a whole and, to some extent, to the public. Table 8.1 shows the use of global imagery (in text and graphics) in the Annual Reports of some Global 500 firms in the 1990s.[17]

Table 8.1 Global imagery in Global 500 Annual Reports

Corporation	Text	Graphics
ABB (1995)	The bigger the local presence in the new markets, the higher the exports out of the old markets – it is a true win/win global strategy (p. 8)	Map of the world with business and geographical sectors and responsible corporate officer
Apple (1995)	One of a handful of globally recognized corporate symbols (p. 15)	3 images of the globe
ARCO (1994)	Five Key Goals: 3. Continue the transformation of ARCO from a predominantly domestic company to a global company (p. 6)	3 images of the globe
BankAmerica (1994)	Boundary-less access, as national economies become globally integrated (p. 3)	Front covers of 3 'Global Corporate Banking' reports
Bankers Trust (1996)	The balance of our global network and local presence in trading and sales provides competitive advantage (p. 18)	none
Bank of China (1995)	Fifth bank in the world in volume of international business to total income (p. 7)	Map of world titled "Global Network" (pp. 14–15)
BCE (1995)	BCE is one of the world's leading communications organizations operating in 90 countries and territories. It is Canada's global communications company (p. 16 pullout)	Images of the globe tilted on its axis with corporate logo, cd-rom with same image.
BHP (1995)	World leader in copper . . . global expansion (p. 1); One of the world's largest diversified resources companies . . . world's best resource company (p. 3); Meeting the global business challenge (p. 4)	none
BP Amoco (1998)	Our aim was to create . . . a global corporation for a global economy . . . We have a world-class set of assets (p. 2); Our pledge is to build a truly global enterprise (p. 4)	none
Chevron (1994)	When you read about Chevron's new opportunities, you'll be taking an armchair global tour (p. 5)	Front cover, sketch map of the world

Table 8.1 (*Continued*)

Corporation	Text	Graphics
DAI–ICHI (1996)	International operations . . . Foundation for Advancement of Life & Insurance Around the World (FALIA) (p. 3)	3 images of globe (pp. 28–30)
Daimler-Benz (1995)	As part of our efforts to globalize our corporate units, it is our goal to continue to increase foreign purchasing (and) global sourcing structures for our foreign production sites (p. 10)	none
Delhaize "Le Lion" (1995)	5 countries/13 trade names/1,610 sales outlets/89,700 staff members/ sales of BEF 369 billion (p. 2)	2 maps of the Western hemisphere highlighting Europe and N. America
Electrolux (1995)	The Global Appliance Company; one of the world's leading manufacturers . . . the largest or second largest in the global market . . . sold in more than 90 countries . . . over 90% of sales outside Sweden (p. 1)	Map of the world with group sales by geographical region illustrated.
Elf (1995)	Goal is to rank among the world leaders in petroleum, chemicals and pharmaceuticals (p. 1)	Photograph of the globe (front cover); same image throughout report (16 in all)
Fiat (1995)	Important element in this process of globalization was the manufacturing program (p. 22)	none
Fluor (1996)	Core strength: a strong global presence (p. 4). As we see it, there are no boundaries, no barriers, no borders, no limits. Our thinking, our strategies, our approach to the marketplace has no limits (p. 5)	none
General Motors (1995)	Building a global corporation through teamwork. I have made global integration one of my top priorities. We have to make more progress in global integration, and fast. (CEO, p. 1)	none
Hewlett-Packard (1996)	An active, global commitment to social progress strengthens HP's ability to compete and is the right way to conduct business as we approach the 21st century (p. 27)	none

Table 8.1   (*Continued*)

Corporation	Text	Graphics
Hitachi (1996)	Globalization – Hitachi is promoting its international operations by viewing the world as a single market . . . endeavoured to globalize its operations (p. 4)	Front cover 4 "global" images of map-globe (p. 22)
Indian Oil (1995–6)	Only Indian company in Global 500 (p. 1)	none
ING (1995)	ING is active on a worldwide scale (cover/p. 1); ING holds leading global market positions (p. 36)	Globe (map on a ball, with the ING Lion superimposed)
Intel (1994)	People must be able to work together effectively – whether they are in the next building or halfway around the world (p. 3)	Pentium processor "takes off" from surface of the globe
Itochu (1996)	Itochu: committed to the global good . . . management plan Global 96 (p. 2)	3 images, globe in centre, maps
Jardine Matheson (1995)	Cultivating partnerships with major international corporations (p. 3)	none
J. P. Morgan (1996)	J. P. Morgan is a leader in global finance and investment . . . solutions that transcend conventional thinking and traditional boundaries (p. 1 pullout)	Globe image consisting of latitude/longitude lines with label "Crossing Boundaries"
Kanematsu (1995)	Global information support . . . new corporate identity . . . rapidly changing conditions of global environment (cover); Global operations section (p. 5)	none
Marubeni (1995)	Global business network global, borderless company (p. 3); corporate citizens of the world (p. 4); borderless market (p. 34)	2 maps of world, 3 images of globe (pp. 34–7)
Matsushita Electric (1996)	One of the world's largest manufacturers of quality electric and electronic products (cover); basic global management policy, global efficiency (p. 3); customer satisfaction on a global basis (p. 4)	none

Table 8.1 (*Continued*)

Corporation	Text	Graphics
Merrill Lynch (1996)	Singularly positioned and strategically committed to global leadership (p. 5); our perennial leadership in global underwriting . . . our top rankings in global research and trading (p. 6)	Half-circle of latitude/ longitude lines and outline of N. American continent; photograph of globe
Mitsubishi (1996)	Principles that guide Mitsubishi: globalizing human resources (p. 1); vast global network of business relationships (p. 5); merchant banking network that spans the globe (p. 6); global leader (p. 9); globalization (p. 14); MC Globe Magazine	Globe, satellite (cover); 1 globe, 1 world map
Mitsui (1996)	Global enterprise (pp. 3, 5); global information network (p. 4); promoting trade and industrial development globally (p. 13)	6 globe-map images
Nestlé (1995)	From 15 factories in 1900 to 489 today . . . Nestlé brands have long been known on all five continents . . . products . . . sold in more than 100 countries (p. 43)	2 maps of the globe
News Corporation (1994)	Preeminent supplier . . . around the world (p. 1); global leader . . . worldwide group (p. 5); global scale (p. 11)	Satellite dish on globe (cover); foldout back cover of companies on world map.
Nichimen (1996)	One of the world's leading general trading companies . . . 93 cities around the globe, global society, global scale (pp. 4–5); reduce dependence on business related to Japan (pp. 4–5)	Map of the world (cover); 10 globes (pp. 8–18); 3 maps of the world (pp. 21–2)
Nippon Life (1996)	World's largest life insurance company, world's largest institutional investor (cover)	3 maps of continents (pp. 28–30)
Nissho Iwai (1995)	One frontier ahead (cover); Economic, political and social conditions around the globe . . . Global human network (cover); global scale, global human society (p. 3)	Products, transport, satellite take off from surface of globe (p. 5); 3 images of globe with satellite maps of world (p. 8)

Table 8.1   (*Continued*)

Corporation	Text	Graphics
Norsk Hydro (1995)	"Worldwide network" (p. 2); Global consumer trends show a long-term demand for [Hydro's] products (p. 10)	Possibly global image of natural gas flames and waterfall (cover)
Novartis (1998)	Global Performance in the Life Sciences (cover); Continued success in global competition (p. 5)	Global images (cover, p. 4)
PDVSA (1996)	Global exports were directed mainly at USA, Latin America, and Europe (p. 34)	Picture of people looking at a large globe-map (p. 54)
Philips (1995)	An important part of our portfolio strategy . . . is to grow fastest in the high growth areas of the world. (p. 10)	Maps of the world with sales, income, shipments, and personnel listed (p. 12)
Procter & Gamble (1995)	Global Opportunities/Global Growth (cover); Faster, more effective globalization (p. 6); Turning Local Successes Into Global Winners (p. 7)	Two-hemisphere globe (cover and throughout)
Repsol (1995)	Engaged in "the extension of international marketing activities" (p. 4); global market . . . strategic alliances with other companies in the sector (p. 21)	none
Rockwell (1995)	Rockwell vision: 1. Create the world's most successful customers; 2. Aggressively pursue global growth (p. 4)	2 global images
Royal Bank of Canada (1996)	The Financial Institutions and Trade group manages the bank's global relationships . . . the bank offers trade lines for more than 120 countries (p. 22)	Cartoon of the globe
Shell (1996)	With increasing globalisation . . . growing focus on roles and responsibilities (p. 2); leading global marketers (p. 18)	none
Siemens (1995)	Secure the company's future global competitiveness . . . world-class expertise (p. 2); intend to speed our global market growth (p. 4)	Image of globe, map of the globe

Table 8.1   (*Continued*)

Corporation	Text	Graphics
Sinochem (1996)	Creating a truly international transnational corporation (p. 3)	Map of the world (pp. 26–7)
Sony (1996)	Global environment (cover); reinvent itself to meet the needs of a new era (p. 2); global business development (p. 4); globalizing R&D (p. 6); global environmental policy (p. 8)	none
Solvay (1997)	20 global Strategic Business Units (p. 6); increased globalization (Bulgaria, Argentina, Finland) (p. 19)	Employees in procession over the globe (p. 10)
Sumitomo (1996)	One of the world's leading traders and distributers . . . growing economic globalization . . . becoming more international in our thinking (p. 5); Reach out globally, think globally (p. 6)	Global cartoon with satellite rainbow circles globe, accompanying text is "global mind, global reach" (p. 5); globe with satellite (p. 5)
Sumitomo Life (1996)	Pre-eminent global investor (p. 6); global corporate citizen (p. 7); 4 references to the global (pp. 6–7)	Map of world (p. 7)
Taiwan Power (1995)	Global economic trend toward internationalization and liberalization (p. 7)	none
Teneo (1995)	Continuing Teneo's contribution towards establishing the presence of Spanish companies on the international market (p. 3)	5 images of the globe, 3 with satellites
Tomen (1996)	6 mentions of globe/world (cover, p. 1); vision to become a diversified yet highly integrated global enterprise [theme of report] . . . business enterprises on a global scale (p. 1); global business with continued solid growth based on sound profitability (p. 11)	Image of map-globe (cover); text superimposed over map of world (p. 45)
Toshiba (1996)	Progress continues within the world community . . . global environment (cover); accelerating globalization (p. 2); global logistics (p. 3)	Possibly global electronic image (cover)

Table 8.1   (*Continued*)

Corporation	Text	Graphics
Toyota (1996)	Here's how we're getting better: . . . globalization (cover); globally: localize our far flung activities even further . . . global business plan, global efficiency (p. 1)	Compass/globe image (cover); map of world operations (p. 21)
Unilever (1995)	Around the world Unilever has operations in more than 90 countries spanning every continent (p. 5); global brand, global potential (p. 7); multilocal multinational (p. 11)	2 map images of world
Volvo (1995)	Global take-off for Volvo FH (truck); FH model was presented in 1993 with the idea that it would be used globally; global supply of components . . . local assembly (pp. 22–3)	Map of world, text superimposed (pp. 22–3)

The Visionary Executive

Many major corporations, particularly those domiciled in the USA, give the impression that boards of directors are more concerned with corporate governance than visions. In the words of one respondent, Boards tend to leave "the vision thing" to company presidents and Chief Executive Officers. It was clear from interviews and documentary research that in most globalizing corporations the main human (as distinct from institutional) driver of globalization was the visionary CEO. (Though this could also mean, in the words of an expatriate banker, that "visions tend to last as long as CEOs or chairmen, normally about 4–5 years.") Nevertheless, many global visions have lasted and new CEOs have reinforced the vision of the founder in many companies. This could be clearly seen in the lore surrounding the founders of Hewlett-Packard, David Hewlett and Bill Packard. From small beginnings in their legendary garage in Silicon Valley, California, these men had a vision of the global economy, expressed in their decision to take the company into Europe in 1960. David Hewlett, in particular, thought that the Treaty of Rome (in which the foundations of the European Union were laid) would make a significant difference to the pace and formation of the global economy, and he also anticipated the rapid growth of the

Japanese economy. The founders of HP always saw themselves as "global players" in emerging markets. Three key elements stood out in this strategy: going early into new markets, investing for the long-run, and establishing local teams. By the 1990s, almost two-thirds of the company's business came from outside of the USA. It is part of the company's history (or mythology) that even though it was not in style in the 1960s, Hewlett and Packard showed global vision from the very beginning.

By the 1990s, it was not uncommon for new CEOs to be brought in specifically to globalize the company,[18] following the models of the great success stories of corporate globalization. A leading example was ABB and its visionary creator, Percy Barnevik. Barnevik's credo was repeated many times after he had been appointed chairman of the hybrid company he forged out of Swedish and Swiss engineering groups in 1987. "Our vision was to create a truly global company that knows no borders, has many home countries, operates with mixed nationality teams and offers opportunities for all nationalities." On his retirement in 1998, ABB was by common consent well on the way to adopting a culture of "continuous change," reliant on the creation of "a new breed of future global managers," notably Barnevik himself. With "The Art of Being Local . . . Worldwide," a slogan broadcast in countless talks, newspaper and magazine articles and sound bites, Barnevik provided a European counterpart to the notion of "global localization" popularized by another globalizing visionary, Morita the founder of Sony. Barnevik, like Morita, was an early adopter of the innovative "think global, act local" technique, designed to hold vastly dispersed conglomerates together while at the same time taking maximum advantage of the economies of scale and market opportunities of the globalizing corporation. In the case of ABB, this was achieved through Barnevik's subtle management of the decentralization issue (allowing ABB's 5,000 profit centers and 1,000 legal entities to compete without destroying the company). Complementing this strategy, Barnevik encouraged multiculturalism (particularly the principle of multicultural management), flat organization (normally no more than four layers between the CEO and the shopfloor), and putting the abstract idea of a borderless world into practice. ABB claimed to have no geographic center and, thus, "no national axe to grind".[19]

Barnevik left ABB in 1998 to run Investor, a Swedish-based company owned by the Wallenberg family (themselves global visionaries), with a substantial stake in ABB and interests in more than 1,000 firms worldwide. When he was running ABB, Barnevik had introduced English as the language for senior managers and subsequently did the same for the Swedish-based companies Electrolux, SKF and Scania, all controlled by Investor. English, he said, "must be the mother tongue for a management which is serious about becoming international [read global]" (quoted in "English Adopted by Swedish Boards," *Financial Times*, March 19, 1998).

Rupert Murdoch of NewsCorp has also been seen as a global visionary. Murdoch's message in the Annual Report for 1994 of the parent company in Australia set out his vision in unmistakable terms. "News Corporation's future is to be the preeminent supplier of first class creative and editorial products to readers and viewers around the world. We believe that we are uniquely positioned to fulfil this destiny." One of the most discussed executives of the late twentieth century, since the 1980s Murdoch and his extensive media networks have spanned the globe and provided much media "product." Murdoch abandoned his Australian citizenship for a US passport to further his media ambitions in the USA, a clear message that the fundamental interests of globalizing capitalists and their corporations lay not with any particular nation-state but in the best access to global markets.

Helmut Maucher, who ran Nestlé for almost twenty years, was another visionary leader of a globalizing corporation. Maucher came to Nestlé in 1981 when the company seemed to have lost its way and turned it into one of the biggest and most successful food companies in the world. While Nestlé outgrew its parochial Swiss origins almost as soon as it was established, its aggressive global strategy of acquisitions and marketing (referred to in chapter 4 as global shift) marked Maucher's period of tenure in the top job as a genuine phase of globalization for the company. His business autobiography (Maucher 1994) explained the process. According to the company, demands for translations of the German language edition of his book from employees all over the world confirmed his status as a visionary leader. Employees (and, no doubt many others) wanted to know what made him and Nestlé tick, and the book has been used by Nestlé (and other companies) to inspire new young recruits. It is, thus, a valuable document for the study of the visionary CEO. This is particularly the case for the concluding chapter, titled "The Global Vision for the Next Millennium," where Maucher highlights the fact that only "about 20 percent of Nestlé's sales are generated by the countries that contain 80 percent of the world's population" (ibid, p. 137). Maucher's vision for Nestlé, therefore, was to ensure that the company captured all those billions of consumers.[20]

Tetsuro Matsuda, President of Mitsubishi until 1995, also exemplified the visionary CEO. He projected a vision that has been widely interpreted as an attempt to take Mitsubishi away from its Japanese roots via a deliberate policy of globalization. Evidence has already been presented to suggest that there was serious resistance to this vision among Mitsubishi employees in Japan. Matsuda retired as President in 1995 and was succeeded by Minoru Makihara, CEO of the company since 1992. The future of Mitsubishi as a globalizing corporation was said to be in the balance at that time. This sentiment was very publicly expressed in a major article in *Fortune* magazine in 1995, strategically placed at the beginning of the report on that year's Global 500, under the title: "Japan: does the world's biggest company have a future" (Smith 1995). This article is a representative text on how the globalizing corporation and the key role of the visionary executive were constructed in what is probably the most influential business magazine in the world.

The sense of crisis that provoked the article derived not from problems about the growth of Mitsubishi (in the newly amalgamated industrial and services Global 500 list in 1995, the company actually ranked number one, with the highest revenues of any corporation in the world).[21] The problem was profits, or rather the embarrassing lack of them. While the article purported to be about the future of Mitsubishi it was just as much about Makihara, with the lead illustration a flattering picture of the (shirt-sleeved) man himself. At 65 years of age, Makihara was portrayed as a product of the West as much as a product of the East. While he was a "true Mitsubishi man" – his father had been a company executive and his wife a descendant of the founding Iwasaki family – Makihara was actually born in England where his father had been posted. He attended a prestigious preparatory school in the USA, and eventually graduated from Harvard. He was so comfortable with Western ways, *Fortune* reported, that he invited a dozen foreign journalists into his private office for a sandwich and wine lunch. That was taken to be an extraordinary gesture in a land where outsiders rarely penetrate beyond formal meeting rooms and tea.

The visionary executive has to be a natural leader and for global capitalism natural leaders have to lead in the global arena. Since Morita, founder of Sony, had become ill, *Fortune* argued, the Japanese business community had lacked a voice that could command attention globally. The obvious question was whether or not Makihara could fill that role. The answer might depend on his success in making Mitsubishi more profitable and that, by common consent, depended on the company's globalizing efforts. In 1995, the success of Mitsubishi's efforts to globalize was far from certain. Makihara's particular passion was to push the company more deeply into multimedia (Mitubishi then owned eight cable TV systems in Japan, two communications satellites in orbit, and equity in long-distance telephone companies). Mitsubishi's most ambitious media project, still in an embryonic phase, was called the MC Cybermarket. This aimed to give customers access, via a computer network, to a vast range of products and services – from second-hand packaging machinery to fleets of cars – a truly visionary project, focused largely on the culture-ideology of consumerism. A particularly significant example of how the global was highlighted was an illustrated booklet "Your Road to Success" (released around 1995), targeted at Mitsubishi's business partners. It opens with a conversation between Makihara and an unnamed interlocutor based on eight questions and answers. For each, the global dimension is explicitly raised. By 1999, the Annual Report makes little reference to globalization, being focused on a new program – MC2000, Taking Charge of Our Future – directed explicitly to corporate restructuring under a new President and CEO. Globalization appears to be taken for granted

The visionary leadership of John Powers of Pfizer was clearly linked to the globalizing efforts of a major corporation with deep roots in the USA (see chapter 3 above). In a speech on "The Vision that Built Pfizer" delivered in 1993, the President of Pfizer's International Pharmaceuticals Group argued that Powers "has been called the architect of Pfizer's transformation into a multinational company, and I think that is an understatement. It's true that he started Pfizer's business overseas, but of greater significance is that he had the first real vision of a global organization – not only in Pfizer but, I would argue, in our industry." The CEO who succeeded Powers in 1991, John Steere, was also seen as a leader keen to facilitate globalization in Pfizer. For example, he propagated his own version of a global vision for the company through a video feed distributed to all Pfizer facilities around the world (and his status was boosted by the success of Viagra globally).

Another CEO who clearly articulated a global vision was Al Zeien of Gillette. In 1998 he explained his vision in terms that will by now be familiar to readers of this book. "A multinational has operations in different countries . . . A global company views the world as a single country. We know Argentina and France are different, but we treat them the same. We sell them the same products, we use the same production methods, we have the same corporate policies. We even use the same advertising, in a different language, of course" (quoted in "As Close as a Group Can Get to Global," *Financial Times*, April 7, 1998). What makes this "reverse parochialism" work, Zeien argued, are the economies of scale and flexibility of supplying a few basic goods (razors, batteries, pens) to the world market combined with the will to transfer ideas. Thus, managers joining Gillette could expect to be relocated three or four times in their first dozen years, which made them (or, at least, those whose families survived the experience) "idea ambassadors." The fact that Gillette's share price rose by an average of 33 percent between 1987 and 1998 gave this vision some credibility. Nevertheless, it is legitimate to question how representative of major corporations this global vision is.

The *Financial Times* commissioned a leading firm of management consultants to discover the most respected companies and executives in the world in 1998. The sample was 3,500 chief executives in 53 countries, from which 648 useable responses were derived, and the findings were weighted by the GDP of the countries in which the respondents were based (an interesting if unorthodox methodology). The top 16 most respected companies were all *Fortune* Global 500 corporations (and 12 of those were in the first 100 places of the Global 500). Of the 40 most respected companies, only 7 were not in the Global 500). This suggests that companies with the biggest revenues are more likely to win respect from their peers. This is even more strongly confirmed by the findings on the most respected chief executives. Eighteen of the top 20 business leaders were from *Fortune* Global 500 corporations, 13 of which were in the top 100 (see table 8.2).

It is clear, therefore, that the CEOs of the largest corporations were much more likely to be more highly respected by their peers than the

Table 8.2 World's most respected business leaders and Global 500 rank of their corporations (1998)

Jack Welch (General Electric, 12)
Bill Gates (Microsoft, 400)
Jurgen Schrempp (Daimler-Benz, 17)
Lou Gerstner (IBM, 14)
Andy Grove (Intel, 125)
Percy Barnevik (ABB, 83)
Nobuyuki Idea (Sony, 30)
Warren Buffett (Berkshire Hathaway, n/a)
Helmut Maucher (Nestlé, 36)
John Browne (British Petroleum, 20)
Jack Smith (General Motors, 1)
Herb Kelleher (Southwest Airlines, n/a)
Kazuo Inamori (DDI, 476)
Lee Iacocca (formerly Chrysler, 25)
Hiroshi Okuda (Toyota, 11)
Goran Lindahl (ABB, 83)
Hugh McColl (Bank of America, 145)
Doug Ivester (Coca-Cola, 201)
John Reed (Citicorp, 68)
Sandy Weill (Travelers Group, 58)

Note: n/a = not applicable (not in Global 500 due to privately-held status of company and/or lack of sufficient revenues).

Sources: adapted from *Financial Times* (Nov. 30, 1998) and *Fortune* magazine (Aug. 3, 1998).

CEOs of smaller corporations.[22] The text that accompanied the results of the survey reported that the three most admired qualities of the top CEOs were clarity of vision, dynamic leadership and tenacity. Profiles of some of these most respected executives (and those running the most respected companies outside North America and Europe), indicated that extensive overseas experience appeared to be the norm. Another interesting finding was that while the CEOs ranked successful change management and globalization of business bottom of a short list of attributes characteristic of the most respected companies of the future, "these last two attributes come up frequently in relation to companies that are today ranked among the most respected." This suggested ambiguity among the CEOs over globalization. The Survey reported that CEOs thought that globalization was not appropriate for all companies, but that those companies that were globalizing successfully were liable to gain respect (*Financial Times* [Survey Section] Nov. 30, 1998, p. vii).[23]

While this reported research is open to question from a methodological standpoint, the direction of the findings is difficult to dispute. CEOs with global vision in successfully globalizing corporations, which tend to be at the top end of the *Fortune* Global 500 (20 of the 40 most respected companies were in the top 100), were most respected by their peers.

Global Vision as a Globalizing Practice

A global vision becomes a globalizing practice when it is mobilized by the transnational capitalist class to further the interests of those who own and control major corporations, with direct or indirect reference to the culture-ideology of consumerism. The most directly globalizing visions are what were termed consumerist visions. Their connections to the culture-ideology of consumerism are obvious. These visions are transformed into globalizing practices when they contribute to global capitalist hegemony against its (anti-consumerist) rivals. The struggle for hegemony, unlike crass struggles for power, involves an element of ideological persuasion as well as the exercise (or the threat) of physical force. The struggle for global hegemony, therefore, involves an element of ideological persuasion at the global level. The consumerist visions of globalizing corporations, daily transmitted through the mass media and by other, more subtle, means play a central role for the hegemonic agenda of the transnational capitalist class.

Many but by no means all of the companies proclaiming a global vision originated in the USA. This fact has led some students of globalization to identify global visions and globalization itself with Americanization, especially in the realm of global brand consumer goods. There are two main problems with this argument (paralleling the differences between global reach and global shift discussed in chapter 4). First, the origins of mass marketing are not exclusively American, they can be found in several societies.[24] Second, it is difficult to maintain the state-centrist dependency view that globalization is an American plot to dominate the world through domination of mass culture with US goods and services. The relationship between globalization and Americanization cannot simply be read off from the fact that most global brands originated with corporations domiciled in the USA. A provocative study of Nike puts this idea across very well and connects it with several themes that this chapter has been exploring.

> Within this system of [global capitalist] images, *Nike* stands for participation in the global community through sports, *Benetton* [originating in Italy] through political awareness, *Microsoft* through imagination synergized by its software, *IBM* through technological power, *Coca-Cola* through the celebration of harmony, the *Body Shop* [originating in Britain] through ecological and global concern. Corporate signs of global unification construct images of global citizenship, multicultural respect, and social and environmental concern. Such advertising encourages consumers to view themselves as citizens of the world, while the corporations appear as a unifying force in a world otherwise experienced as increasingly fragmented and conflictual. (Goldman and Papson 1998: 186n28)

The significance of this statement is that it takes us beyond the theory of cultural and media imperialism propagated to powerful effect by dependency theorists towards a more nuanced theory of the role of culture and media in the global system (see Tomlinson 1997). The difference between these positions can be fruitfully pursued through an analysis of the strengths and weaknesses of the theory of US media imperialism. The market power of Disney, Hollywood and Madison Avenue is clearly not restricted to the USA. Nevertheless, the attempt to read off the hegemonic aspirations of the American state directly from this market power is unconvincing for the reasons suggested in the discussion of "national" interest above.

There are also more technical issues that must be raised. First, the media (especially TV) clearly influence people in many ways, but this influence is problematic, as much audience research has shown (see Neuman 1991). Second, the argument over the ubiquity and popularity of TV has to contend with the remarkable transformation of new electronic media since the 1980s. Local input into TV programming through cable and the "sidestep function of video" (Tracey 1988) suggests that the homogeneity thesis on which US media imperialism rests has been overtaken by mass media plurality. While it is true that the "overwhelming use of VCRs remains for the viewing of movies not political tracts" (Tracey 1988: 13) and that cable and satellite (and now the internet) give people more choices, plurality and homogeneity are in a dialectical not a mutually-exclusive relationship. Tracey himself cites a study of German public service TV with commercials which shows: "In general, the programs for framing the commercials are selected more carefully to attract those audience segments particularly middle-aged and younger people, in whom the advertisers are interested" (ibid, 23). Such trends have intensified since the 1980s. Tracey, and many other media scholars impressed by the liberating potential of new media, miss the central point that if the *imperialism* in media imperialism is conceptualized not as American imperialism but in terms of the commercial interests of TNCs (and the transnational capitalist class), then all the evidence on diversity and declining preference for Hollywood is irrelevant, even where it is true. Movies (and all other forms of mass media communications) become "political tracts" for the culture-ideology of consumerism when they are used directly to sell products (through advertising) or indirectly (through product placements, advertorials, or advocacy advertising) to sell the consumerist way of life. The consumerist content of most corporate global visions, therefore, is a central component for the survival and growth of globalizing corporations, but this has no necessary connection with the "national interest" of the USA or any other country.

One place where this theoretical battle has been fought out in practice is the realm of the soap opera. Research on Brazil's TV Globo network suggests that the genre might have reached its climax there. Oliveira (1993) reports that everyone interviewed by the Brazilian Polling Institute in Rio and Sao Paulo one particular evening in 1973 had been watching *Selva de Pedra*, a soap opera (*telenovela*) on Globo TV. Primetime all over the world is dominated by soap operas of various types. Globo alone has exported its programs to over 100 countries, including China, Cuba and Eastern Europe. While some analysts see this as creolization of US cultural products, Third World copies of Western values and models of social relations, Oliveira concludes that the overwhelming majority of Brazilian soaps have the same purpose as their US counterparts, that is to sell products, hardly a uniquely America value, and to promote consumerism. Oliveira's work does not make the common error of identifying US cultural imperialism and capitalist consumerism. He demonstrates how indigenous companies in Latin America, often in alliance with TNCs, are just as adept at transmitting the culture-ideology of consumerism as Holly-wood and Madison Avenue. The same is true for TNCs and business in general in other parts of the world. This is precisely the point that can be made against arguments about the positive educational effects of Latin American *telenovelas* and pro-development soap operas (Brown 1992) from Africa and India (see Sklair 1995, ch. 5). As with TV Globo, this is not all one-way traffic. The "do you dream in Sony" campaign and the Sony PlayStation II range, with its built-in "emotion engine," represent the globalizing of the culture-ideology of consumerism, not Americanization.

The picture that has been painted here might, understandably, be criticized for its apparent acceptance of capitalist global triumphalism. Major corporations, after all, mostly base their global visions on con-sumerism in the sure knowledge that most people want to increase rather than reduce their consumption. Nevertheless, my purpose has been concerned less with rendering a verdict on who has won the struggle between capitalism and democratic socialism[25] than on locat-ing consumerism within a more general theory of how the capitalist global system works. It would be foolish to deny that capitalism appears to have triumphed, particularly in Eastern Europe and most formerly socialist states in Africa and Asia. However, until we have a more adequate account of how the culture-ideology of consumerism fits into this triumph, we shall be unable to evaluate adequately its world-historical significance.

Notes

1 This chapter does not directly discuss consumerist elites (merchants and media) but focuses on how the globalizing corporations, some of which fall under these categories, operate. This analysis has been guided by Ewen (1976) on advertising and marketing and Herman McChesney (1997) on media in global capitalism.

2 There may be some transnational corporations whose global vision explicitly abjures any connection with the culture-ideology of consumer-ism, but I have not come across any of them in the course of my research. Even the much-praised Body Shop and Ben & Jerry's exhort people to consume as much cosmetics and ice-cream as they can! Amelio and Simon (1996, ch. 1) is a useful account of the uses and misuses of corporate visions.

3 Hewlett-Packard appointed Carly Fiorina as CEO in 1999. Her compensa-tion package of $90 million (mostly stock and options) made her the highest-paid woman in corporate history.

4 Kanter claims that this creates "customer power," but fails to convince. On

the contrary, Ritzer (1996: 54) shows how the McDonaldization of shopping "offers many examples of imposing work on consumers."

5 All unattributed quotations are taken from company publications in the 1990s, where many slogans such as this can be found.

6 The declining importance of labor costs in the production of many consumer products has undermined the older versions of the new international division of labor thesis.

7 Intel paid some of the costs of advertising campaigns for products displaying the "intel inside" stickers (its annual advertising budgets in the late 1990s were around $1 billion). IBM has also considered the possibility of marketing its components in other manufacturers" machines with "IBM Technology Inside" logos.

8 Though state-centrist, the distinction between information dependent and information independent societies discussed by Hamelink (1988) is useful. For further discussion of the relationships between access to information and class, gender, ethnicity and age, see Castells (1998). Schiller (1999) shows how the new digital capitalism favors rich, largely corporate, internet and cross-border users over ordinary phone customers (rate rebalancing), locally and globally. See also, Tehranian (1999).

9 This turned out to be ironic as, subsequently, MCI merged with WorldCom and was pressured to sell off its internet business in order to comply with antitrust regulation in the US and the EU. In January 2000 the service provider AOL merged with Time Warner, creating the first integrated content provider and new media conglomerate and a similarly motivated merger of Warner Music and EMI followed soon after.

10 With the classic culture-ideology of consumerism technique of brand-stretching, Iridium came with its dedicated magazine, *roam* [*sic*], its own range of jackets, shirts, bags, watches, and baseball caps, and a Global Partnership Eco-Challenge program on the Discovery Channel. It is interesting to note that Industrial Bank of Japan took a stake in Iridium.

11 The 1998 Annual Report pays a generous tribute to the retiring CEO, Alex Trotman, as a pragmatic visionary. Trotman is quoted as saying: "In this business a visionary had better show up in work clothes." His successor, Jac Nasser, left no doubt that the consumer-focused global vision remained central. His "Let's Chat about the Business" invoked Disney, American Express, P&G, Wal-Mart, Coca-Cola, Fedex, Dell Computer, Microsoft and 3M.

12 See also from 1999, "An issue of responsibility: BT's social report." In late 1999, BT was caught collaborating with cigarette manufacturers in a scheme to target young people and immediately apologized.

13 Another example of environmental rebound BT cites is when savings from increased energy efficiency encourage people to buy more goods thus increasing the total impact on resources and the environment. See also, Brower and Leon (1999).

14 See the discussion of ICI's global shift in chapter 4. As the *Financial Times* (July 15, 1997) pointed out, the irony was that ICI had originally been

created as part of a British state industrial strategy to compete with the American company DuPont and the German company IG Farben (itself subsequently split into BASF, Bayer and Hoechst). These nationalist considerations are no longer relevant for globalizing corporations though they may be for some governments.

15 Similar sentiments were expressed in the 1996 Annual Report of Sumitomo, the major Japanese trading house. Reflecting on the need to change and adapt in an "era of growing globalization and megacompetition" the company surmised that it was "more important for us to reevaluate continuously our reasons for being," i.e. corporate introspection.

16 The attempt to persuade line managers and workers that they "own" corporate objectives is a common technique used throughout business sectors and locations. For example, I observed exactly this in the Samsung television factory outside Tijuana, Mexico in 1999. Here, workers on the assembly-line were said to have "ownership" of core production values, notably quality targets. I am indebted to Oscar Contreras for arranging this contact with Samsung.

17 I am grateful to Peter Robbins for his assistance with this figure. Pritchard (1999) on corporate websites suggests another source of material.

18 For example, BCE (the leader in Canada's telecommunications industry) recruited Jean Monty specifically to globalize the company; and George Trumbull was recruited from Cigna Insurance in Philadelphia in the mid-1990s to demutualize and globalize AMP (the leading insurer in Australia). AMP was not then in the Global 500, but by 1999 it was ranked 238, only 70 places below Cigna, and was buying up banks in Europe.

19 An interesting aspect of this is the increase in the number of people born in one country becoming CEOs of major companies domiciled in other countries. Notable additions to Jacques Maisonrouge at IBM, were Geoffrey Bible (New Zealand) at Philip Morris, Roberto Guizueta (Cuba) at Coca-Cola, Helmut Maucher (Germany) at Nestlé, Ron Sommer (Israel) at Deutsche Telekom, Alex Trotman (Scotland) followed by Jacques Nasser (Lebanon) at Ford, and Tony O'Reilly (Eire) at Heinz, plus many US-born CEOs of corporations domiciled in other countries.

20 One insight into his mentality is worth quoting at length: "I willingly accept the critical scrutiny of the media, even with all its limitations, because the public and the press can do much to promote moral thinking within a company. But let us never forget that the profit motive is the controlling element in a market economy. Ethics must not simply write it off as egoism or greed, for profit is the driving force behind our economic system. This is precisely the fact that disturbs so many people and leads them to the attack again and again. I remember a discussion I had with a sociology professor many years ago. We had disagreed, and I had brought out all my arguments. At the end he said, 'Mr Maucher, I've understood now; nevertheless inside I'm still against it.' That is the really tragic thing about intellectuals: they simply cannot, or will not, understand the profit mechanism" (Maucher 1994: 107).

21 Mitsubishi's loss of first place in the Global 500 in subsequent years was due as much to the declining value of the yen as to loss of revenues relative to its main contenders, GM, DaimlerChrysler, and Ford (but not Itochu and Mitsui, the largest trading companies in 1999).

22 I am assuming that the weighting technique was not applied retrospectively to avoid a result that made obscure CEOs from obscure corporations in poorer economies the most respected in the world. For an interesting account of the top 100 billionaires in Asia and some of their globalizing practices, see Hiscock (1997).

23 The brief report of "Attributes" suggests that the Survey would provide strong support for the argument that corporations that have success in achieving all of the four criteria of globalization discussed in this book are considered highly deserving of respect by this sample of CEOs. As I was unable to gain access to the raw data, I cannot say more.

24 There is a lively debate on the origins of and relations between advertising, mass marketing, art, and consumer society, insightfully discussed and beautifully illustrated in Varnedoe and Gopnik (1990).

25 My opinion, perhaps unfashionably, is that while Stalinist Communism has been decisively defeated, the jury is still out on the issue of democratic socialism, and will remain out for some time. The contemporary version of this debate around the Third Way often neglects the fact that not all Third Ways are the same. It is important to distinguish between those coming from democratic socialism, and those coming from the liberal capitalist version of social democracy (the New Labour Project in Britain, for example) which consign the opposition between left and right to the historical dustbin.

Chapter 9
Conclusion

This has been a long book and this will be a short conclusion. The book has attempted to articulate a set of ideas about a transnational capitalist class and propose a method to study it. This method assumes that those who own and control the most significant economic resources (principally through transnational corporations) will be in a position to further their interests to an extent and in ways not available to most other groups in society. However, those who run the TNCs cannot achieve their ends alone. They require help from other groups, notably, globalizing bureaucrats, politicians and professionals, consumerist elites and the institutions in which they operate, to carry out their work effectively. Together, all these people constitute a transnational capitalist class. They are a *class* in that they are defined in terms of their relationship to the means of production, distribution, and exchange, and they are a *capitalist class* in that they own and/or control, individually or collectively, the major forms of capital. They are a *transnational capitalist class* in that they operate across state borders to further the interests of global capital rather than of any real or imagined nation-state. Global system theory offers an explanation of how this transnational capitalist class works, how corporate and other elites cross local and state boundaries to become globalizing manifestations of the transnational capitalist class in action.

Communication between the four fractions of the transnational capitalist class is facilitated in a variety of ways, notably through interlocking directorates and cross-memberships of groups in different institutional complexes (business, government, politics, professions, media, etc.). The influence of the TCC is exercised through the leadership roles of its members in other social spheres, in think-tanks, charities, universities, medical, arts and sports foundations, and the like. In these ways the idea that the business of society is business is promulgated in every community with the consequence that nonbusiness activities become more and more commercialized and models of best practice derive increasingly from the practices of the major corporations. This can be clearly demonstrated for social services, the arts, sports, science, education, and many other aspects of social life in more and more communities and countries.

The case studies of how environmental problems have been handled in Global 500 corporations demonstrate how and why, even under threats to its very existence, the transnational capitalist class has managed to defend itself, prosper, and organize to assure its future. The methodology and findings of global system theory as applied to the transnational capitalist class suggest that detailed case studies on resource allocation, material rewards, key decisions, institutional changes, and agenda-building would provide further evidence that the TCC has acted as the dominant class in the global system since the 1960s. But what of the future prospects of the global capitalist system?

While capitalism increasingly organizes globally, resistances to global capitalism can only be effective where they can disrupt its smooth running (accumulation of private profits and claims of hegemony) locally and can find ways of globalizing these disruptions. No social movement appears even remotely likely to overthrow the three fundamental institutional supports of global capitalism that have been identified, namely the TNCs, the transnational capitalist class, and the culture-ideology of consumerism. Nevertheless, in each of these spheres there are resistances expressed by social movements and by transnational networks that have the potential to grow into social movements that could challenge the hegemony of global capitalism as a whole or of one or more of its essential supports. The TNCs, if we are to believe their own propaganda, are continuously beset by opposition, boycott, legal challenge, and moral outrage from disappointed or injured consumers of their products, by disruptions from their workers, and by protests from communities adversely affected by their actions. The transnational capitalist class often finds itself opposed by vocal coalitions when it tries to impose its will in the old and new ways. And what is widely referred to as the spiritual crisis of our era, from both theological and secular perspectives, has a root-and-branch critique of the culture-ideology of consumerism at its core. The problem for global capitalism is that each of its economic, political, and culture-ideology victories throws up mass movements on the local, national, and global scales to challenge its hegemony.

These movements come from inside and outside the capitalist system. While movements against capitalism as a whole clearly strike at the heart of the system, the wearing-down effect of critical movements within it (for example, against child labor or for stricter environmental controls) should not be underestimated. Some nervous members of the transnational capitalist class around the world are correct, to some extent, when they label as subversive consumer movement activists who are broadly supportive of the capitalist system but critical of consumerism, particularly those propagating green ideology.

Opposing capitalism, from households, communities, cities, all the way up to and beyond the level of the nation-state, has always been practically difficult in terms of resources, organization, and ideology. In most capitalist societies movements for social democracy have led to many uneasy alliances between those who are hostile to capitalism, those who struggle to alleviate its worst consequences, and those who simply want to ensure that capitalism works with more social efficiency than the so-called free market allows. This has inevitably meant that anticapitalists (principally socialists) of many kinds have seen no alternative to using capitalist practices to achieve anticapitalist ends. The findings of this book suggest that capitalism can only be successfully challenged through social movements that target global capitalism through its three main institutional supports, the TNCs, the transnational capitalist class, and the culture-ideology of consumerism.

Challenging global capitalism in the economic sphere involves disrupting the TNCs' capacity to accumulate profits at the expense of their workforces, their consumers, and the communities that are impacted by their activities. These communities are the truly global contexts of the TNCs, the places where their raw materials come from, where these raw materials are processed, through which they are transported, where the components are made and assembled, where the final consumer goods are designed, manufactured, sold, and used, and eventually disposed of. As discussed above, an important part of economic globalization today is the increasing dispersal of the manufacturing process into many discrete phases carried out in many different sites. Being no longer dependent on the production of one factory and one workforce gives capital a distinct advantage, particularly against the strike weapon, which once gave tremendous negative power to the organized working class. Global production chains can be disrupted by strategically planned stoppages, but this generally acts more as an irritation than as a decisive weapon of labor against capital. The global division of labor builds flexibility into the system so that not only can capital migrate anywhere in the world to find the cheapest source of labor, but also few workforces can decisively "hold capital to ransom" by withdrawing their labor. In this respect, at least, the global organization of the TNC has generally, though not always, proved to be too powerful for the local organization of labor.

But TNCs can be and have been successfully challenged. Where the TNCs have been disrupted and they have been forced to change their ways and compensate those who have grievances against them, it has usually been due to local campaigns that have attracted worldwide publicity. Prominent examples of these are the campaigns against the thalidomide tragedy caused by Distillers' Company, the Bhopal disaster caused by Union Carbide, environmental catastrophes caused by oil companies, sickness and deaths of babies for which Nestlé and other infant formula companies have been held responsible, and ecological damage caused by Mitsubishi and other logging companies. There are many other less well-publicized cases, as noted in the preceding chapters. The knowledge that worker, citizen, religious, and other concerned groups in communities all around the world are monitoring their activities clearly encourages some TNCs to act more responsibly than they otherwise might be doing. New technologies of communication help transform local disruptions of TNC activities into global challenges to capitalist hegemony. And as these challenges have become more effective, the response of the TNCs has become more systematic.

Global system theory argues that capitalism is organized politically on a global scale through the transnational capitalist class. Each of the four fractions of the TCC tends to be represented, to a greater or lesser extent, in movements and campaigns on behalf of the interests of the global capitalist system. Local, national, international, and global trade and industry associations are mainly composed of TNC executives and their affiliates all over the world. Chambers of commerce and business, educational, and philanthropic organizations are also prime sites for the study of how TNC executives and their local affiliates work in the community on behalf of the capitalist global project. The political activities of what are wryly called civil servants in some societies provide ample evidence of the role of globalizing state bureaucrats in procapitalist movements all around the world, including many countries officially hostile to global capitalism in previous decades. Not all bureaucrats in all government departments and agencies are entirely and wholeheartedly in favor of the global capitalist project – far from it. Global system theory sets out to explain the transition from a capitalism that is circumscribed by national interests to one in which globalizing bureaucrats and politicians in local and national governments increasingly begin to see their interests best served by a more open adherence to the practices of global capitalism and in more open alliance with the TNCs. Substantial lobbying efforts by globalizing bureaucrats and politicians on behalf of corporate interests in the GATT, WTO, and the MAI, for example, are a particularly important marker of this transition. The point of all this activity is to defuse and marginalize the class polarization crisis and the ecological crisis.

As the preceding chapters have documented, most major corporations nowadays acknowledge some form of responsibility for corporate citizenship; many make specific reference to this in their annual reports and other corporate literature. In the 1990s, many of the Fortune Global 500 corporations (for example, 3M, DuPont, Dow Chemical, General Motors, Mitsubishi, Shell, BP, and Unilever) began to publish reports to allow interested parties to monitor their performance in safety, health, and environment. The pressure for global corporate responsibility is closely related to the struggle to establish formal global codes of conduct for transnational corporations, a struggle that has had, to date, little success. The evidence from the Global 500 is that industry-specific pressures (for example, technical staff shortages in electronics, environmental hazards in the oil and chemical industries, and threats to brand-name equity and reputation in consumer goods industries) rather than any other forces will drive changes in this sphere. As detailed in chapters 6 and 7, the history of the Responsible Care initiative of the global chemicals industry, the resolution of the dispute between Mitsubishi and the Rainforest Action Network, and labor and human rights issues for Nike and Levi Strauss, for example, illustrate these processes at work.

Paradoxically for positivists but unsurprisingly for dialecticians, the very forces that promote globalization, namely foreign direct investment in global commodity chains, the globalization of finance, the ever-increasing global reach of the privately owned mass media, and the penetration of more and more human relationships by the culture-ideology of consumerism, also serve to undermine it. For every act of foreign investment there is a potential for local groups in contact with global networks to expose exploitation of labor, violation of human rights, and the degradation of the environment. Daily evidence of casino capitalism brings forth daily expressions of moral outrage. The global village of the mass media is vilified for its violence and lack of taste and educational value, and the culture-ideology of consumerism is frequently cited as depressing evidence for the lack of meaning that is claimed to characterize our epoch.

These themes were well illustrated in the campaign against the Multilateral Agreement on Investment (MAI) of the OECD and the demonstrations against the WTO meeting in Seattle at the end of 1999. The MAI campaign was the first major worldwide campaign against globalization, bringing together a network of hundreds of organizations from all over the world, many mobilizing on a local basis, united (notably through the internet) in their opposition to what was widely broadcast as a license for TNCs to do as they please. The events in Seattle at the end of 1999 provided further evidence that the opposition to global capitalism was increasingly well-organized. The internet, of course, gives the possibility to those with access (a small but significantly increasing number all over the world) to find out about anticapitalist and antiglobalization struggles, as the regular mass media either ignore or marginalize such protests. On just one site (Corporate Watch) we can hear the voices of Medha Patkar from the National Alliance of People's Movements in India campaigning against the Enron corporation; Dolores Huerta of the United Farm Workers in California campaigning against carcinogenic pesticides; the Irian Jaya Amungme leader Tom Beanal documenting the malpractices of the Freeport-McMoRan Copper and Gold mining corporation in Indonesia; Bronwen Manby of African Human Rights Watch on the oil corporations in Nigeria; and many others.

It is not for a sociological theorist and researcher to lay down a blueprint for a successful challenge to global capitalism. None exists, or could exist. However, if we wish to change a system, just as if we wish to fight an illness, we have to find out what is wrong and to ensure that the cure does not kill the patient. This truism brings me to my last point, namely the centrality of democracy to any viable challenge to global capitalism.

The issue of democracy is central to the practice and the prospects of social movements against capitalism, local and global. The rule of law, freedom of association and expression, freely contested elections, transparency in public affairs, as minimum conditions and however imperfectly sustained, are as necessary in the long run for mass-market-based global consumerist capitalism as they are for any viable socialist alternatives. This applies in two ways. First, social movements against capitalism have to be democratic in their own practices, even when this appears to be disadvantageous in the short term. Large majorities of people will only take alternatives seriously if they are persuaded that they are serious alternatives. Second, holding those in power and authority over the whole range of capitalist institutions (including some agencies of government) to democratic account on every issue on every single occasion does force changes that can shift the balance of social advantage from more privileged capitalist interests to less privileged popular interests. However small these shifts might be (for example, the establishment of a ridiculously low minimum wage, or marginally progressive antiracist or antisexist legislation, or making taxation systems slightly more fair to the poor), and however often they may be reversed and have to be won again, they are worth fighting for.

Just as important as the material victories of democratic alternative policies and practices imposed on the transnational capitalist class in the corporate, political, and culture-ideology spheres, are the demonstration effects of popular victories in the struggle to undermine capitalist hegemony on a global scale and replace it with a more genuine democracy. In this respect, the terrible lessons of Stalinist and other forms of Communist and Fascist totalitarianisms have much to teach us in the quest for a peaceful transition out of global capitalism and into other forms of local and global organization that could reverse the tendencies of the system to class polarization and ecological crisis. As the preceding pages have shown, this will not be easy to do, but if these two crises are unresolved by peaceful means it is likely that they will provoke unpeaceful responses. They have already begun to do so and desperate people often take desperate remedies. Members of the transnational capitalist class and the institutions in which they operate are certainly acting rationally, even if too little and too late, in their attempts to resolve the class and ecological crises on their doorsteps, but they are doomed to fail. The tremendous productive powers of the transnational corporations inextricably bound up with the ceaseless quest of those who own and control them for maximum profits guarantees at best the persistence and at worst the intensification of the class polarization crisis on a global scale. As the culture-ideology of consumerism created many of the components of the ecological crisis, it is not likely that any system predicated on it will be able to resolve this crisis.

Sometimes it is necessary to look backwards in order to move forwards. I am content to let the last words be those of John Ruskin, like global capitalism itself a mass of contradictions. Ruskin introduced his own simple account of political economy, *Unto this Last,* in 1862 with the credo: "There is no Wealth but Life. Life, including all its powers of love, of joy, and of admiration. That country is the richest which nourishes the greatest number of noble and happy human beings."

Appendix 1:
Fortune Global 500 Corporations (and Subsidiaries) Interviewed, by Business Sector

The following is based on 88 interviews in headquarters and/or subsidiaries of 82 corporations. Numbers in parentheses are totals for consolidated business sectors based on the *Fortune* Global 500 in 1996. Subsidiaries are identified by location.

Consumer Goods And Services (153)

BAT
Colgate-Palmolive
Ford (Visteon Mexico)
General Motors (GM-Delphi Mexico) and GM-Holden (Australia)
Fiat
Johnson & Johnson
Kimberly-Clark (Australia)
McDonald's (Australia)
McKesson
Mitsubishi (Australia)
Mitsui (Australia)
Nestlé
Newscorp
Nissho Aiwa (Hong Kong)
Pfizer
Procter & Gamble
RJR Nabisco
Roche (Ireland)
Unilever
Viacom
Woolworths Australia

Financial Services (132)

AMP
Australia and New Zealand Bank
Bank of America
Citigroup (Citicorp Australia)
Deutsche Bank (Hong Kong)
Fannie Mae
HSBC
Industrial Bank of Japan (Australia)
J. P. Morgan
Merrill Lynch
Metlife
National Australia Bank
New York Life
Prudential (Australia)
Royal Bank of Canada
Salomon Brothers
Swiss Bank Corporation (Australia)

Heavy Industries (84)

Arco
Alcan
BP and BP (Australia)
BHP
Chevron
Dupont and Dupont (Australia)
Exxon (Esso Australia)
Hanson (Renison Goldfields Australia)
ICI and ICI (Australia)
Mitsubishi Chemical (MC Infonics Ireland)
Mobil (Australia)
Shell
Sumitomo (Sumicem Ireland)
Texaco (Caltex Australia)
RTZ and RTZ-CRA (Australia)

Infrastructure (88)

ABB (Australia)
AlliedSignal (Hong Kong)
AT&T (Europe)
BT
Edison International
Fluor Corporation
Lockheed Martin
Lufthansa (Lufthansa Shannon Turbine Technologies Ireland)
MCI
Nynex
P&O (Australia)
PG&E
Telstra
Tokyo Electric Power Company (USA)
Tyco (Raychem Ireland)

Electronics (43)

Apple
BCE
Dell (Ireland)
General Electric (Hong Kong)
Hewlett-Packard
Hitachi (Mexico)
Intel
Motorola (Hong Kong)
NEC (Hong Kong)
Philips and Philips (Australia)
Rockwell
Samsung (Mexico)
Sony (Hong Kong)
Thomson (Mexico)

Appendix 2:
Other Corporations and Organizations Interviewed

Corporations Not in the *Fortune* Global 500

Analog Digital (Ireland)
Bechtel (California)
Boston Consulting Group (Australia)
Burson-Marsteller (New York)
Burson-Marsteller (Australia)
Chief Executive Magazine (New York)
Citic (Australia)
Federal Mogul (Mexico)
Fortune Magazine (New York)
Foster's Brewing Group (Australia)
Korn/Ferry International (Australia)
Mallesons Stephen Jacques (Australia)
McKinsey (Australia)
Tellabs (Ireland)

Organizations with Globalizing Agendas

Business for Social Responsibility (California)
China Council for the Promotion of International Trade (Hong Kong)
Corporate Watch (Washington)
Economist Intelligence Unit (Australia)
Environmental Protection Agency (Washington)
International Forum On Globalization (London)
Infact (Boston)
Information Age Town (Ennis, Ireland)

Multifunction Polis (Australia)
Multinational Monitor Magazine (Washington)
Resources for the Future (Washington)
Trilateral Commission (New York)
US Agency for International Development (Washington)
United States Council for International Business (Washington)
World Business Council for Sustainable Development
Worldwatch Institute (Washington)

References

Adam, B. 1998. *Timescapes of Modernity*. London: Routledge.

Aharoni, Y. (ed.) 1997. *Changing Roles of State Intervention in Services in an Era of Open International Markets*. Albany: State University of New York Press.

Alley, P. and S. Taylor. 1999. "From the Dragon's Tail." *Earthmatters* (Spring): 24–6.

Al-Moneef, M. A. 1999. "Vertical Integration Strategies of the National Oil Companies." *The Developing Economies* XXXVI: 203–22.

Althusser, L. 1971. *Lenin and Philosophy and Other Essays*. London: New Left Books.

Amelio, G. and W. Simon. 1996. *Profit from Experience: The National Semiconductor Story of Transformation Management*. New York: Van Nostrand Reinhold.

Amin, A. and N. Thrift (eds.) 1994. *Globalization, Institutions, and Regional Development in Europe*. Oxford, New York: Oxford University Press.

Angell, M. 1996. *Science on Trial: The Clash of Medical Evidence and the Law in the Breast Implant Case*. New York: Norton.

Avery, N., M. Drake, and T. Lang. 1993. *Cracking the Codex: An Analysis of Who Sets World Food Standards*. London: National Food Alliance.

Ayala, J. and R. Lai. 1996. "China's Consumer Market: A Huge Opportunity to Fail?" *The McKinsey Quarterly* 3: 56–71.

Banerjee, S. 1998. "Corporate Environmentalism: Perspectives from Organizational Learning." *Management Learning* 29: 147–64.

Bannock, G., R. Baxter, and R. Rees. 1972. *The Penguin Dictionary of Economics*. Harmondsworth: Penguin.

Barad, M. 1997. "Total Quality Management." In Warner, *op cit*.

Barlett, D. and J. Steele. 1998. "Corporate Welfare." *Time*, 9 Nov.: 36–54.

Barnet, R. and R. Muller. 1974. *Global Reach: The Power of the Multinational Corporation*. New York: Simon and Schuster.

Barnett, H. 1994. *Toxic Debts and the Superfund Dilemma*. Chapel Hill: University of North Carolina Press.

Barovick, R. 1980. "The Public Interest Goes International." *Business & Society Review* (Summer): 53–4.

Bartlett, C. and S. Ghoshal. 1989. *Managing Across Border: The Transnational Solution*. Boston, Mass.: Harvard Business School Press.

Bartu, A. 1999. "Redefining the Public Sphere through Fortified Enclaves: A View from Istanbul." *WALD International Conference*, Istanbul.

Baudrillard, J. 1988. *Selected Writings*, ed. M. Poster. Oxford: Blackwell.

Beder, S. 1997. *Global Spin: The Corporate Assault on Environmentalism*. Totnes, Devon: Green Books.

Behrman, J. 1970. *National Interests and Multinational Enterprise: Tensions among the North Atlantic Countries*. Englewood Cliffs, NJ: Prentice-Hall.

Benedick, R. 1991. *Ozone Diplomacy: New Directions in Safeguarding the Planet*. Cambridge, Mass.: Harvard University Press.

Berggren, C. and M. Nomura. 1997. *The Resilience of Corporate Japan*. London: Paul Chapman.

Bhargava, A. 1988. "The Bhopal Incident and Union Carbide: Ramifications of an Industrial Accident." *Bulletin of Concerned Asian Scholars* 18: 2–19.

Bourdieu, P. 1996. *The State Nobility: Elite Schools in the Field of Power*. Cambridge: Polity Press.

Bratcher, D. (ed.) 1999. *The Corporate Examiner* number 28 (whole issue).

Brazier, C. 1999. "The Great Education Scandal." *New Internationalist*, Aug.: 7–11.

Brecher, J. and T. Costello. 1994. *Global Village or Global Pillage: Economic Reconstruction from the Bottom Up*. Boston: South End Press.

Brewer, T. and S. Young. 1998. *Multilateral Investment System and Multinational Enterprises*. Oxford: Oxford University Press.

Brower, M. and W. Leon. 1999. *The Consumer's Guide to Effective Environmental Choices*. New York: Three Rivers Press.

Brown, W. 1992. "Sociocultural Influences of Prodevelopment Soap Operas in the Third World." *Journal of Popular Film and Television* 19: 157–64.

Browning, B. 1990. *The Network: A Guide to Anti-Business Pressure Groups*. Victoria: Canonbury Press.

Budros, A. 1997. "The New Capitalism and Organizational Rationality: The Adoption of Downsizing Programs, 1979–1994." *Social Forces* 76: 229–50.

Bunker, S. 1988. *Underdeveloping the Amazon: Extraction, Unequal Exchange, and the Failure of the Modern State*. Chicago: University of Chicago Press.

Burch, P. 1981. "The Business Roundtable: Its Make-up and External Ties." *Research in Political Economy* 4: 101–27.

Burch, P. 1997. *Reagan, Bush and Right-Wing Politics: Elites, Think Tanks, Power and Policy*. Greenwich, Conn.: JAI Press.

Byrne, J. 1995. *Informed Consent: A Story of Personal Tragedy and Corporate Betrayal*. New York: Random House.

Callon, S. 1995. *Divided Sun: MITI and the Breakdown of Japanese High Tech Industrial Policy, 1975–1993*. Stanford: Stanford University Press.

Carey, P. 1990. "The Making of a Global Manager." *North American International Business* June: 36–41.

Carroll, P. 1994. *Big Blues: The Unmaking of IBM*. New York: Crown.

Castells, M. 1998. *End of Millennium*. Oxford: Blackwell.

Charkham, J. 1994. *Keeping Good Company: A Study of Corporate Governance in Five Countries.* Oxford: Clarendon Press.

Clapp, J. 1998a. "The Privatization of Global Environmental Governance: ISO 14000 and the Developing World." *Global Governance* 4: 295–316.

Clapp, J. 1998b. "Foreign Direct Investment in Hazardous Industries in Developing Countries: Rethinking the Debate." *Environmental Politics* 7: 92–113.

Cockburn, A. and K Silverstein. 1996. *Washington Babylon.* London: Verso.

Cockett, R. 1995. *Thinking the Unthinkable: Think-Tanks and the Economic Counter-Revolution, 1931–1983.* London: Harper Collins.

Cole, R. (ed.) 1995. *The Death and Life of the American Quality Movement.* New York: Oxford University Press.

Cole, R. 1998. "Learning from the Quality Movement: What Did and Didn't Happen and Why?" *California Management Review* 41: 43–73.

Connell, R. W. 1977. *Ruling Class, Ruling Culture.* Cambridge: Cambridge University Press.

Cox, R. W. 1987. *Production, Power, and World Order: Social Forces in the Making of History.* New York: Columbia University Press.

Craig, T. 1997. "Location and Implementation Issues in Support Function FDI: The Globalisation of Matsushita Electric Industrial Co., Ltd." *Asia Pacific Journal of Management* 14: 143–64.

Dalby, S. 1996. "Reading Rio, Writing the World: The New York Times and the 'Earth Summit.'" *Political Geography* 16: 593–613.

Daly, H. and J. Cobb. 1994. *For the Common Good.* Boston: Beacon Press.

Danahar, K. (ed.) 1994. *Fifty Years is Enough: The Case Against the World Bank and the IMF.* Boston: South End Press.

Davis, G. and H. Greve. 1997. "Corporate Elite Networks and Governance Changes in the 1980s." *American Journal of Sociology* 103: 1–37.

Davis, M. 1999. *Ecology of Fear: Los Angeles and the Imagination of Disaster.* New York: Metropolitan Books.

Davis-Floyd, R. 1998. "Storying Corporate Futures: The Shell Scenarios." In *Corporate Futures: The Diffusion of the Culturally Sensitive Corporate Form,* ed. George Marcus. Chicago: University of Chicago Press.

Deal, C. 1993. *The Greenpeace Guide to Anti-Environmental Organizations.* Berkeley, Calif.: Odonian Press.

Dedmon, E. 1984. *Challenge and Response: A Modern History of Standard Oil Company.* Chicago: Mobium Press.

Delphos, W. 1997. *Inside the World Bank Group: The Practical Guide for International Business Executives.* Washington, DC: Venture.

Dewey, S. 1998. "Working for the Environment: Organised Labor and the Origins of Environmentalism in the United States, 1948–1970." *Environmental History* 3: 45–63.

Dicken, P. 1998. *Global Shift: Transforming the World Economy.* London: Paul Chapman, 3rd edn.

Dion, M. 1998. "A Typology of Corporate Environmental Policies." *Environmental Ethics* 20: 151–162.

Dobson, A. 1990. *Green Political Thought.* London: Unwin Hyman.

Dobson, A. 1998. *Justice and the Environment.* Oxford: Oxford University Press.

Domhoff, W. G. 1981. "Provincial in Paris: Finding the French Council on Foreign Relations." *Social Policy,* March/April: 5–13.

Domhoff, W. G. 1996. *State Autonomy or Class Dominance? : Case Studies on Policy Making in America.* Hawthorne, NY: Aldine de Gruyter.

Dominguez, J. (ed.) 1997. *Technopols: Freeing Politics and Markets in Latin America in the 1990s.* University Park, Penn.: University of Pennsylvania Press.

Dorfman, A. and A. Mattelart. 1975. *How to Read Donald Duck: Imperialist Ideology in the Disney Comic.* London: International General.

Dowie, M. 1995. *Losing Ground: American Environmentalism at the Close of the Twentieth Century.* Cambridge, Mass. and London: MIT Press.

Dreier, P. 1982. "Capitalists vs. the Media: An Analysis of an Ideological Mobilization Among Business Leaders." *Media, Culture and Society* 4: 111–32.

Dunn, S. W. 1979. *How Fifteen Transnational Corporations Manage Public Affairs.* Chicago: Crain Books.

Dunning, J. (ed.) 1992–1994. *The United Nations Library on Transnational Corporations.* London: Routledge, 20 vols.

Dunning, J. 1997. *Alliance Capitalism and Global Business.* London and New York: Routledge.

Easton, G. 1995. "A Baldridge Examiner's Assessment of US Total Quality Management." In Cole, ed., op. cit.

Eisenhower, D. and D. Johnson. 1973. "The Low Profile Swings a Big Stick." In *The Chilean Road to Socialism,* ed. D Johnson. New York: Anchor Books.

Elkington, J. 1997. *Cannibals with Forks: The Triple Bottom Line of 21st Century Business.* London: Capstone.

Evans, P. 1997. *Embedded Autonomy.* Princeton: Princeton University Press.

Ewen, S. 1976. *Captains of Consciousness.* New York: McGraw-Hill.

Feenstra, R. C. 1996. "Globalization, Outsourcing and Wage Inequality." *American Economic Review* 86: 240–5.

Fennema, M. 1982. *International Networks of Banks and Industry.* The Hague: Martinus Nijhoff.

Fluor, J. R. 1978. *Fluor Corporation: A 65-Year History.* New York: Newcomen Society.

Fox, S. 1991. *Toxic Work: Women Workers at GTE Lenkurt.* Philadelphia: Temple University Press.

Frank, A.G. 1972. *Lumpenbourgeisie: Lumpendevelopment.* New York: Monthly Review Press.

Fraser, J. and J. Oppenheim. 1997. "What's New about Globalization?" *The McKinsey Quarterly* 2: 168–79.

Friedmann, J. and C. Weaver. 1979. *Territory and Function.* London: Edward Arnold.

Frynas, J. G. 2000. "Shell in Nigeria: A Further Contribution." *Third World Quarterly* 21: 157–64.

Gantz, D. 1998. "Globalizing Sanctions against Foreign Bribery: The Emergence of a New International Legal Consensus." *Northwestern Journal of International Law & Business* 18: 457–97.

Garsten, C. 1994. *Apple World : Core and Periphery in a Transnational Organizational Culture.* Stockholm: Dept. of Social Anthropology, Stockholm University.

Gereffi, G. and D. Wyman (eds.) 1990. *Manufacturing Miracles: Paths of Industrialization in Latin America and East Asia.* Princeton: Princeton University Press.

Gerlach, M. 1992. *Alliance Capitalism: The Social Organization of Japanese Capitalism.* Berkeley and Los Angeles: University of California Press.

Gibbs, L. 1995. *Dying from Dioxin.* Boston: South End Press.

Giddens, A. 1990. *The Consequences of Modernity.* Cambridge: Polity Press.

Gill, S. 1990. *American Hegemony and the Trilateral Commission.* Cambridge: Cambridge University Press.

Gjording, C. 1991. *Conditions Not of Their Choosing: The Guayami Indians and Mining Multinationals in Panama.* Washington, London: Smithsonian Institution Press.

Gladwin, T. 1987. "Environment, Development, and Multinational Enterprise." In Pearson, ed., op. cit.

Gladwin, T. 1993. "Envisioning the Sustainable Corporation." In *Managing for Environmental Excellence: The Next Business Frontier,* ed. E. Smith. Washington, DC: Island Press.

Gladwin, T. and I. Walter. 1980. *Multinationals Under Fire.* New York: Wiley.

Glassman, J. 1999. "State Power Beyond the 'Territorial Trap': The Internationalization of the State." *Political Geography* 18: 669–99.

Goldman, R. and S. Papson. 1998. *Nike Culture: The Sign of the Swoosh.* London: Sage.

Gomes-Casseres, B. 1996. *The Alliance Revolution: The New Shape of Business Rivalry.* Cambridge, Mass.: Harvard University Press.

Goodman, T. 1987. "Foreign Toxins: Multinational Corporations and Pesticides in Mexican Agriculture." In Pearson, ed., op. cit.

Gordon, D. 1996. *Fat and Mean: The Corporate Squeeze of Working Americans and the Myth of Managerial "Downsizing."* New York: The Free Press.

Gottdiener, M. and N. Komninos (eds.) 1989. *Capitalist Development and Crisis Theory: Accumulation, Regulation and Spatial Restructuring.* New York: St. Martins Press.

Gramsci, A. 1971. *Selections from the Prison Notebooks.* London: Lawrence and Wishart.

Graziano, L. 1989. "How Business Ethics Became 'Issues Management.'" *Propaganda Review* (Summer): 29–31.

Greeno, J. (ed.) 1998. *Making Business Sense of Sustainable Development.* Cambridge, Mass.: Arthur D. Little.

Greer, J. and K. Bruno. 1996. *Greenwash: The Reality Behind Corporate Environmentalism.* Penang: Third World Network.

Grieco, J. 1984. *Between Dependence and Autonomy: India's Experience with the International Computer Industry.* Berkeley, Los Angeles: University of California Press.

Grossman, P. 1998. "The Trade–Environment Linkage in the North American Free Trade Agreement." Unpublished paper, World Congress of Sociology, Montreal.

Hall, A. 1996. "The Ideological Construction of Risk in Mining: A Case Study." *Critical Sociology* 22: 93–116.

Hall, P. and A. Markusen (eds.) 1985. *Silicon Landscapes*. Boston: Allen and Unwin.

Hamelink, C. 1988. *Cultural Autonomy in Global Communication*. Lund: Studentliteratur.

Harry, M. and R. Schroeder. 2000. *Six Sigma*. New York: Currency.

Hartley, R. 1993. *Business Ethics: Violations of the Public Trust*. New York: Wiley.

Harvey, D. 1982. *The Limits to Capital*. Oxford: Blackwell.

Held, D. 1995. *Democracy and the Global Order*. Cambridge: Polity Press.

Henderson, J. 1989. *The Globalisation of High Technology Production*. London: Routledge.

Henderson, J. 1999. "Uneven Crises: Institutional Foundations of East Asian Economic Turmoil." *Economy and Society* 28: 327–68.

Herman, E. and R. McChesney. 1997. *The Global Media: The New Missionaries of Corporate Capitalism*. London: Cassell.

Hildyard, N. 1996. "Public Risk, Private Profit: The World Bank and the Private Sector." *The Ecologist* 26: 176–8.

Hill, S. and A. Wilkinson. 1995. "In Search of TQM." *Employee Relations* 17: 8–25.

Hirst, P. and G. Thompson. 1996. *Globalization in Question: The International Economy and the Possibilities of Governance*. Cambridge: Polity Press.

Hiscock, G. 1997. *Asia's Wealth Club: Who's Really Who in Business – the Top 100 Billionaires in Asia*. London: Nicholas Brealey.

Hoffman, R. and C. Gopinath. 1994. "The Importance of International Business to the Strategic Agenda of US CEOs." *Journal of International Business Studies*, Third Quarter: 625–37.

Holton, R. 1998. *Globalization and the Nation-State*. London: Macmillan.

Holzer, B. forthcoming. "Transnational Protest and the Corporate Planet: The Case of Mitsubishi Corporation vs. the Rainforest Action Network." *Southeast Asian Journal of Social Science* .

Horovitz, B. 1990. "The Real Thing in Brand Power is Coke, Global Survey Shows." *Los Angeles Times* (Sept. 13).

Houck, J. and O. Williams (eds.) 1996. *Is the Good Corporation Dead? Social Responsibility in a Global Economy*. Lanham, Md.: Rowman and Littlefield.

INFACT. 1997. *The 1997 People's Annual Report*. Boston: INFACT.

Interbrand. 1990. *Brands: An International Review*. London: Interbrand.

Interbrand. 1997. *Naming*. London: Interbrand.

Jardine Fleming. 1993. *Trading Companies: Creatures of a Bygone Age*. Tokyo: Jardine Fleming Securities Ltd.

Johnson, C. 1982. *MITI and the Japanese Miracle*. Stanford: Stanford University Press.

Juniper, T. 1999. "Supping with the Devil." *Earthmatters* (Summer): 10–12.

Kakabadse, A. L. and A. M. Okasaki-Ward. 1996. *Japanese Business Leaders*. London: International Thomson.

Kanter, R. M. 1996. *World Class: Thriving Locally in the Global Economy*. New York: Simon and Schuster.

Kapstein, E. 1994. *Governing the Global Economy: International Finance and the State.* Cambridge, Mass.: Harvard University Press.

Karliner, J. 1997. *The Corporate Planet: Ecology and Politics in the Age of Globalization.* San Francisco: Sierra Club Books.

Karliner, J. 1999. "Co-opting the UN." *The Ecologist* 29: 318–21.

Keck, E. and K. Sikkink. 1998. *Activists Beyond Borders: Advocacy Networks in International Relations.* Ithaca, NY: Cornell University Press.

Kester, C. 1991. *Japanese Takeovers: The Global Contest for Corporate Control.* Boston: Harvard Business School Press.

King, A. 1999. "Suburb/Ethnoburb/Globurb: Framing Transnational Urban Space in Asia." *WALD International Conference,* Istanbul.

Kloppenberg, J. 1988. *First the Seed: The Political Economy of Plant Biotechnology, 1492–2000.* Cambridge: Cambridge University Press.

Kluger, R. 1997. *Ashes to Ashes: America's Hundred-Year Cigarette War, the Public Health and the Unabashed Triumph of Philip Morris.* New York: Knopf.

Knox, P. and P. Taylor (eds.) 1995. *World Cities in a World-System.* Cambridge: Cambridge University Press.

Konings, P. 1998. "Unilever, Contract Farmers and Co-operatives in Cameroon: Crisis and Response." *Journal of Peasant Studies* 26: 112–38.

Korten, D. 1995. *When Corporations Rule the World.* San Francisco: Herrett-Koehler.

Korzeniewicz, R. P. and T. P. Moran. 1997. "World-Economic Trends in the Distribution of Income, 1965–1992." *American Journal of Sociology* 102: 1000–39.

Kroc, R. and R. Anderson. 1977. *Grinding it Out: The Making of McDonald's.* New York: St. Martin's Press.

Krugman, P. 1996. *Pop Internationalism.* Cambridge, Mass.: MIT Press.

Langman, L. 2000. "Globalization and National Identity Rituals in Brazil and the USA: The Politics of Pleasure or Protest?" In *Globalization and National Identities,* ed. Paul Kennedy. London: Macmillan.

LaPalombara, J. and S. Blank. 1976. *Multinational Corporations and National Elites: A Study in Tensions.* New York: The Conference Board.

Lechner, F. and J. Boli (eds.) 2000. *The Globalization Reader.* Boston and Oxford: Blackwell.

Lenskyj, H. 1998. "Sport and Corporate Environmentalism: The Case of the Sydney 2000 Olympics." *International Review for the Sociology of Sport* 33: 341–54.

Leonard, H. J. 1988. *Pollution and the Struggle for the World Product.* Cambridge: Cambridge University Press.

Lipset, S. M. and W. Schneider. 1983. *The Confidence Gap: Business, Labor and Government in the Public Mind.* New York: The Free Press.

Logan, D. 1998. "Corporate Citizenship in a Global Age." *RSA Journal* 3: 65–71.

Luthans, F. and R. Hodgetts. 1997. "Management in North America." In Warner, ed., op. cit.

MacIntyre, A. (ed.) 1994. *Business and Government in Industrializing Asia.* Ithaca: Cornell University Press.

Madeley, J. 1999. *Big Business, Poor Peoples: The Impact of Transnational Corporations on the World's Poor.* London: Zed.

Magaziner, I. and R. Reich. 1983. *Minding America's Business: The Decline and Rise of the American Economy.* New York: Vintage Books.

Main, B., C. O'Reilly, and J. Wade. 1995. "The CEO, the Board of Directors and Executive Compensation: Economic and Psychological Perspectives." *Industrial and Corporate Change* 4: 292–332.

Mair, A. 1994. *Honda's Global Local Corporation.* London: Macmillan.

Maisonrouge, J. 1988. *Inside IBM: A European's Story.* London: Collins.

Mallin, C. and Rong Xie. 1998. "The Development of Corporate Governance in China." *Journal of Contemporary China* 7: 33–42.

Mander, J. and E. Goldsmith (eds.) 1996. *The Case Against the Global Economy: And for a Turn Toward the Local.* San Francisco: Sierra Club.

Manes, C. 1990. *Green Rage: Radical Environmentalism and the Unmaking of Civilization.* Boston: Little, Brown and Co.

Mann, M. 1997. "Has Globalization Ended the Rise and Rise of the Nation-state?" *Review of International Political Economy* 4: 472–96.

Marceau, J. 1989. *A Family Business? The Making of an International Business Elite.* Cambridge: Cambridge University Press.

Maucher, H. 1994. *Leadership in Action: Tough-minded Strategies from the Global Giant.* New York: McGraw-Hill.

McCormick, J. 1992. *The Global Environment Movement: Reclaiming Paradise.* London: Belhaven.

McGovern, P. and V. Hope-Hailey. 1995. "Inside Hewlett-Packard: Corporate Culture and Bureaucratic Control." In *Cultural Complexity in Organizations*, ed. Sonja Sackman. London: Sage.

McManus, P. 1996. "Contested Terrains: Politics, Stories and Discourses of Sustainability." *Environmental Politics* 5: 48–53.

Meadows, D. H., D. L. Meadows, J. Randers, and W. W. Behrens. 1972. *The Limits to Growth.* New York: New American Library.

Medawar, C. and B. Freese. 1982. *Drug Diplomacy.* London: Social Audit.

Meiksins, P. and C. Smith. 1996. *Engineering Labour: Technical Workers in Comparative Perspective.* London: Verso.

Mills, C. W. 1956. *The Power Elite.* New York: Oxford University Press.

Minor, M. 1994. "The Demise of Expropriation as an Instrument of LDC policy: 1980–1992." *Journal of International Business Studies* 25: 177–88.

Mitchell, A. 1996. "Marketing-Brands Play for Global Domination." *Marketing Week*, 2 February: 26–7.

Mizruchi, M. and M. Schwartz (eds.) 1987. *Intercorporate Relations: The Structural Analysis of Business.* Cambridge: Cambridge University Press.

Mokhiber, R. and A. Wheat. 1995. "1995's 10 Worst Corporations." *Multinational Monitor*, Dec.: 9–16.

Mol, A. 1995. *The Refinement of Production: Ecological Modernization Theory and the Chemical Industry.* Utrecht: Van Arkel.

Moody, R. 1996. "Mining the World, the Global Reach of Rio Tinto Zinc." *The Ecologist*, March/April: 46–52.

Morita, A. and E. Reingold. 1987. *Made in Japan: Akio Morita and Sony.* London: Collins.

Murphy, P. 1998. *Eighty Exemplary Ethics Statements.* Notre Dame, Ind.: University of Notre Dame Press.

Nader, R. and L. Wallach. 1996. "GATT, NAFTA, and the Subversion of the Democratic Process." In Mander and Goldsmith, ed., op. cit.

Naess, A. 1973. "The Shallow and the Deep, Long-range Ecology Movement, a Summary." *Inquiry* 16: 95–100.

Nash, J. and M. P. Fernandez-Kelly (eds.) 1983. *Women, Men, and the International Division of Labor.* Albany: SUNY Press.

Nelson, J. 1996. *Business as Partners in Development.* London: Prince of Wales Business Leaders Forum.

Neuman, W. R. 1991. *The Future of the Mass Audience.* Cambridge: Cambridge University Press.

Newell, P. and M. Paterson. 1998. "A Climate for Business: Global Warming, the State and Capital." *Review of International Political Economy* 5: 679–703.

O'Connor, J. "Is Sustainable Capitalism Possible?" In M. O'Connor, ed., op. cit.

O'Connor, M (ed.) 1994. *Is Capitalism Sustainable?* New York: Guildford Press.

OECD. 1996. "Recent Trends in Foreign Direct Investment." *Financial Market Trends* 64: 37–61.

Ogliastri, E. and C. Davila. 1987. "The Articulation of Power and Business Structures: a Study of Columbia." In Mizruchi and Schwartz, ed., op. cit.

Ohmae, K. 1990. *The Borderless World.* London: Collins.

Oliver, N. 1997. "Benchmarking." In Warner, ed., op. cit.

Oliver, R. 1995. *George Woods and the World Bank.* Boulder, Colo.: Lynne Rienner.

Oliveira, O S. 1993. "Brazilian Soaps Outshine Hollywood: Is Cultural Imperialism Fading Out?" In *Beyond National Sovereignty: International Communications in the 1990s*, eds. K. Nordenstreng and H. Schiller. Norwood: Ablex.

Omvedt, G. 1993. *Reinventing Revolution: New Social Movements and the Socialist Tradition in India.* Armonk: M. E. Sharpe.

O'Riordan, T. 1991. "The New Environmentalism and Sustainable Development." *Science of the Total Environment* 108: 5–15.

Overbeek, H. (ed.) 1993. *Restructuring Hegemony in the Global Political Economy: The Rise of Transnational Neo-liberalism in the 1980s.* London: Routledge.

Packard, D. 1995. *The HP Way: How Bill Hewlett and I Built our Company.* New York: Harper Business.

Palast, G. 1999a. "Ten Years After but Who was to Blame?" *Observer* [Business Section], March 21.

Palast, G. 1999b. "Native Inc Oils Wheels in Alaska." *Observer* [Business Section], April 4.

Panjabi, R. 1997. *The Earth Summit at Rio : Politics, Economics, and the Environment.* Boston: Northeastern University Press.

Pearson, C. (ed.) 1987. *Multinational Corporations, Environment and the Third World.* Durham, NC: Duke University Press.

Peet, R. and M. Watts (eds.) 1996. *Liberation Ecologies: Environment, Development, Social Movement.* London and New York: Routledge.

Pendergrast, M. 1993. *For God, Country and Coca-Cola.* New York: Macmillan.

Piott, S. 1985. *The Anti-Monopoly Persuasion.* Westport, Conn.: Greenwood Press.

Poole, W. 1989. "How Big Business Bankrolls the Left." *National Review,* March 10: 34–39.

Porter, M. 1990. *The Competitive Advantage of Nations.* London: Macmillan.

Prasad, M. 1998. "International Capital on 'Silicon Plateau': Work and Control in India's Computer Industry." *Social Forces* 77: 429–53.

Pritchard, W. 1999. "Local and Global in Cyberspace: The Geographical Narratives of US Food Companies on the Internet." *Area* 31: 9–17.

Proctor, R. 1995. *Cancer Wars: How Politics Shapes What We Know and Don"t Know about Cancer.* New York: Basic Books.

Pusey, M. 1991. *Economic Rationalism in Canberra: A Nation Building State Changes its Mind.* Cambridge: Cambridge University Press.

Ramesh, N. 2000. "Boom Time in Electronic City." *The Guardian,* Feb. 26.

Ranney, D. 1994. "Labor and an Emerging Supranational Corporate Agenda." *Economic Development Quarterly* 8: 83–91.

Rattigan, A. 1987. *Industry Assistance: The Inside Story.* Melbourne: Melbourne University Press.

Ray, L. 1993. *Rethinking Critical Theory: Emancipation in the Age of Global Social Movements.* London: Sage.

Reader, W. J. 1980. *50 Years of Unilever 1930–1980.* London: Heinemann.

Redclift, M. 1984. *Development and the Environmental Crisis.* London: Methuen.

Reich, R. 1991. *The Work of Nations.* New York: Simon and Schuster.

Rich, B. 1994. *Mortgaging the Earth: The World Bank, Environmental Improvement and the Crisis of Development.* London: Earthscan.

Ritzer, G. 1996. *The McDonaldization of Society.* Newbury Park, Calif.: Sage.

Robbins, P. 1996. "TNCs and Global Environmental Change: A Review of the UN Benchmark Corporate Environmental Survey." *Global Environmental Change* 6: 23–44.

Robinson, W. 1996. *Promoting Polyarchy.* Cambridge: Cambridge University Press.

Robison, R. and D. Goodman (eds.) 1996. *The New Rich in Asia: Mobile Phones, McDonalds and Middle-class Revolution.* London: Routledge.

Ross, R. and K. Trachte. 1990. *Global Capitalism: The New Leviathan.* Albany: SUNY Press.

Rowell, A. 1996. *Green Backlash: Global Subversion of the Environmental Movement.* London: Routledge.

Ryan, M., C. Swanson, and R. Buchholz. 1987. *Corporate Strategy, Public Policy and the Fortune 500: How America's Major Corporations Influence Government.* Oxford: Blackwell.

Sabin, P. 1998. "Searching for Middle Ground: Native Communities and Oil Extraction in the Northern and Central Ecuadorian Amazon, 1967–1993." *Environmental History* 3: 144–68.

Sachs, W. (ed.) 1992. *The Development Dictionary.* London: Zed Press.

Salas-Porras, A. 1996. "The Mexican Business Class and the Process of Globalization: Trends and Counter-Trends." Unpublished Ph.D. thesis, London School of Economics and Political Science.

Sassen, S. 1988. *The Mobility of Labor and Capital: A Study in International Investment and Labor Flow.* Cambridge: Cambridge University Press.

Saxenian, A. 1994. *Regional Advantage: Culture and Competition in Silicon Valley and Route 128.* Cambridge, Mass.: Harvard University Press.

Schiller, D. 1999. *Digital Capitalism: Networking the Global Market System.* Cambridge, Mass.: MIT Press.

Schmidheiny, P. 1992. *Changing Course: A Global Business Perspective on Development and the Environment.* Cambridge, Mass.: MIT Press.

Schmidheiny, S. 1990. "The Entrepreneurial Mission in the Quest for Sustainable Development." In Willums, ed., op. cit.

Schrecker, T. 1990. "Resisting Environmental Regulation: The Cryptic Pattern of Business-government Relations." In *Managing Leviathan: Environmental Politics and the Administrative State,* eds. R. Paehlke and D. Torgerson. London: Belhaven.

Schuler, R. 1997. "Human Resource Management." In Warner, ed., op. cit.

Scordis, N. and F. Katrishan. 1997. "The Changing International Insurance Industry." In Aharoni, ed., op. cit.

Scott, A. 1990. *Ideology and the New Social Movements.* London: Unwin Hyman.

Scott, J. 1997. *Corporate Business and Capitalist Classes.* Oxford: Oxford University Press.

Scott, J. (ed.) 1990. *The Sociology of Elites.* Aldershot: Edward Elgar, 3 vols.

Servan-Schreiber, J.-J. 1968. *The American Challenge.* Harmondsworth: Penguin.

Sethi, S. 1971. *Up Against the Corporate Wall: Modern Corporations and Social Issues of the Seventies.* Englewood Cliffs, NJ: Prentice-Hall.

Sethi, S. 1977. *Advocacy Advertising and Large Corporations.* Lexington: D. C. Heath.

Sethi, S. 1996. "Moving from a Socially Responsible to a Socially Accountable Corporation." In Houck and Williams, eds., op. cit.

Shawcross, W. 1992. *Murdoch.* Sydney: Random House.

Shoup, L. and W. Minter. 1977. *Imperial Brain Trust.* New York: Monthly Review Press.

Shrivastava, P. 1996. *Greening Business: Profiting the Corporation and the Environment.* Cincinnati: Thomson Executive Press.

Silva, E. 1996. "From Dictatorship to Democracy: The Business-State Nexus in Chile's Economic Transformation." *Comparative Politics* 28: 299–320.

Sklair, L. 1993. *Assembling for Development: The Maquila Industry in Mexico and the United States.* San Diego: University of California Center for US–Mexican Studies.

Sklair, L. 1994. "The Culture-Ideology of Consumerism in Urban China: Some Findings from a Survey in Shanghai." *Research in Consumer Behavior* 7: 259–92.

Sklair, L. 1995. *Sociology of the Global System.* London and Baltimore: Prentice-Hall and Johns Hopkins University Press.

Sklair, L. 1996. "Conceptualizing and Researching the Transnational Capitalist Class in Australia." *The Australian and New Zealand Journal of Sociology* 32: 1–19.

Sklair, L. 1998. "The Transnational Capitalist Class and Global Capitalism: The Case of the Tobacco Industry." *Political Power and Social Theory* 12: 3–43.

Sklair, L. 1999. "Globalization." In *Sociology: Issues and Debates*, ed. S Taylor. London: Macmillan.

Sklair, L. 2000. "Global Capitalism and Sustainable Development: Exploring the Contradictions." In *Shared Space: Rethinking the US–Mexico Border Environment*, ed. L. Herzog. San Diego: University of California, Center for US–Mexican Studies.

Sklair, L. and P. Robbins. forthcoming. "Big Business in Developing Countries."

Sklar, H. (ed.) 1980. *Trilateralism: The Trilateral Commission and Elite Planning for World Management*. Boston: South End Press.

Sklar, R. 1987. "Postimperialism: A Class Analysis of Multinational Corporate Expansion." In *Postimperialism*, eds. D. Becker, J, Frieden, S, Schatz, and R, Sklar. Boulder, Colo.: Lynne Rienner.

Smart, B. (ed.) 1992. *Beyond Compliance: A New Industry View of the Environment*. Washington DC: World Resources Institute.

Smith, L. 1995. "Does the World's Biggest Company Have a Future?" *Fortune*, Aug. 7.

Smith, P. and L. Guarnizo (eds.) 1998. *Transnationalism from Below*. Brunswick, NJ: Transaction Books.

Sobel, R. 1983. *IBM: Colossus in Transition*. New York: Bantam.

Sorkin, M. (ed.) 1992. *Variations on a Theme Park*. New York: Noonday.

Southwest Organizing Project. 1995. *Intel Inside New Mexico: A Case Study of Environmental and Economic Injustice*. Albuquerque, N.Mex.: SWOP.

Stallings, B. (ed.) 1995. *Global Change, Regional Response: The New International Context of Development*. Cambridge: Cambridge University Press.

Stiffler, A. 1985. "Management, Consulting Services Continue Rapid Overseas Growth." *Business America* 8: 13–14.

Stokman, F. N., R. Ziegler, and J. Scott (eds.) 1985. *Networks of Corporate Power: A Comparative Analysis of Ten Countries*. Cambridge: Polity Press.

Strange, S. 1994. "Wake up, Krasner! The World *Has* Changed." *Review of International Political Economy* 1: 209–19.

Strange, S. 1996. *The Retreat of the State: The Diffusion of Power in the World Economy*. Cambridge: Cambridge University Press.

Sugden, J. and A. Tomlinson. 1998. *FIFA and the Contest for World Football*. Cambridge: Polity.

Swasy, A. 1994. *Soap Opera: The Inside Story of Procter and Gamble*. New York: Simon & Schuster.

Sykes, T. 1994. *The Bold Riders: Behind Australia's Corporate Collapses*. St Leonards, NSW: Allen & Unwin.

Taira, K. and T. Wada. 1987. "Business–government Relations in Modern Japan: A Todai-Yakkai-Zaikai Complex." In Mizruchi and Schwartz, eds., op. cit.

Tanzer, M. 1969. *The Political Economy of International Oil and the Underdeveloped Countries*. Boston: Beacon Press.

Taylor, W. 1991. "The Logic of Global Business: An Interview with ABB's Percy Barnevik." *Harvard Business Review* 69: 90–105.

Tehranian, M. 1999. *Global Communication and World Politics*. Boulder, Colo.: Lynne Rienner.

Thacker, S. 1999. "NAFTA Coalitions and the Political Viability of Neoliberalism in Mexico." *Journal of InterAmerican Studies and World Affairs* 41: 57–89.

Tolchin, M. S. 1993. *Buying into America.* Washington, DC: Farragut.

Tomas, W. 1990. "What is Motorola 's Six Sigma Product Quality?" American Production & Inventory Control Society, Conference Proceedings: 27–31.

Tomlinson, J. 1997. "Cultural Globalization and Cultural Imperialism." In *International Communication and Globalization,* ed. A. Mohammadi. London: Sage.

Tracey, M. 1988. "Popular Culture and the Economics of Global Television." *Intermedia:* 9–25.

Tsalikis, J. and D. Fritzsche. 1989. "Business Ethics: A Literature Review with a Focus on Marketing Ethics." *Journal of Business Ethics* 8: 695–743.

Tsuru, S. 1993. *Japan's Capitalism: Creative Defeat and Beyond.* Cambridge: Cambridge University Press.

United Nations. 1988. *Transnational Corporations and Environmental Management in Selected Asian and Pacific Developing Countries.* New York: ESCAP/UNCTC Series B, no. 13.

United Nations. 1998. *Workshop on Indicators for Changing Consumption and Production Patterns.* New York: Division for Sustainable Development.

United Nations Development Programme. 1998. *Human Development Report.* New York: Oxford University Press.

Useem, M. 1984. *The Inner Circle.* New York: Oxford University Press.

Useem, M. 1992. *Executive Defense: Shareholder Power and Corporate Reorganization.* Cambridge, Mass.: Harvard University Press.

van der Pijl, K. 1993. "The Sovereignty of Capital Impaired: Social Forces and Codes of Conduct for Multinational Corporations." In H. Overbeek, ed., op. cit.

Vandervoort, S. (1991) "Big 'Green Brother' is Watching." *Public Relations Journal,* April: 14–26.

Varnedoe, K. and A. Gopnik. 1990. *High and Low: Modern Art and Popular Culture.* New York: Museum of Modern Art.

Venkataramani, R. 1990. *Japan Enters Indian Industry: The Maruti–Suzuki Joint Venture.* London: Sangam Books.

Vernon, R. 1971. *Sovereignty at Bay.* New York: Basic Books.

Vidal, J. 1999. "India Zaps the GM Food Giants." *Guardian* (Weekend), June 19: 10–19.

Vietor, R. 1994. *Contrived Competition: Regulation and Deregulation in America.* Cambridge, Mass.: Harvard University Press.

Wallach, L. and R. Naiman. 1998. "NAFTA: Four and a Half Years Later: Have the Promised Benefits Materialized." *The Ecologist* 28: 171–6.

Warner, M. (ed.) 1997. *Concise Encyclopedia of Business & Management.* London and New York: Thompson Business Press.

Waters, M. 1995. *Globalization.* London: Routledge.

Watson, G. 1993. *Strategic Benchmarking.* New York: John Wiley.

Watson, J. (ed.) 1997. *Golden Arches East: McDonald's in East Asia.* Stanford: Stanford University Press.

Weiss, E. B. and H. Jacobson. 1998. *Engaging Countries: Stengthening Compliance with International Environmental Accords.* Cambridge, Mass.: MIT Press.

Wells, P. and M. Jetter. 1991. *The Global Consumer: Best Buys to Help the Third World.* London: Gollancz.

Wernick, A. 1991. *Promotional Culture.* London: Sage.

Westra, L. and P. Wenz (eds.) 1995. *Faces of Environmental Racism: Confronting Issues of Social Justice.* Lanham, Md.: Rowman and Littlefield.

Whyte, W. H. 1956. *The Organization Man.* New York: Simon & Schuster.

Willums, J. (ed.) 1990. *The Greening of Enterprise: Business Leaders Speak Out.* Bergen: International Chamber of Commerce.

Wilson, R. 1998. "Society's Changing Expectations of the Mining Industry." Rio Tinto (4 May).

World Bank. 1996. *Global Economic Prospects and the Developing Countries.* Washington, DC: World Bank.

Yamamoto, Y. 1998. "Globalization and the State: A Japanese Perspective." *Japan Review of International Affairs* 12: 198–212.

Yearley, S. 1996. *Sociology, Environmentalism, Globalization.* London: Sage.

Zeitlin, M. and R. Ratcliff. 1988. *Landlords & Capitalists: The Dominant Class of Chile.* Princeton: Princeton University Press.

General Index

Author Index